Built on Value

"Huawei is an enterprise that deserves respect and is worth learning from. The great importance placed by this tech company on financial management offers us inspiration and insight."
—Liu Chuanzhi, *Chairman of the Board of Legend Holdings Corporation, and Founder of Lenovo Group Limited*

"Enabling 'lead to cash', engaging in project operations, ensuring internal and external compliance, using the certainty of rules to deal with the uncertainty of results, allowing flexibility while also ensuring standard operations, rapidly striking a balance and then actively disrupting the balance, and inspiring dedication based on customers' interests... These are what Huawei Finance has done. Huawei's financial management practices have redefined the logic behind traditional financial management, and opened a door to a broader world for Chinese enterprises that are working hard to catch up and overtake their global competitors."
—Wu Xiaobo, *Director of the National Institute for Innovation Management, School of Management, Zhejiang University*

"Huawei is a world-class Chinese company that is capable of going head-to-head with the best in the global market. To compete successfully, Huawei focuses on delivering value to customers rather than just reducing costs. Huawei is also able to create value by leveraging the strengths of China. This does not only refer to cheap labor, but also to talented R&D employees who truly grasp core technologies. However, just hiring these talented people isn't a guarantee to unlock their potential. That's why Huawei chooses to distribute shares to its employees. The company knows how to fully motivate employees and inspire dedication. These three points are what have made Huawei what it is today."
—Yang Guoan, *Management Professor at the China Europe International Business School*

Weiwei Huang

Built on Value

The Huawei Philosophy of Finance Management

palgrave
macmillan

Weiwei Huang
School of Business
Renmin University of China
Beijing, China

ISBN 978-981-13-7506-4   ISBN 978-981-13-7507-1 (eBook)
https://doi.org/10.1007/978-981-13-7507-1

© The Editor(s) (if applicable) and The Author(s) 2019 This book is an open access publication
Open Access This book is licensed under the terms of the Creative Commons Attribution-NonCommercial-NoDerivatives 4.0 International License (http://creativecommons.org/licenses/by-nc-nd/4.0/), which permits any noncommercial use, sharing, distribution and reproduction in any medium or format, as long as you give appropriate credit to the original author(s) and the source, provide a link to the Creative Commons licence and indicate if you modified the licensed material. You do not have permission under this license to share adapted material derived from this book or parts of it.
The images or other third party material in this book are included in the book's Creative Commons licence, unless indicated otherwise in a credit line to the material. If material is not included in the book's Creative Commons licence and your intended use is not permitted by statutory regulation or exceeds the permitted use, you will need to obtain permission directly from the copyright holder.
This work is subject to copyright. All commercial rights are reserved by the author(s), whether the whole or part of the material is concerned, specifically the rights of translation, reprinting, reuse of illustrations, recitation, broadcasting, reproduction on microfilms or in any other physical way, and transmission or information storage and retrieval, electronic adaptation, computer software, or by similar or dissimilar methodology now known or hereafter developed. Regarding these commercial rights a non-exclusive license has been granted to the publisher.
The use of general descriptive names, registered names, trademarks, service marks, etc. in this publication does not imply, even in the absence of a specific statement, that such names are exempt from the relevant protective laws and regulations and therefore free for general use.
The publisher, the authors, and the editors are safe to assume that the advice and information in this book are believed to be true and accurate at the date of publication. Neither the publisher nor the authors or the editors give a warranty, express or implied, with respect to the material contained herein or for any errors or omissions that may have been made. The publisher remains neutral with regard to jurisdictional claims in published maps and institutional affiliations.

Cover Image: © Sean Pavone / Alamy Stock Photo

This Palgrave Macmillan imprint is published by the registered company Springer Nature Singapore Pte Ltd.
The registered company address is: 152 Beach Road, #21-01/04 Gateway East, Singapore 189721, Singapore

*The goal of any enterprise is to make itself more competitive, build trust among its customers, and survive market competition.
Huawei's Board of Directors has made it clear that its goal is not to maximize the interests of shareholders or stakeholders (including employees, governments, and suppliers). Rather, it embraces the core values of staying customer-centric and inspiring dedication. This is the foundation for Huawei's survival.
– Ren Zhengfei*

Forewords

"*Don't solve problems.*"
So advised the late patriarch of management theory Peter Drucker.
What could Drucker have meant? Problem-solving is the chief preoccupation and agenda of nearly all business managers and their companies.
But when you solve problems, as this timely book shows, you tend to feed your failures, starve your strengths and sink into costly mediocrity. Problems orient you toward the past. Entrepreneurship is about the future.
"Don't solve problems," said Drucker. "Instead, *pursue opportunities.*" When you pursue opportunities, as Huawei's amazing history demonstrates, you can transform your entire competitive environment. You can turn your previous "problems" into the maps and matrices of a new business strategy. You can launch a juggernaut of innovation and growth.
Exemplifying this transformative wisdom are Huawei's leaders Ren Zhengfei, founder philosopher, and his extraordinary daughter Sabrina Meng, Huawei Chief Financial Officer and guiding light of this book, which launches with her preface. Grasping its visionary principles of finance, you can gain new Druckerian insight into the miracle of Huawei. You may even understand how Ren Zhengfei in just three decades could turn the equivalent of $3 thousand into not just China's telecom equipment champion but into a *multinational* colossus. It now commands $107 billion of revenues, operations in 170+ countries and regions, and 180+ thousand employees from around the world, 30 thousand of them non-Chinese. Its finance division, guided by Meng, commands hundreds of experts and managers from such schools as Harvard, Cambridge, Wharton, and Yale.

In the United States, anxious experts and rivals have offered many explanations and alibis for the Huawei miracle. They depict Zhengfei as an ex-army officer with sinister ties to the Chinese government. They imply he created his company as an elaborately mounted Trojan horse for communist hackers and spies. As the story goes, huge subsidies and gigantic heists of intellectual property account for Huawei's meteoric ascent as a state-owned and state-ruled enterprise.

Zhengfei's army career, however, was routine for Chinese youths of his era and devoted to engineering. As the son of a "capitalist roader" pilloried during the "cultural revolution," Zhengfei launched one of the first fully private firms in mainland China. Long before the creation of any Chinese stock exchange, he founded Huawei with a major financial innovation, what is called in the US an ESOP (Employee Stock Ownership Plan). Far from leaning on the government, Huawei triumphed by outperforming all the state-owned enterprises previously dominating China's telecom industry. Huawei's accountants, KPMG, report no major state subsidies and verify Huawei's private ownership structure with 98.86 percent of the equity owned by employees and 1.14 percent retained by Zhengfei.

Ren Zhengfei built Huawei in admiration for American openness, now ironically in danger of being lost in a siege of xenophobic fear of Huawei. This book quotes his 2014 riff on American success: "Openness is one of the factors that contribute to the success of capitalism. There was no economic success in China when it shut its doors to the outside world. Therefore, we must open up.

"Currently, many people in China hope to grow stronger behind closed doors. This is a mistake. Throughout history, China has shut itself away from the outside world for long periods of time, making it impossible to become strong. The US is the world's most open nation, and thus the world's strongest. Though the US may fall behind from time to time, it has seen constant waves of innovation: Apple, Facebook, and others. As long as the US remains open, who can stop it from moving forward?" (Ren Zhengfei: "Absorbing the Energy of the Universe over a Cup of Coffee," 2014).

Ren Zhengfei is also a supply-sider: "*Reducing taxes encourages investment. It is like digging a trench in the ground, which makes it easy for water to flow...Benefits from increased investment can offset loss of revenue from tax cuts for the government.*"

All major business competitors, necessarily imitating one another and using common components under industry standards, provoke tensions over intellectual property. In Huawei's case the charges of theft mostly reflect rivals' shock at Huawei's success in entering a market shaped by standards and inventions from the United States, made by such companies as Cisco, Bell Labs, and 3Com.

Although one would never know it reading American journals, more than 15 years ago the claims of stolen IP were fully ventilated and litigated. It was an episode that rivals should study today—along with this book—before they disparage Huawei's current constitutional challenge to the U.S. ban of Huawei equipment in U.S. networks.

In January 2003, the American router pioneer Cisco shocked Huawei with a wide-ranging suit for property rights infringement. To prevent any effective response, Cisco unleashed its 70 pages of complaints in a famously patent-friendly venue in a remote District Court in Marshall, Texas. A Cisco executive in Asia was reported to have declared: "This time we need to make Huawei go bankrupt."

To most company leaders, this move would have seemed an insuperable "problem," solvable only by capitulation and retreat to niche markets in China. But in his characteristic inspirational leadership, Zhengfei saw the Cisco suit not as a problem but as a giant opportunity. Declaring that he trusted the fairness of the U.S. court system, he sent Huawei lawyer to Texas to defend his company against all charges. In the end the court vindicated Zhengfei's confidence by upholding the Huawei defense on all key points and barring Cisco from raising the issues again in another venue.

Huawei is now a leading player and stakeholder in the global system of intellectual property rights and standards organizations. In recent years, Huawei has paid Qualcomm of San Diego more than a billion dollars in royalties. Last year Huawei bought $ billions worth of microprocessors from Intel, which also benefited from $4 billion of additional Chinese business.

Today with some 2.5 thousand patents in the relevant technology, Huawei is the world leader in patents for the new industry standard called 5G and offers the only turnkey system. This new standard, the Fifth Generation of wireless architecture, enables a wide range of future industries, from next generation airport surveillance and security to urban traffic management to self-driving automobiles and battlefield robotics, from Internet virtual reality and the Internet of Things to smart cities and intelligent grids. Huawei now has a deep interest in the maintenance of intellectual property rights.

So let's sum it up.

The U.S. has chosen to attack arguably the most creative and powerful and best-led capitalist company in China. The leading supplier of telecom equipment in the world, it is led by Ren Zhengfei, a charismatic philosopher king of global industry with a natural eloquence and insight.

The U.S. government regards Huawei as such an immediate threat that it has reached into Canada to put CFO Sabrina Meng, the founder's elegant daughter, under house arrest in Vancouver. It is no way to treat a lady, regardless of whether Huawei blurred the murky rules of the international boycott of Iran.

In spite of major royalty payments to US companies, it is being indicted for stealing US intellectual property. It is said to be concealing surveillance devices in its smartphones, worldwide best sellers behind only Samsung. It is said to be hiding chips in its routers and switches that enable them to be controlled from China, jeopardizing our networks and power grids.

Now the US is backpedaling the claims, making the more general argument that as a Chinese company Huawei is necessarily under the control of the Chinese government. Chinese law imposes a requirement that businesses comply with the needs of national intelligence bodies.

A flagrant example of "problem" paralysis, this U.S. claim is even more dangerous than the specific smears of Huawei. Such a rule would apply to any nation, including the U.S., and would render impossible most international trade in technology. It would cripple the international fabric of supply chains and standards that underlies most world economic growth and opportunity.

In a letter to his employees in the midst of the crisis over the arrest of his daughter, Zhengfei outlined how to turn this "problem" into an opportunity. He wrote: "*We must be open, transparent, active and courageous to reveal problems and actively promote improvements.* Software development is a creative and artistic work that takes full advantage of our ingenuity and potential. *We need to improve and enhance the transparent, traceable and auditable full process management mechanism to enhance software engineering capabilities and practices from initial design and complete build to product lifecycle management from a credible perspective.*"

It is up to telecom companies and other network managers to do their jobs and negotiate open and defensible contracts for sensitive equipment. If they harbor suspicions, Huawei's carrier customers can entrust independent third parties to view the software source code and conduct security testing. Firmware programming for network hardware systems should be cryptographically signed, just as no iPhone or Huawei app will boot unless it is cryptographically signed.

If the U.S. can't deal with Huawei without craven bars and bans, it might as well retreat to a fetal curl, sealing off its "infant industries" and illusions in a commercial theme park. But let's take inspiration from Peter Drucker. Huawei is not a problem for American technology; it is a huge customer and huge opportunity. It offers a chance to revitalize the U.S. economy and infrastructure with a new competitive challenge and innovative resource.

Tyringham, MA, USA   George Gilder

> Looking back on the path from whence we come, we see only the verdant green shimmering in the majestic setting sun. – Huawei CFO Sabrina Meng's 2017 New Year Greeting

At year-end, our Finance Department generally falls into a flurry of activity. There is an enormous amount of data to review, and it all has to be calculated, tracked, analyzed, verified, and measured. Beginning in October each year, Finance will face a period where overtime becomes the norm. Annual accounting and auditing work begins at the company's subsidiaries around the world. The next year's budget preparation and review also happen during this period. All our finance organizations are generally up to their eyeballs with work relating to these two tasks, sometimes almost drowning in an endless sea of numbers.

As the old Chinese poem goes, "Looking back on the path from whence we come, we see only the verdant green shimmering in the majestic setting sun." As we wave goodbye to the past year, we are filled with unforgettable memories and fruitful results. Especially when we look at where we were a year ago, we will be aware of how much progress we have made over the past year. I am sure that many of our teams and colleagues now have a strong sense of pride.

Looking back at the challenges we have overcome and the peaks we have climbed, it is hard not to feel proud of our hard work. Thinking back on the twists and turns of the past year, how could we not feel inspired by our own perseverance? Of course, our present position only marks the beginning of our next journey.

As we open up boundaries at work, we are there to take up responsibility

Projects are at the core of the company's business operations. The project finance team is now in its third year of development. This year, each region supplied us with many skilled people to engage in work related to project finance. In terms of its "form", our project finance staffing is almost completed. In terms of its "spirit", we still have a long way to go if we are to meet the expectations of corporate management. Even though we are only half way in terms of overall capabilities of project finance, we have come a long way from our humble beginnings over the past three years, and we should be enlivened by our progress. Globally, 1500 project finance staff members are tirelessly handling contracts and projects. Their unremitting effort and perseverance are shedding light on all corners of the globe.

In one representative office I'll call "S", the project finance team's work has been practical and down-to-earth. They have won the recognition of their field office and proven their own value. They braved the scorching sun to reach sites 120 kilometers into the desert. Each month they went out to inspect road repair works, and thus reduced project costs by 3.5 million US dollars. They drove into a valley 2 kilometers deep to survey site locations with site engineers and contractors, and proposed a feasible plan to reduce delivery costs for 10 sites in the valley. They basically lived at the sites, spending time discussing concerns with local villagers, and providing patient explanations. They found ways to use local village power sources instead of consuming diesel fuel, which saved a total of 388,000 US dollars, equivalent to 10 months of fuel for 31 sites.

In 2016, when facing major exchange rate fluctuations in country N, the representative office project finance team volunteered to help out. Before negotiating contracts with customers, they collected information and carried out detailed calculations to get a good idea of the possible foreign exchange losses that the company could face during the period of future contract fulfillment. During contract negotiations, the finance team participated in talks relating to the terms for sharing the exchange rate losses. Even during tough periods in the negotiations, they stayed positive and courteous, and did their best to protect the company's interests. After contracts were signed, they didn't waste any time to follow up on payment collection, delivery plans, and customer payment plans. They proactively coordinated the work and progress on both sides, and played an effective role in fending off potential foreign exchange risks.

As the old Chinese poem goes, "I see the petals falling out in the courtyard, and gaze out at the swirling clouds in the sky." Even though our project finance team achieved some progress, everyone was aware that this was just one step of many on our long journey, and that we shouldn't balk at the road ahead.

We are a tireless and dedicated team. We are confident. We are willing. And more importantly, we are capable. In another two to three years, we will be a project finance team that is viewed as indispensable by field offices in their delivery.

For the finance team, we have to make sure that we are living up to our roles, as this is our compulsory task. Management opportunities that are not in our job descriptions are our optional tasks. The finance team has always worked hard on our compulsory task to demonstrate the best practices in the ICT industry. At the same time, we are working hard on our optional tasks to become the most preferred and most trusted partner of business departments.

As we open up boundaries in management, we are there to seize opportunities

We are still honing our expertise on project finance management. Over the next few years, we will grow through exploration and make changes through adaptation. After many years of hard work, another transformation project related to finance – the development of our internal control system – has found its way through the fog and into the light.

In 2007, internal controls management was kicked off as a sub-project of Integrated Financial Services (IFS), embarking on the road toward transformation. Rome wasn't built in a day, and after 10 years of hard work, we have embedded internal control awareness, mechanisms, and capabilities into all our business activities. Internal controls can be found wherever we do business, forming a global internal control management system based on "process ownership and organizational responsibility".

In the early days of promotion of internal controls, finance was viewed in opposition to business. The goal of internal controls seemed to be to hinder the rapid handling of business. Amidst the confusion, we gradually found our footing and proposed the management goal of "demonstrating the value of internal controls in the improvement of operational results". With this objective in mind, we softened our approach and broke the work down into smaller parts. We went to each region and each organization to talk to them about what we wanted to achieve. We gradually clarified our role and explained the objectives of internal controls for each domain and each organization. Once we had goals, we made commitments. Once we made commitments, we honored them. Internal controls gradually took root and blossomed in operational activities. Field teams also gradually accepted the concepts of internal controls, and became more willing to carry out their work according to management requirements for internal controls.

Aiming to improve the quality of work in the Opportunity to Cash (OTC) process, the internal control team at a representative office I'll call "M" rolled out a system of automated acceptance, billing, and cost offsetting. This shortened billing time from 80 minutes down to 10 minutes, and the incidence of bill refusals by customers dropped by 98%.

The internal control team in representative office "L" likewise focused on OTC process improvements. Focusing on actual pain points in business, they chose to automate the link of Purchase Orders (POs) to customers. Once the project was implemented, the current year discrepancy in accounts receivable was reduced by 32 million US dollars, and losses caused by returned goods were reduced by 11 million US dollars.

These are all examples of how internal controls "imperceptibly" bring about operational returns during the course of their execution. When an enormous machine is operating, internal controls act as the lubricant as well as the brakes. When we improve operations and optimize work, we are the lubricant. When we are ensuring there are checks and balances and that data is visible, we are the brakes. Effective internal controls provide systematic assurances for the "active delegation and effective exercise of authority". Organizations that are closest to customers need to boldly and actively exercise authority. Organizations that have a bigger picture in mind have to appropriately delegate authority and effectively exercise controls. This is the sort of management and control system that we want. The true beneficiaries of internal control mechanisms are the various organizations at the company. They receive more authority and more responsibilities, and boundaries are clearer. Each organization is able to shine within their respective scopes of authority and responsibility, making life better for everyone.

As we open up organizational boundaries, we are where talent is found

Within a dissipative structure, an organization must bravely stretch out its branches and actively absorb new energy in order to obtain new drive for ongoing growth. This is like the process of photosynthesis. A seedling needs light to grow into a towering tree.

Over the past two years, finance has been working hard at opening up organizational boundaries and absorbing fresh energy, welcoming in outstanding talent from around the world. In November 2014, our finance team trialed a finance-focused job fair in the UK for the first time. This was the first step toward expanding our pool of overseas talent. Huawei's finance team now has several hundred graduates from Oxford, Cambridge, Harvard, Yale, and other renowned universities. They are gradually becoming a new driving force for us. Overseas recruitment of finance talent is gradually becoming systematic. From employer brand building to campus talks, from hands-on activities during the summer break to finance contests, we are gradually building our reputation at leading institutions of higher learning. In 2016, we hired nearly 340 international students to fill finance roles, accounting for 38% of this year's campus recruitment headcount.

These students who fill our finance positions have strong aspirations to change the world and to realize their own personal value. They have enthusiasm, drive, strong ability to learn, and extremely open minds. They were admitted to world-class universities as a result of their tangible achievements and outstanding characters. They have lived independently abroad, and have strived to expand their scope of knowledge. Today, they have joined our teams, and they are widely recognized for not being afraid of hard work, cherishing opportunities, having effective time management skills, and easily integrating into teams. The dedication that they exhibit fits very well with Huawei's core values. We hope that these young people will be able to rapidly develop and grow, and bloom in all their brilliance.

At the same time, we build organizations and centers of expertise in places where there is talent.

In 2015, our teams involved in tax planning and connected transactions were relocated as a group to London. More than a year since then, we have found that these two types of high-end talent are noticeably easier to find, and they are more easily integrated into our teams. Highly influential experts are propelling our professional tax capabilities to the next level. Everyone is proud to work alongside such senior experts. Working with them is one of the most valuable non-monetary incentives for our young staff who yearn to learn and grow.

We are opening organizational boundaries and introducing "colleagues without a Huawei badge" into the team. Whether you are an employee or a consultant, and whether you are working full-time or part-time for Huawei, we will work very openly with you. Success is our sole objective.

"Nike Papa", former manager of global connected transactions from British pharmaceutical company GSK, is highly respected. He previously led the handling of the world's largest legal case involving connected transactions. After he became involved in our tax transformation project as a consultant, we resolved to hand him the role of Chief Technical Officer. This decision turned out to be correct, and he delivered a framework technical plan for connected transactions, which was undoubtedly at the forefront of the industry.

As we open up boundaries in thought, we are where methodologies are found

Of all the boundaries out there, the hardest to break down are invisible boundaries of thought. To keep up with this ever-changing era, we have to shake free from the shackles of our thinking and actively experiment with new methods and new tools. We have to break down boundaries in how we do our work, striving to experiment with new perspectives and new stances. We have long since moved beyond the scope of basic financial services. Our teams are equipped with advanced tools and methods from the ICT industry, making limitless vitality possible.

In the field of accounting, we are actively piloting automation and use of AI, handing over the accounting in standard scenarios to machines. Currently, we handle an annual average of approximately 1.2 million expense reimbursements from employees. Employees handle reimbursement processes themselves, and machines directly generate accounting vouchers based on pre-set rules. There are 746 accounts in 98 countries that are now interconnected, with payment orders able to be transmitted to any given bank around the world within 2 minutes. Our payment accuracy is more than 100 times higher than that of banks. In four business scenarios in the accounts payable (AP) field, we have launched automated processing. Pilots have run for half a year, and parallel validations are being done manually. The results have thus far demonstrated an accuracy rate of 100%.

Our global program of radio frequency identification (RFID) asset management through the Internet of Things (IoT) is now implemented across 140,000 fixed assets at 2382 sites in 52 countries. RFID tags are attached to fixed assets that need to be managed. Every 5 minutes, the RFID tags automatically report a location signal, and once per day we update the usage load (or idle) data for the fixed assets. After deploying RFID, the time required to carry out fixed asset inventory work was reduced from a scale of months down to only a few minutes. For each year's asset inventory work and asset inspections, we saved upwards of 9000 person-days of workload. The timely update and sharing of asset location information and asset idle data really got us on track in our asset management.

We have seen impressive innovation from the four big data projects involved in treasury planning. We have now officially launched big data projects for "operating cash flow forecasting" and "cash flow forecasting by currency". Using big data modeling, computers carry out upwards of ten thousand data calculations and model iterations, with 12-month fixed-length rolling forecasting now possible for operating cash flow. From the perspective of matches with historical data, the smallest variance is only 8 million US dollars. For a company with an annual cash settlement volume of approximately 400 billion US dollars, annual revenue of about 80 billion US dollars, and business presence in 170 countries, a variance of 8 million US dollars in rolling forecasts of cash flows is an extremely ideal result.

Working with machines can be that wonderful! Machines thrive when you give them numbers.

As we open up boundaries in capabilities, we are where the artisans are found

There are countless stories to be told of the journeys of growth and development in the finance team. There are tales of perseverance, dedication, craftsmanship, and excellence, supporting the organization as it moves forward in business.

The implementation of consistency of inventory accounts and goods (CIAG) has made inventories visible, identifiable, and manageable for the first time in the company's nearly 30-year history. Site CIAG rose from 76% in 2014 to 98.62% in 2016. We were able to re-use off-book materials worth 88 million US dollars in global central warehouses, and we cleared 75 million US dollars' worth of overdue inventory. We significantly improved the material storage periods at central warehouses and sites. Inventory Turnover (ITO) was improved by 44 days over the prior year. Each of these tangible achievements has proven that we are a team that does what it says it will do. In 2014, we made a commitment to the company that within three years we would achieve CIAG globally. We vowed to walk the talk. And we have lived up to that commitment.

We now have a 24/7 cyclical account settlement system for our accounting on a global scale. We have made full use of the advantages of time differences at our Shared Services Centers (SSCs). On the same data platform and using the same account settlement rules, the SSCs work together to handle settlement work, which has significantly reduced the number of calendar days required for account settlement. The system works around the clock to automatically dispatch account settlement data on a rolling basis. Over 170 systems are seamlessly connected, with 40 million lines of data processed every hour. As we like to say, "the sun never sets on the SSCs" as they cyclically handle account settlement, providing support at the fastest possible speed to more than 130 representative offices so that they have timely access to operating data.

The company's 259 subsidiaries around the world each have to follow local accounting rules, Chinese accounting rules, as well as international accounting rules, and issue three financial reports that meet the requirements of these rules respectively. In addition, our SSCs also have to release operating reports by product, region, BG, and customer group. These reports can all be produced with high quality within five days.

One tax expert named Maria Carlos Paula in Brazil found that the National Social Security Institute (INSS) rules made the company eligible to apply for a rebate on paid social insurance taxes. Therefore, she sacrificed her spare time, spending over two months collecting more than 150 tax refund proofs from the mountain of paperwork in the warehouse. The hard work and perseverance of Maria won back 30 million US dollars from the Brazilian tax authorities in overpaid taxes by the company.

During peak periods, one of our payment specialists named Ma A'li has to stamp 3000 documents every single day. That is equivalent to stamping one document every 15 seconds. She is so busy during those times that she continues stamping the documents while eating her lunch. Despite facing such an intense and high-pressure job, Ma A'li has never made a mistake in over 10 years at the company, with hundreds of millions of US dollars having passed across her desk. What incredible effort and what an impressive contribution this is to the company!

Traditional finance services have long since fallen to the wayside as the primary target of our work. Gone are the days where a finance worker would be a bespectacled old fellow with a bent back hunched over a desk, a cup of tea beside him as he crunched the numbers.

Finance is now a part of all business activities. Finance moves along with the company as it grows, from contract estimation to project payment collection, from product planning to market analysis, from business travel applications to expense reimbursement, from asset management to inventory management, from sales financing negotiations to implementation of financing planning, and from tax planning to the design of pricing. Finance organizations have developed from a state of "utter backwardness" to being "somewhat backward", and on to the present day where we can confidently say that we are "somewhat advanced". Confucius once asked his disciples about their aspirations. One of them, whose name was Yan Yuan, said: "It is best to refrain from self-praise, and to avoid professing one's own accomplishments." Even though we have a low-key culture, the continued effort and ongoing achievements of the finance team are still things to be proud of. Today, our professional financial capabilities are at the forefront of the industry across the board, with some sectors even leading the industry.

Just like Shu Ting describes in her poem "To the Oak Tree", finance and business organizations are two independent and mutually complementary entities, like the oak tree and the ceiba tree.

As we welcome in the new year, I will borrow from the words of Shu Ting to conclude this new year message. I dedicate this to finance colleagues all around the world, and thank you for your unswerving effort and dedication. I am confident that we will not be a "clinging vine" hanging on the great oak's branches, nor an "infatuated bird" singing endless praise. We are a proud and self-sufficient ceiba tree in our own right!

> ...
> I must be a ceiba tree beside you,
> Be the image of a tree standing together with you,
> Our roots, entwined underground,
> Our leaves, touching in the clouds,
> ...
> You have your copper branches and iron trunk,
> Like knives, like swords,
> Like halberds, too,
> I'll have my crimson flowers,
> Like heavy sighs,
> And valiant torches,
> We'll share cold spells, storms, and thunder,
> We'll share mists, hazes, and rainbows...
> ...

In the coming year, let's continue to work hard, and continue to be proud about what we will be accomplishing!

Shenzhen, China   Sabrina Meng

Contents

Part I	**Expansion and Control**	1
1	**Huawei's Business Goal**	3
1.1	Pursuing Sustainable and Profitable Growth	4
1.1.1	Seeking to Survive as a Legal Entity Beyond Life-Span Constraints of Natural Persons	4
1.1.2	Huawei Only Exists to Serve Its Customers	6
1.1.3	Inspiring Passion Across the Company Through Steady Growth	7
1.1.4	Being an Industry Leader and Leading Industry Development	8
1.2	The Meaning of Sustainable and Profitable Growth	11
1.2.1	Pursuing Profitable Growth, Healthy Cash Flow, and Light-Asset Operations	11
1.2.2	Continuously Improving Huawei's Core Competencies	15
1.2.3	Building a Healthy and Friendly Business Ecosystem	18
1.2.4	Pursuing Huawei's Long-Term Value	20
1.2.5	Sharing Gains Based on the Capital and Labor Invested	21
1.2.6	Passing Market Pressure Down Through Each Layer of the Company to Make Sure Our Internal Response System Remains Active	26

2 Huawei's Competition Strategy: A Financial Perspective — 31

- 2.1 Continuing to Invest Boldly to Seize Strategic Opportunities — 32
  - 2.1.1 Seizing Strategic Opportunities Ensures Success While Missing Them Leads to Failure — 32
  - 2.1.2 Increasing Future-Oriented Investment When the Market Is Experiencing a Cyclical Downturn — 34
  - 2.1.3 Avoiding Opportunism and Having Strategic Patience in an Era of Big Opportunities — 36
- 2.2 Working Together Towards the Same Goal and Deciding What Not to Do in Order to Do Something Great — 39
  - 2.2.1 Concentrating High-Quality Resources on Core Business and Strategic Opportunities to Establish and Reinforce Strengths — 39
  - 2.2.2 Narrowing Strategic Focus to Become an Industry Leader — 41
  - 2.2.3 Maintaining a Narrow Focus to Make Breakthroughs — 45
  - 2.2.4 Never Wasting Strategic Resources on Non-strategic Opportunities — 48
- 2.3 Innovating to Create Greater Value for Customers and the Company — 53
  - 2.3.1 Placing More Emphasis on Value Creation Than on Cost Savings — 53
  - 2.3.2 Changing the R&D Spending Structure and Increasing the Proportion of Investment in Research and Innovation — 54
  - 2.3.3 Ensuring Sufficient Customer-Facing Budgets — 56
- 2.4 Digging In and Widening Out — 58
  - 2.4.1 "Digging In": Ensuring Investments in Improving Core Competencies and Preparing for the Future — 58
  - 2.4.2 Constantly Tapping into Internal Potential and Lowering Operating Costs to Provide Higher Value Services to Customers — 59
  - 2.4.3 Sharing More Value with Customers and Treating Upstream Suppliers Generously — 60
  - 2.4.4 Never Pursuing Low Prices, Low Costs, or Low Quality — 61

2.5	Openness, Competition, and Collaboration		63
	2.5.1	Nothing Can Stop Us If We Remain Open	63
	2.5.2	Competition in the Future Will Be Between Supply Chains	65
	2.5.3	Value Sharing Is Vital to a Robust Business Ecosystem	67
2.6	Becoming a Truly Global Company		70
	2.6.1	Building a Global Business Ecosystem to Keep Growing	70
	2.6.2	Leveraging Relative Advantages in Global Competition	71
	2.6.3	Locating Strategic COEs in Places Rich with Strategic Resources	72
	2.6.4	Attracting Global Talent and Building a Global Management Structure	76

3 Remaining Flexible to Seize Opportunities Amidst Uncertainties — 83

3.1	Maintaining Flexibility When Investing in Projects of Uncertainty		84
	3.1.1	Never Putting All Eggs in One Basket When Making Strategic Decisions	84
	3.1.2	Large Investment Along Multiple Paths in Multiple Waves	85
	3.1.3	Absorbing the Energy of the Universe over a Cup of Coffee	90
3.2	Technological Innovation Without Boundaries Can Take Company Strategy in the Wrong Direction		95
	3.2.1	Product Innovation Must Focus on the Core Business and Must Always Be Driven by Business Needs	95
	3.2.2	Research and Innovation on Uncertainties Must also Have Boundaries and Serve the Core Business	96
3.3	Identifying and Creating Certainty Out of Uncertainty		98
	3.3.1	The Role of a Leader: Setting a Clear Direction Amidst Uncertainties	98

  3.3.2 *In Field Offices Are Highly Competent Lean Teams Dealing With Uncertainties; In Back Offices Are Functional Departments and Shared Services Centers Dealing with Certainties* 100
 3.4 *Success Is Not a Reliable Guide to Future Development* 102
  3.4.1 *The Only Thing that Is Constant Is Change* 102
  3.4.2 *We Are the Only Ones Who Can Defeat Ourselves* 103
  3.4.3 *The Best Defense Is a Good Offense; Moving beyond Existing Advantages to Create New Ones* 105

4 Enhancing Core Competencies through Strategic Mergers and Acquisitions and Corporate Venture Capital Investment 107
 4.1 *Bridging Gaps in Core Competencies Through Strategic Mergers and Acquisitions* 108
  4.1.1 *Capital Investment Should Serve the Strategic Purpose and Help Huawei Acquire Key Technologies and Capabilities* 108
  4.1.2 *Focusing CVC Investments on Developing Cutting-Edge Technologies, Preventing Technological Risks, and Supporting Development Strategies in Our Core Business* 108
  4.1.3 *The Purpose of Acquisitions Is to Make Up for Weaknesses in Our Core Business Rather Than Diversifying Our Business* 109
 4.2 *Principles for External Investments and M&As* 110
  4.2.1 *Never Making Principal Investments Aimed Solely at Achieving Financial Returns* 110
  4.2.2 *Strengthening Post-Investment Management to Ensure Investment Goals Are Achieved* 111
  4.2.3 *No Support for Employees Starting a Business: No Investing or Engaging in Such Activities* 111

5 Strengthening Risk Control and Compliance Management 113
 5.1 *Controlling Risks During Expansion: The Purpose of Control Is to Ensure Sustainable and Profitable Growth* 114

	5.1.1	Can Huawei Keep Its Balance in an Unbalanced World? How Can It Do So?	114
	5.1.2	Do Not Focus Exclusively on Opportunities Without Considering Risks	115
	5.1.3	Pursuing Sustainable and Profitable Growth and Curbing Blind Expansion	117
	5.1.4	Balancing Expansion and Control	118
5.2	A Multi-faceted System for Controlling Financial Risks at Huawei	119
	5.2.1	The "Four Threes" System for Risk Control	119
	5.2.2	Two Perspectives of Financial Risk Control	122
	5.2.3	Three Financial Risk Control Centers	122
5.3	Financial Risk Prevention and Control	124
	5.3.1	We Need to Have Contingency Plans to Deal with Financial Crises, But the Key Is Improving Contract Quality	124
	5.3.2	Taking Diversified Approaches to Financing and Settlement	126
	5.3.3	Do Not Stop Progressing Because of Risks or Ignore Risks in Order to Progress	126
5.4	Business Continuity Management	127
	5.4.1	Huawei's Primary Obligation: Maintaining Stable Network Operations	127
	5.4.2	Building Strategic Reserves to Prevent Supply Risks	128
	5.4.3	Avoiding the Inclusion of Countries and Regions Affected by War, Civil Unrest, or Epidemics into Emergency-Triggered Management Cycles	129
5.5	Using the Certainty of Legal Compliance to Deal with the Uncertainty of International Politics	130
	5.5.1	Legal Compliance Is the Most Important Basis on Which We Survive, Provide Services, and Contribute Worldwide	130
	5.5.2	Focusing on Protecting User Privacy in the Same Way We Have Done in Cyber Security	132
5.6	Compliance Management and Subsidiary Boards' Oversight Responsibilities	132
	5.6.1	Strengthening Compliance Management to Harvest More Crops	132

    5.6.2   *Subsidiary Boards: Performing Integrated Oversight in the Field on Behalf of the Company Without Interfering in Business Operations*   134

6 Finding the Right Amount of Openness, Compromise, and *Huidu*, and Properly Balancing Expansion and Control   141

6.1 *Opportunity-Driven Versus Resource-Driven*   142
    6.1.1 *More Emphasis on Opportunity-Driven Resource Allocation*   142
    6.1.2 *Channeling High-Quality Resources to Valued Customers, Valued Countries, and Mainstream Products*   144
    6.1.3 *Managing Investment Portfolios and the Pace of Investment Based on Corporate Strategy, Investment Capacity, and Business Opportunities*   146
    6.1.4 *Keeping the Costs of Resources in Mind and Acquiring Resources to Achieve Growth Goals*   148
    6.1.5 *Guiding Resource Allocation with Differentiated Value Assessments*   149

6.2 *Growth Versus Profits*   151
    6.2.1 *Focusing on Long-Term Strategic Development to Turn Today's Cash into Tomorrow's Profits*   151
    6.2.2 *Focusing on Both Opportunity-Driven Scaled Growth and Profit-Driven Sustainable Growth*   151
    6.2.3 *Company Operations: A Dissipative Structure*   153
    6.2.4 *Pursuing Rapid Growth on the Basis of a Reasonable Profit Margin*   154

6.3 *Long-Term Versus Short-Term Interests*   155
    6.3.1 *Short-Term Interests Ensure Survival*   155
    6.3.2 *Striking a Balance Between Long-Term and Short-Term Interests*   156

6.4 *Centralization Versus Decentralization*   158
    6.4.1 *Development: Staying Focused, Involving Little Uncertainty, and Supporting Business Success*   158
    6.4.2 *Research and Explore Across a Wide Scope*   160
    6.4.3 *Narrowing Our Strategic Focus and Setting Ourselves Apart from Competitors in Our Core Business*   164

6.5	Opportunities Versus Risks		165
	6.5.1	Managing Both Opportunities and Risks, with More Attention Paid to Risks	165
	6.5.2	Inaction Has No Risk, But Will Leave Us Behind	166
	6.5.3	Promoting Sales Growth While Effectively Managing Risks	167
6.6	Creating Order Out of Chaos Versus Creating Chaos Out of Order		169
	6.6.1	Purpose of Fine-Grained Management: Preventing Chaos During Business Expansion	169
	6.6.2	Striking and Disrupting a Balance	171

Part II Value Management   175

7 Guidelines for Value Management   177

7.1	Huawei's Most Valuable Asset: An Enduring Management System		178
	7.1.1	Management Is Key to Ending Reliance on Talent, Technology, and Capital, and Enabling the Company to Evolve from the Realm of Necessity to the Realm of Freedom	178
	7.1.2	Goal of Transformation: To Harvest More Crops and Increase Soil Fertility	180
7.2	Business Plays a Leading Role and Accounting Plays an Oversight Role		183
	7.2.1	When We Say That "Business Plays a Leading Role and Accounting Plays an Oversight Role", We Mean That We Do Not Focus Solely on Financial Returns on Investment	183
	7.2.2	Accurately Recognizing Revenue, Accelerating Cash Inflows, Ensuring Visibility of Project Profits and Losses, and Managing Business Risks	184
	7.2.3	How Can Financial Personnel Effectively Serve and Oversee Business If They Do Not Understand It?	188
	7.2.4	Oversight Means Firm Commitment to Process Management	189
	7.2.5	Everything We Do Must Support Field Operations, Serve Business, and Contribute to Business Success	191

	7.3	Using the Certainty of Rules to Deal with the Uncertainty of Results	192
		7.3.1 Setting Rules to Prevent Chaos	192
		7.3.2 Using the Certainty of Rules to Deal with the Uncertainty of Results for Major Processes, Allowing Flexibility at the Endpoints	193
		7.3.3 Using the Certainty of Rules to Deal with the Uncertainty of Execution	194
	7.4	Effectively Conducting Oversight While Further Delegating Authority to the Field	195
		7.4.1 Centralized Authority Over Treasury, Accounting, and Auditing Management	195
		7.4.2 Delegating Command Authority to the Field and Giving Field Commanders the Final Decision-Making Authority	196
		7.4.3 Moving Oversight to the Field While Delegating Authority to the Field	199
		7.4.4 Oversight Is the Means to Our End Goal: Business Success	201
	7.5	Streamlining Our Organizations and Processes to Create Value for Customers	203
		7.5.1 Simplicity Is Key: Standardizing and Streamlining Routine Management	203
		7.5.2 Any Department or Process That Doesn't Create Value for Customers Is Redundant	206
8	**Financial Management Throughout End-to-End Business Processes**		211
	8.1	Financial Management Throughout the OTC Process	212
		8.1.1 KCPs Throughout the OTC Process	212
		8.1.2 Controlling Contract Quality at the Very Beginning	217
		8.1.3 Integrating Payment Collection, Revenue Recognition, and Project Budgeting and Accounting Based on Customer Contracts/POs	221
		8.1.4 Setting Up a Contract Support Office That Offers One-Stop-Shop Services to Support Contract Fulfillment	225

8.2		Financial Management Throughout the IPD Process	227
	8.2.1	The Essence of IPD: From Opportunity to Commercial Success	227
	8.2.2	Key Control Points Throughout the IPD Process	231
	8.2.3	Industry Business Plans and Product Investment Portfolio Management	233
	8.2.4	Integrating IPD and Other Business Processes	235
8.3		Financial Management Throughout the PTP Process	237
	8.3.1	KCPs Throughout the PTP Process	237
	8.3.2	Integrating Procurement and Financial Processes	240
	8.3.3	Automation and Payment Security of the PTP Process	243

9 Project Financial Management 247

9.1		Shifting from Being Function-Centered to Being Project-Centered	248
	9.1.1	Projects Are the Basic Units and Cells of Business Management	248
	9.1.2	Establishing a Corporate-Level Project-Centered Management System	250
	9.1.3	Back Offices Need to Collaborate to Provide Timely and Accurate Support for Field Operations	253
9.2		Key Activities for Project Financial Management	254
	9.2.1	Closed Loop Operations: Project Estimation, Budgeting, Accounting, and Final Accounting	254
	9.2.2	Building an Awareness of Project Operations and a Project Operations Management Mechanism	261
	9.2.3	Integrating Pre-sales and Post-sales Activities	263
	9.2.4	Closed-Loop Management of Project Risks and Assumptions	265
9.3		Matching Project Managers and Project Management Teams' Authority with Their Responsibilities	266
	9.3.1	Matching Project Managers' Authority with Their Responsibilities	266
	9.3.2	Further Developing Project Management Teams and Inspiring Passion Across Field Operating Units	269
9.4		Project Appraisals and Incentives	270

        9.4.1   Adopting an Appraisal and Incentivization Mechanism Based on Final Project Results   270
        9.4.2   Exploring Project Bonuses and Implementing the Contribute and Share System   271

10 Optimizing the Management Control System for Responsibility Centers   275
   10.1 Every Operating Mechanism Is Ultimately Value-Driven   276
        10.1.1 Making Accounting Granularity Small as Needed   276
        10.1.2 Using the Value Distribution System to Drive Business Units to Operate on Their Own, Responsible for Profits and Losses, and Incentives and Constraints   281
        10.1.3 Leveraging the Value Sharing Mechanism and Strategic Investment to Reinforce Our Culture of "Toasting Those Who Succeed and Offering a Helping Hand to Those Who Fail"   283
   10.2 Methods for Managing Responsibility Centers   285
        10.2.1 We Establish Responsibility Centers to Define Responsibilities, Streamline Management, and Motivate the Workforce   285
        10.2.2 Incorporating Checks and Balances into Responsibility Center Management   288
        10.2.3 Responsibility Centers Must Adopt Different Approaches to Manage Certainties and Uncertainties   293
   10.3 Operating Mechanisms for Profit Centers   295
        10.3.1 Focusing on Business Operations, Making Decisions Independently, and Never Rigidly Setting Job Grades Based on Scale and Levels   295
        10.3.2 Positioning HQ as a Resource Pool and Adopting a Resource Buy & Sell Mechanism   297
        10.3.3 Authority Delegation and Responsibility for Profit Centers   299

11 Developing a Better Planning, Budgeting, and Accounting System — 303

11.1 Aligning Planning, Budgeting, and Accounting with Strategy and Business Operations — 305
- 11.1.1 The Primary Purpose of Budget Management: Pushing the Company Forward Rather Than Only Determining What Can Be Done with the Resources Available — 305
- 11.1.2 Establishing a Planning, Budgeting, and Accounting System to Support Business Success — 306
- 11.1.3 Linking Budgets to Contributions and Strategies — 308
- 11.1.4 Shifting the Focus of Business Management from BPs to SPs — 310
- 11.1.5 Establishing a Budget Allocation Mechanism Based on the "SP–Project–Budget" Logic — 312

11.2 Preparing Plans and Budgets from the Bottom Up — 314
- 11.2.1 Projects and Customers: The Focus of Planning, Budgeting, and Accounting — 314
- 11.2.2 Proper Planning: Integrated Operating Plans Are the Foundation of Effective Management — 315
- 11.2.3 Making Business Forecasts More Reliable — 317
- 11.2.4 Continuously Optimizing Expense Baselines, Reducing Operating Costs, and Improving Management to Increase Efficiency — 318

11.3 Implementing Flexible Budgeting to Adapt to Opportunities and Changes — 320
- 11.3.1 Reasonableness Analysis of Detailed Business Department Budgets and Strict Control of Functional Department Budget Caps — 320
- 11.3.2 Preparing Flexible Budgets to Allow Field Teams to Obtain More Resources After Their Business Grows — 322
- 11.3.3 Strictly Implementing a Process for Granting and Increasing Budgets — 324

11.4 Accounting: An Important Indicator of Management Improvement — 325

		11.4.1	Overseeing the Exercise of the Delegated Authority Through Accounting to Ensure Field Teams Have Command Authority	325
		11.4.2	Improving Management Through Scientific Accounting	326

12 Service and Oversight Functions of Accounting — 329

12.1 Keeping Accounting Independent from the Top Down and Letting It Serve as a "Dam" — 330
    12.1.1 Roles of Accounting: Service and Oversight, with the Latter Being More Important — 330
    12.1.2 Oversight by Accounting: Comprehensive Oversight Throughout All Processes — 332
    12.1.3 "Accounting Plays an Oversight Role": Incorporating Service and Oversight into End-to-End Processes; Exercising Oversight While Providing Services — 333

12.2 Accounting Must Get Deeply Involved in Business Operations and Implement Integrated Financial Management While Serving Business — 335
    12.2.1 Accounting Must Be Proactive While Serving Business — 335
    12.2.2 Accounting Must Get Close to Business and Establish a Multi-level Shared Service Model Based on Business Scenarios — 337

12.3 Payment Management — 339
    12.3.1 Basing Performance Appraisals of Payment Personnel on the Quality of Their Work and Maintaining Appropriate Redundancy in the Headcount — 339
    12.3.2 Establishing a Mechanism to Ensure Daily Reconciliation at Three Organizational Levels — 340
    12.3.3 Having a Correct Understanding of Error Rates — 342

12.4 Complying with Accounting Ethics and Rules — 342
    12.4.1 Being Bold and Able to Stick to Principles — 342
    12.4.2 Complementing Institutional Oversight with Ethical Constraints — 344

13 Treasury Management — 347
13.1 Exploring a Capital Structure for the Company's Long-Term Development — 348
13.1.1 Growing from Within Is the Core and Major Driving Force Behind Huawei's Future Development — 348
13.1.2 Improving Working Capital Efficiency and Quality to Ensure the Continuity and Robustness of Operating Cash Flow — 350
13.2 Building a Global Treasury Management System to Better Manage Fund Risks — 355
13.2.1 Scaling Up Financing, Enriching the Financing Structure, and Dispersing Financing Risks — 355
13.2.2 Establishing Diversified Financing Systems and Cash Settlement Centers — 356
13.2.3 Guaranteeing Financing Capabilities with Stable Financial Policies — 357
13.3 Centrally Managing Funds to Ensure Fund Security — 357
13.3.1 Centrally Managing Funds and Enhancing the Process Ownership System — 357
13.3.2 Standardizing Account Management and Establishing a Unified Treasury Management System — 359
13.3.3 The Ability to Deal with Strict Foreign Exchange Controls Helps to Guarantee the Company's Fund Security. It Is Also a Core Competency That Helps Affected Regions Maintain Their Competitive Advantages and Robust Business Performance — 361

14 Tax Management — 363
14.1 Paying Taxes Is a Corporate Social Responsibility — 364
14.1.1 A Company's Biggest Contribution to Society Is to Pay Taxes and Do Its Work the Best It Can — 364
14.1.2 Abiding by Applicable Tax Laws in All Business Activities — 364
14.1.3 Performing Intercompany Transactions in a Standard and Effective Way Based on External Laws and Industry Practices — 366

14.1.4 Establishing a Long-Term Transformation and Operation Management Mechanism to Ensure Taxes Are Paid According to Law ... 367
14.1.5 Creating a Positive Business Environment to Support Huawei's Global Operations ... 368
14.2 Proactively, Effectively, and Appropriately Managing Tax Risks and Costs ... 369
14.2.1 Clarifying Goals and Responsibilities of Tax Risk Management ... 369
14.2.2 Effectively Developing Global Tax Plans and Keeping the Company's Taxes at a Reasonable Level ... 370

15 Internal Controls and Internal Audit ... 373
15.1 The Company's Oversight System: The Governance Structure and Three Lines of Defense ... 374
15.1.1 The Oversight System: Governance Structure ... 374
15.1.2 Internal Controls: Three Lines of Defense ... 375
15.2 Process Controls ... 378
15.2.1 Oversight Aims to Prevent Corruption, Improve Operations, and Establish Deterrence ... 378
15.2.2 "Wearing American Shoes" and Starting from Scratch to Build Huawei's Internal Control System ... 381
15.2.3 Internal Control Management: Objectives and the Framework ... 383
15.2.4 Implementing the Process Ownership System ... 385
15.2.5 Internal Control Ownership System ... 387
15.3 Internal Controls Over Financial Reporting (ICFR) ... 391
15.3.1 Building Sustainable and Profitable Growth with High-Quality Process Controls and ICFR ... 391
15.3.2 ICFR Is a Means, and Consistency of Business and Accounts Is an End ... 392
15.3.3 ICFR: Starting by Managing the Quality of Business Data to Ensure the Quality of Financial Reports ... 395
15.3.4 ICFR Management Should Shift Its Focus from Moving Targets to Fixed Targets ... 396

	15.3.5	Finance: Building an Effective Internal Control System; Business Departments: Rigorously Fulfilling Their Internal Control Responsibilities	397
	15.3.6	ICFR Is Designed to Continuously Improve the Quality of Financial Reports, Not Merely to Hold People Accountable	399
15.4	Internal Audits and Investigations		400
	15.4.1	Establishing Deterrence Through Internal Audits	400
	15.4.2	Strengthening Legal Deterrence and Tightening Accountability Criteria Every Year	403
	15.4.3	Separating Investigations from Disciplinary Actions	404
	15.4.4	Oversight Is the Best Way to Care for and Protect Our Managers	407
	15.4.5	Audit: Assuming Innocence Until Proven Guilty and Taking Appropriate Disciplinary Actions Against Mistakes at Work	410

16 Digital Financial Management — 417

16.1	Data Is a Strategic Resource		418
	16.1.1	Managing Data in the Same Way as Managing Capital	418
	16.1.2	Fully Leveraging Data Resources to Create New Competitive Advantages	419
16.2	Data Cleaning Is the Most Effective Approach for Internal Controls		421
	16.2.1	Ensuring Data Quality from the Source	421
	16.2.2	Whoever Creates Data Must Be Responsible for Data Quality	422
16.3	Making Routine Financial Management Automated and Intelligent, and Leveraging Big Data Analytics to Improve Financial Management		424
	16.3.1	The Basis of Scientific Management: Rational Analyses Based on Data and Facts	424
	16.3.2	Establishing a Future-Proof Data Governance System	426
	16.3.3	Leveraging Automation, AI, and Big Data Analytics to Reduce the Complexity and Uncertainty of Financial Management	428

17 Making Financial Management Process-Based and Professional — 433

17.1 Financial Personnel Should Understand Business and Business Personnel Should Understand Finance — 434

17.1.1 Financial Personnel Can Help Business Grow Only by Understanding Business — 434

17.1.2 Managers Are Also About Managing Finance — 435

17.1.3 Financial Personnel Can Become Well-Rounded Managers Only by Knowing How to Manage Projects — 437

17.1.4 Developing a Mixed Financial Team — 439

17.2 Building a Process-Based, Professional Financial Management System — 440

17.2.1 Reducing Costs Through Process-Based and Professional Financial Management — 440

17.2.2 Building a Professional Financial Team That Has Solid Integrity, Dares to Shoulder Responsibilities, and Sticks to Principles — 442

17.3 Progress in Finance Is the Basis for All Management Advances — 443

17.3.1 Financial Transformation Is Not Limited to the Finance System, But a Company-Wide Effort — 443

17.3.2 There Will Not Always Be Flowers Along the Road Ahead — 445

Epilogue — 447

Acronyms — 451

PART I

Expansion and Control

To achieve sustainable and profitable growth, we need to consider financial indicators in the short term; in the medium term, we need to look at capability improvement; in the long term, we need to focus on the industry landscape, the health of the business ecosystem, and the sustainability of the industry. Business success will always be an issue of concern throughout our company's lifecycle. Management is about weighing the present against the future, balancing the short term and the long term. – Ren Zhengfei

CHAPTER 1

Huawei's Business Goal

A company must first have a clear business goal. Huawei's business goal is to make itself more competitive, build trust among its customers, and survive market competition. These are actually the most basic goals of any enterprise. Without any of the three, an enterprise will find it hard to survive. An enterprise should first ensure that its most basic goals are continuously achieved, rather than seeking to meet a certain target or maximize the interests of a certain group. In reality, any attempt to maximize interests will yield the opposite result.

Huawei pursues sustainable and profitable growth, rather than maximizing the interests of its shareholders or employees. Huawei only exists to serve its customers. Financially speaking, this refers to the value created for the company. For Huawei, a non-public company, value is not the same as capital market valuation. Rather, it relates to the deeper essence of value, reflecting the company's current and potential capabilities to make profits.

At Huawei, sustainable and profitable growth first means that business performance is robust, with profitable revenue, healthy cash flow, and light assets. Second, sustainable and profitable growth means the company is constantly enhancing its core competencies. Third, it means building a healthy and friendly business ecosystem. Business performance must be steady and balanced if it aims to support the company's long-term survival and development. Huawei's business model is one that maintains a long-term state of hunger for the company and doesn't seek to make big money.

Huawei does not overly focus on profits. Rather, it adopts a long-term perspective for company development and pursues rapid growth at a reasonable profit rate. Growth is fundamental to any enterprise. In the information and communications industry, you either take the lead or get wiped out. There are no other paths.

All cooperation between people is actually about value sharing. Huawei stresses that every factor of production should be rewarded according to the value it creates for the company. If a certain factor of production is not rewarded, it will become a factor that constrains value creation. Value sharing that is based on the capital and labor invested is what drives Huawei's ongoing growth over the years. Today, this value sharing mechanism is gradually extended to also include its customers and suppliers. This has propelled the entire ecosystem into a positive cycle.

How can everyone at a company, from the founder to each ordinary employee, feel the pressure of market competition, think what customers think, and address what customers are most concerned about? This might be the biggest challenge for enterprise management. That's why an enterprise needs to transfer market pressure to every employee to keep the entire organization vibrant. This is Huawei's management philosophy – placing itself in a desperate position in order to survive.

This chapter thoroughly describes the major ways that Huawei adopts to achieve sustainable and profitable growth.

1.1 PURSUING SUSTAINABLE AND PROFITABLE GROWTH

1.1.1 Seeking to Survive as a Legal Entity Beyond Life-Span Constraints of Natural Persons

We are currently considering how we can develop the company comprehensively. At present, we rely heavily on technology, capital, and individual employees. As we move forward, we need to reduce this reliance in order to shift from the realm of necessity to the realm of freedom. *(Ren Zhengfei: Victory Is Inspiring Us, 1994)*

The purpose of drafting *The Huawei Charter* is to help establish rules and regulations, ultimately ensuring the company's sustainable development. This means that the company's development doesn't rely on any one individual; this is the only way for Huawei to have a future. *(Ren Zhengfei: Minutes of the CEO's Staff Team[1] Meeting, 1997)*

Our company must continue to survive, yet the law of nature indicates that all men eventually die. Even if it is not constrained by the law of nature, a legal entity is still constrained by social norms. Even if a person is not successful, he or she may still live a long life. An enterprise, however, cannot survive for even a week if it lacks key capabilities. If an enterprise can adapt to both the law of nature and social norms, it may survive for centuries. *(Ren Zhengfei: Survival Is Fundamental to an Enterprise, 2000)*

The survival of an enterprise depends on the enterprise itself. If it does not survive, it is not because others do not allow it to – it is because it cannot find a way to carry on. Survival doesn't mean dragging out an ordinary existence or simply existing for the sake of existing. To survive is not easy and to thrive is even more difficult. This is because we face a constantly changing environment and a highly competitive market. This is further complicated by interpersonal relationships within our company. An enterprise can survive only if it is constantly improving. *(Ren Zhengfei: Survival Is Fundamental to an Enterprise, 2000)*

The goal of any enterprise is to make itself more competitive, build trust among its customers, and survive market competition. *(Ren Zhengfei: Deepening Our Understanding of the Corporate Culture of Staying Customer-centric and Inspiring Dedication, 2008)*

Achieving sustainable growth is the biggest challenge that all companies face. To overcome this challenge, we need to identify the major driving forces behind Huawei's development, and figure out how to sustain and improve these forces. Now, people are beginning to understand that a company's core values are what power the joint efforts of all employees. We need to ensure that our successors embrace our core values, and take the initiative to grow by reflection. We need to mold our successors through our core values. This is necessary to ensure the sustainable growth of our company. *(Ren Zhengfei: Managers Should Live and Pass on Huawei's Core Values—Speech at the First Workshop on Human Resource Management Outline, Huawei Executive Office Speech No. [2010] 009)*

---

[1] Staff Team, or ST for short, is a daily business coordination and decision-making team which operates with the CEO being responsible for the decisions made through collective discussions. Currently, there are STs in business departments and functional departments of the company.

Although a company's survival depends on many different factors, I think that maintaining sustainable and profitable growth and providing quality services are the most important. *(Ren Zhengfei: Speech and Comments at the Carrier Network BG's Strategy Retreat in Huizhou, Huawei Executive Office Speech No. [2012] 010)*

Whether or not Huawei is an Internet company is not important. Whether or not the Huawei spirit can be called an "Internet spirit" is not important, either. What matters most is whether the Huawei spirit can help us survive. The tortoise as described in the fable titled *A Tortoise and a Hare* is determined to move forward, doesn't hesitate, and doesn't rely on others. Similarly, we must have a firm belief in our own values, and adhere to development at a reasonable rate. We must not envy others for their rapid success. *(Ren Zhengfei: Applying the Spirit of the Tortoise to Catch up with the Dragon Spacecraft—Speech at Huawei Annual Management Conference 2013, Huawei Executive Office Speech No. [2013] 255)*

In the future, we will adopt a business model that allows us to maintain our own advantages, strengthen openness and collaboration, and ensure sustainable profitability. Survival is the ultimate victory. Our business model should ensure that we continuously make profits. This doesn't necessarily mean that we earn more than others. Our ultimate goal is to survive. We will firmly hold onto our advantages and continue to move forward. This is what BMW is doing. In addition, we pay sufficient attention to Tesla and learn about its competitive advantages. We should have a positive view of the changes that are taking place worldwide. As long as a strategic opportunity emerges, we will throw sufficient resources to seize it. *(Ren Zhengfei: Speech and Comments at the Carrier BG's 2013 Strategy Retreat, Huawei Executive Office Speech No. [2014] 016)*

The war-torn days of Genghis Khan are long gone. Modern society is not completely free from chaos, but it will eventually find peace. Survival is the ultimate victory. *(Ren Zhengfei: Avoiding Opportunism in the Era of Big Opportunities—Speech at the Luncheon with the Administrative Team of the Consumer BG, Huawei Executive Office Speech No. [2014] 025)*

1.1.2 Huawei Only Exists to Serve Its Customers

Huawei is not solely focused on profits. We aim for long-term development. We always act with integrity in regards to our customer engagement, operations, and corporate development. It is integrity that helps us earn customer satisfaction, trust, and loyalty. By not overly focusing on profits, we can spend more of our energy on diligently pursuing long-term development, rather than on hype or speculation. Admittedly, if we act with integrity and avoid hype, certain customers may not think highly of us, but they will eventually see the value we bring. *(Ren Zhengfei: Huawei's Opportunities and Challenges, 2000)*

There is only one way to satisfy customers and maintain good customer relationships. That is to provide premium services. This is the basis for Huawei's survival. What does premium service mean? It means customers will continue to praise us even after they have paid us. *(Ren Zhengfei: Enlarging Teams to Prepare for a Big Battle, 2000)*

Huawei doesn't aim to maximize the interests of its shareholders or employees. Huawei only exists to serve its customers. This is why Huawei has and will continue to succeed. *(Ren Zhengfei: Minutes of a Briefing on Marketing Goals, 2002)*

Only after customers fully understand us will they realize how we are different from our competitors and see the type of future we can help them create. Then they will buy our products and help us to survive. *(Ren Zhengfei: Being Future-oriented, Focusing on Customers' Pain Points, and Displaying Huawei from a Global Perspective, Huawei Executive Office Speech No. [2012] 046)*

Huawei's Board of Directors has made it clear that its goal is not to maximize the interests of shareholders or stakeholders (including employees, governments, and suppliers). Rather, it embraces the company's core values of staying customer-centric and inspiring dedication. This is the basis on which Huawei survives. *(Ren Zhengfei: Clarifying the Rotating CEO System Under the Leadership of the Board of Directors, 2012)*

To provide quality services, we need to allocate high-quality resources to valued customers. This means that after we earn money from a customer, we will invest some of the money back in the customer. How can we do this? By improving our services. *(Ren Zhengfei: Remarks at a Briefing by Southeast Africa Multi-country Management Department, Huawei Executive Office Speech No. [2013] 003)*

1.1.3 *Inspiring Passion Across the Company Through Steady Growth*

If Huawei had ceased to develop two years ago, we would be cleaning up a mess today and be preparing for bankruptcy. If we cease to develop today, we will face the same situation in two years' time. Our competitors are too strong, so we have no choice but to press forward. *(Ren Zhengfei: There's No Guarantee for Success, But Boldness Makes a Difference, 1996)*

By maintaining growth at a reasonable rate, Huawei provides its employees with opportunities for personal development. Our increasing profits enable us to compensate employees generously and attract global talent. This is how we achieve optimal resource allocation. So, in this sense, a reasonable growth rate is necessary to inspire passion across the company. *(Ren Zhengfei: How Long Can Huawei Survive?, 1998)*

Huawei must maintain steady growth. So how can we grow faster? The answer lies in management and services. Without effective management, we would not be able to gain traction, and without high-quality services, we would be lost. *(Ren Zhengfei: Do Not Be a Temporary Hero, 1998)*

As long as we constantly improve upon our core competencies, our market share will increase and we will rise above the rest. Then we can push even further, get even better, and continue to grow. And before you know it, we will have surpassed the competition. *(Ren Zhengfei: Focusing on a Down-to-earth Approach to Seize Opportunities for Development, 2000)*

Our goal is very clear: We need to develop further. If we don't, we will collapse. *(Ren Zhengfei: Human Resources Must Facilitate Business Development and Refrain from Being Rigid, 2008)*

1.1.4 Being an Industry Leader and Leading Industry Development

We must find our strategic direction amid chaos. Huawei will definitely approach the edge of a cliff one day. What do I mean by this? I mean that we will be ahead of our global peers. No one will then be able to tell us clearly what our future will be and we will have to rely on ourselves to shape the future. It is impossible for us not to approach the edge of the cliff. Nothing good will come out of trying to avoid this situation. *(Ren Zhengfei: Remarks at a Meeting at the Shijing Mountain Park in Zhuhai, 1997)*

In the information and communications industry, you either take the lead or get wiped out. There are no other paths. *(Source: The Huawei Charter, 1998)*

What do we strive for? We strive to become a global leader and provide quality services to our customers. You might think it sounds funny. How could Huawei have put forward such an ambitious slogan, especially in its early years when it was still a small company? However, this goal has enabled us to become what we are today. If we hadn't set this goal, we would have been unable to build customer trust and develop a grand goal while keeping our staff down-to-earth. What people have been and will continue to be concerned about is whether electronic and network products can be upgraded in the future, whether new technology will emerge and develop, and whether the networks they have invested in will be phased out because of technological progress. If Huawei doesn't want to collapse, we must strive to be a global leader. *(Ren Zhengfei: How Long Can Huawei Survive?, 1998)*

In the future, the global market will be shared by several dominant telecom equipment providers. Huawei's overall strategy is to both compete and cooperate with strong competitors in an ordered and controlled manner to gain a favorable position and firmly counter competitors who aggressively move against us. This is how we can establish a landscape of two or three major players in each segment of the market, namely, regions, products, and customer groups, within the next two years. *(Source: Guidelines on Sales Priorities, EMT Meeting Minutes No. [2008] 014)*

The First Emperor of the Qin dynasty was able to unify the country after 600 years of chaos because the state finally reached a consensus on their goals and interests. Guan Zhong[2] said that if all people of a state received income from the same source, that state would stand unrivalled. We must be fully aware of our goals and responsibilities, be resolute in achieving these goals and fulfilling these responsibilities, and at the same time periodically re-examine these goals and responsibilities. We have gathered a team of exceptional talent from each nation. However, in this great era, we have done something that requires great efforts but is not very profitable. Over two decades of hard work, we have established a platform that has tremendous potential value. We must not destroy it because of corruption or lack of resolve. We must hold tight to our oath in the EMT declaration, and at least those 2000 to 3000 people at the core must be strictly self-disciplined. We must remain dedicated and work together towards the same goal and receive income from the same source. *(Ren Zhengfei: EMT Meeting Minutes No. [2012] 002)*

At best, Huawei can become one of the world's top three players. There is no way we will become the sole global leader. *(Ren Zhengfei: Speech and*

---

[2] Guan Zhong (c. 720–645 BCE) was a chancellor and reformer of the State of Qi during the Spring and Autumn period of Chinese history.

Comments at the Carrier Network BG's Strategy Retreat in Huizhou, Huawei Executive Office Speech No. [2012] 010)

There are four requirements for being an industry leader. First, a leader needs to be able to envision the future, including the direction, trends, and changes of the industry. But this is not enough. A leader should also be able to shape the future, guiding the entire industry and always playing a leading role. Second, a leader should adopt a value sharing mechanism that covers the entire value chain. If industry players have the opportunity to earn more profits while facing fewer risks, they will be more willing to follow that leader. Why does Apple have so many followers? The company does a huge volume of business. This gives its partners access to a huge market space and a bright future. Apple's high profits mean it can be generous to its suppliers and partners, who are able to earn a lot of money with limited risk. Third, a leader must make trade-offs between what it will and won't do, and remain committed to its choices. Why didn't Ericsson develop WiMAX[3]? Because if it had, its followers might not know what it, as a leader, was going to do. If it changes its mind often, its followers may lose confidence in it. Fourth, a leader needs to build an environment that promotes competition and ensures profitability of the entire industry. If a leader snatches up all of the market shares by setting extremely low prices, there will be no room left for other players. *(Ren Zhengfei: Speech and Comments at the Carrier Network BG's Strategy Retreat in Huizhou, Huawei Executive Office Speech No. [2012] 010)*

To develop our business in the future, we need to lead industry development and serve as an advisor for our customers. *(Ren Zhengfei: Speech and Comments at the Carrier BG's 2013 Strategy Retreat, Huawei Executive Office Speech No. [2014] 016)*

We must focus on a "needle-tip" strategy for our pipe business, achieve sustainable and profitable growth, and become an ICT leader through peaceful means. *(Ren Zhengfei: Speech at the Briefing on HR Work, Huawei Executive Office Speech No. [2014] 057)*

To be an industry leader, we must not be so narrow-minded as to throw stones on highways to stop others and develop our own unique strengths. This will harm other market players and impede global progress. This is not what we want to achieve. Our aim is to become an industry leader and

---

[3] WiMAX, worldwide interoperability for microwave access, also known as "802.16 Wireless Metropolitan Area Network" or "802.16", is an emerging mobile broadband access technology that provides fast Internet connections.

contribute to the world. Then what makes a leader? Being a leader means making the world a better place, contributing to the broader architecture of global information networks, and sharing benefits with others. Huawei is a large, responsible company. How could we block network information flow? Even if we could, people would still find other ways to reach their destination, and we will be marginalized in the end. *(Ren Zhengfei: Speech at a Meeting with Employees of the Legal Affairs Department, Secretariat Office of the Board of Directors, and Wireless Network Product Line, Huawei Executive Office Speech No. [2015] 015)*

1.2 The Meaning of Sustainable and Profitable Growth

1.2.1 Pursuing Profitable Growth, Healthy Cash Flow, and Light-Asset Operations

Without economies of scale, it will be increasingly difficult to develop the company

We are in an information age where, thanks to the widespread exchange of information, human intelligence is enhanced and unleashed on an unprecedented scale. As a result, we can produce more new products and technologies to serve the world. As information networks continue to expand at greater speeds, the lifecycle of new products and technologies will become shorter and shorter. If we can't grasp these fleeting windows of opportunity and achieve economies of scale, we will find it increasingly difficult to develop the company. Without a massive global service network, and a management system to support that network, we won't be able to generate enough profit to survive and maintain rapid development. For Huawei, letting opportunities like this slip can only be attributed to issues with our services and management. This is a strategic inflection point for Huawei. *(Ren Zhengfei: Do Not Be a Temporary Hero, 1998)*

Due to advances and rapid changes in the information industry, we must achieve economies of scale to shorten the time invested in new products. Scale is an advantage. This advantage is based on effective management. A company that downsizes will become less competitive while a company that scales up but is unable to effectively manage itself will face bankruptcy. Management is an internal factor and can be improved. However, external factors are beyond our control. Small companies, when exposed to these factors, will find themselves very vulnerable. To survive, we must continuously improve our management and services. These are the strategic starting points for Huawei to increase scale and inspire passion. *(Ren Zhengfei: What Can We Learn from the American People?, Improvement Issue No. 63, 1998)*

If we can stay ahead of our competitors and control our costs after we seize a large market share, we might be able to maintain that share of the market. The costs I am talking about are not just the costs for technologies and products. If we can't control costs or hold on to our market share, our competitors will easily catch up even if we are achieving technological breakthroughs. Like the "mile-a-minute weed"[4], whoever can lock up this space will lock in this industry. *(Ren Zhengfei: Speech at the 2008 Mid-year Report by Regions to the EMT, EMT Meeting Minutes No. [2008] 028)*

Centering our business operations on profits, but not pursuing maximum profits

For many years, Huawei's growth has been oriented towards sales. In a bubble economy, this growth model is understandable. This is what happens in the real estate market. When prices are very high, whoever controls more land will earn more. In Huawei's early years, our net profit reached 23%. At that time, as long as we won a contract, we would turn a profit. This is why we have developed a sales-focused culture. However, this culture hasn't changed with the times. We must change now. During this historic period, selling more is no longer enough. We need to increase our operating efficiency and project management capabilities. We need to shift our focus towards three things: sales revenue, contribution gross profits, and cash flow. These are necessary for us to maintain a balance in the long run. *(Ren Zhengfei: Adapting the Manager Appraisal System to Challenges Facing the Transforming Industry, Huawei Executive Office Speech No. [2006] 036)*

In our first two decades as a company, the market was huge and profits were high. At that time, we focused on scale because it guaranteed profits. But things are changing. Now, when we assess the performance of each representative office, region, and product line, we focus more on positive cash flow, positive profit margins, and improvements in per capita efficiency. I believe significant changes will take place over the next three

---

[4] "Mile-a-minute weed" is an extremely vigorous plant that can survive and grow quickly even in harsh conditions.

years. If we continue to focus on scale, the company will spin out of control. *(Ren Zhengfei: Remarks at a Meeting with Senior Managers at a Project Management Summit, Huawei Executive Office Speech No. [2009] 007)*

The paramount goal of a company is to serve its customers and earn profits. After 20 years of development, we are finally able to say that our business operations are centered on profits. However, there are short-term, mid-term, and long-term profits. There is no rule for when profits need to be gained. Profits gained this year are profits, and profits that take 10 years to gain are still profits. Being profit-centered is an important aspect of our management transformation. The entire organization and the people responsible may experience significant changes because of our emphasis on profits. So why am I so confident? I think the ultimate result we want from the transformation is that Huawei will be able to perform a little bit better than it did the day before. This slight difference in performance is what will enable us to survive. Sometimes, the difference between life and death might be only a second or two. *(Ren Zhengfei: Speech at the Regular Meeting of the Reserve Pool, 2009)*

Maximum profits are not what we pursue. In fact, maximizing profits will bleed the future dry, which in turn will harm our strategic position. *(Ren Zhengfei: Speech at the EMT ST Meeting, 2010)*

When Huawei was still a small company, we saw profits each year despite our goal to become a big company. If we didn't have money to distribute, the company would have collapsed long ago. Every one of you wants to grow our company into those like Cisco and Apple, and every one of you speaks louder the richer you become. It would have been fine if we just focused on what we had and made breakthroughs. But we insisted on becoming a large world-class company. That is why we have unfolded all of our businesses. However, we failed to do a good job in some key areas. We must not continue to expand to areas where we can't create value. We must focus on creating value. *(Ren Zhengfei: Speech at the EMT ST Meeting, 2012)*

Cash flow is the lifeline of a company

I once took our senior executives for a visit to the Hakka fortified houses. How were the Hakka people able to safeguard their fortified houses? Why were these big houses able to survive? The key lies in the fact that every big house had a well that functioned effectively. This is like cash flow. Our senior managers must be fully aware of the importance of cash flow. There is no sign of collapse for Huawei even today. This is because we've always had cash flow. We can store materials like food. However, without water, we won't be able to survive. The biggest characteristic of fortified houses is that each of them has a well. Castles outside of China all needed water supply, as it was crucial to both war and life. At Huawei, this well is the cash flow in our financial management. *(Ren Zhengfei: Speech at the Third Quarter Meeting Regarding Marketing in China, 2004)*

The biggest danger in the future will lie in cash flow. We must pay great attention to this. If we encounter a big problem in the future, that will be a drain on cash. This is a bottleneck for any company's survival, and many companies in the industry have collapsed because of this problem. What happened to the company D'LONG International Strategic Investment? It went bankrupt because a soft landing was impossible for many of its projects due to a drain on cash. All the banks asked the company to pay back their loans, which disrupted the company's chain of operations. This is why we say "cash is king". Therefore, if we collapse, it will probably be caused by a drain on cash. We won't collapse because of lack of profits. Without profits, we can sell our buildings or land. That will sustain us for several years. But without cash, we will quickly go bankrupt. *(Ren Zhengfei: Strengthening Payment Collection and Improving Cash Flow—Speech at the EMT ST Meeting on February 28, 2006, Huawei Executive Office Speech No. [2006] 007)*

Only robust and balanced financial results will be able to support the company's long-term survival and development

We should not overemphasize any single indicator in our appraisals, because doing so will not guarantee our company's sustainable development. If we only focus on sales revenue, some regional offices and product lines will do whatever they can to get strategic subsidies and price cuts from the company. We usually see this behavior in incompetent sales people and managers who can only sell products at low prices. Using this approach, the more we sell, the sooner we will perish. *(Ren Zhengfei: Speech at the Mid-year Market Conference, Huawei Executive Office Speech No. [2006] 036)*

We must continue to base our performance appraisals on factors such as sustainable and profitable growth, profits, cash flow, and per capita efficiency improvements. (In areas where operations are mature, we can use total compensation packages as the basis of this accounting.) In cases where departments fail to exceed the average score for corporate-level per capita efficiency improvements, the heads of areas, regions, representative offices, product lines, and other departments will be held accountable.

Departments that exceed the average score must be ranked by positive profits, positive cash flow, and strategic goal attainment; senior managers that rank the lowest will be removed from their positions. This is different from our past practice of not penalizing senior managers and will allow us to assign people with successful field experience to our HQ. *(Ren Zhengfei: Who Calls for Artillery and How Do We Provide Timely Artillery Support?—Speech at the Awards Ceremony of Sales & Services, Huawei Executive Office Speech No. [2009] 001)*

The purpose of sales is not merely to sign contracts. Any exciting opportunity has to generate revenue, and all revenue has to bring profit and cash. Otherwise, temporary success will lead to the company's demise. *(Ren Zhengfei: Guidelines on the Analysis of the Business Environment and Key Business Strategies, Corp. Doc. No. [2012] 081)*

Huawei is an asset-light company, and doesn't have the capacity or experience to manage assets. If we own heavy assets, our fluidity will become increasingly poor. Then we will face the problem of demise, not profitable and sustainable growth. *(Ren Zhengfei: Comments at a Meeting with Sales Financing Experts, Huawei Executive Office Speech No. [2012] 025)*

"With survival as our bottom line, we aim to achieve profitable growth and healthy cash flow, and avoid asset-heavy operations." This goal should be made clear and we need to focus on achieving this goal over the next two to three years. *(Source: Minutes of the Report on the 2016 Work of the Finance Committee, Board of Directors Meeting Minutes No. [2017] 006)*

1.2.2 Continuously Improving Huawei's Core Competencies

Increasing forward-looking, strategic investments to build the company's future technological advantages and lead industry development

Business operations and management should center on our core competencies, not on short-term interests. Huawei will never do anything that is not conducive to enhancing our core competencies. When faced with opportunities outside the scope of our core competencies, we can resist the temptation. Some might say that we've let so many opportunities slip through our fingers in an attempt to maintain a strong hold on our core competencies. But I would argue that, without our core competencies, we would lose the opportunity to develop entirely. Sure, we have a lot of opportunities right within our grasp, but only by approaching them with caution can we achieve something that no one else could possibly achieve.

We only have one standard for ourselves: Continue to improve upon our core competencies. With them, we can do many, many things. Without them, we can't achieve anything. This is why we're constantly trying to cut down on superfluous activities. *(Ren Zhengfei: Huawei's Opportunities and Challenges, 2000)*

We must invest more in strategic goals. Our investments today can only produce effects in two years' time. If we reduce investment today, we will lack the seeds and fertilizer we will need when spring comes. *(Ren Zhengfei: Speech at the CEO's Staff Team Meeting, 2001)*

We will increase forward-looking, strategic investments, and build up our technological advantages for the future to lead industry development. We must increase our technology-centric strategic investments to maintain a leading position in the industry. After all the talk about customer centricity, it is possible that we go from one extreme to the other and ignore our forward-looking technology-centric strategy. In the future, our concept of technology centricity will be intertwined with our concept of customer centricity. We will be customer-centric when developing products, and technology-centric when developing next-generation architectural platforms. *(Ren Zhengfei: Guidelines on the Analysis of the Business Environment and Key Business Strategies, Corp. Doc. No. [2012] 081)*

Moving forward on two wheels – technological innovation and management transformation – to drive the ongoing improvement of the company's core competencies

Short-term improvements to management should be guided by the long-term goal of enhancing the company's core competencies. With this in mind, we will not get lost in the midst of short-term management improvements, and our short-term and long-term goals will not contradict each other. As a result, our core competencies will improve, and we will discover what we need to survive and what value our survival brings. *(Ren Zhengfei: Survival Is Fundamental to an Enterprise, 2000)*

What can help us to survive a "hard winter"? The answer is high quality and low costs. Whoever delivers the highest quality at the most affordable price and is the most responsive to customer needs will be able to survive the winter. Therefore, the top priority for managers in charge of R&D is to improve quality and reduce costs. Only when they have achieved these two things can they start to explore the direction of technological innovation. The three pillars that support technological innovation are: quality, cost, and time. Technological innovation that does not satisfy these conditions is worthless. We should never innovate for the sake of innovation. We must be both bold and cautious when doing research. We must also be bold enough to spend money yet cautious about quality and technological validation. *(Ren Zhengfei: Speech at a Meeting with the R&D Managers of Huawei Technologies and Avansys, 2001)*

How can we succeed in our globalization and maintain our competitive advantages? Huawei's core values have told us what our goals, strategies, and approaches are. We have survived through dedication and technological innovation. Isn't there an end to technological innovation? Will Moore's law carry on forever? Can we win in all markets with the same approach? In my opinion, when wired and wireless broadband access reaches a certain bandwidth, and have a certain degree of coverage, innovation in network technology will slow down. At that time, companies that have a very large market presence will be managed effectively and that can provide low-cost high-quality services will be able to survive. Huawei has to become such a company before a decline. In the past ten years, we have strived to change ourselves, modestly learn from Western companies, improve efficiency, develop an exceptional human resource management mechanism, and motivate all our staff to remain dedicated. This is the only way for us to survive. As long as we are not complacent, we will surely become a winner over the long term. *(Ren Zhengfei: The Market Economy Is Best for Competition; Economic Globalization Is Inevitable—Speech at the Commendation Meeting of Finance, Huawei Executive Office Speech No. [2009] 005)*

We have two principles for innovation. First, we must emphasize value. We must not innovate for innovation's sake; rather, we must innovate to create value. Second, we must be more tolerant of failures in innovation. *(Ren Zhengfei: Speech at the Meeting with Staff from the 2012 Laboratories, Huawei Executive Office Speech No. [2012] 035)*

What is the downside of engineers being managers? Engineers-turned-managers tend to neglect management and emphasize technological innovation so much that they end up making products that no customer wants. We should not always prioritize technology. We must also emphasize management and shift our focus from technology to business. A project manager must be a business leader, not a technical expert. *(Ren Zhengfei: Speech at the EMT ST Meeting, 2012)*

1.2.3 Building a Healthy and Friendly Business Ecosystem

We need to possess strategic thinking when building a business ecosystem

As Huawei continues to grow, it may be impossible to always have friends around us; we do have foes, as we may have caused the collapse of many smaller companies. We need to change this situation; we need to achieve a win-win scenario through open collaboration. We have turned some friends into foes during the past 20 years; in the next two decades we will strive to turn foes into friends. When we have numerous friends across the value chain, we will surely achieve even greater success. *(Ren Zhengfei: Customer Centricity, Increased Platform Investments, and Open Collaboration for Shared Success—Speech at the 2010 PSST Managers' Meeting, Huawei Executive Office Speech No. [2010] 010)*

Any strong man is balanced. Can we survive when we become extremely strong, but have no friends around us? No. Why should we force out other players in order to dominate the market? Many people throughout history wanted to conquer the whole world, but in the end they perished before their goals were achieved. Huawei will surely fail if we have the same mentality. Why shouldn't we work with our partners, especially strong ones? We must not be so narrow-minded as to force out other players. Rather, we should cooperate with our peers while competing alongside them, as long as such cooperation is in the interest of both parties. *(Ren Zhengfei: Customer Centricity, Increased Platform Investments, and Open Collaboration for Shared Success—Speech at the 2010 PSST Managers' Meeting, Huawei Executive Office Speech No. [2010] 010)*

As our business continues to grow and change, the business environment will become increasingly tough. We must have measures in place to help us handle tough situations. Although we are already very strong, there are still many problems within our organization. We must be strong internally and soft externally and learn to make concessions. In addition, we must avoid being arrogant and learn to appropriately handle internal and external relationships. What looks strong on the surface is not always strong throughout. *(Ren Zhengfei: Success Is Not a Reliable Guide to Future Development—Speech at the Huawei Market Conference on January 17, 2011, Huawei Executive Office Speech No. [2011] 004)*

Huawei's future success relies on two factors: One is organizational capabilities and vitality; the other is a favorable business ecosystem. Will we have the capacity to run a company with revenue of US$100 billion? Will we have the vitality to cope with future challenges? Will the business ecosystem be tolerant of us and allow us to become big and strong? What measures will we take to improve the business ecosystem? *(Ren Zhengfei: Do Not Expand Blindly and Do Not Assume That We Are Already Strong Enough, Huawei Executive Office Speech No. [2012] 006)*

In this era of heroes, we must dare to lead on a global scale; but once we establish our advantages, we cannot afford to make enemies. We must instead cooperate with others. Someone asked me, "What is your business philosophy?" I replied, "We do not have a business philosophy. We simply serve our customers." *(Ren Zhengfei: Speech at the Corporate Strategy Retreat, 2015)*

Exchanging land for peace

Managers at Huawei do not have to cater to the needs of employees, but should adopt appropriate methods to achieve company goals. Temporarily, we may need to sacrifice our short-term interests, but in the long run, our company will grow. *(Ren Zhengfei: Huawei's Hard Winter, 2001)*

When we were cooperating with a world-class company, which was also one of our all-around competitors, I told them I was a disciple of Yitzhak Rabin, and that we should be interdependent and seek the help of each other to coexist. I mentioned my respect for Rabin to illustrate our long-term strategic relationship with competitors. *(Ren Zhengfei: Huawei's Hard Winter, 2001)*

About seven or eight years ago, we began to implement a "land for peace" strategy, seeking to cooperate with competitors at the cost of our market share. This cooperation complements our strengths and creates greater value for customers. Also, we have become more recognized, and our competitors have begun to treat Huawei as their friend. While we vie with competitors for the opportunities to provide customers with superior services, we collaborate with competitors to drive down product development costs. This change in the paradigm has added fuel to our growth momentum and will significantly reshape our future development. *(Ren Zhengfei: Seeing the Situation Clearly and Accelerating Organizational Building and Reserve Pool Development to Embrace Huawei's New Development—Speech at a Meeting for HR Directors, 2005)*

1.2.4 Pursuing Huawei's Long-Term Value

Value reflects an enterprise's current and potential capabilities to make profits

Although a product may not be profitable at first, it can still become profitable in the future. We must adopt a long-term profitable strategy for products that are not yet producing profit in the short-term. The key is to set up a point of marginal cost so that once we exceed that point, we will become profitable. *(Ren Zhengfei: Speech at a Briefing on Developing the IP Microwave Business, 2009)*

During our current restructuring, we should prioritize market opportunities first, and then per capita efficiency. If we only emphasize per capita efficiency, based on our business performance this year, per capita efficiency will increase as long as we don't increase the size of our workforce. But we won't have achieved sufficient growth. To truly increase per capita efficiency, we need to first guarantee sustainable and profitable growth – a mechanism centered on self-coordination. We can't focus single-mindedly on per capita efficiency, or we will definitely fail. We need to have a strategic mindset – focus our attention on growth, as well as the total amount of profit we generate – and then we can assess per capita efficiency. Otherwise, we're doomed to failure. *(Ren Zhengfei: Speech at the Regular Meeting of the Reserve Pool, March 25, 2009)*

We must focus on our core business. Value – not technology – must be at the center of everything we do. *(Ren Zhengfei: Speech at a Work Report of the Network Energy Product Line, Huawei Executive Office Speech No. [2012] 043)*

Huawei's business model: always staying hungry, not seeking to earn big money

In this era, it doesn't matter if we cannot influence market demand. Rather, we must be able to adapt to changes. Many of our existing assets are a legacy of the voice era. Our success over the past two decades will not ensure our future success. We need to put our past success behind us and move forward. I don't think we should consider technology to be a threshold, because competitors will catch up with us sooner or later. Customers might not remain loyal to us all the time, because we might not treat them the same as time goes by. What actually matters, in my opinion, is the business model. Why do I insist on earning small money, instead of big money? It's because of our business model. We have managed to catch up with other vendors because many of them decreased their investment in areas that generated lower profits. If we continue to earn small money after we become the industry leader, it will be impossible for other players to earn big money in the industry. Will they remain dedicated if they can only earn small money? If not, we will remain the industry leader. If we always stay hungry and do not seek to earn big money, we will keep earning small money and survive. If we give employees decent pay, they will stay and we can keep the company running. If we only focus on short-term interests and seek to earn big money, we will be digging our own grave. Although a company's survival depends on many different factors, I think that maintaining sustainable and profitable growth and providing quality services are the most important. *(Ren Zhengfei: Speech and Comments at the Carrier BG's 2013 Strategy Retreat, Huawei Executive Office Speech No. [2014] 016)*

Huawei has been swayed many times in the past. I think that to succeed, one has to focus on the things that one is good at. Just now, a colleague said making chips doesn't make much money. Those who make semi-conductors earn a lot of money. But those who earn big money won't be able to sustain it, because people will become jealous of the profits and want to get in the game. What about earning modest profits? We work hard, but our profit margins are lower than those of real estate companies. It would be unfair if we perished first. When I talked to the vice president of the EU, he asked me how Huawei could develop when the global economy is in such bad shape. My answer was that, first of all, we are dealing with small amount transactions, which are not particularly influenced by economic crises. For example, if you owe me money, I still have to make a call to ask you to pay me back. That telephone call costs a small amount of money. Secondly, our profit rate is lower than restaurants or real estate companies. Since we can survive with such a low profit margin, we won't collapse that easily. While the whole world is anxious, the management team of Huawei is not. We are going on with the transformation. Although the overall economy is not good, we have still managed to offer our employees pay raises over the past few years. How have we managed to remain stable? The answer is that we insist on earning small money. *(Ren Zhengfei: Speech at the Meeting with Staff from the 2012 Laboratories, 2012)*

1.2.5 Sharing Gains Based on the Capital and Labor Invested

Cooperation between people is actually based on interest distribution. If our initial aim were to get rich alone, we would have fewer partners, our organization would be less effective, and our profits would be lower. In that case, we would have a higher distributable percentage out of a smaller sum. When these two factors are multiplied, the outcome would be small. Our aim is to make the overall pie bigger and decrease our own slice of the pie. This adheres to the principle of interest sharing. *(Ren Zhengfei: Speech Regarding Corporate Organizational Goals and System Blueprints for the Future, 1994)*

Resources can be exhausted; only culture endures. Huawei does not have any natural resources to depend upon. What we do have is the brainpower of our employees. This is our oil, our forests, and our coal. Human ingenuity is the creator of all wealth. *(Source: The Huawei Charter, 1998)*

We must establish a value distribution system where the income of each employee is linked to the company's overall performance. When the company performs well, we must dare to expand and share risks together. When the company experience difficulty, we need to get through the hard times together. In this way, we can share the pressure among all employees across the company. *(Ren Zhengfei: Key Points for Management, 1999)*

To achieve growth, an enterprise must create results for its customers, capital providers, and employees. Therefore, it is essential to satisfy customer needs, and cultivate employees who are passionate and work hard to meet these needs. We should base salaries on employees' real contributions and potential to continually contribute, and base bonuses on short-term contributions. We should also emphasize individual contributions to capital. Any increase in headcount should be accompanied by added value. An enterprise must satisfy its customers, as this is the basis for its survival. It must also satisfy its shareholders, as this is the purpose of their investment. The enterprise must satisfy its value contributors, and value the contributions of dedicated employees, as they are the driving force behind sustainable growth. *(Ren Zhengfei: Guidelines for Human Resources Management Transformation, 2005)*

Who will Huawei recognize, dedicated employees or shareholders? People outside Huawei say that Huawei shares are valuable because Huawei employees are dedicated. If no one works hard, these shares will become valueless. Your efforts are saving the company and ensuring the interests of financial investors. Financial investors should be rewarded adequately, but dedicated employees should receive higher rewards. This is a reasonable value distribution mechanism. *(Ren Zhengfei: Remarks at a Meeting with Members of the Project & Financial Management Enablement Program for High Potentials, Huawei Executive Office Speech No. [2014] 054)*

One employee posted an article from an external critic on our *Xinsheng Community*, saying, "If Huawei fails to make profits continuously, a bubble will emerge in its Restricted Phantom Shares, which will burst sooner or later." This article speaks the truth. Therefore, Huawei must work hard to improve itself, focus on strategy, simplify management, reduce redundancy, and dismiss underperformers. This is the only way for us to inspire passion across the company. Similarly, public companies will collapse if they don't make profits. Without profit, private companies won't grow either. We don't have a different fate. What we can do is work hard. *(Ren Zhengfei: Comments to Staff of the Enterprise BG, Huawei Executive Office Speech No. [2014] 006)*

Our Restricted Phantom Shares plan was approved by the Chinese government and is therefore legal. Several top government officials have asked about this plan and wondered whether it can promote industry development. Even though we are abiding by the law, any investment has risks. We bundle our risks with employee dedication. If employees are confident in their own dedication, then they voluntarily buy company shares. Of course, they can choose not to buy. If they are worried, any of them can withdraw from the plan completely, during the period of the company's steady development. However, once they withdraw, they will not be allowed to buy back their shares. If they want to buy shares later, they have to follow the share distribution plan, which is based on contributions, and this has ceilings. *(Ren Zhengfei: Comments to Staff of the Enterprise BG, Huawei Executive Office Speech No. [2014] 006)*

Huawei has been successful over the past 20 years because it has implemented a value sharing mechanism based on the capital and labor employees invest. This mechanism should be extended to also include our suppliers and customers. The ultimate result is that we share the world market. *(Ren Zhengfei: Remarks at the Strategic Reserve's Oath-taking and Awards Ceremony, Huawei Executive Office Speech No. [2015] 083)*

Yang Lin: Just now you mentioned Huawei's mechanisms. There are many discussions in China about Huawei's mechanisms and corporate culture. May I hear your own perspectives on this? Ren Zhengfei: Our culture is very simple: staying customer-centric and inspiring dedication. In this world, our customers treat us best, so we need to devote ourselves to serving them. As we want to earn money from our customers, we must treat our customers well, and make them willing to give us their money. In this way, we establish good relationships with them. How can we serve our customers well? By working hard despite all the hardships we might encounter. We need to motivate our dedicated employees and set a reasonable ratio between gains from capital and labor. *(Source: A Chat in the Garden with Huawei Founder Ren Zhengfei, Huawei Executive Office Speech No. [2015] 098)*

Yang Lin: Huawei has achieved great success, especially in Europe. How has Huawei emerged from a small unknown Chinese company to a top player in the European market? How has Huawei eaten away the market share of its competitors, including established companies like Nokia and Ericsson? Ren Zhengfei: Actually, you're wrong. You should say how we have worked together with these companies to contribute to the world. The information society is developing faster than our own capabilities. If this weren't the case, we could be playing golf and relaxing in cafés. During this period, our global peers have also grown, and the apple has become too big to peel. Our strategy is to collaborate and grow to meet social needs. Our value sharing mechanism has allowed us to share our gains from capital and labor with our employees, which is now gradually extending to sharing success with our customers and suppliers. In addition, we are cooperating with world-leading companies to formulate standards and set roadmaps. Together, we can make a greater contribution to society. We are not so insular as to want to wipe others out. The reason that some companies burn money is to dominate the market when their competitors have no money to burn. We don't intend to dominate the market. We haven't eaten away at our competitors. Neither have we ever intended to do so. Instead, we have tried our utmost to help them become strong. For example, we are very happy to learn that Nokia will merge with Alcatel-Lucent. I think Nokia's spirit of dedication is stronger than any other company. That's why it is able to return to the world stage. We will enhance cooperation with these companies to serve society. *(Source: A Chat in the Garden with Huawei Founder Ren Zhengfei, Huawei Executive Office Speech No. [2015] 098)*

We have only one core value at Huawei, which is contributing more to earn more. The Contribute and Share system applies to all dedicated employees, no matter what positions they hold. Driven by benefits, the company will move forward. Due to a lack of attention, the compensation of staff in our visa handling department used to be very low. In the future, we will raise the compensation level so that we are able to attract more outstanding people to help us deploy more of our staff in field offices. Monetizing visa processing will motivate staff to work harder. *(Ren Zhengfei: Speech at the Annual Meeting of the Employee Relationship Dept, Huawei Executive Office Speech No. [2016] 058)*

I view core values like this: Each element that contributes to value creation should be rewarded accordingly. "Freedom, equality, and fraternity" are all very good ideas. However, it is unclear who will actually make the "cake". Without a cake, how can you ensure "freedom, equality, and fraternity"? Many people say that network equipment will become white boxes, and will be very cheap. However, who will cook the "free lunch"? And who will maintain these white boxes? Can white boxes be of high quality and with good maintenance services? If an element contributes to value creation but is not rewarded, it will not be sustainable. A free lunch does not comply with the rules for the market economy. If people cannot make money in one domain, they will leave and go somewhere else. This kind of innovation concerns business model innovation, whereas the US tends to focus on technological innovation. *(Ren Zhengfei: Remarks at Meetings with Huawei Fellows, Huawei Executive Office Speech No. [2016] 069)*

Capital may play a role in creating our world, but labor still plays the biggest role. We have benefited from reading communications standards in the past 20-plus years and have instilled them into the brains of our employees. We "weighed" each brain and distributed company shares accordingly. This helped us develop a new mechanism. Those who read these standards are very capable. Even if several people left, our standards system still remains. If our company collapses one day, we will no longer have the same standards as before even if we gather everyone together again. This is because standards can sustain only when they have life. Because our management and standards systems are lifeless, without support from people, these systems would be useless. So, we must not allow Huawei to collapse. Otherwise, the management system we have spent more than ten billion dollars developing over the last few decades will be useless, and our understanding of technical standards will also be of no use. *(Ren Zhengfei: Remarks at Meetings with Huawei Fellows, Huawei Executive Office Speech No. [2016] 069)*

Over the past 28 years, we have adhered to working together towards the same goal and receiving income from the same source, and investing long-term to make strategic breakthroughs. We have also adopted a value sharing mechanism for capital and labor, and collective dedication is our unique competitive advantage. *(Ren Zhengfei: There Will Not Always Be Flowers Along the Road Ahead—Speech at the H1 Huawei Market Conference, Huawei Executive Office Speech No. [2016] 079)*

There are rumors circulating online that Huawei employees retire at the age of 34. If this is the case, I wonder who will pay for their pensions.

Huawei doesn't have a pension fund. The company purchases social insurance, health insurance, and accidental injury insurance for employees. Concerning retirement, you have to comply with national policies. Even if you leave the company, you still have to pay the premiums; otherwise, your insurance will be cut off. You won't receive your pensions if you don't comply with national policies. Of course, you could try to ask the heroic and dedicated employees working in Tibet or Bolivia, or in regions subject to war and disease, if they are willing to pay for your retirement. After all, employees working in such regions have higher bonuses. They struggle through rain and ice, and endure bitter hardship. Will they give you some money for your retirement? Huawei doesn't have much money. The company will collapse if we do not remain dedicated. We won't pay anything to people who are not dedicated. Do you really think it is realistic that at thirty-something years old, in the prime of your life, you don't have to work hard, and can just lie on your bed counting money? *(Ren Zhengfei: Speech at Meetings in Thailand with Regional Supervisors and in Nepal with Staff, Huawei Executive Office Speech No. [2017] 026)*

We need to gradually increase our efficiency, and ensure that our spending on people grows more slowly than sales revenue and profits. We expect three people to do the work of five and earn the income of four. We need to enhance the Contribute and Share system, and develop a team with collective interests and common beliefs despite having diverse cultural backgrounds. *(Ren Zhengfei: Huawei's Success Is Also the Success of Our HR Policies—Speech at a Dinner with Some CHR Staff, Huawei Executive Office Speech No. [2017] 037)*

1.2.6 Passing Market Pressure Down Through Each Layer of the Company to Make Sure Our Internal Response System Remains Active

Core values can be passed down only after they are turned into a benefit-driven mechanism

All enterprises are benefit-driven. This requires a fair value distribution system preceded by objective value assessments, which in turn need to be underpinned by a positive corporate culture. This is necessary to ensure that outstanding people who have made contributions to the company will be paid fairly. *(Ren Zhengfei: Seizing Opportunities, Adjusting Management Systems, and Meeting Challenges, 1997)*

"Staying customer-centric, inspiring dedication, and persevering" is a benefit-driven mechanism. To sustain our culture of inspiring dedication, we must reward our dedicated employees. We will not forget those who have a sense of mission and proactively contribute. That might be our corporate culture. We cannot build our culture and make it sustainable with empty talk. Instead, we must incorporate this culture into our appraisal system. *(Ren Zhengfei: From "Philosophy" to Practice—Speech at Huawei Annual Management Conference 2011, Huawei Executive Office Speech No. [2011] 016)*

Other companies may be people-centered, but our company focuses on dedicated employees. We are increasing our market share through hard work, not through a monopoly. Therefore, we distribute value to our dedicated employees. We are opening our doors to all kinds of talent. We can increase the size of the pie only by uniting as many people as possible. As long as you work hard, the slice of the pie you get will only increase. Don't be afraid that it will be snatched away by a newcomer who's been here only two months. If we are open-minded like this, we will grow even stronger. *(Ren Zhengfei: Speech at a Meeting with Elite Teams at the Training Camp on July 23, 2013, Huawei Executive Office Speech No. [2013] 174)*

We must widen the gaps in employee compensation based on the value that each employee contributes. We must fully fuel the engines in the organization so that they can drive the train to run faster and deliver more. To truly live out our core values, we must have a group of people who set the example. Employees' compensation is not based on their scope of management; it has to be based first and foremost on contributions, results, and responsibilities, and second on the spirit of dedication. *(Ren Zhengfei: Applying the Spirit of the Tortoise to Catch up with the Dragon Spacecraft—Speech at the Huawei Annual Management Conference, Huawei Executive Office Speech No. [2013] 255)*

Huawei protects the interests of its dedicated employees. If you are tired and want to retire, we are there for you. We must not say that previous dedicated employees are no longer entitled to company benefits. If we do, who will be willing to fight in the battlefield? But who will be willing to work hard if we give more to retired employees and less to dedicated employees? I will also retire in the future, so I should be among those who support the policy of giving more to the retired employees and ask you to do more work, so that I can get more money. But wouldn't you be a fool to accept that? So, our core values won't change much. Those who circulated this rumor must be underperformers. *(Ren Zhengfei: Remarks at a Meeting with Members of the Project & Financial Management Enablement Program for High Potentials, Huawei Executive Office Speech No. [2014] 054)*

Our assessment system should focus on results and responsibilities, and we should motivate heroes in a timely manner. We should dare to fast track outstanding employees and widen the income gap between high performers and low performers. First, our incentives for heroes should be offered promptly. This means that we should focus on goal fulfillment and must not appraise employees based on the leadership model. Those who have achieved success in a project should be given an incentive. As to whether they should become managers, we need to measure them against the leadership model. Currently, there is a tendency of using key performance indicators for every type of assessment. What does success have to do with these indicators? Those who achieve success are heroes. We should reward them for their contributions, and should not consider irrelevant shortcomings. But we will take their shortcomings into account when we consider promoting them to managerial positions or raising their personal grades. Second, we should dare to widen the income gap between high performers and low performers, and dare to fast track employees who have made outstanding contributions. Outstanding employees should be rewarded more and fast tracked. If we don't widen the income gap, outstanding seeds will not be able to grow. If these employees are suppressed and not promoted, there will be backlash and the morale of their teams will be low. Strong teams are made in battles. Once a team achieves success, promotions should quickly follow so that morale will be boosted and the team will become even stronger. We need to select several outstanding employees as role models, to motivate others to fight in the battlefield and outperform the role models. This will boost morale. Those who don't make progress, fall behind, or perform poorly will gradually be removed. *(Ren Zhengfei: Speech at a Meeting with Employees of the Central Asia & Caucasia Region, Huawei Executive Office Speech No. [2016] 063)*

Transferring market pressure to every process and every employee to inspire passion across the organization

At its current stage of development, the problems Huawei faces will only continue to grow. We will either stagnate and die off, or work harder, achieve more, and stand shoulder-to-shoulder with other great companies of the world. Managing a company is like rowing upstream: If we don't advance, we will be driven backwards. We need to instill a sense of urgency into every single Huawei employee. *(Ren Zhengfei: Toasting Those Who Succeed and Offering a Helping Hand to Those Who Fail, 1997)*

There's no way back; we have to burn our boats. We need to transfer a sense of urgency and pressure to every employee. We need to pass market pressure down through each layer of the company to make sure our internal response system remains active. *(Ren Zhengfei: How Long Can Huawei Survive?, 1998)*

Outside China, we were often offered opportunities to participate in telecom privatization projects, but we didn't. Because of this, we may encounter greater difficulty in selling equipment in the future. This has forced us to develop products that are of the best quality, with the best performance and service, but at the lowest costs. If we fail to do this, we will find it hard to sell them. Poor performance in any segment will be subject to criticism from other segments. Through this transfer of market pressure, we can ensure our internal operations are always vigorous and activated. Placing ourselves in a desperate position can force us to become a world-class equipment provider. *(Ren Zhengfei: How Long Can Huawei Survive?, 1998)*

Junior and middle managers should have a sense of urgency. What does it mean by this? It means 10% of managers will be removed from their positions each year. As a manager, you have been given trust and opportunities. If you fail to put these to good use, the company will have no choice but to remove you from your position. We must resolutely remove unqualified managers. Only in this way can we rank and screen managers, drive them to remain passionate under pressure, and help our teams maintain their effectiveness. *(Ren Zhengfei: Staying Customer-centric, Inspiring Dedication, and Persevering Are Key to Our Success—Speech at the 2010 Huawei Market Conference, Huawei Executive Office Speech No. [2010] 002)*

Our future value assessment system must be oriented towards business success. Managers who create long-term losses for the company must be removed from their positions, along with personal grade decrease and pay cuts, to deter others from following in their footsteps. Even if they are outstanding seeds, why not demote them and place them in the Strategic Reserve as ordinary employees? They can rise again after further contributions are made. First, their pay needs to be lowered and positions adjusted. After they do a good job, they can rise again. Therefore, managers with poor business performance need to be replaced. If managers are weak, the entire team will be weak. Managers who fail to make strategic contributions must not be promoted. *(Ren Zhengfei: Growing from a Soldier to a General Within Three Years, Huawei Executive Office Speech No. [2014] 031)*

Open Access This chapter is licensed under the terms of the Creative Commons Attribution-NonCommercial-NoDerivatives 4.0 International License (http://creativecommons.org/licenses/by-nc-nd/4.0/), which permits any noncommercial use, sharing, distribution and reproduction in any medium or format, as long as you give appropriate credit to the original author(s) and the source, provide a link to the Creative Commons licence and indicate if you modified the licensed material. You do not have permission under this license to share adapted material derived from this chapter or parts of it.

The images or other third party material in this chapter are included in the chapter's Creative Commons licence, unless indicated otherwise in a credit line to the material. If material is not included in the chapter's Creative Commons licence and your intended use is not permitted by statutory regulation or exceeds the permitted use, you will need to obtain permission directly from the copyright holder.

CHAPTER 2

Huawei's Competition Strategy: A Financial Perspective

Huawei creates value primarily through its business operations. The primary task of its financial management department is to support and oversee business departments in creating value. Financially, what are the key points that Huawei focuses on as it creates value?

First, Huawei looks at business from an investment perspective and views opportunities strategically. The window of strategic opportunity is usually very short. To seize strategic opportunities, Huawei has the courage to win, is willing to make massive investments, and is skilled at achieving success.

Second, Huawei directs all its efforts towards the same goal and is selective about what it does and what it doesn't do. Focusing on its core business and keeping a sharp focus are the principles that Huawei has always followed in resource allocation. These principles are the key to Huawei's success and also guide Huawei as it allocates financial resources.

Third, Huawei refuses to be opportunistic in the face of big opportunities. The company is not distracted by short-term interests and temptations and does not dwell on sunk costs that may be incurred.

When there are conflicts between opportunities and costs, which is more important? Huawei's answer is opportunities. The company believes that, in the tech industry, the value opportunities bring is higher than their costs. If a strategic opportunity is seized, the company will succeed no matter how much money it spends. However, if it misses a strategic opportunity, it will fail even if it doesn't spend a penny. Being frugal will lead

© The Author(s) 2019
W. Huang, *Built on Value*,
https://doi.org/10.1007/978-981-13-7507-1_2

Huawei nowhere. Therefore, in financial management, Huawei places more emphasis on value creation than on cost savings.

The concept of "Digging In and Widening Out" developed by Li Bing for water management is the key to the longevity of the Dujiangyan Irrigation System in Sichuan Province, China. The wisdom it contains can be applied to far more than just irrigation. Huawei views this concept as a vivid illustration of its business model, and believes that it is also applicable to Huawei if the company wants to survive and thrive in the long run. Huawei's approach is to keep a reasonable profit margin, invest more in the future, and share more value with its customers, suppliers, and partners.

Openness, competition, and collaboration are the basic principles Huawei adopts to enhance its core competencies and build a favorable business ecosystem. An enterprise supply chain is actually a business ecosystem that ties together customers, partners, suppliers, and manufacturers. An enterprise can survive over the long term only when it strengthens cooperation with others, focuses on the interests of its customers and partners, and pursues success for all. Only when Huawei helps its customers create value can it find its position in the value chain.

Economic globalization is the end state of a market economy. This is an unstoppable historical trend. Huawei's development has been a process from going international to going global. In its first 20 years, Huawei was involved in a process of international expansion from China. In its second 20 years and beyond, Huawei operates on a global scale by bringing in talent from around the world and setting up its strategic centers of expertise (COEs) in places rich with strategic resources.

The above key points form the general strategy that guides Huawei's business and financial operations. This chapter elaborates further on these key points.

2.1 Continuing to Invest Boldly to Seize Strategic Opportunities

2.1.1 Seizing Strategic Opportunities Ensures Success While Missing Them Leads to Failure

We must consider the company's current development from a strategic perspective. Development requires investment, which incurs costs. Hiring new people may impact business results and salary growth. But we must look into the future to gain new perspectives. We must seize the right opportunities to develop rapidly. *(Ren Zhengfei: Speech at the Mobilization and Training Meeting Regarding Recruitment of New Graduates of 2001, 2000)*

The overall goal of our operations is to expand more rapidly. We are facing an unprecedented opportunity. We witnessed a similar opportunity about seven or eight years ago. However, back then we were still small and didn't have the ability to seize it. Now that we're capable of seizing the current opportunity, we must have the courage to win – this is necessary for us to achieve success. *(Ren Zhengfei: Eight Points Made After Receiving the "2008 Business Plan and Budget" Report at the EMT ST Meeting on January 31, EMT Meeting Minutes No. [2008] 009)*

We are bound to encounter some difficulties because of the lag effect of heavy investments. But this is not a problem as long as we are able to survive. If we could not even survive, no matter how large we are, we still have a problem. *(Ren Zhengfei: Working Together Towards the Same Goal, Concentrating Advantageous Resources on Our Core Business, and Having the Courage to Seek Greater Opportunities and Further Widen the Gap—Minutes of the Work Report on the Wireless Business, Huawei Executive Office Speech No. [2011] 039)*

The amount of data traffic may grow faster than we can imagine. As long as there is data traffic, we will have opportunities. Huawei is tasked with transmitting data traffic, and we need to build bigger, wider, and faster data pipes. This is the biggest opportunity we have and it is the core of our business. The platform that we have built over the past 25 years outperforms any of those built by other companies. We can no longer make data pipes wider just by stacking a dozen smaller ones. A bigger platform is now needed for the future. This is a strategic opportunity for us, as smaller companies do not have the capacity to create a big platform. *(Ren Zhengfei: Speech and Comments at the Carrier BG's 2013 Strategy Retreat, Huawei Executive Office Speech No. [2014] 016)*

When we spot a strategic opportunity, we can pour in huge amounts of resources to bring ourselves up to speed. We must boldly try different methods of investment, not just by adding people. This is different from the way small companies approach innovation. *(Ren Zhengfei: Applying the Spirit of the Tortoise to Catch up with the Dragon Spacecraft—Speech at Huawei Annual Management Conference 2013, Huawei Executive Office Speech No. [2013] 255)*

We now need to make heavy, focused investment in our strategic areas. Once we seize the strategic high ground, we can sell our products at higher prices and generate more profits, which can then be invested in advanced research. *(Ren Zhengfei: Comments to Staff of the Enterprise BG, Huawei Executive Office Speech No. [2014] 006)*

We must be willing to make investments and use modern technologies to develop modern products to seize the strategic high ground. Today, we need to rely on tools to win in the market. In the past, we didn't have money, so we emphasized self-reliance. We did our best to achieve success on our first try, and independently develop testing tools. This is now an outdated approach. We should be willing to invest and use the most advanced tools available to produce the most advanced products. This is the only way for us to increase our share in the market and earn more money. We have to spend money on the tools that we need to secure the strategic high ground. Once we gain control, the valuable resources all around will be ours. We need to be willing to invest and prepare for the future. *(Ren Zhengfei: The Best Defense Is a Good Offense—Remarks at a Briefing on the Wireless Network Business, Huawei Executive Office Speech No. [2013] 232)*

2.1.2 Increasing Future-Oriented Investment When the Market Is Experiencing a Cyclical Downturn

We should have a good understanding of the fluctuations in industry cycles and increase our investment in future opportunities. R&D doesn't have to be fully aligned with marketing and sales. There should be a two-year gap between R&D and marketing and sales. If we don't increase investment now, what will we sow when spring comes, and how will we create new opportunities? We must increase R&D investment when the market declines so that we can develop when the market recovers. To make that happen, we must be resolute in investing heavily in R&D. *(Ren Zhengfei: Speech at the Work Report of the Product Line Management Office, 2000)*

We've recently adopted a strategy of overtaking our competitors on the inside track. This means we should be bold enough to overtake our competitors when global competition is at an inflection point. When we watch a Formula One race, we rarely see racers overtake others on the straight, because this is almost a "mission impossible". Everyone is accelerating on the straight. How could you overtake anyone? Our Western peers have decades of experience in management, branding, and building customer trust. If everything goes well for them, and they speed up, they will leave us far behind, making it impossible for us to overtake them. But at a turn, a wrong decision could cause them to fall behind, as people can easily get confused and hesitant at a turn in the road. Nowadays, there is a surplus of electronic products, much like watermelons in autumn. There are just too many of them, so their prices are incredibly low. Nobody knows if the products will ever generate profits again. As long as we maintain our strengths and are bold enough to increase investment at a turn in the road, we are likely to overtake our competitors in some areas. The telecom industry is now at such a turn in the road and is undergoing transformations in technology, networks, business, and business models. *(Ren Zhengfei: Seeing the Situation Clearly and Accelerating Organizational Building and Reserve Pool Development to Embrace Huawei's New Development—Speech at a Meeting for HR Directors, 2005)*

We are now expanding rapidly in spite of a decline in the overall economy. For a period after the year 2000, we almost collapsed due to challenges both at home and abroad. Logic would have dictated that we should have reduced investments, reshaped our team, and consolidated our markets for future recovery. But we didn't. Instead, we increased investment and grew in the tough environment. When the financial crisis was over, our competitors noticed us. We were still small, but had grown. Following the first round of counter-cyclical growth, we stepped onto the global stage. Now we are experiencing a second round of counter-cyclical growth. I am not sure what we can achieve this time, but at the very least we will have some pricing power. *(Ren Zhengfei: Speech at the PSST[1] Managers' Meeting, 2008)*

When the IT bubble burst, transmission products' sky-high prices collapsed. Many leading companies in the industry cut investment in this field. But we didn't, even in the face of extreme financial difficulties. This helped us become the world's second largest company in transmission products. *(Ren Zhengfei: Making Youth Shine Out—Speech at the Dedication Conference of the Network Product Line, 2008)*

---

[1] PSST: Products & Solutions Staff Team.

2.1.3 Avoiding Opportunism and Having Strategic Patience in an Era of Big Opportunities

In an era of big opportunities, we must avoid opportunism and must have strategic patience. *(Ren Zhengfei: Avoiding Opportunism in the Era of Big Opportunities—Speech at the Luncheon with the Administrative Team of the Consumer BG, Huawei Executive Office Speech No. [2014] 025)*

When a window of big opportunity opens before us, what should we do? I hope you will keep improving yourselves. I'm very pleased to see your tremendous progress within such a short period of time. Recently, I told the Consumer BG that in an era of big opportunities, we must avoid opportunism and must have strategic patience. You should keep up the good work, and work towards our common goals. The more the company earns, the more we will invest in the future. This will help us hone our strategic competitive edge. When we become stronger, we will be able to earn more and attract the best people from all over the world, who will help us hone our edge further, and repeat this cycle. *(Ren Zhengfei: Speech at the Japan Research Center's Work Report, Huawei Executive Office Speech No. [2014] 034)*

Huawei must have the spirit of a marathon runner and run steadily to sustain profitability. Massive amounts of standardized, digital content are currently being transmitted more easily than before thanks to the Internet. This has driven the real economy to improve after acquiring and digesting information. Information drives the progress of society, the real economy, and services. The Internet is not just about the use of the Internet itself. As long as our smartphones are of high quality and meet the needs of consumers, we can strive to sell them online. We are different from JD and Alibaba in that we can control the quality of our transactions and we have a broad portfolio of intellectual property to protect us in the global market. It is risky to simply be a platform for transactions. You need to understand that cars have to be cars first. The same is true for all things, from finance to tofu. Nothing except Aladdin's magic carpet could ever replace a car. *(Ren Zhengfei: Avoiding Opportunism in the Era of Big Opportunities—Speech at the Luncheon with the Administrative Team of the Consumer BG, Huawei Executive Office Speech No. [2014] 025)*

While we were moving forward slowly like a tortoise, we ignored the flowers everywhere along the road in China. We remained dedicated, up until today. Our Consumer BG has gone through ups and downs with us for many years. It should continue to walk down the right path, with enough money to be distributed to employees. We need to identify our own problems and weaknesses, understand who we are, and be ourselves in order to succeed and build our own future. If we can continue to survive 20 years down the road, we will succeed, because many others will have been left behind. *(Ren Zhengfei: Avoiding Opportunism in the Era of Big Opportunities—Speech at the Luncheon with the Administrative Team of the Consumer BG, Huawei Executive Office Speech No. [2014] 025)*

Some people will say that we are opportunistic. We are actually trying to force you to change in the same way as we did to Consumer BG CEO Richard Yu several years ago – The Consumer BG managed to change after that. At that time, I told Richard, "I believe that in the next two to three years the Consumer BG will greatly improve its product quality, and will continue to do so in the years ahead. You should focus on things like business models and planning management." I also made a suggestion to him, "You must be able to grow watermelons on this peach tree of yours; you can't just grow peaches. One business model is not enough." The tree's trunk is the company's joint support platforms, like service, maintenance, and finance platforms. Its root system needs to be divided among different customers so that the tree can absorb different kinds of nutrients. You need to try different business models. Many companies know the tricks of the trade. As for how to grow watermelons on a peach tree, this is something you'll have to figure out for yourself. *(Ren Zhengfei: Heroes Are All Around Us—Speech at the Q4 Regional Presidents' Meeting, Huawei Executive Office Speech No. [2014] 086)*

We should not rush into commercializing our new technologies. We must have strategic patience and win as a late mover. We are closely watching the trends in customer demands, and we are not becoming complacent. We are poised to move, like a cat ready to pounce, as soon as market conditions are mature enough. We are not a slow mover that will miss big opportunities when they come. We also need to figure out how to protect customer investments as much as possible. We should not always think about disruption and starting anew every time. *(Ren Zhengfei: Remarks at Meetings with the UK R&D Center, Beijing Research Center, and Financial Risk Control Center in London, Huawei Executive Office Speech No. [2015] 075)*

We keep on stressing that strategic patience is key in our consumer business. You must have patience and perseverance. If you rush things, a problem with a single component could cause a malfunction in hundreds of thousands – or even millions – of our phones. This could ruin our consumer business, making it very hard to recover. So we have to stay realistic, control our ambitions, and develop at a reasonable pace. Too much excitement is always followed by a mistake. We are in a new age of "Warring States". No matter how fierce the competition becomes, I don't encourage you to engage in destructive price wars. I want you to keep improving quality, and keep running the hard race. That's the right way to ultimate victory. Don't worry if someone else has quickly won a share in a certain market. People switch their phones every two or three years, so just make sure that they buy a Huawei phone next time. That way, in three years' time, we can rise above the waterline and show our true colors. *(Ren Zhengfei: Pounding the Streets, We Are the Marathoners Who Always Push for More—Speech at the Consumer BG's Mid-year Conference, Huawei Executive Office Speech No. [2015] 107)*

In an era of big opportunities, we must avoid opportunism and must have strategic patience. Advances in basic science are essential to social development. And the development of basic science requires patience and perseverance. Some great people remained dedicated all through their lives despite the fact that they were not recognized. It also took several hundred years before gene technology really took off. Huawei has over 80,000 R&D employees. Each year, we allocate about 20% to 30% of our R&D spending to research and innovation, and 70% to product development. We have been investing over 14% of our annual revenue in R&D. Over the next few years, our annual R&D investment will gradually increase to US$10–20 billion. *(Ren Zhengfei: Dedicated to China's Century-old Dream of Revitalizing Science and Technology, Huawei Executive Office Speech No. [2016] 067)*

Huawei is forging ahead into the industry's uncharted territory. In this territory, we have no pilot, no rules, and no one to follow. Huawei will gradually slow down its pace as a "follower", and will assume the responsibility of creating guiding theory. We cannot just harvest what others have sown or cultivated. And we should thank Western companies for their piloting over the past 30 years. *(Ren Zhengfei: Dedicated to China's Century-old Dream of Revitalizing Science and Technology, Huawei Executive Office Speech No. [2016] 067)*

Why have we always stressed that we must focus on our core business? Because we are confident that our assumptions for the window of big opportunity that will open in the future are correct. We must not lose direction or miss the big opportunities because of our greed for small and short-term interests. *(Ren Zhengfei: There Will Not Always Be Flowers*

Along the Road Ahead—Speech at the H1 Huawei Market Conference, Huawei Executive Office Speech No. [2016] 079)
Because of our 28 years of unremitting effort, we have been able to make breakthroughs and become what we are today. And we will be likely to enter uncharted territory for transmission of massive amounts of data. Therefore, we must establish strategic confidence. We believe that we will be able to seize opportunities in this era of big opportunities. We believe that our team can achieve the goal of generating US$200 billion in revenue. Of course, we must not be burdened by the US$150 billion or US$200 billion goal. We must not put on our red dancing shoes. We set this goal to guide our transformation in organizational structures, systems, and processes, so as to develop capabilities that will be required in the future. It is not a key performance indicator (KPI). Rather, it is our core competency. Simply stressing this goal is meaningless. *(Ren Zhengfei: There Will Not Always Be Flowers Along the Road Ahead—Speech at the H1 Huawei Market Conference, Huawei Executive Office Speech No. [2016] 079)*

2.2 Working Together Towards the Same Goal and Deciding What Not to Do in Order to Do Something Great

2.2.1 *Concentrating High-Quality Resources on Core Business and Strategic Opportunities to Establish and Reinforce Strengths*

We must seize the opportunities presented by industry transformation, have the courage to increase investment, and seize strategic opportunities. With sustainable and profitable growth as the ultimate goal, we need to stay strategically focused and seize the strategic high ground, thus laying the foundation for survival and development over the long term. *(Ren Zhengfei: Guidelines on the Analysis of the Business Environment and Key Business Strategies, Corp. Doc. No. [2012] 081)*

We must strengthen internal transformation and focus our efforts on building an advantageous position in our core business and strategic markets. We should be cautious about developing in other businesses or markets, as it will compromise our ability to develop our core business and strategic markets. With clear strategic goals, we must focus on vertical business integration and do everything we can to increase efficiency. We can strategically reinforce our long-term strengths only by achieving sustainable and profitable growth and higher profitability. If we don't transform or improve our efficiency, we will not be able to seize the opportunities that will pop up over the next several years. *(Ren Zhengfei: Speech at the Self-reflection Session of the Executive Committee of the Board of Directors, 2012)*

What is a *core business*? Everything in the world follows a normal distribution curve. The most populous portion of this curve is our core business. We won't go after opportunities on either side of the curve, even if they are highly profitable. There's simply not enough demand. We just focus on our core business and follow major trends. As long as there is data traffic, there is an opportunity for us to succeed. *(Ren Zhengfei: Speech and Comments at the Consumer BG's Strategy Retreat in Sanya, 2012)*

We must focus on our core business. Value – not technology – must be placed at the center of everything we do. As an auxiliary product line, our Network Energy Product Line needs to show what you contribute to our core business. *(Ren Zhengfei: Speech at a Work Report of the Network Energy Product Line, Huawei Executive Office Speech No. [2012] 043)*

Sometimes the happier their customers are, the more difficult things are for carriers and equipment providers. But as long as we stay the course in *big rivers* – that is, our core business – we will eventually reach the ocean. *(Ren Zhengfei: Staying Customer-centric and Communicating Huawei at the Strategic Level—Speech at Huawei's Branding Strategy and Communication Retreat on April 12, 2012)*

If we cannot survive, there won't be any future! Our value assessment system needs to shift its focus from technology to business success. The Consumer BG is now part of the company's core business, where you must create value. However, value is not just about having leading technology. You still have a very long way to go. You should contribute energy to the core business rather than be a drag on it. If the energy of our core business gets dispersed, it will be very difficult to bring it back together to achieve our goals. *(Ren Zhengfei: Avoiding Opportunism in the Era of Big Opportunities—Speech at the Luncheon with the Administrative Team of the Consumer BG, Huawei Executive Office Speech No. [2014] 025)*

Huawei has made it clear that we will stick to our needle-tip strategy and be selective about what we do and what we don't do. We have defined the company's strategic roadmap and will follow it through. We will increase investment in massive data traffic and snap up a market share in areas beyond network products. We need to increase our share of data traffic and help customers monetize their data. The size of their networks is fixed, but if more traffic flows through their networks than their competitors', this is also a success. We must not waste our strategic resources on non-strategic opportunities. *(Ren Zhengfei: Speech at a Meeting with Trainees at the First Training Session for the Global Solutions Elite Team, Huawei Executive Office Speech No. [2014] 064)*

We must focus on our core business. Non-strategic areas of business must first be profitable, and we must have the courage to abandon loss-bearing projects and seize strategic opportunities. *(Ren Zhengfei: Heroes Are All Around Us—Speech at the Q4 Regional Presidents' Meeting, Huawei Executive Office Speech No. [2014] 086)*

We need to be like the Yangtze River: Keep to our course and flow forward, while generating massive potential along the way. Every product, large or small, should focus on our core business. New sprouts should also take root and grow in our core business. Don't deviate from this path, or our company will be split into two separate management platforms. *(Ren Zhengfei: Innovating to Create Global Value—Speech at the Corporate Strategy Retreat, Huawei Executive Office Speech No. [2015] 006)*

2.2.2 Narrowing Strategic Focus to Become an Industry Leader

Harnessing major trends successfully to truly lead global trends

We must not pursue multiple businesses at the same time, or we will become exhausted. Our focus should be on where our key customers are heading. If they change direction, we need to change with them. *(Ren Zhengfei: Speech at the Meeting with the R&D Managers of Huawei Technologies and Avansys, 2001)*

Our investment and HR management policies must be geared towards the most prominent needs of customers and society – essentially the most populous portion of a normal distribution curve. Sure, Huawei stands out in certain domains, but if we want to lead global trends, we need to successfully harness the major trends in our own industry. So for the time being, we will invest in our customers' most prominent needs. This approach will keep us aligned with major trends. *(Ren Zhengfei: Still Waters Run Deep—Continuously Improving Ourselves Based on Customer Needs, 2002)*

We need to work together towards the same goal. Greater force can only be generated when we focus our efforts on a very small area. Internally, we're good at limiting ourselves to the same source of income, but we're not so good when it comes to working together towards the same goal.

Our competitors have caught up with us because our R&D efforts are too spread out. At Huawei, every product line and every engineer is hungry for success, so there are far too many small projects going on here and there. This has weakened us. The Wireless Network Product Line must work together towards the same goal and increase investment in our core business to improve our capabilities and set ourselves apart from our competitors. *(Ren Zhengfei: Working Together Towards the Same Goal, Concentrating Advantageous Resources on Our Core Business, and Having the Courage to Seek Greater Opportunities and Further Widen the Gap—Minutes of the Work Report on the Wireless Business, Huawei Executive Office Speech No. [2011] 039)*

We must reduce or remove products that are not profitable from our portfolios. I will not invest in non-strategic products unless the investment is made on a rolling basis and can yield high profits. To make breakthroughs, we need to maintain a sharp focus across the company. A company without focus is like a dull knife: We'll never be able to carve out a piece of strategic markets. *(Ren Zhengfei: Speech at a Work Report of the Network Energy Product Line, Huawei Executive Office Speech No. [2012] 043)*

To become an industry leader, we must narrow our strategic focus and concentrate all our resources on seizing the strategic high ground in our core business and strategic markets. *(Ren Zhengfei: Speech and Comments at the Carrier Network BG's Strategy Retreat in Huizhou, Huawei Executive Office Speech No. [2012] 010)*

We must stay ahead of the demand curve. We have no other choice but to stay focused. We should learn from successful US companies. Most of them maintain a laser-like focus, but why? Do they lack the capabilities to engage in other businesses? At the moment, we are not ahead of demand; in fact, we are still trying to catch up. We're at the forefront of the industry, but we can't say with confidence that we are able to set its pace going forward. However, as long as we stay focused, odds are we can make ourselves irreplaceable. *(Ren Zhengfei: Our Transformation Goals Are to Harvest More Crops and Increase Soil Fertility—Speech at the 2015 Huawei Market Conference, Huawei Executive Office Speech No. [2015] 016)*

For our enterprise business, we should consolidate our position in areas where we have been successful, and further hone our competitive edge vertically before expanding into other areas. Smart cities are emerging. The finance industry is moving its IT to the cloud. Power grids are going digital, and there is an increasing demand from governments and enterprises for cloud services. These are all strategic opportunities. Our Safe City solutions are key to establishing our market presence in the smart city domain. But we must not expand too widely; otherwise, we will not be able to focus on strategic opportunities. *(Ren Zhengfei: Firm Belief and Strong Focus Lead to Greater Success—Speech at the 2016 Huawei Market Conference, Huawei Executive Office Speech No. [2016] 007)*

Developing a clear strategy by boldly letting go of non-strategic areas of business

Strategy is all about focus, and focus isn't just about what you pay attention to, but what you choose to ignore. This is key to being competitive. There are plenty of opportunities to choose from, but we need to decide what we won't do in order to do something great. When deciding whether to go for an opportunity, we have only one criterion: Whether it can help us constantly improve our core competencies. *(Ren Zhengfei: Huawei's Opportunities and Challenges, 2000)*

We must have a clear product strategy. We can't do everything ourselves, and we need to have the courage to give up certain things. Only by knowing what to give up can we have a clear strategy. We can consider researching and developing products that have large demand, huge potential for growth, and mature technology. For other products, we can consider joint R&D. *(Ren Zhengfei: Building the Competitiveness of Low-end Access Products with High Quality and Low Costs, 2009)*

In order to succeed, we need to learn the art of making strategic trade-offs. If we find it difficult to succeed in a certain region despite consistent effort, we could reassign our people to places where it's easier for us to succeed. We only need to build a presence in some parts of the world. If we remain stuck in a region that proves to be challenging, we might miss strategic opportunities in other regions. We will make trade-offs while keeping the big picture in mind. The next three to five years may be the best time for us to seize a share of the global market. We must stay focused during this period and seize the strategic high ground of massive data traffic. Once we secure this position, it will be difficult for others to reach our level, and we will have a brighter future. *(Ren Zhengfei: Comments to Staff of the Enterprise BG, Huawei Executive Office Speech No. [2014] 006)*

In the future, the Internet of Things, smart manufacturing, and big data will generate massive demand for ICT infrastructure. Our responsibility is to provide connections – specifically, equipment that enables connections. The global market is huge, and we won't be able to succeed in every single country. But we'll do what we can, where we can, and it will be no small feat. *(Source: A Chat in the Garden with Huawei Founder Ren Zhengfei, Huawei Executive Office Speech No. [2015] 098)*

In Chinese, the word for strategy can be broken into two parts. The first part is to "take action" or "take to the field". We won't be able to take action or take to the field in the right place at the right time if we lack strategic direction. Interestingly, the second part means to "omit" or let go of something. If you don't give up something, then your strategy won't be complete. We must dare to give up markets with bleak prospects and stay focused. As long as there are profits, that is fine. *(Ren Zhengfei: Speech at a Meeting with Employees of the Central Asia & Caucasia Region, Huawei Executive Office Speech No. [2016] 063)*

Resisting easy money utside the confines of core competencies

Shenzhen has experienced two economic bubbles: one in real estate, and one in the stock market. Huawei didn't get swept up in either. This is not because we're any better than those around us, but because we're serious about technology. When these bubbles swelled up, we certainly had opportunities. But we believe that the future world will be built on knowledge, not on bubbles. So we decided to hold our ground. *(Ren Zhengfei: How Long Can Huawei Survive?, 1998)*

We cannot allow ourselves to be lured away by the tempting opportunities all around us. With a gloomy outlook for the global economy, we cannot expand everywhere. Doing so will lead to chaos. We must narrow our strategic focus, and ICT infrastructure will always be our area of focus. This will never change. We can only maintain our strategic high ground by giving up non-strategic areas of business. Our Carrier Network BG, Enterprise BG, and Consumer BG must focus on the core business, harness the major trends in their own domains, and establish systematic forces instead of betting on winning in non-strategic areas. Everything in the world follows a normal distribution curve. The most populous portion of this curve is our core business. We concentrate our investment on our strategic direction. To prevent our non-strategic areas of business from developing blindly, we require them to produce a profit margin that is higher than that of our core business. *(Ren Zhengfei: Guidelines on the Analysis of the Business Environment and Key Business Strategies, Corp. Doc. No. [2012] 081)*

We can only make breakthroughs and move to the forefront of the world in a very narrow domain. We can't allow ourselves to be lured away from our core business. Straying too far into other domains and overdiversification will not help Huawei seize the strategic high ground when strategic opportunities emerge. We need to shift our operational focus from the blind pursuit of scale to long-term, sustainable growth – profitability, efficiency, and quality. Product lines and business units in non-strategic domains need to set high profitability targets. This is to inhibit their expansion and avoid spreading our human resources too thin. We must gradually learn how to seize the strategic high ground in markets, and adopt a top-down approach, where we start with high-end markets and allow that success to radiate down through the mid- to low-end markets. Of course, the precondition is that we have very good products and services. If we cannot offer low-end and mid-range products that are affordable and of high quality, we will be unable to seize the mid- to low-end markets and earn much profit. As these businesses grow, our people must grow even faster. *(Ren Zhengfei: Building a Highly Competitive Team—Speech at the Q3 Regional Presidents' Meeting, Huawei Executive Office Speech No. [2013] 093)*

While developing high-end technologies for the future, the 2012 Laboratories should dare to forge ahead in our core business. The more difficult the artificial intelligence technology, the harder we should work on its R&D. We must not make small commodities aimed at earning small amounts of money. We have made a lot of money in the last several years, so we should invest heavily and accelerate our pace of tool development to provide the most advanced tools to our service staff. It takes time for these tools to be ready. We should have strategic patience. *(Ren Zhengfei: Speech at a Meeting with Employees of the Noah's Ark Laboratory, Huawei Executive Office Speech No. [2016] 083)*

2.2.3 Maintaining a Narrow Focus to Make Breakthroughs

Narrowing the scope of focus and making massive investments to achieve key breakthroughs and create positive business cycles

Huawei's policy is one of concentrating resources to the greatest extent possible. By concentrating all of our strengths on a single point, we can achieve major breakthroughs. Why do we need to stick to this approach? Because business success relies on two factors: customer trust and a company's capabilities. AT&T has what it takes to make personal computers, but an AT&T branded PC wouldn't appeal to consumers. When we first launched our transmission products, many people might have thought they weren't as good as those produced by the Wuhan Research Institute of Posts and Telecommunications, which was the market leader at the time. We had to spend a lot of manpower, resources, money, and time before our products earned the trust of our customers. A company can only do well in a few areas at a time. You can't be great at everything. Focusing on our strengths will help our business grow exponentially. *(Ren Zhengfei: Staying Focused to Make Breakthroughs, 1994)*

The telecom market is huge, and we can't afford to invest in every single domain. We need to focus all of our resources – manpower, materials, and money – on the strategic areas of business where Huawei is capable of leading the pack, just like our competitors overseas do. All we need is a small inroad, and we can gain market share. Once we have earned money, we will invest more in the market, which in turn will lead to greater breakthroughs and a larger market share. This will form a positive business cycle. If our products continue to take the lead, and we have a large enough market, we can use a cookie-cutter approach to reduce costs. We can replicate our software and reuse it in other products. This approach will increase profit and give us room to thrive. *(Ren Zhengfei: Maintaining Technological Leadership to Expand into New Areas, 1996)*

As we know, muddy roads can support tanks, but hard floors will shatter when struck with a needle that has enough concentrated force. In other words, if we don't have much money, we should put all we've got into a single point – and I mean *everything* we've got. This might just help us make breakthroughs. Back in the day, people may have laughed at us for this approach, but focusing all of our resources on a single point is exactly what we have to do. *(Ren Zhengfei: Seizing Opportunities, Adjusting Management Systems, and Meeting Challenges, 1997)*

When it comes to resource allocation, Huawei has a very sharp focus. We allocate more resources than our major competitors to factors that are critical to our success and to strategic areas of growth. If there is no strategic value, we won't do it. But when we do decide to do something, we go all in – focusing all of our manpower, materials, and money on achieving major breakthroughs. *(Source: The Huawei Charter, 1998)*

From day one, Huawei bound its mission to the R&D of core communications network technologies. We invested almost all our profits from re-selling the equipment of other vendors in the research of private branch exchanges. By concentrating all our resources on these products, we managed to make partial breakthroughs, gradually achieved technological leadership, and generated higher profit margins. Our technological leadership created a window of opportunity for increased profit. We then reinvested the profits in the R&D of the next generation of products. By repeating this process, we continuously improve and innovate. Although we have become much stronger now, we still maintain this approach. We concentrate all our resources on core network R&D, to develop our core technologies. In this way, Huawei has progressed step by step, steadily growing into a global leader. *(Ren Zhengfei: Innovation Is an Inexhaustible Driving Force Behind Huawei's Growth, 2000)*

Compared with large companies, small companies are more flexible and responsive to market changes. They can identify new markets and opportunities more rapidly and earn a certain amount of profit before their competitors can react. Large companies are unwieldy and less responsive. But once they enter a market, they can leverage their strengths in platform and scale, concentrate their resources to make breakthroughs, and occupy the market with strong capabilities as a late mover. *(Ren Zhengfei: Delegating Authority and Boldly Innovating to Rapidly Respond to Customer Needs, 2001)*

We are a company with limited capabilities. We can only catch up with and surpass US companies if we keep our focus narrow. A broad focus would weaken our position, and if we don't keep our focus narrow, we can't generate the force required to make breakthroughs. My guess is that our Strategy & Development Committee is confident in our profitability over the next few years; they want to invest more in strategic domains. So they want us to give it a try and surpass US companies. We only stand a chance if we narrow our focus down to the size of a needle tip. If our focus expands to the size of a match-head or the end of a stick, there's no way we'll surpass them. *(Ren Zhengfei: Applying the Spirit of the Tortoise to Catch up with the Dragon Spacecraft—Speech at Huawei Annual Management Conference 2013, Huawei Executive Office Speech No. [2013] 255)*

Focusing all strategic resources on cracking big markets

We emphasize details too much in our company, and we lack strategists. Our goal is to enter a strategic market. I don't care how much force this takes. We need to break through, secure our presence, and reap the rewards. I am not saying that we should not cut costs or improve quality. But we should also look at strategic opportunities and determine which is more important. We must focus our resources on making breakthroughs in our core business and strategic markets. *(Ren Zhengfei: Working Together Towards the Same Goal, Concentrating Advantageous Resources on Our Core Business, and Having the Courage to Seek Greater Opportunities and Further Widen the Gap—Minutes of the Work Report on the Wireless Business, Huawei Executive Office Speech No. [2011] 039)*

I don't think our enterprise business needs to become big and strong within a very short period of time. I think it is more important to be down-to-earth and profitable. The one who outlives others will live best. Huawei is not one of the world's great companies. It became strong because it survived and outlived its competitors. Therefore, I still don't believe it is a good idea to blindly stretch ourselves too thin. Instead, we should focus on a few valued customers and a few competitive products and make breakthroughs in these areas. We don't need to extend our reach to too many areas. Instead, we need to stay focused and make breakthroughs. After we manage to make a breakthrough, it could set an example and generate huge profits when the practice is extended to the entire industry. So we should focus on making breakthroughs in high-value areas rather than shifting our resources to other places as soon as we make some progress. If we divided our resources and allocated them in different directions, this would be a sure path toward ruin. *(Ren Zhengfei: Comments to Staff of the Enterprise BG, Huawei Executive Office Speech No. [2014] 006)*

2.2.4 Never Wasting Strategic Resources on Non-strategic Opportunities

Never wasting strategic resources on minor goals

In his memoirs about World War II, *Lost Victories*, German Marshal Erich V. Manstein writes, "The offensive capacity of the German Army was our trump card on the Continent, and to fritter it away on half-measures was inadmissible." The strategic principle I learned from this was to never waste strategic resources on non-strategic opportunities. Our company must focus on achieving its strategic goals. We have separated our R&D from regional operations so that R&D becomes independent. Bundling R&D and regional offices together only satisfies low-end customer needs, which means abandoning strategic opportunities. We should channel high-quality resources to valued customers and abandon a certain portion of low-end customer needs. In the future, we will not take the lead in every business domain and may narrow our focus to a single domain. Therefore, if we are not earning a profit in non-strategic areas of business, we should gradually withdraw from them. *(Ren Zhengfei: Heroes Are All Around Us—Speech at the Q4 Regional Presidents' Meeting, Huawei Executive Office Speech No. [2014] 086)*

We must not waste our strategic resources on non-strategic opportunities. It's fine if a non-strategic area of business is beyond our capacity. We simply can't address every single customer need. However, we must gradually open up the interface with our customers, giving our partners room to meet the needs that we can't meet on our own. *(Ren Zhengfei: Speech at a Meeting with Trainees at the First Training Session for the Global Solutions Elite Team, Huawei Executive Office Speech No. [2014] 064)*

Instead of wasting strategic resources on small market segments, we focus all our strategic resources on cracking big markets. Take our storage business as an example. If we spent a large amount of energy trying to understand all sorts of industries, we would be wasting our strategic resources on non-strategic opportunities. Then we would lack the resources required to make breakthroughs in our areas of focus. Our storage business is currently bleeding money. We need to reduce investment in industries where we can't replicate our experience or expand on a large scale. *(Ren Zhengfei: We Can't Fit the Pacific Ocean in a Tea Cup—Speech at a Work Report of the IT Storage Product Line, Huawei Executive Office Speech No. [2014] 045)*

We can't focus too much on non-strategic opportunities; otherwise, small interests may weaken our overall strategic strength. The window of strategic opportunity lasts three to five years. Based on how we're doing right now, can we get our foot in the door? There's no point in complaining that our performance appraisal system is cruel. Some people might say, "I think I'm doing fine", but "doing fine" is not enough. We have different expectations for managers at different levels. As managers, you need to think about how to live up to these expectations. If your revenue and profits don't reach the targets, I'm not the one who's going to kick you out. When profits drop, your team's bonuses will shrink. Your team members will earn less under your leadership and will push you aside for sure. *(Ren Zhengfei: Why Can't Water from the Himalayas Flow to the Amazon River?—Remarks at the Work Conferences of the Latin America Region, Key Account Departments, and Carrier BG, Huawei Executive Office Speech No. [2014] 044)*

We need to continue with our needle-tip strategy. That means focusing our efforts on making breakthroughs that will help us take the lead in the era of massive data traffic. We must not waste too many strategic resources on non-strategic opportunities. *(Ren Zhengfei: Our Transformation Goals Are to Harvest More Crops and Increase Soil Fertility—Speech at the 2015 Huawei Market Conference, Huawei Executive Office Speech No. [2015] 016)*

Focusing on innovation in our core business is extremely difficult. I've noticed that all of your research and innovation projects are solid additions to our core business. This is precisely what we need. Breakthroughs only come with continuous buildup of capabilities and achievements. The massive data flows that we're seeing these days are the first of their kind in history. The systems and equipment that we provide to support these data flows are now among the best around the world. This is a rare honor and it is also a tough responsibility. We will strive to lead the pack in the future. If we fail to do so, we will fall behind and gradually wither away. And all our hard work will have been for nothing. So we must focus on innovation in our core business and must not waste strategic resources on non-strategic opportunities. It's true that even if we focus our efforts, we may not necessarily succeed. But if we lack focus, we will definitely fail. Technology is advancing so fast that if we hesitate for even a second, we will be brushed aside. *(Ren Zhengfei: Remarks at Meetings with the UK R&D Center, Beijing Research Center, and Financial Risk Control Center in London, Huawei Executive Office Speech No. [2015] 075)*

We don't expect our teams in small countries to make big money, but they must be capable of surviving, turning a profit, and building a strategic buffer zone. To survive, we must put ourselves in our customers' shoes and ensure network quality. We need to figure out customers' pain points about their networks. This requires us to look at data traffic maps, network topologies, satellite maps, economic charts, demographic distribution charts, and other types of charts. We should look at them every month, and see what customers' pain points are and where data traffic is highly concentrated. We will then persuade our carrier customers to invest in these areas to reduce the pressure on their networks and increase their revenue. This will boost their confidence. We cannot hard sell our assumptions to carriers. To avoid ineffective investment, we need to invest mainly in high-value regions, and pass over low-value regions for the time being. We need to have a clear focus in smaller countries. *(Ren Zhengfei: Speech at a Briefing by the Tajikistan, Turkey, and Belarus Representative Offices of the Central Asia & Caucasia Region, Huawei Executive Office Speech No. [2016] 091)*

Channeling high-quality resources to valued customers

We can provide good services to our customers only when we survive. Only when valued customers share more value with us can we become more capable, hire more people, and provide quality services. We have shared interests with our customers. *(Ren Zhengfei: Speech at the Awards Ceremony for Small Countries, Huawei Executive Office Speech No. [2013] 039)*

I have been saying recently that we must channel high-quality resources to valued customers. Serving valued customers well is the best we can do for them. Today, I told the executives of a carrier customer in China's Guangdong Province that making money is the foundation for Huawei to survive and thrive. I said the best we could do for valued customers is to channel high-quality resources to serve them and help them achieve greater success. This will create a positive cycle. Our overarching guideline is to serve customers well. The aim of our transformation is to channel high-quality resources to valued customers. For employees working in outstanding teams and on good service platforms, we can give them higher personal grades. We don't need to overemphasize balance across representative offices. If your representative office earns profit, I will assign service staff of higher grades to you to help you better serve customers. In that case, customers will see the value of Huawei and realize that they can succeed only by working with Huawei. As CFOs, you must understand the importance of channeling high-quality resources to valued customers. After making money from valued customers, you should do something for them in return. When I say high-quality resources, I mean we need to raise the personal grades of junior managers in field offices. Their personal grades can be increased again and again. In this way, we will have high-quality resources serve our valued customers. *(Ren Zhengfei: Comments to Staff of the Guangzhou Representative Office, Huawei Executive Office Speech No. [2013] 057)*

We must channel high-quality resources to valued customers. Who are our valued customers? Customers who give us more money. We will assign people with a major-general's capabilities as company commanders to serve our valued customers. This will increase our service cost. Major-general company commanders will definitely provide better service than company commanders at lower levels. *(Ren Zhengfei: The Best Defense Is a Good Offense—Remarks at a Briefing on the Wireless Network Business, Huawei Executive Office Speech No. [2013] 232)*

We must channel high-quality resources to valued customers and prioritize strategic customers. We need to concentrate our strengths on high-value areas. In the future, Huawei should have the right to choose customers. This doesn't mean that we will place undue pressure on our customers. There are so many customer needs, and it's impossible for us to meet all of them. *(Ren Zhengfei: Speech and Comments at the Carrier BG's 2013 Strategy Retreat, Huawei Executive Office Speech No. [2014] 016)*

We must channel more high-quality resources to valued customers and send more capable employees to serve them and improve our service quality. These high-paying employees will erode some of the money we make from our valued customers. These customers will realize that Huawei has not made much money from them and will feel good about that. In addition, we will help them become much more competitive. *(Ren Zhengfei: Growing from a Soldier to a General Within Three Years, Huawei Executive Office Speech No. [2014] 031)*

We will be a driver of order in the industry, and seize strategic opportunities in the era of massive amounts of data. We will channel high-quality resources to valued customers and work to satisfy their high-value needs by focusing on profits, our core business, and strategic markets. By channeling high-quality resources to valued customers, we are helping these customers seize the market. The market is determined by end customers. If we help our customers seize more of the market and earn more profits, they will buy more products from us and we will succeed as well. *(Ren Zhengfei: Comments to Staff of the Brazil Representative Office and Brazil Supply Center, Huawei Executive Office Speech No. [2014] 050)*

In the future, our elite teams should focus on designing solutions. As the times change, we must provide carriers with integrated solutions. The price will be a bit higher, but of course the service will also be better. When we say we will channel high-quality resources to valued customers, we do not mean we will only serve valued customers and ignore others. It means that we assign a *major general* to serve our valued customers, and a *lieutenant* to serve our regular customers. That is where the difference lies. But we should serve all our customers with the same passion. A *major general* will certainly perform a little bit better, enabling our valued customers to make more money. In return, we can also make more money. This is what we mean by channeling high-quality resources to valued customers. People and organizations are different, so resources to be invested will also be different. *(Ren Zhengfei: Building Advanced Tools and Enhancing Core Competencies to Achieve Success at a Higher Level—Speech at a Carrier BG Briefing on the Service Experience and Phased Acceptance of the "Three Cloud" Platform, Huawei Executive Office Speech No. [2015] 099)*

Serving valued customers well is the best we can do for them. We must have the courage to channel high-quality resources to valued customers and further improve our services. We need to optimize our resource allocation strategies and base our resource investment decisions on contracts

rather than complaints. *(Source: Resolution on Improving Services for Valued Customers, EMT Resolution No. [2015] 010)*
We need to adjust our presence and channel high-quality resources to our valued customers. We may begin this process with a few select customers in several select countries. In this way, we can build strong ties with one or two strong customers and jointly develop our capabilities. *(Ren Zhengfei: Innovating to Create Global Value—Speech at the Corporate Strategy Retreat, Huawei Executive Office Speech No. [2015] 006)*

2.3 INNOVATING TO CREATE GREATER VALUE FOR CUSTOMERS AND THE COMPANY

2.3.1 Placing More Emphasis on Value Creation Than on Cost Savings

The overall objective of our company is to increase sales and profits. We must increase R&D investment. If the investment turns out to be worthwhile, it will bring us more opportunities, and we must cherish these opportunities. We must also increase investment in marketing and sales, as this can help us obtain new opportunities. We must seize these opportunities, as the value they bring will be higher than their costs. When there are conflicts between opportunities and costs in the company, which is more important? Our answer is opportunities. I always believe that, in the tech industry, the value opportunities bring is higher than their costs. As long as opportunities bring value, an increase in costs is acceptable. *(Ren Zhengfei: Minutes of a Work Report on Annual Taxes and Budgets, 2001)*

What currently matters the most is whether or not we can seize strategic opportunities; costs are not our primary concern. If we seize a strategic opportunity, we will succeed no matter how much money we spend. However, if we miss a strategic opportunity, we will fail even if we don't spend a penny. Being frugal will lead Huawei nowhere. *(Ren Zhengfei: Speech at the Shanghai Research Center, 2007)*

When it comes to innovation, we must emphasize value. We must not innovate for the sake of innovation; rather, we must innovate to create value. *(Ren Zhengfei: Speech at the Meeting with Staff from the 2012 Laboratories, Huawei Executive Office Speech No. [2012] 035)*

Internet companies always talk about disruptive innovation. But Huawei's aim is to create value for the world. We innovate in order to create value. When it comes to innovation, we should focus on the needs of society over the next five to ten years. Most of our people should not be looking any further into the future than that. For most of our products, we should focus on sustaining innovation, and we must stick to this approach. At the same time, we will allow a small number of our younger employees to pursue disruptive innovation – exploring whatever seems interesting – within certain boundaries. Such disruptive innovation is open, from which sustaining innovation can absorb energy. When disruptive innovation grows strong enough, it can absorb energy from sustaining innovation. *(Ren Zhengfei: Innovating to Create Global Value—Speech at the Corporate Strategy Retreat, Huawei Executive Office Speech No. [2015] 006)*

To adapt to changes in future networks, we must innovate continuously. We innovate to help the world move forward and to create value. As we continue to focus on sustaining innovation, we should be more open-minded to different ideas and different types of innovation. *(Ren Zhengfei: Our Transformation Goals Are to Harvest More Crops and Increase Soil Fertility—Speech at the 2015 Huawei Market Conference, Huawei Executive Office Speech No. [2015] 016)*

2.3.2 Changing the R&D Spending Structure and Increasing the Proportion of Investment in Research and Innovation

Stored program control exchanges are high-tech products that require massive investments. Manufacturers have to keep up with the most advanced technology available and invest heavily in R&D to make sure their equipment is world-class. On top of this, they need to invest in marketing, sales, training, and services to make sure that their equipment can function well in switching networks, and that it's well suited for quality communications networks. *(Ren Zhengfei: Opinions on the Rural Telephone Network and Switch Industry in China, 1994)*

We're known for our customer centricity and reliable products. Beyond that, our emphasis on R&D is the most important factor for us to stand out in the competition with global giants in China's highly competitive telecom market. *(Ren Zhengfei: Sticking to Customer Centricity and Keeping up with Global Trends, 1996)*

To explore and build our presence in future markets, Huawei earmarks 10% of its annual sales for R&D and maintains a tight focus on *strategic* development. Only by consistently increasing investment can we narrow

the gap between Huawei and other global players. *(Ren Zhengfei: Standing Against Pride and Complacency and Being Mentally Dedicated, 1996)*
Every year, the company invests 10% of its sales in R&D – even more, if necessary. *(Source: The Huawei Charter, 1998)*
Our research budget accounts for 10% of our R&D investment, which is the maximum amount we allow ourselves. It doesn't matter if the money is wasted, but we can't go beyond our budget – and if the budget runs out, that's it. When it comes to investment, it's important to pay attention to normal distribution curves. Investment should be driven by two things: customer needs and technology. We can't rely on just one or the other – both are important. *(Ren Zhengfei: Corporate Development Should Focus on Meeting the Current Needs of Customers—Speech at a Meeting with Key Employees of the Optical Network Product Line on April 18, 2002)*
The money set aside for research must not be used for any other purposes, or mixed with other R&D budgets. We say over and over again that we're a customer-centric company. If we don't give research its proper due, then the technology-driven side of our business will become very weak. Meeting customer needs is our guiding light. But if we hope to meet these needs, we need the right technology. So we have to guarantee the right amount of investment in technological innovation. *(Ren Zhengfei: Comments at the Meeting Regarding the Planning and Budgeting Work for 2005, 2004)*
Our overall principle is to continue increasing R&D investment. We just need to ensure a certain degree of profitability. We need to spend a reasonable amount of our short-term profits and increase investment in R&D to enhance our long-term ability to compete. I recommend that we increase our investment in network R&D to 12% of our annual revenue. The R&D department must use up this investment. *(Ren Zhengfei: EMT Meeting Minutes No. [2010] 025)*

1. Product development is a well-defined task, and should be subject to disciplined planning, budgeting, and accounting. If R&D staff make mistakes in product development, they can reapply for budgets.
2. We should change the budget mix for R&D and increase the percentage of investment in research and innovation. For example, 70% of our R&D budgets go to product development and the remaining 30% to research and innovation. We can consider increasing the percentage of our total R&D spending to 14% of our annual revenue.

3. Research and innovation should be forward-looking, carried out along multiple paths and in multiple waves. Product development should become a task of certainty, following the roadmap defined by the IPMT[2] of each product line.

(Ren Zhengfei: Scale New Heights and Forge Ahead into Uncharted Territory Along Multiple Paths in Multiple Waves—Key Messages of Discussions at Mobile World Congress and in Ukraine, Huawei Executive Office Speech No. [2016] 068)

2.3.3 Ensuring Sufficient Customer-Facing Budgets

1. Business units must focus on short-term business goals, and more importantly, on the long-term return on investment and business development potential of our customers. They need to prepare reasonable customer-facing budgets based on the baselines set by the company and the actual needs of business development. They must avoid only seeking to reduce the expense rate.
2. Customer-facing and internal operations budgets should be prepared and granted separately. Customer-facing budgets cannot be used for other purposes, and savings in such budgets will not be included in the profits of the current period. Those who use customer-facing budgets for internal operations will be disciplined by the Internal Audit Department.
3. Customer-facing budgets are linked to performance KPIs and managed flexibly. If customer-facing budgets are expected to exceed the quarterly or annual budgets granted, and if the performance KPIs and expense rates are expected to remain acceptable over the coming period (e.g., 6–12 months), the departments whose budgets are to be overrun can apply to borrow the budgets from the subsequent quarters or to increase their annual budgets.

(Source: Resolution on Managing Customer-facing Budgets, Finance Committee Resolution No. [2013] 003)

---

[2] IPMT: Integrated Portfolio Management Team is a cross-functional team that manages the profit, loss, and business success of a product line on behalf of Huawei.

To do business with customers over the long term, we must not reduce customer-facing budgets. Instead, we must ensure that our budgets cover all carrier customers. We need to allocate enough account managers and CC3 roles targeting customer CIOs and CMOs to ensure good sales of our IT products. The headcount of account managers will be set based on need rather than efficiency. How many account managers will be needed for a customer must be clearly managed using checklists, and the number cannot be reduced. *(Source: Implementing Corporate Strategy to Ensure Solid Operations of the Carrier Business and Effectively Develop Enterprise and Device Businesses—Speech by Xu Zhijun[3] at a Meeting with Staff from the Southern Pacific Region, SDC[4] Office Speech No. [2014] 008)*

Whether or not customers will transform successfully is a very complex issue. It is not something we can help them with, and we should not be in any rush to change how our customers operate. We just need to assign more people to engage with customers. It is understandable if these people do not achieve quick results. *(Ren Zhengfei: Speech at the Oath-taking and Awards Ceremony of the Transformation Elite Team, Huawei Executive Office Speech No. [2015] 047)*

We must maintain sufficient customer-facing budgets. *(Source: Notice on Launching the Annual Corporate Planning and Budgeting for 2017, Corp. Notice No. [2016] 398)*

We need to improve the ability of representative offices to deliver a "One Customer, One Solution" experience. We will move our solutions to the field. Representative offices can select products based on the company's product lineup and develop them into solutions. They can also set their own prices based on their actual conditions and long-term business plans. We need to establish elite teams that aim to deliver this "One Customer, One Solution" experience. We should recruit employees who have planning experience, extensive experience in Global Technical Services (GTS), and a strong sense of responsibility from across the company to join in this effort. With extensive experience and a sense of responsibility, these people are an asset to be cherished in the company. We can enroll two or three hundred people to build customized solutions that

---

[3] Xu Zhijun was the Rotating CEO of Huawei at the time.
[4] SDC: Strategy & Development Committee was a professional committee under Huawei's Board of Directors. With the authority delegated by the Board of Directors, the SDC set the company's strategic directions and ensured that concerted efforts were made to sustain the company's growth.

meet customers' needs in the current period. These people need to work alongside contract scenario experts. This will allow us to have more in-depth operations within a country. Each solution could have two or three people acting as seeds. A local sales team will develop during the course of customization. The seeds can be taken to representative offices around the world, and by doing so, our global sales will become standardized on the basis of customization. *(Ren Zhengfei: Speech at a Briefing on the Progress of the ISC+ and CIF Projects, Huawei Executive Office Speech No. [2017] 035)*

2.4 DIGGING IN AND WIDENING OUT

2.4.1 *"Digging In": Ensuring Investments in Improving Core Competencies and Preparing for the Future*

The concept of "Digging In and Widening Out" was developed by Li Bing and his son over 2000 years ago. Other marvels of the time – such as the Hanging Gardens of Babylon and the Roman aqueducts and bathhouses – have long fallen to ruins, but the Dujiangyan Irrigation System in China's Sichuan Province is still working well and continues to benefit people living in the Chengdu Plain. Why? The concept of "Digging In and Widening Out" is the key to the longevity of the Dujiangyan Irrigation System. The wisdom it contains can be applied to far more than just irrigation. This concept is also applicable to Huawei if we want to survive and thrive in the long run. *(Ren Zhengfei: Digging In, Widening Out—Speech at the Commendation Meeting of the Operations and Delivery Division, Huawei Executive Office Speech No. [2009] 009)*

"Digging In" means ensuring investments in improving core competencies and preparing for the future, even in times of financial crisis. It also means tapping into internal potential and lowering operating costs to provide higher value services to our customers. "Widening Out" means curbing our greed for profits, avoiding sacrificing long-term interests for short-term interests, and sharing more value with our customers, all while treating our upstream suppliers generously. *(Ren Zhengfei: Digging In, Widening Out—Speech at the Commendation Meeting of the Operations and Delivery Division, Huawei Executive Office Speech No. [2009] 009)*

Everything we do is for our customers. But ultimately, we are the ones who benefit from doing so. Some people say we treat our customers so generously that they are just taking our money. We must understand the meaning of "Digging In and Widening Out". We don't need so much money. We only need enough profits to survive; the rest can be given to our customers, partners, and competitors. This is how we can become bigger and stronger. You must understand the meaning of "Digging In and Widening Out". It relates to guaranteeing everyone's survival. *(Ren Zhengfei: Customer Centricity, Increased Platform Investments, and Open Collaboration for Shared Success—Speech at the 2010 PSST Managers' Meeting, Huawei Executive Office Speech No. [2010] 010)*

2.4.2 Constantly Tapping into Internal Potential and Lowering Operating Costs to Provide Higher Value Services to Customers

To improve the quality of our internal operations and reduce operating costs, we must build a robust management system that includes a series of highly-effective platforms for assessment and incentives and excludes ineffective elements. *(Ren Zhengfei: Speech at a Meeting with the Steering Committee on Self-reflection, 2006)*

Low prices require low internal operating costs, which should be achieved by optimizing each aspect of operations and reasonably controlling employee compensation. Customers will not pay for the high salary and comfort of our employees. *(Source: Huawei's Core Values, 2007)*

We must consider internal operating costs no matter what we do. We have to avoid high-cost endeavors that do not create value. *(Ren Zhengfei: Speech at a Meeting Regarding General Procurement and Information Security, 2007)*

The impact of new technologies on business success will decrease. Low operating costs will be critical to competition, and our future survival and development will rely on management improvement. We must keep our costs low and keep our feet on the ground. We must seize territory first and then take root and blossom. *(Source: Minutes of the Discussion on Huawei's Business Strategy for 2009, EMT Meeting Minutes No. [2009] 017)*

During current budget assessments, we try to reduce internal operating costs rather than management expenses relating to customers and suppliers. Each department needs to fully understand this. Cutting internal operating costs is conducive to organizational streamlining at HQ and process optimization and simplification. *(Ren Zhengfei: Focusing on Strategy and Streamlining Management, Huawei Executive Office Speech No. [2012] 041)*

We must keep our feet on the ground. The earth is our mother, the source of our strength. We must stick to our strategy of high quality and low costs. *(Ren Zhengfei: Building the Competitiveness of Low-end Access Products with High Quality and Low Costs, 2009)*

In the future, the value of the Internet may not be in helping ICT infrastructure providers and Internet companies make money. Rather, its value will lie in helping companies in the real economy make money by mining and using data. Both ICT infrastructure providers and Internet companies are working to build a better future for the world. Our business model should guarantee sustainable profitability rather than profitability higher than others. We will succeed as long as we can survive. *(Ren Zhengfei: Speech and Comments at the Carrier BG's 2013 Strategy Retreat, Huawei Executive Office Speech No. [2014] 016)*

2.4.3 Sharing More Value with Customers and Treating Upstream Suppliers Generously

We need to pursue a reasonable profit margin. If our prices are too high, competitors will join the game; if our prices are too low, they will destroy the industrial environment and make our own survival impossible. Any product can be unprofitable at first and then become profitable later. We need to use our long-term profitable strategy to support our short-term strategy that is not profitable. The key is to set up a point of marginal cost so that once we exceed that point, we will become profitable. *(Ren Zhengfei: Building the Competitiveness of Low-end Access Products with High Quality and Low Costs, 2009)*

We are dedicated to the philosophy of "Digging In and Widening Out". We don't want to earn too much money, but we can't afford to lose money for too long. We only need reasonable profits for survival. We will give the rest to our customers and suppliers. We will become the big shot in the industry if we can outlive all of our competitors. Since we are competing with strong competitors, all those who survive are heroes. *(Ren Zhengfei: Being a Tolerant and Broad-minded Hero with the Spirit of Openness, Cooperation, and Self-reflection, 2010)*

We need to stick to the philosophy of "Digging In and Widening Out", overcoming difficulties on our own and sharing value with others. We need to plant more flowers and less thorny bushes and make more friends and fewer enemies. We must unite as many people as possible to achieve

shared success rather than becoming the sole winner. *(Ren Zhengfei: Over Earth and Ocean, Clouds Roam with Gentle and Swift Motion, 2010)*
We must improve our customer services rather than lower prices. Competition on excessively low prices will destroy the entire business ecosystem, which will definitely cost quality in the end. All industries in China are facing this issue right now. We must work hard to improve our profitability, but the extra profit we earn cannot be completely distributed to employees. Part of it must be used to provide high-quality services to our customers. By improving our service quality, we can become more competitive than small companies and reinforce our competitive position. *(Ren Zhengfei: Minutes of the Report on the 809 Strategic Guidelines, EMT Meeting Minutes No. [2012] 016)*

2.4.4 Never Pursuing Low Prices, Low Costs, or Low Quality

My long-term view is that we need to improve the quality of our services from within and avoid significantly lowering prices. If we don't improve the quality of our services, customers will only focus on prices when choosing suppliers. In that case, we will not be able to set ourselves apart from others even if we offer low prices. We need to improve the quality of our products to compete in the market and avoid cornering Western companies through low prices. *(Ren Zhengfei: Speech at the EMT ST Meeting, July 2010)*

When we select partners for project delivery, quality must be a key factor. As we seek high quality, we also need to pay attention to costs and avoid recklessly pursuing low prices. *(Source: EMT Meeting Minutes No. [2010] 022)*

We have already established a favorable presence in the device market, and need to develop steadily on the basis of good profitability. In this market, we need to avoid price wars. Previously, we tried to compete on price. We need to stop doing that, or we will destroy order in the marketplace. We need to win customers with high-quality products and services rather than low prices. Price wars will lead Huawei nowhere. *(Ren Zhengfei: Comments to Staff of the Guangzhou Representative Office, Huawei Executive Office Speech No. [2013] 057)*

In a scarcity economy, a company could earn lots of money by scaling up production capacity to meet demand. But we are now in a surplus economy where supply exceeds demand. In this context, some companies compete ferociously on price, and some churn out fake or substandard products. Both of these approaches are shortsighted and short-lived. Some companies squander huge sums of money not on serving customers well, but on forcing out their competitors, aiming to profit handsomely from their customers. At Huawei, one of our core values is to stay customer-centric. Our high-quality offerings benefit our carrier customers, so they choose to stay with us. But we will not offer low prices; otherwise, we might have to offer lower pay and in that case, many of our staff might leave our company. Therefore, we must be committed to improving quality because it is essential to our competitiveness. *(Ren Zhengfei: Speech at the Q4 Regional Presidents' Meeting, Huawei Executive Office Speech No. [2015] 113)*

Even though we are unable to develop a technological edge for some products, we can still standardize and simplify these products so they are maintenance-free. To achieve success, we must also create advantages and set ourselves apart from others in terms of business and management models, as well as the spirit of dedication, capabilities, and sense of responsibility of our employees. We must not follow the path of low prices, low costs, or low quality. If we do so, the strategic advantages we have established over the past 20 years will be destroyed, and we will lose our competitiveness. *(Ren Zhengfei: Our Transformation Goals Are to Harvest More Crops and Increase Soil Fertility—Speech at the 2015 Huawei Market Conference, Huawei Executive Office Speech No. [2015] 016)*

We must change our focus from low costs to high quality. We must leave our component suppliers a reasonable level of profits and use high-quality components to make high-quality products. We must provide customers with high-quality services and a superior experience. High quality may incur higher costs, but it will also create greater value. With high-quality products, we will be better positioned to mitigate risks and maintain stable operations in the face of international competition and economic fluctuations. *(Source: BOD Executive Committee Meeting Minutes No. [2015] 023)*

Do low-end products yield low profit? Not necessarily. Once we get the quantity up and ensure zero maintenance, profit doesn't necessarily have to be low. We cannot force the price down. We don't have to drop our prices just because others drop theirs. That's just driving them into the ground. We have to first show consumers our quality, then we can allow our prices to be a little higher. And every year, some mature hardware and software can filter down from our high-end products to the low-end products. Last year's high-end model is this year's low-end device. That way, users who don't have as much money to spend can still enjoy good quality. That's also success for us. So we shouldn't underestimate or simply ignore the low-end phone market. *(Ren Zhengfei: Pounding the Streets, We Are the Marathoners Who Always Push for More—Speech at the Consumer BG's Mid-year Conference, Huawei Executive Office Speech No. [2015] 107)*

In the future, we must remain absolutely committed to two things. One is intellectual property, and the other is product quality. As soon as we make money, we will reinvest it in improving services. That's what we mean when we talk about the "Van Fleet Load". We have to rapidly build up a global service system. If we can't build it fast enough, then we can train people in China, and send the best service people overseas to develop service capabilities. Once the capabilities overseas are built up, then we can have local service staff provide high-quality services to local customers, and the Chinese staff we assigned there can gradually come back home. We need to constantly innovate our service models, because in mobile phones, the focus of competition is slowly shifting away from R&D. Once a certain level of usability has been reached, further improvements to these products will no longer deliver much value to consumers. R&D will start to lose traction. Apple will also struggle to find ways to improve their phones. This is a sign that the technology is getting close to the point of saturation. Once the hare makes it to the saturation point, it has nowhere else to go, and all it can do is wait for the tortoise to catch up with him. This is the time when we have to speed up the rollout of our service network, and prepare to lead the world. *(Ren Zhengfei: Consumer BG Services Should Be "Genghis Khan's Horseshoes": The Firm Footing for Our Global Ambitions—Speech at the Consumer BG Services Strategy Report, Huawei Executive Office Speech No. [2016] 012)*

2.5 Openness, Competition, and Collaboration

2.5.1 *Nothing Can Stop Us If We Remain Open*

A closed culture cannot absorb the strengths of others and will gradually be marginalized. A closed organization will eventually become like stagnant water. We must openly learn from others in every area, such as R&D, sales, services, supply management, and financial management. We must not cling to what has worked in the past and become self-centered. In our process of innovation, we need to stand on the shoulders of giants and absorb as many external strengths as possible in the same way as a sponge absorbs water. We must not pursue independent innovation behind closed doors. With openness, Huawei will be able to survive in the long run. Without openness, it will soon perish. *(Ren Zhengfei: Deepening Our Understanding of the Corporate Culture of Staying Customer-centric and Inspiring Dedication, 2008)*

An integral part of Huawei's core values is openness and initiative, but our EMT members were divided on this for quite some time when we were determining our core values. Huawei is already a strong innovator. Is openness so important? Due to our past successes, our confidence, pride, and complacency have increased, and we are becoming increasingly self-absorbed. We need to change. We need to be open and learn more from others. Only by doing this can we set new goals, truly examine ourselves, and develop a sense of urgency. *(Ren Zhengfei: Openness, Compromise, and Huidu, 2010)*

Why do we emphasize openness? The global market is enormous and ICT infrastructure is as wide as the Pacific. It is so large a market that no single company can dominate. Failure to stay open will lead us into a dead end. So why are some people against openness? They are blinded by their vested interests. We must get rid of vested interests. This is what we have always been doing. We are getting rid of what makes money for us. If we don't do this, others will ultimately replace us. The Stone Age did not end because there were no stones left in the world. We must remain open and stay committed to openness, no matter whether we are weak or strong. When we are open, our advantages will be gone, so we will have to work even harder to gain new ones. *(Ren Zhengfei: Speech and Comments at the Carrier Network BG's Strategy Retreat in Huizhou, Huawei Executive Office Speech No. [2012] 010)*

We must build an open system rather than a closed one. Lack of openness will only lead to decline. If we do not learn from the Americans, we will never surpass US companies. *(Ren Zhengfei: Speech at the Meeting with Staff from the 2012 Laboratories, Huawei Executive Office Speech No. [2012] 035)*

Openness is one of the factors that contribute to the success of capitalism. There was no economic success in China when it shut its doors to the outside world. Therefore, we must open up. Currently, many people in China hope to grow stronger behind closed doors. This is a mistake. Throughout history, China has shut itself away from the outside world for long periods of time, making it impossible to become strong. The US is the world's most open nation, and thus the world's strongest. Though the US may fall behind from time to time, it has seen constant waves of innovation: Apple, Facebook, and others. As long as the US remains open, who can stop it from moving forward? *(Ren Zhengfei: Absorbing the Energy of the Universe over a Cup of Coffee, 2014)*

Many companies and research institutes around the world are very good at one particular area of R&D. But we have the strongest integration capabilities, so we shouldn't be afraid of opening up to the outside world. On average, only one out of every 1000 academic papers has commercial value. People in academia will be happy if we approach them and ask them to tell us about their problems. Our Thought Research Center should be up and running soon. In this center, there will be only one department – the Secretariat Office, which is a meeting coordination team responsible for preparing meeting minutes after brainstorming sessions. We must invest in the future, and this is the only way for us to secure a position in this area in three to five years' time. *(Ren Zhengfei: Speech at a Meeting with Employees of the Noah's Ark Laboratory, Huawei Executive Office Speech No. [2016] 083)*

We should be highly open-minded when it comes to research on artificial intelligence. You are right by conducting research yourselves. Otherwise, you won't be able to know whether you're moving in the right direction, or which research results are valuable. There are companies that are doing better than us. We can incorporate what they have done. The Google system has scanned lots of books from Spain and Latin America, so its translations from English into Spanish are very accurate. We should bring in such machine translation capabilities. In terms of natural language processing, can we partner with the industry's leading companies? We can sponsor them and use the systems they develop. To be a global leader, we must be open-minded and inclusive. *(Ren Zhengfei: Speech at a Meeting with Employees of the Noah's Ark Laboratory, Huawei Executive Office Speech No. [2016] 083)*

2.5.2 Competition in the Future Will Be Between Supply Chains

The price we offer to our suppliers must be high enough for their survival. It is not a good idea to create a vicious market environment, as it makes it impossible for both sides to survive. If we lose our suppliers, we will have to find new ones. Doesn't qualifying new suppliers incur extra cost? *(Ren Zhengfei: Remarks at a Meeting with Procurement Managers, 2000)*

When a company grows to a certain size, it must build strategic partnerships with its suppliers to ensure the ongoing supply of materials and components. This is also necessary for the company to develop rapidly. *(Ren Zhengfei: Speech at the Report on Supply Situations, 2000)*

Competition in modern times is no longer between individual enterprises; it's between supply chains. An enterprise supply chain is actually a business ecosystem that ties together customers, partners, suppliers, and manufacturers. An enterprise can survive over the long term only when it strengthens cooperation with others, focuses on the interests of its customers and partners, and pursues success for all. *(Source: Huawei's Core Values, 2007)*

Future competition will be between supply chains. The robustness of the entire supply chain – upstream and downstream – is vital to Huawei's survival. *(Ren Zhengfei: Digging In, Widening Out—Speech at the Commendation Meeting of the Operations and Delivery Division, Huawei Executive Office Speech No. [2009] 009)*

The value of enterprise management lies in the effective, market-oriented integration of all resources and elements, such as capital, technology, talent, markets, R&D, manufacturing, and supply chains, to help the company compete successfully in the market. This is also the goal of enterprise management. *(Ren Zhengfei: News Release, 2009)*

We need to enhance strategic cooperation with high-quality resources in the industry, and we can also form alliances with our peers to jointly create value for the world. As we do this, we also need to protect customer resources.

First, we need to stress joint value creation and contribution, rather than disruption. If we can work with Cisco and make our equipment compatible, it will be a success for us. We should not reject Cisco. In certain domains, we need to establish alliances with Cisco. We can have a look at what path Cisco has chosen and provide necessary support. We need to be more open-minded. We have become what we are today by turning our competitors into allies.

Second, to stay competitive, we need to strengthen strategic cooperation with top industry players. We can buy from any vendor who delivers to our standards. We need to be open-minded. If we don't buy from these vendors, they may sell to our competitors, who, by integrating resources of companies that have no dealings with us, will become as competitive as us. This will be bad for our company. Therefore, we need to be open, collaborate with European and US vendors, and share value with them. *(Ren Zhengfei: Speech at the Briefing on Industry Trends and Progress in Fixed Networks, Huawei Executive Office Speech No. [2015] 109)*

2.5.3 Value Sharing Is Vital to a Robust Business Ecosystem

Only when we help our customers create value can we find our position in the value chain. Only when we truly understand the needs and challenges of our customers and provide them with good services to help them hone their competitive edge, will they grow with us in the long run and agree to long-term partnerships. As a result, we will survive and thrive. So we need to focus on the challenges our customers face and provide them with competitive communications solutions and services. *(Source: Huawei's Core Values, 2007)*

While working with others, Huawei must not act like a black widow, a kind of spider that eats its mate in order to gain nutrition for its offspring. In our past dealings with partners, Huawei either "ate" or "dumped" our partners after collaborating for one year or two. Now that we have grown strong enough, we should become more open-minded and modest, and look at issues with a deeper insight. We must pursue more effective models of collaboration for shared success. Our R&D teams are open, but I expect to see even greater openness, both internally and externally. It has not been easy for Huawei to grow into what we are today. As we continue to progress, we need to absorb as many ideas as possible from the outside world and get inspiration from them. Do not be narrow-minded. *(Ren Zhengfei: Customer Centricity, Increased Platform Investments, and Open Collaboration for Shared Success—Speech at the 2010 PSST Managers' Meeting, Huawei Executive Office Speech No. [2010] 010)*

We are increasingly aware that the purpose of our global business operations is not just to increase sales and profits. More importantly, we need to invest over the long term in countries where we operate, to create jobs, pay taxes, and promote local technological advances. At the same time, we should make the local industry more competitive, help communities prosper, and make due contributions to the development of every country where we have a presence. In this way, we can create a mutually beneficial business ecosystem. The obstacles we face in the business environment today are something we must experience as we grow from a small company to a big one. We must adopt an open mind to face difficulties and setbacks ahead of us, think proactively, and act calmly. This is the only way to gradually improve our business environment and ultimately get the industry, government, and society to accept our development. *(Ren Zhengfei: Guidelines on the Analysis of the Business Environment and Key Business Strategies, Corp. Doc. No. [2012] 081)*

We must learn to share value with our allies and look at the world with an open mind. Through this, we will eventually win over the world. We need to be open. Huawei will soon be number one in the ICT industry. If we only want to dominate the world without sharing any value with our partners, we will ultimately fail. Many people throughout history who wanted to dominate the world perished before their goals were achieved. Those who are unwilling to give up markets are not strategists. I suggest that you watch a movie called *From Victory to Victory*. Don't be too concerned about the temporary gains and losses of individual projects or markets, because our goal is the global market. *(Ren Zhengfei: The Best Defense Is a Good Offense—Remarks at a Briefing on the Wireless Network Business, Huawei Executive Office Speech No. [2013] 232)*

Senior managers should read three corporate documents very carefully. The first is *Resolution on Improving Services for Valued Customers*. For the Consumer BG, we have to do just that – improving the quality of services for our valued customers in every phase of user service, including product quality, sales, and after-sales. The second document is *Resolution on Sharing Value with Suppliers*. The purpose of this document is to improve our relationship with suppliers, especially with our strategic suppliers. In the past, we supported small companies as our suppliers, and of course it was impossible to ensure high quality. We are producing enormous quantities of products now, so we need to find key suppliers, and build strategic partnerships with them. We need to share value with our suppliers to motivate them to offer us parts of even higher quality, so that we can better serve our consumers. Huawei is firm in its policy of openness: opening up to external partners and promoting open source internally. We don't necessarily have to invest in production lines of other manufacturers or build our own. We just need to sincerely share value with our suppliers and we will then succeed together. *(Ren Zhengfei: Pounding the Streets, We Are the Marathoners Who Always Push for More—Speech at the Consumer BG's Mid-year Conference, Huawei Executive Office Speech No. [2015] 107)*

The Consumer BG should implement an elite team strategy. We don't want to expand the team too much; otherwise, it will collapse in the end.

When we implement our Contribute and Share system in the Consumer BG, it's not just for employees or suppliers; we also need to share value with sales channels, retail partners, and other parties involved. The strategy of sharing value widely means we don't need to build a huge organization. We need to correctly assess our own situation. Don't think that we are omnipotent. We need to keep self-reflecting on our weaknesses. This way, we will find the right approach for the Consumer BG to develop. I think that if we are going to hire more people, we should also add new capabilities. We need to focus on details when planning human resources for the Consumer BG. For example, ask yourself a few questions: Where do you need to increase headcount? What standards do new people need to reach? What contributions should they make? You need to prepare a list of such questions first. *(Ren Zhengfei: Pounding the Streets, We Are the Marathoners Who Always Push for More—Speech at the Consumer BG's Mid-year Conference, Huawei Executive Office Speech No. [2015] 107)*

I hope that our Consumer BG will use the world's best cameras, acoustics, and computing capabilities to create the world's best mobile phones. We don't need to develop all components by ourselves. Instead, we should integrate our research system with the platforms of our strategic suppliers so that we can share value together. Even if we conduct research on most of these components, we should give our partners the opportunity to produce and supply them. We must not do everything on our own. We have shared value with our employees. Why can't we share value with our strategic partners as well? We must not do everything independently, as that will turn us into an international orphan. *(Ren Zhengfei: There Will Not Always Be Flowers Along the Road Ahead—Speech at the H1 Huawei Market Conference, Huawei Executive Office Speech No. [2016] 079)*

You need to study the meeting minutes sent to the Capital Construction Management Department – *Sharing Our Success Beyond Huawei*. We must be open-minded and allow high-quality suppliers to become our partners and grow together with us. The mechanism adopted in the Capital Construction Management Department makes workers feel respected, and this has greatly boosted their initiative and motivated them to deliver high-quality projects at a faster pace. We must share our success with all of our partners. *(Ren Zhengfei: Remarks at a Meeting at the National Academy of Sciences of Belarus, Huawei Executive Office Speech No. [2016] 087)*

2.6 Becoming a Truly Global Company

2.6.1 Building a Global Business Ecosystem to Keep Growing

As the Chinese economy goes global, our country can prosper only by learning the best practices of other countries. In this era, a company can only thrive by having a global strategic outlook and can only keep growing by building a global business ecosystem. Likewise, to have a successful career, employees need to have a global perspective and the ability to work globally. *(Ren Zhengfei: Speech at a Farewell to Employees Heading Overseas, 2001)*

Currently, many big companies think they are not big enough, and seek to become bigger by constantly acquiring other companies. Why are companies obsessed with mergers and acquisitions? It's because the world of the future will be dominated by big companies, not small ones. US politics in fact serve big companies. The aim of the US's globalization strategy is to help big companies sell their products all over the world. But products can be sold globally only when they are of high quality. Small companies can't benefit much from globalization. Only big companies can make big money through market monopolies. They can reinvest the money they make in new functional domains like R&D, marketing, sales, and management, thereby sustaining their profitability. This is well understood the world over, and is leveraged by many players as they ride the wave of globalization. *(Ren Zhengfei: Comments to Staff of the Technical Support Department, 2002)*

We are facing very good opportunities in the international market. The addressable market in China may shrink in one or two years, but the overseas market is developing rapidly. I've been to some countries, which are just like what China was ten years ago, and have very bright prospects. There are many opportunities out there. We have never faced such promising markets. In the past, we always waited to snap up a small share after others had taken up almost all of the market. Now we are able to enter national markets as they open. Take Russia as an example. It is double the size of China. Just imagine how many optical fibers will be needed there. Isn't this a great opportunity for us? We have to pick up our pace to grow into an international company, and all departments must understand the market issues. *(Ren Zhengfei: Speech at a Meeting with Key Employees of the Optical Network Product Line, 2002)*

Economic globalization is the end state of a market economy. This is an unstoppable historical trend. Capital seeks out the best places to grow. It is like a migrating bird, always seeking out the best niche to settle in. *(Ren Zhengfei: The Market Economy Is Best for Competition; Economic Globalization Is Inevitable—Speech at the Commendation Meeting of Finance, Huawei Executive Office Speech No. [2009] 005)*

After the original global economic landscape is disrupted, protectionism is inevitable. We must be able to cope with it. With a gloomy outlook for the global economy, we must resolve issues surrounding globalization at the cost of some short-term interests. *(Ren Zhengfei: Guidelines on the Analysis of the Business Environment and Key Business Strategies, Corp. Doc. No. [2012] 081)*

Globalization demands that ideas, cultures, and nations become more global. Each nation has its unique qualities. For example, Germany and Japan are advanced manufacturing powers; the French are romantic and have a keen sense for color and mathematics. That is why we can locate our fuzzy mathematics research center and color research center in France. *(Ren Zhengfei: Speech at the Japan Research Center's Work Report, Huawei Executive Office Speech No. [2014] 034)*

2.6.2 Leveraging Relative Advantages in Global Competition

For Huawei, globalization does not mean we simply hold ourselves to European and US standards, especially in terms of compensation and cost. If our labor costs run out of control, we could lose our fundamental competitive advantage. Our compensation policy must be designed in a way that ensures we remain profitable globally. *(Source: Minutes of the Report on the Globalized HR Management Project, EMT Meeting Minutes No. [2006] 018)*

Thanks to the large number of talented individuals in China, we have gained a unique competitive advantage – low R&D costs. Our business model is to grow our network equipment business, and build world-class platforms for marketing, sales, service, R&D, and management. Based on these platforms, we are cultivating our managers, developing new businesses, and earning profits through capital investments in these new businesses. *(Source: Guidelines on Global Competition Strategies, EMT Resolution No. [2007] 021)*

We must develop targeted strategies to help us compete in different locales, product sets, and customer groups. We cannot expand everywhere and adopt a "one-size-fits-all" approach around the world. In addition, we must think strategically in the areas of government relations, customer relations, and competitive and cooperative relations. We must clarify the strengths we need to build to set us apart from our competitors and be clearly felt by our customers. *(Source: Guidelines on Sales Priorities, EMT Meeting Minutes No. [2008] 014)*

The correct path forward is to recognize that there will always be a division of labor, and that we must leverage our relative advantages in the international division of labor. This will help us gradually improve our weaknesses. Complaining won't solve anything. *(Ren Zhengfei: The Market Economy Is Best for Competition; Economic Globalization Is Inevitable—Speech at the Commendation Meeting of Finance, Huawei Executive Office Speech No. [2009] 005)*

2.6.3 Locating Strategic COEs in Places Rich with Strategic Resources

I think we should build COEs based on the cultural characteristics of specific regions around the world. If a region has the most talented people in a certain domain, we should build a COE in that region for that particular purpose. For instance, there is a lot of talent in India with very good negotiation and bidding skills, so we should build our COEs for negotiation and bidding in India. *(Ren Zhengfei: Speech at the EMT ST Meeting, 2009)*

Based on business needs, we should build different COEs in different countries around the world. The building of COEs is a global strategy that addresses global business needs rather than only the needs of a particular country. *(Ren Zhengfei: Integrating Project Estimation, Budgeting, Accounting, and Final Accounting to Support Project Operations—Speech at a Briefing on the IFS Project, Huawei Executive Office Speech No. [2010] 007)*

COEs must be built on an ongoing basis based on a unified plan. The plan for building global COEs will be developed in line with the company's strategy management process. If the direction of a COE is clear, it can be built immediately. *(Source: Requirements for Building Global Centers of Expertise and Recruiting Talent, EMT Meeting Minutes No. [2010] 033)*

Our business is going global. While we tap into China's resources and market strengths, we need to rapidly pool together, allocate, and share our global talent, capabilities, experience, and resources around the world. *(Source: Requirements for Building Global Centers of Expertise and Recruiting Talent, EMT Meeting Minutes No. [2010] 033)*

Why not step up efforts to build different COEs around the world? For example, we can establish a shared services center for auditing in the UK or the Netherlands. When I said we should build COEs, the Human

Resource Management Department prepared a form, which was completely R&D-centric. This is still technology-oriented, and they have not shifted their focus to balanced, comprehensive capability improvement. In our Financial Risk Control Center, why not do project risk analysis and control in collaboration with experts from Wall Street? We have many fellows now, some of whom are exceptional young people from outside of China. I think our operations management department, financing department, and audit department can also bring in some talented individuals, but they don't have to be as senior as fellows. When it comes to COE building, we are still technology-oriented and are not fully improving our managerial capabilities. *(Ren Zhengfei: Success Is Not a Reliable Guide to Future Development—Speech at the Huawei Market Conference on January 17, 2011, Huawei Executive Office Speech No. [2011] 004)*

In its first 20 years, Huawei was involved in a process of international expansion from China. In its second 20 years, Huawei will go global by building COEs that focus on global talent and address global needs. *(Ren Zhengfei: Minutes of the Meeting Regarding How to Share Value with Dedicated Employees, Huawei Executive Office Speech No. [2011] 010)*

Our R&D department operates dozens of COEs around the world. These centers are not responsible for local or regional operations (e.g., Europe). They are there to lead Huawei's global business. We will continue our efforts to plan and build global COEs, which will gradually bridge the capability gaps of our specialized teams. *(Ren Zhengfei: Comments at a Meeting with Sales Financing Experts, Huawei Executive Office Speech No. [2012] 025)*

I said in January that we will establish settlement centers in Japan and Europe focusing on Japanese yen and euro, respectively. We will diversify our financing channels and make some change in our capital settlement efforts. *(Ren Zhengfei: Comments at a Meeting with Sales Financing Experts, Huawei Executive Office Speech No. [2012] 025)*

The top priority for the Japan Research Center is to increase investment and take bigger steps in development. You do not have to focus only on the applied sciences for materials. You can also delve into the area of quality management. People in Japan take things very seriously. This is their biggest advantage. We can establish testing centers in Japan and Germany, integrate our three testing centers in China, Japan, and Germany, and increase investment in large capacity, high speed, and data security assurance. *(Ren Zhengfei: Speech at the Japan Research Center's Work Report, Huawei Executive Office Speech No. [2014] 034)*

We need to adopt a more open approach in our manufacturing. We need to continue to make good use of Japanese lean production consultants and German consultants. We can also directly bring in manufacturing managers, engineers, and technicians from leading companies in developed countries like Japan and Germany to rapidly make Huawei's manufacturing technology and management world-class. *(Ren Zhengfei: Speech at the Factory at Songshan Lake, Huawei Executive Office Speech No. [2014] 052)*

We need to place our strategic COEs in areas rich with strategic resources. Large companies should boldly channel their resources in a specific direction to shorten the catch-up period and extend the window of opportunity. This is the business version of a Van Fleet Load. *(Ren Zhengfei: Remarks at Meetings with the UK R&D Center, Beijing Research Center, and Financial Risk Control Center in London, Huawei Executive Office Speech No. [2015] 075)*

Quality is a top priority for our products, including hardware and software. Of the top software companies in the world, one is in Germany and all the others are in the US. Therefore, we should set up a software research center in Seattle and separate research in physics from that in logic. Without measures like this, we won't be able to produce the best possible software. The US has a robust innovation system, backed by an uncompromising spirit and strong momentum. We must not cling to what has worked in the past. We need to place our strategic COEs in places rich with strategic resources. *(Ren Zhengfei: Pounding the Streets, We Are the Marathoners Who Always Push for More—Speech at the Consumer BG's Mid-year Conference, Huawei Executive Office Speech No. [2015] 107)*

When we develop high-end devices, we should locate technology development in Japan, put the brain in the US, and carry out hands-on development activities in Suzhou, China. If we want to produce better high-end products, we need to build an ecosystem for the development of high-end devices. What are high-end products? They are products that align well with consumer demand and are apace with the times. One of the very important technologies of the future is going to be image processing, and in Japan there are many specialists in this area, because they have been cultivating people in image processing for decades. Japanese companies working on images are dying, but the DNA is still there. We should set up an image research center in Japan to absorb the Japanese philosophy of "small, light, precise, and compact" and its strengths in image processing. This will give a huge boost to our phones features. We can do the development in smaller cities in China. Average pay is relatively low there, so with the same salary, our staff in smaller cities can have a higher standard of living than in Shanghai. *(Ren Zhengfei: Pounding the Streets, We Are the Marathoners Who Always Push for More—Speech at the Consumer BG's Mid-year Conference, Huawei Executive Office Speech No. [2015] 107)*

We should place our COEs in regions rich with industrial resources. We need a global vision for this: Don't just focus on Beijing, Shanghai, and Shenzhen. We must not just operate in China; we should have a global presence. When I talk about first-tier cities, I don't just mean Beijing and Shanghai; I mean global first-tier cities, including those in the US. Employees can choose the locations where they want to work. Second-tier cities will be our R&D delivery bases in the future. *(Ren Zhengfei: Focusing on the Core Business and Seizing Strategic Opportunities—Speech at the Product Investment Strategy Review Meeting, Huawei Executive Office Speech No. [2015] 123)*

We should support technological development in Russia and former Soviet republics (mainly Belarus and the Ukraine), because these countries were very strong in technology. Today, those foundations are still there, and people in these countries are down-to-earth and apply themselves to what they do. They are different from many in China, who are often restless and busy speculating in real estate, stocks, or P2P lending. Few people conduct scientific research in a down-to-earth manner. China is vast, but there isn't a single quiet desk. Down-to-earth people can devote themselves to scientific research in the same way the Japanese aim to win Nobel Prizes. We must support their research – and they will be of great help to us when they manage to accomplish something in the future. *(Ren Zhengfei: Remarks at a Meeting at the National Academy of Sciences of Belarus, Huawei Executive Office Speech No. [2016] 087)*

Over the years, we have gradually set up our COEs in areas rich with strategic resources. So far, we have established 26 COEs around the world, and this figure is increasing each year. These COEs have gathered together many world-class scientists, who provide guidance to our company across every facet of our business. These COEs themselves are also evolving. The talent pyramid at Huawei used to be a closed system. We have blown open the top of this pyramid to absorb the energy of the universe. We must strengthen our communication and cooperation with scientists from all over the world, sponsor the research of those who move in the same direction as us, get actively involved in international industry and standards organizations, and attend all kinds of academic seminars. We should drink more coffee with bright minds to absorb their brilliant ideas and sense the direction of future development. Only long-term, persistent investment will ultimately lead to strategic breakthroughs. As breakthroughs become more complex, cross-field cooperation will become more important than ever. Therefore, we should blur the boundaries between organizations and between specialized fields and prepare the soil for breakthroughs. In addition to developing managers and experts internally, we should also introduce more capable ones from outside of Huawei. Russian scientists are more willing to take on long-term challenging projects, so we can integrate them with our Chinese employees who prefer short-term success. Japanese scientists are attentive to details; French scientists are romantic; Italian scientists are committed to work; and scientists from the UK and Belgium are great world leaders. These are all qualities that are extremely valuable to Huawei. *(Ren Zhengfei: Dedicated to China's Century-old Dream of Revitalizing Science and Technology, Huawei Executive Office Speech No. [2016] 067)*

We need to search extensively outside Huawei and set up our COEs in places rich with strategic resources. We also need to establish aggregating platforms by geography and by area of expertise. The role of these platforms is to digest ideas. We will invest in universities and sponsor the research of professors. We don't want to own their papers or their patents. We don't want to own anything, and their research projects don't have to be successful. It doesn't matter if they fail, as long as they tell us why and how they have failed. They just need to give us some lectures on their research process and the progress at certain milestones. If the research does not go well, we want them to tell us where and how it has gone wrong. Our aggregating platforms will summarize key takeaways from these scientists. *(Ren Zhengfei: Scale New Heights and Forge Ahead into Uncharted Territory Along Multiple Paths in Multiple Waves—Key Messages of Discussions at Mobile World Congress and in Ukraine, Huawei Executive Office Speech No. [2016] 068)*

2.6.4 Attracting Global Talent and Building a Global Management Structure

Stepping up efforts to build a global presence of technology and new business

To future-proof our business, we need to adapt to the requirements for new technologies like mobile Internet, new consumer electronics, ICT, and cloud computing. We also need to expand into new business domains, including enterprise business, new energy, and chips for consumer electronics. Therefore, we need to look at this from a global perspective, and step up efforts to plan new technologies and new businesses accordingly. *(Source: Requirements for Building Global Centers of Expertise and Recruiting Talent, EMT Meeting Minutes No. [2010] 033)*

We will not change the path of our globalization. Huawei's facilities in Europe are European companies and our facilities in Japan are Japanese companies. They are not Chinese companies. We should gradually localize them in terms of mindset. *(Ren Zhengfei: Comments at a Meeting with Sales Financing Experts, Huawei Executive Office Speech No. [2012] 025)*

When establishing our Strategic Advisory Council, we should first adopt an international approach. The ideas from one region do not represent the entire world. The strategic direction drawn from these ideas may not be correct, and we may pay a price for pursuing it. We should not take a wrong path when the strategic direction is correct, and we also don't want to be the only one who succeeds in this strategic direction. We want to be just part of the correct strategic direction, not the only one. We must share value with others, and incorporate this into our core values. This way, we will have fewer conflicts with other players in the world. *(Ren Zhengfei: Speech at the EMT ST Meeting, 2012)*

There are two things that I'm very worried about. First, we have not established a good presence around the world. Second, we aren't acquiring enough new technology. If we become self-obsessed and complacent, we may miss the best opportunities. If we do everything on our own, we will soon be cast aside by history. *(Ren Zhengfei: We Can't Fit the Pacific Ocean in a Tea Cup—Speech at a Work Report of the IT Storage Product Line, Huawei Executive Office Speech No. [2014] 045)*

We need to establish an architecture for a broad quality system. We should set up broad quality COEs in China, Germany, and Japan. Materials science in Japan is extremely advanced. Don't underestimate Kyocera.[5] Their gallium nitride is a ceramic and the main material used in radio communications. We should use materials in Japan to develop the world's best products. Germany is known for its culture of extreme rigorousness, and its technology and management capabilities are excellent; many Chinese tend to let their minds wander but are good at structural thinking.

---

[5] Kyocera is a Japanese multinational ceramics and electronics manufacturer headquartered in Kyoto, Japan.

Combining the strengths of the three cultures together will support Huawei's broad quality strategy. We can also replace people with tools and methods, produce irreplaceable and unrivalled products using the best tools in the world, and ultimately become a global leader. *(Ren Zhengfei: Speech at a Work Report on Corporate Quality, Huawei Executive Office Speech No. [2015] 067)*

We can set up a delivery capability research center in Japan, which should not be located in the same places as our two existing research centers in the country. The Japanese are well-known for their attention to detail, so our service team can bring onboard many of them to help us win on the front line. This research center should be able to help us find keys to engineering delivery and quality assurance. Our GTS should also leverage the strengths of local resources around the world. *(Ren Zhengfei: Speech at a Briefing on Business Strategies for Professional Services, Huawei Executive Office Speech No. [2016] 062)*

Bringing in talent from around the world regardless of their background

We are in the process of aligning ourselves with international standards. In this process, we should not ask non-Chinese people to make compromises to the Chinese. Rather, this is a process in which Chinese people integrate into the world. *(Ren Zhengfei: Speech at a Briefing by the Corporate Information Security Department, 2001)*

Huawei will step up its pace of internationalization to embrace the trends of economic globalization. We require our employees to spend more time learning and improving themselves. IPD,[6] ISC,[7] and financial IT systems are all important steps we take to go international. We will continue to develop our Chinese employees into international talent. At the same time, we will work harder to develop non-Chinese local employees, cultivate a batch of key non-Chinese employees, and place them in our management and decision-making teams at all levels. *(Ren Zhengfei: Key Points for Management, 2002)*

---

[6] IPD: Integrated Product Development is a set of models, concepts, and methodologies for managing the full lifecycle of research into innovative technologies and product development.

[7] ISC: Integrated Supply Chain is a system for managing the supply chain. Comprised of manufacturers and suppliers of raw materials and components, it provides products and services to customers through planning, procurement, manufacturing, order fulfillment, and other associated activities.

To meet the challenges of going international, we need to bring in international and professional talent in different areas, including technical services, supply chain, procurement, strategic cooperation, branding, overseas public relations, human resources, and commercial affairs. We only need to hire a limited number of high-end employees, who will act as seeds to improve our overall capabilities. *(Source: EMT Resolution No. [2005] 005)*

In sales and services, we will speed up the localization of our staff working outside China. This is a general principle of the company. This principle has been effectively implemented in the service domain, and sales should catch up as soon as possible. The Chinese employees we send to work outside China face a challenge as they try to integrate into local communities. Cross-cultural communication is difficult for them. In addition, the cost of local employees is much lower. Therefore, localization of employees outside China is a goal we will pursue over the long term. *(Ren Zhengfei: Strengthening Professionalization and Localization, 2005)*

We will hire more high-end professionals with global vision and appoint them as department directors. Our supply chain department should hire a vice president from Japan or Germany. Our audit department should recruit high-end talent from the US. We aim to have non-Chinese members in the Staff Team (ST) of every level-1 department and regional office in 2008. We should be open-minded towards external talent. All employees who follow company policy and contribute more than they cost will be recognized at Huawei, regardless of their country of origin or seniority. At Huawei, employees are evaluated according to policies, not based on their experience. We should get rid of our narrow-minded views of talent. *(Source: Guidelines for Delivery, Working Capital Management, and Team Building, EMT Meeting Minutes No. [2008] 013)*

We should deploy more non-Chinese managers. We can do this if we have a sound oversight system in place. When we do public relations in India, why not hire Indians to engage with Indians? We can provide advice behind the scenes. Our PR positions should be gradually filled by local employees. At the Shanghai World Expo 2010, I hope we will have many non-Chinese employees to host foreign delegations. This will make them feel better. Of course, there can be a Chinese employee accompanying the delegations. However, we must definitely not have a group of Chinese employees host a group of non-Chinese. We should have visionary and politically savvy people working in public relations. *(Ren Zhengfei: Speech at the EMT ST Meeting, 2009)*

We should bring in talent from around the world regardless of their background. As Huawei is going international, we will gradually raise the compensation packages for exceptional employees to international levels. This is the only way for us to attract world-class experts to Huawei. Why is the US such a developed country? It's because the US has a nurturing environment. Talent in the US comes from around the world. At Huawei, most employees are Chinese. Huawei has developed by hiring people from all parts of China, and the next step is to hire people from all over the world. *(Ren Zhengfei: Focusing on Business Success and Attracting Global Talent, Huawei Executive Office Speech No. [2014] 026)*

A company cannot become great by relying on only one person. It must learn to unleash the potential of outstanding people. In the R&D process of our product lines, we must develop a large number of maintenance experts and build elite teams. In the future, maintenance may play a more important role than R&D. We must create an environment where world-class talent can survive and thrive. In sales and marketing departments, it is very difficult for externally hired managers who are dropped into the middle of a tightly-knit "band of brothers" to succeed, because the "band of brothers" may refuse to follow their orders. However, scientists can survive at Huawei. Their work does not involve so many interpersonal relationships. We will establish elite teams in our sales and marketing departments. Externally hired managers in these departments will be sent to the elite teams for training and practice and form their own "bands of brothers". *(Ren Zhengfei: We Can't Fit the Pacific Ocean in a Tea Cup—Speech at a Work Report of the IT Storage Product Line, Huawei Executive Office Speech No. [2014] 045)*

At our recent management conference, we said we will change and improve our talent pyramid. Why? Japan and Germany are the two countries that are the best at electronic manufacturing. We will improve our manufacturing processes in line with Japanese standards. We will hire Japanese technicians and ask them to build a production line at Huawei. Our Chinese technicians need to be benchmarked against their Japanese counterparts. If they meet Japanese standards, they can receive a salary as high as that of Japanese technicians. Currently, we aim to set the salary of our key marketing, sales, and R&D staff by referring to US standards, and the salary of our key manufacturing staff by referring to Japanese standards. This will give us a higher standard to look up to in every domain. *(Ren Zhengfei: Speech at a Training and Practice Session of LTC Trainers in Germany, Huawei Executive Office Speech No. [2014] 061)*

The US is still the strongest when it comes to software. It has a strong sense of innovation. We need to increase our investment in future outstanding talent in the US, and place the outpost units of our Noah's Ark Laboratory in the US or Canada. Ireland is close to the east coast of the US. Is it possible for us to find great architects in Ireland? The average age of our experts outside of China is 40 to 50, so we should begin to bring onboard young seeds. These seeds do not have to be all Chinese. They can be non-Chinese PhD holders. They will be in the prime of their life a decade later and play a pivotal role at Huawei. If we don't bring them onboard now, we will soon be short of successors in our experts' team. There are also many outstanding people in Hong Kong and Taiwan who have returned from studying in other countries. However, there aren't any big industries in these two regions, so we can attract more of them to the company. These days, there is a lot of hype around artificial intelligence, and some bubbles might burst soon. We should source talent as soon as possible. When the river floods, we can catch fish in the street. *(Ren Zhengfei: Speech at a Meeting with Employees of the Noah's Ark Laboratory, Huawei Executive Office Speech No. [2016] 083)*

Building a global management structure

The company must go international. Finance has already gone international, and we need to do the same for Supply Chain and GTS – and quickly. We have no other choice. *(Ren Zhengfei: Employees Will Never Become Generals If They Don't Know Where They've Gone Wrong, Huawei Executive Office Speech No. [2007] 033)*

We must have a global view when establishing our HR presence. We should select several countries with a nurturing legal environment and a good price-performance ratio in employee compensation, and assess the feasibility of making them our low-end R&D bases or other business bases. We need to make a comparative analysis of policies and environments in advance. *(Ren Zhengfei: Minutes of a Briefing by HR, 2007)*

Our business structure in India can refer to our model in the US. We can consider bringing in independent directors who are influential in society. In addition to that, we need to streamline our business and governance structures to meet our market expansion needs in India. *(Source: Minutes of the Report on the Proposal for the Business and Organizational Structures in the US, EMT Meeting Minutes No. [2010] 007)*

We need to go global at a faster pace and establish a global management structure. We need to develop and promote a large batch of managers around the world who have a strong sense of mission, strategic thinking, business acumen, and strong motivation, and place them in our management teams at all levels. We need to create mechanisms that encourage healthy competition between managers. *(Ren Zhengfei: Guidelines on the Analysis of the Business Environment and Key Business Strategies, Corp. Doc. No. [2012] 081)*

Open Access This chapter is licensed under the terms of the Creative Commons Attribution-NonCommercial-NoDerivatives 4.0 International License (http://creativecommons.org/licenses/by-nc-nd/4.0/), which permits any noncommercial use, sharing, distribution and reproduction in any medium or format, as long as you give appropriate credit to the original author(s) and the source, provide a link to the Creative Commons licence and indicate if you modified the licensed material. You do not have permission under this license to share adapted material derived from this chapter or parts of it.

The images or other third party material in this chapter are included in the chapter's Creative Commons licence, unless indicated otherwise in a credit line to the material. If material is not included in the chapter's Creative Commons licence and your intended use is not permitted by statutory regulation or exceeds the permitted use, you will need to obtain permission directly from the copyright holder.

CHAPTER 3

Remaining Flexible to Seize Opportunities Amidst Uncertainties

As Huawei evolves from a follower into an industry leader, a new challenge it faces is how to manage uncertainties. The ICT industry is full of change and uncertainty, and a moment of hesitation will cause any company to fall behind. The consequences will be more serious if that company is happy with the status quo, and refuses to make progress or listen to criticism.

The more uncertain the future is, the more opportunities there are in store. Uncertainty is exactly where profits stem from. The history of high-tech companies shows that a major determinant of market value is the strategic value of growth opportunities amidst uncertainties. According to modern finance theories, a company's strategic value depends on the flexibility with which it invests in opportunities amidst uncertainties. The value of such flexibility can be interpreted and evaluated by the real options theory.

In the face of a highly uncertain future, making a strategic decision is different from making a bet. When making a future-oriented strategic decision, Huawei does not bet everything it has on a single opportunity – this is too risky. Betting everything on a single opportunity is what small companies do, because they lack money to invest in anything else. Huawei is a large company, and it is increasing investment in research along multiple paths in multiple waves. Only when things become clearer will it dedicate a large team to the area it has selected. The word "failure" is not in the vocabulary of Huawei explorers. Research and innovation on uncertainties are what scientists are most interested in, but they need to be confined within boundaries and serve the company's core business. Technological innovation without boundaries can take company strategy in the wrong direction.

The company needs to ramp up investment in research on uncertainties. It should also develop the ability to distinguish between businesses of certainty and those of uncertainty, create certainty out of uncertainty, and make the elements of certainty standardized, process-based, and automated to achieve higher efficiency and better results. These are the major tasks of management transformation.

From the perspective of strategic value management, this chapter thoroughly discusses how Huawei remains flexible to seize opportunities amidst uncertainties and face future challenges.

3.1 Maintaining Flexibility When Investing in Projects of Uncertainty

3.1.1 Never Putting All Eggs in One Basket When Making Strategic Decisions

When we decide to move in a certain strategic direction, we need to invest strategically in an opposing direction to guard against potential risks and help to buy us some time if the strategic direction we choose turns out to be wrong. If we lack a clear direction amidst chaos, we must make balanced investments in multiple directions to guard against risks. Only when things become clearer can we dedicate a large team to the area we have selected. Despite this, we need to carefully study the areas in which we can seek international cooperation. We must not do everything on our own. Every company needs to focus on its area of expertise. *(Ren Zhengfei: Speech at the Work Report of the Product Line Management Office, 2000)*

When we make strategic decisions, we must not put all our eggs in one basket. It is too risky to select only one product for investment. *(Ren Zhengfei: Comments to Staff of the CDMA2000[1] Base Station Team, 2001)*

---

[1] CDMA: code division multiple access, a communications scheme that uses frequency expansion technology to form different code sequences. When the CDMA scheme is used, subscribers with different addresses can use different code sequences for multi-address connections. This mobile telephony system is applicable to ultrahigh frequencies including 800 MHz and 1.9 GHz.

No one knows how large data traffic will be in the future. In this era of massive data traffic, fixed networks will have an integral role to play. There will be plenty of market opportunities. Since we have set our strategic direction, we need to seize multiple opportunities to achieve our objectives. We cannot bet everything on a single opportunity. This is what small companies do, because they lack money to invest in anything else. Huawei is a large company with enough money, so we should dare to invest. To achieve our objectives, we can select multiple paths, develop multiple technical solutions, and move in multiple waves in our research and innovation. Similarly, in our core business, we can use multiple methods to *row our boat*. However, this doesn't mean we will diversify our investments, or deviate from our core business. In such a rapidly changing world, we should never rely on chance. Companies that bet everything on a single opportunity may find it hard to succeed. If they choose the wrong strategic direction, they will suffer badly. *(Ren Zhengfei: Speech at the Briefing on Industry Trends and Progress in Fixed Networks, Huawei Executive Office Speech No. [2015] 109)*

3.1.2 Large Investment Along Multiple Paths in Multiple Waves

As long as there is sufficient demand in the market, we must seize the opportunities it brings. Since we don't know what will happen in the market in the future, we need to compete on a wider front and must not give up easily. When things become clearer, we should immediately shift our investments to key areas. Therefore, I think we should be business or product-driven. Profitability is also important, but we must not be completely profit-driven. What we need are future opportunities. *(Ren Zhengfei: Meeting Minutes of the R&D Management Committee, 2001)*

We need to create a protection system to ensure the Blue Team[2] is in an important position within Huawei. The Blue Team may seem irrational at times. Some of its members have the courage to think, speak, and act out in ways we are not familiar with. We should show leniency towards them after their debates with the Red Team. It's very likely that they can create a unique way forward. I can think of two examples of defensive lines that

---

[2] As part of its ongoing effort to identify potential weaknesses, Huawei employs a "Red Team and Blue Team" method of self-reflection. The Blue Team plays the role of a competitor, always challenging the Red Team and exposing its faults to help the Red Team improve.

failed to live up to their purposes. One was the Maginot Line built by the French to protect France against Germany. The German army didn't attack the line directly, but instead attacked France through Belgium, making the Maginot Line useless. The other was the defensive line of 17 fortresses built by Japan in northeast China. This was designed to prevent the Soviet Union from attacking Manchuria, but the Japanese didn't realize that the Soviet Union would traverse the Greater Khingan Range instead. Unexpectedly, the Soviet troops had passed through the mountains and bypassed the Japanese fortresses. I think offense is more important than defense, and this means we need to value the role of the Blue Team. The Blue Team must try its best to challenge the Red Team. Even if it fails, it has to try. The success of the Three Gorges Dam would have been impossible without opposing voices. Although their role was not recognized explicitly, the design of the dam was revised based on their opinions. We must recognize the value and role of those with different ideas and welcome their input. *(Ren Zhengfei: The Best Defense Is a Good Offense—Remarks at a Briefing on the Wireless Network Business, Huawei Executive Office Speech No. [2013] 232)*

Greater leaders are made through practice, rather than by thinking. We need to get everyone involved in real operations. For some enterprises that emphasize scale and service, both market demand and development space are limited. Due to commoditized competition, other companies can edge in to grab market shares, and shrink that development space. However, the telecom industry is rapidly growing and it is a place where real strengths count. If you cannot deliver something advanced, and if you have no forward-looking strategy, you will quickly collapse. Many companies similar to Huawei have collapsed. Huawei is not a public company, so our top management develops strategies with an eye on the next five to ten years, without worrying about short-term gains. Therefore, we move faster than others and are more forward-looking. To make breakthroughs, we must have strategic patience. If we cannot make breakthroughs within 10–20 years, or even within our own lifetimes, we would be left in a secondary position. We are not currently betting on any particular technology or direction. Betting on a single business opportunity is something small companies do, because they don't have enough money to invest in multiple areas. Large companies have sufficient funds to advance in their core business along multiple paths in multiple waves, and can be investment-intensive to reduce the time needed to explore the direction. Of the multiple opportunities we explore, some might become major industry trends. We can then focus more on these opportunities and less on others. That being said, we don't need to close the door on other opportunities. We can transfer experienced managers to major fields while deploying new managers in minor fields so that they can continue to push forward. This will give us multiple perspectives. Reflecting on failures will also be helpful. Having multiple perspectives will enable us to climb to the top. In order to win battles, the US military doesn't calculate how much ammunition it uses. Some people think they waste ammunition, but in fact they are concentrating energy to advance. We also have a mechanism in place to attract talent. When our 150,000 employees work towards the same goal, we can only succeed. *(Source: A Chat in the Garden with Huawei Founder Ren Zhengfei, Huawei Executive Office Speech No. [2015] 098)*

For research and verification of uncertainties, we advocate multiple waves of exploration along multiple paths, with large and focused investment when things become clearer. The Blue Team should also have their physical organization. In addition, we don't make assessments based on success or failure. We must extract success factors from failed projects, affirm achievements, praise those who deserve it, and encourage ongoing exploration. The word "failure" is not in the vocabulary of Huawei explorers. *(Ren Zhengfei: Dedicated to China's Century-old Dream of Revitalizing Science and Technology, Huawei Executive Office Speech No. [2016] 067)*

The word "failure" is not in the vocabulary of Huawei explorers. When monkeys lived in trees, there were no paths on earth. After they evolved into human beings, they walked and left behind small zigzagging paths. Numerous explorers made the world a place with countless crisscrossing paths. No one can ever walk the entire length and breadth of the world. Those who manage to cover just one section of a long path are heroes. A total of 3.5 million ships sank along the sea route from Europe to Asia. Those who sank along with the ships were heroes of globalization. Flawed heroes are still heroes. This idea inspires people to continuously explore and make sacrifices for science. If people who have "failed" remain in our team with their experiences, we will become more mature. We should understand geniuses who might seem eccentric, and allow "black swans" to fly out of our coffee cups. We will either succeed or fail in innovation. We should boldly embrace "disruptive" ideas. Broken from the outside, eggs will be fried. Broken from the inside, peacocks will emerge. *(Ren Zhengfei: Dedicated to China's Century-old Dream of Revitalizing Science and Technology, Huawei Executive Office Speech No. [2016] 067)*

There are also heroes in failed projects. We must be open-minded to accommodate more talent, and explore the future along multiple paths. Certain paths might fail, but they may well produce great people, or heroes. Flawed heroes are still heroes. We should be good at extracting success factors from failed projects. In this sense, failure will also mean success. In areas of certainty, we can assess if a person is a hero purely by the outcome he or she delivers. But in areas of uncertainty, there are heroes in failed projects as well, as long as they are good at summarizing what they've done right and what they haven't. Therefore, when assessing a person, don't jump to conclusions. Disruption is often performed by outsiders, who rarely follow the same logic as the insiders. Take old China as an example. It was two doctors, Sun Yat-sen[3] and Lu Xun,[4] who brought disruptive changes to the country. *(Ren Zhengfei: Scale New Heights and Forge Ahead into Uncharted Territory Along Multiple Paths in Multiple Waves—Key Messages of Discussions at Mobile World Congress and in Ukraine, Huawei Executive Office Speech No. [2016] 068)*

Society has undergone many twists and turns. We have already touched the feet of truth. Don't always think that we fail in what we are doing. What is failure and what is success? If you walk on a path and find that it is wrong, but you tell your colleagues about it and they then try another one, this is also success. Your experience will be greatly enriched during these so-called failures. ... When assessing employees, we must not use a simple black-or-white mindset. I am referring to you guys working in research projects, not projects of certainty. *(Ren Zhengfei: Speech at a Meeting with Employees of the Noah's Ark Laboratory, Huawei Executive Office Speech No. [2016] 083)*

In scientific research, we must not suppress people with different opinions. This is what I mean by multiple paths. We must respect different opinions, which is necessary to make multiple paths possible. The paths we take in the future will thus become wider and wider. If we want to become a global leader, we must be open-minded. *(Ren Zhengfei: Remarks at*

---

[3] Sun Yat-sen (1866–1925), known as the father of modern China, was influential in overthrowing the Qing dynasty and served as the first president of the Republic of China in 1912. He started his career as a medical doctor.

[4] Lu Xun (1881–1936) was an important literary critic known for his sharp and unique essays on the historical traditions and modern conditions of China. He is widely considered China's greatest modern writer of the twentieth century. He received medical training in Japan between 1904 and 1906.

Meetings with Huawei Fellows, Huawei Executive Office Speech No. [2016] 069)
Huawei pushes its employees through a "bottleneck". This is part of our core values. After being pushed through the bottleneck, employees can run faster and faster, propelling the Huawei "machine" to move forward. We are now making changes, so that all of you can unleash your potential and be inspired. *(Ren Zhengfei: Remarks at Meetings with Huawei Fellows, Huawei Executive Office Speech No. [2016] 069)*

Innovation in the future must be multidisciplinary. However, it is impossible for Huawei to have so much multidisciplinary talent, so Hu Houkun[5] said that we should weaken the "staff badge culture". Previously, we used the term "narrowband and high amplitude", meaning that each employee is very strong in one area, but his or her scope of knowledge is rather narrow. However, if we combine the expertise of all of our employees, we will achieve "broadband and high amplitude". How can we become multidisciplinary? Through all kinds of combinations. These measures will be how we approach research in the future. *(Ren Zhengfei: Remarks at Meetings with Huawei Fellows, Huawei Executive Office Speech No. [2016] 069)*

People in the first echelon may not have time to read books or corporate documents, and they might be worn out within a couple of years. So the second echelon, or the rising stars of the future as we call them, will take the baton, build on what the first echelon has achieved, and continue to press forward. From the comments posted on our Intranet, I see our younger generation is catching up and picking up the baton from the first echelon. But we still need to prepare our second echelon and recruit top students in China majoring in lasers, physics, and chemistry. Lasers are fast, and students studying lasers tend to think fast as well. Zheng Baoyong[6] is one such example. The second echelon should not do exactly the same thing as the first echelon; that's not what they are there for. The second echelon should be able to identify the problems that already exist, and resolve issues that the Red Team has never thought about or has no capacity to resolve, or even issues that are very different from the Red Team's thinking. *(Ren Zhengfei: Scale New Heights and Forge Ahead into Uncharted Territory Along Multiple Paths in Multiple Waves—Key Messages*

---

[5] Hu Houkun was the Rotating CEO of Huawei at the time.
[6] Zheng Baoyong was an Executive Vice President of Huawei at the time.

of Discussions at Mobile World Congress and in Ukraine, Huawei Executive Office Speech No. [2016] 068)

Huawei holds tight to the pipe strategy, remains open and collaborative, and aims to unite as many people as possible to explore the future direction and keep uncertainties under control. *(Ren Zhengfei: Remarks at Meetings with Huawei Fellows, Huawei Executive Office Speech No. [2016] 069)*

In addition to achieving success in the marketplace, we should also accomplish something in technology. On top of the more than 8 to 9 billion US dollars invested in development, we are also investing more than 3 billion US dollars in research each year. Why are we expanding our efforts into basic research? Because this is a rapidly-developing era. The whiplash pace of network progress has made it impossible for us to continue the slow practice of understanding scientific papers, conducting engineering experiments, and then developing products. Now we need to get involved in scientists' exploration and research, and think about how we can turn their research results into products. We will encourage scientists and engineers in our dozens of centers of expertise (COEs) to proactively explore, and will assure them that they don't need to be afraid of failure. In addition, we will transcend the limits of our "staff badge culture" and sponsor scientists worldwide who are moving in the same direction as us. We don't invest for a narrow purpose. As I noted at the National Academy of Sciences of Belarus, we support scientists selflessly. We don't aim to own their papers, patents, or other achievements. We simply wish to keep abreast of their progress, including both successes and failures. Similar to a lighthouse, scientists can illuminate us, and also others. We don't seek to own the lighthouses or interfere in how their research results are applied. *(Ren Zhengfei: Be First to Know When Springtime Comes. Vow Not to Return Till We Reach Our Goals—Speech at an Oath-taking Rally for Reassigned Senior R&D Experts and Managers, Huawei Executive Office Speech No. [2016] 093)*

3.1.3 Absorbing the Energy of the Universe over a Cup of Coffee

We must be more open-minded. We can exchange ideas with others in coffee houses or share ideas online to inspire the next generation of talent. *(Ren Zhengfei: Speech at the Meeting with Staff from the 2012 Laboratories, Huawei Executive Office Speech No. [2012] 035)*

Our senior managers and experts are expected to attend more international conferences, and sit down for a coffee with others, aiming to find inspiration by communicating and exchanging ideas with others. After returning from conferences, they need to write down their thoughts on what they saw. They may not think this is a big deal, but what they write may inspire other people and help them succeed. They contribute if they help someone else in the company succeed. The reason we have so many strategy retreats is that we want to explore the correct strategic positioning. This is what we call "absorbing the energy of the universe over a cup of coffee". *(Ren Zhengfei: The Best Defense Is a Good Offense—Remarks at a Briefing on the Wireless Network Business, Huawei Executive Office Speech No. [2013] 232)*

We need to absorb the energy of the universe over a cup of coffee. Why don't our Fellows[7] communicate their technological ideas with the seeds for the future, like PhDs and doctoral students? If you can have coffee with experts, why not have coffee with those seeds as well? The expense on coffee can be reimbursed. It's okay if the experts don't join Huawei. They can still contribute to humanity. By communicating with these high-potential people, we are creating a huge group of like-minded experts and exerting influence on the world. It is like creating ripples in a pond. If one Fellow makes five friends like this and each of these people has hundreds of followers, a lot of people will be influenced. Communicating with others is also an effective way to improve ourselves. We don't know what the future will look like. The network inside Huawei is very small. If our Fellows stay in the office all day and don't go out to drink coffee with others, our company may eventually fail. Scientists should not be too restricted by our attendance rules. They might not always be able to clock in and clock out at the right times if they are busy communicating with people outside the company. All in all, we must be open-minded in our management. *(Ren Zhengfei: Absorbing the Energy of the Universe over a Cup of Coffee, 2014)*

Huawei must strive to become a world-class company. Currently, we lack thinkers and strategists and only have generals who are good at operations. If our philosophy and direction are wrong, the better we are at

---

[7] Fellow is the highest honor for technical professionals at Huawei. This title is presented to employees who have made creative achievements in and significant contributions to products, technologies, engineering, and other domains, and have sufficient influence in the industry.

operations, the more problematic things will become. So besides technical experts I hope some of you can become thinkers to help build the future world. *(Ren Zhengfei: Absorbing the Energy of the Universe over a Cup of Coffee, 2014)*

Our senior managers and experts need to become more open-minded, broaden their horizons, and change their narrow mindsets. They need to communicate more and drink more coffee with others. The US's IT industry is the world's most advanced. While we continue to bring in high-end experts, our senior managers and experts need to go out and communicate with their counterparts all over the world. They need to learn how to absorb the energy of the universe over a cup of coffee rather than only working hard all on their own. We attend many international conferences and forums. On these occasions, it may only take five minutes for us to get inspired and absorb a lot of energy over a cup of coffee. You won't know what the world is like if you don't change your mindset and interact with the world. Sometimes, we may be inspired by only a few words. *(Ren Zhengfei: Taking a Long-term View When Making Decisions—Speech at a Briefing by the Chengdu Research Center, Huawei Executive Office Speech No. [2014] 027)*

As we move forward, it is not enough to focus only on cutting-edge technologies. We also need to cultivate a group of technology ambassadors. These "ambassadors" should be outstanding experts who not only specialize in a single domain, but also have an extensive knowledge base and strong comprehensive capabilities. While our Fellows are committed to developing new technologies, our technology ambassadors can travel around the world to have coffee with others as assistants to our Fellows and keep up with the latest trends. They can capture new information about the industry through such exchanges and interactions and bring that information back to our platform for analysis. Scientists can then discuss and analyze such information at strategy retreats. If they conclude that the direction is correct, the information discussed will become the main points of the retreats and be sent to our 2012 Laboratories. From there, the 2012 Laboratories will begin technological research for the next decade or two. After we see research achievements after a period of time, we can send them to the strategy marketing department to help with our business planning. *(Ren Zhengfei: Speech at the Briefing on Industry Trends and Progress in Fixed Networks, Huawei Executive Office Speech No. [2015] 109)*

We will either succeed or fail in innovation. We should boldly embrace "disruptive" ideas. Broken from the outside, eggs will be fried. Broken from the inside, peacocks will emerge. Today, technology advances very rapidly, and uncertainties are on the rise. We are going to be deeply engaged in product development, which is part of our known and certain territory. However, in order to keep pace with the times, we need to increase our investment in uncertainties. We encourage scientists, experts, and engineers – tens of thousands of them – in our COEs to strengthen communication with the outside world in order to absorb the energy of the universe over a cup of coffee. We aim to turn our Strategy and Technology Workshop into a "Roman Square", an open platform for scientific and technological discussion, so that sparks of ideas will turn into burning fires. Our company should have ideals, and discard the mindset of calculating profits in particular areas. It is hard to plan major innovations. Staying stuck in a rut would be the easiest option, but this would keep us from seizing big opportunities. *(Ren Zhengfei: Dedicated to China's Century-old Dream of Revitalizing Science and Technology, Huawei Executive Office Speech No. [2016] 067)*

"Black swans" might appear but, when they do, we hope that they will appear in "our coffee cups". We must be open-minded, support scientists who are moving in the same direction as us, and understand and support geniuses who may seem eccentric. We welcome "black swans" to fly in our company; they could represent a chance to reinvent ourselves. *(Ren Zhengfei: Scale New Heights and Forge Ahead into Uncharted Territory Along Multiple Paths in Multiple Waves—Key Messages of Discussions at Mobile World Congress and in Ukraine, Huawei Executive Office Speech No. [2016] 068)*

We should find and support some professors with opinions different from the mainstream. Then we should create a team to follow them, and that team will become part of the second echelon. Quantum communications is a good example. Several years ago, it was widely criticized as something unrealistic and far away down the road. Look at it now. China has already done it. Can we include things like this in one of our paths as we explore the future? We must be bold in supporting people who are intelligent, including PhD candidates and seemingly eccentric geniuses. And we need to spot them early on, say, in universities. We can begin to support them when they are still students, but they don't have to join Huawei after graduation. If they later make inventions that can help resolve our problems, we can pay them for the use of these inventions. *(Ren Zhengfei: Scale New Heights and Forge Ahead into Uncharted Territory Along Multiple Paths in Multiple Waves—Key Messages of Discussions at Mobile World Congress and in Ukraine, Huawei Executive Office Speech No. [2016] 068)*

To absorb the energy of the universe over a cup of coffee, you don't have to bring all top experts on board or make them part of Huawei. What truly matters is their ideas. Can we set up a Thought Research Institute that mainly comprises Fellows? Fellows must be involved in multiple fields, exchange ideas with others, and be powerful sources of inspiration. This institute will be positioned to conduct research into ideas and directions, not just into technologies. Fellows should not just work on specific tasks, or just care about products. We would like them to just sit down with the right people for a cup of coffee, and share each other's inspirations to continuously generate streams of ideas. Each research center should have some budgets of their own; it's a brilliant idea. Xu Wenwei[8] said that we will not touch content or data. That is a major direction, and it's also a brilliant idea. However, this doesn't mean we will draw a clear demarcation line. We must develop the capacity to support massive amounts of content and data, but we won't monetize them. *(Ren Zhengfei: Scale New Heights and Forge Ahead into Uncharted Territory Along Multiple Paths in Multiple Waves—Key Messages of Discussions at Mobile World Congress and in Ukraine, Huawei Executive Office Speech No. [2016] 068)*

We need to use American bricks to build our own "Great Wall" and allow the eccentric to dance on it. We should be very open-minded when it comes to research on artificial intelligence (AI). Conducting research yourselves is also a good idea; otherwise, you won't be able to know whether you're moving in the right direction, or on which areas you should focus. There are companies who are doing better than us. We can bring in what they have made to our company. *(Ren Zhengfei: Speech at a Meeting with Employees of the Noah's Ark Laboratory, Huawei Executive Office Speech No. [2016] 083)*

---

[8] Xu Wenwei was the Chief Strategy Marketing Officer of Huawei at the time.

3.2 TECHNOLOGICAL INNOVATION WITHOUT BOUNDARIES CAN TAKE COMPANY STRATEGY IN THE WRONG DIRECTION

3.2.1 Product Innovation Must Focus on the Core Business and Must Always Be Driven by Business Needs

What do we mean by freedom? For us, freedom means setting rules and making things work by following the rules. For a train, freedom means traveling on the tracks and reaching its destination without being derailed. Freedom comes from awareness of the laws of nature. It is the opposite of necessity, which is the result of a lack of knowledge or mastery of the laws of nature. *(Ren Zhengfei: Shifting from the Realm of Necessity to the Realm of Freedom, 1998)*

We have boundaries for our research and innovation. We must only focus on our core business, or areas closely related to it. Our product innovation must always be driven by business needs. Bell Labs ultimately came apart because of its reckless innovation. Although Bell Labs specialized in communications, some of its scientists invented the electron microscope because of personal interests. Discarding the invention makes its heart ache, so Bell Labs established an organization to put the microscope into commercial use. This story tells us that technological innovation without boundaries can take company strategy in the wrong direction. Product innovation should be done within certain boundaries. Research and innovation can be a bit broad, but not boundless. We need to achieve Huawei's ideals, not the ideals of humanity. Our innovation should have boundaries. *(Ren Zhengfei: Absorbing the Energy of the Universe over a Cup of Coffee, 2014)*

Innovation should have boundaries. We will continue our needle-tip strategy and focus our efforts on the core business to make breakthroughs and take the lead in the era of massive data traffic. *(Ren Zhengfei: Our Transformation Goals Are to Harvest More Crops and Increase Soil Fertility—Speech at the 2015 Huawei Market Conference, Huawei Executive Office Speech No. [2015] 016)*

We have two decision-making systems: One is an idealistic system, which focuses on technology. The other is a realistic system of Strategy Marketing, which focuses on customer needs. We encourage fierce debate between these two systems and would like to see them reach consensus on

product development goals. *(Ren Zhengfei: Remarks at Meetings with Huawei Fellows, Huawei Executive Office Speech No. [2016] 069)*
We don't know what the future information society will look like. We need to develop assumptions about it. Without correct assumptions, there will be no correct direction. Without a correct direction, there will be no correct thoughts. Without correct thoughts, there will be no correct theories. Without correct theories, there will be no correct strategies. The Thought Research Institute will explore future ideas and directions. The 2012 Laboratories will develop them into theories and then verify them. In other words, the 2012 Laboratories conducts experiments with future assumptions and ideas. No matter what, we must figure out where we should be heading. *(Ren Zhengfei: Scale New Heights and Forge Ahead into Uncharted Territory Along Multiple Paths in Multiple Waves—Key Messages of Discussions at Mobile World Congress and in Ukraine, Huawei Executive Office Speech No. [2016] 068)*

3.2.2 Research and Innovation on Uncertainties Must also Have Boundaries and Serve the Core Business

We focus on our core business, with sustaining innovation at the core, complimented by disruptive innovation. On the Internet, disruptive innovation is a hot topic, but we aim to create value for the world and innovate to create greater value. We should still focus on social demand for the next five to ten years; most of our people should not be looking any further into the future. For most of our products, we should focus firmly on *sustaining innovation*. At the same time, we should allow a small part of our younger employees to engage in *disruptive innovation*: to "talk nonsense" and explore new ideas. These employees can be as disruptive as they please, but they must remain within certain boundaries. Such disruptive innovation is openly accessible, allowing sustaining innovation to continuously absorb energy from it; after disruptive innovation has grown into a strong sapling, it can turn around and absorb energy from sustaining innovation. *(Ren Zhengfei: Innovating to Create Global Value—Speech at the Corporate Strategy Retreat, Huawei Executive Office Speech No. [2015] 006)*

Our mission is to create value for humanity. Our innovation must serve this purpose. We must not innovate just for the sake of innovation. I think the concept of independent innovation is one-sided. We need to stand on the shoulders of giants in order to move forward. If we have to climb upward from the ground by ourselves, it could take millennia for us to reach our goals. To reach our goals faster, we must take advantage of all past achievements, as this will increase efficiency. ... During the course of innovation, we need to absorb as much energy as possible to save on time and resources needed to create value. Using other people's intellectual property by paying them reasonable fees is more cost-effective for us. Innovating blindly on our own is far more expensive. Every year we invest 10% of revenue in R&D, and much of the funds are spent on purchasing intellectual property from others and on research projects that are terminated in their early stages. To be an industry leader, we must not be so narrow-minded as to throw stones on highways to stop others and develop our own unique strengths. This will harm other market players and impede global progress. This is not what we want to achieve. Our aim is to become an industry leader and contribute to the world. Then what makes a leader? Being a leader means making the world a better place, contributing to the broader architecture of global information networks, and sharing value with others. *(Ren Zhengfei: Speech at a Meeting with Employees of the Legal Affairs Department, Secretariat Office of the Board of Directors, and Wireless Network Product Line, Huawei Executive Office Speech No. [2015] 015)*

We need to reduce the workload that our management system has to handle, because there is beauty in simplicity. Our management system doesn't need to handle too many things. During this year's budgeting process, we won't earmark much money for product development, which is a job of certainty and needs to focus on the target and efficiency. We will increase our investment in future growth and breakthroughs in uncharted territory. An investment-intensive approach must not be used randomly. We need to review it carefully. Research and innovation on uncertainties must also have boundaries and serve our core business. We need to limit research and innovation initiatives that don't serve our core business. *(Ren Zhengfei: Speech at the EMT ST Meeting on January 25, 2016, Huawei Executive Office Speech No. [2016] 054)*

Our AI should be confined to our core business, and we should not pursue applications beyond them. Our AI should be bundled with our core business. Within the core business, we can invest heavily and work together to generate more ideas and unleash greater potential. I won't give you money if you deviate from our core business. Huawei will not make AI products for public use or small AI commodities. I am afraid that you might act on impulse and compare your AI with AI outside of Huawei. If I don't use your AI products, some of you may start a business with them. This will hollow our company out. If you are talented, you should come to work in our core business. AI products for public use are the major business of other companies, not of our company. We should not engage in this business. We can just buy such products from others after they succeed in producing them. *(Ren Zhengfei: Speech at a Meeting with Employees of the Noah's Ark Laboratory, Huawei Executive Office Speech No. [2016] 083)*

3.3 IDENTIFYING AND CREATING CERTAINTY OUT OF UNCERTAINTY

3.3.1 *The Role of a Leader: Setting a Clear Direction Amidst Uncertainties*

The uncertainty of the future poses lots of risks to us. In the face of uncertainties, managers at all levels must focus on the most important issue and the key factor that influences it, set a clear direction, control the pace, and apply *huidu*[9] to achieve goals. We must do more self-reflection and be more alert to changes in our surroundings. This is what I mean when I say "Digging In and Widening Out". *(Ren Zhengfei: Who Calls for Artillery and How Do We Provide Timely Artillery Support?—Speech at the Awards Ceremony of Sales & Services, Huawei Executive Office Speech No. [2009] 001)*

Huawei's goal of establishing committees is to make collective, high-quality decisions on key issues and uncertainties in the business environment. Regarding routine business operations with relative certainty, business commanders need to make decisions to increase operating efficiency. *(Source: EMT Meeting Minutes No. [2013] 009)*

To deal with uncertainties, we need to identify them first. Every year, our company discusses and determines key uncertainties we face. Our strategy department and other relevant departments then study and analyze these uncertainties, work out measures to address them, and follow up on the progress of their handling. *(Source: BOD Executive Committee Meeting Minutes No. [2015] 005)*

In the face of economic, financial, and market uncertainties, we must systematically identify the operational, financial, and compliance risks posed to Huawei, create a corporate risk management map, and assign

---

[9] *Huidu* is a Chinese term used at Huawei to describe the shades of grey that exist between black and white, which implies flexibility and balance without losing sight of direction.

owners for major risks. The goal is to effectively reduce the impact of uncertainties on our operations. *(Source: EMT Resolution No. [2015] 013)*

The external environment is changing. To become the world leader over the next five years, we need to drive further transformation in our own business domains of certainty, develop capabilities to cope with future risks, and adapt to changes in the external environment. This transformation in domains of certainty will support us in dealing with uncertainties. *(Source: EMT Meeting Minutes No. [2015] 007)*

We now face severe challenges in our management transformation. Most members of our transformation teams are engaged in businesses of certainty, and they should have the confidence to study the issues that Huawei faces. In Europe, why does the installation of a base station cost 20,000 Euros in certain countries, but 3000 Euros in other countries? The higher costs result from our failures to effectively manage businesses of certainty, make these businesses process-based and standardized, and consistently integrate data. These costs directly impact our bonus packages. If we eliminate these costs, then they could become bonuses for us. Doesn't that make sense? We must strive to improve in this aspect, so as to further increase our efficiency and make more contributions. This will enable our company to enter a positive cycle. Our turnkey projects are good examples. In the past, we had no clue about these projects. But things have changed: We now have a general understanding of them. In the future, we will need to study how to do better in all our business domains to make further improvements. *(Ren Zhengfei: Speech at the Oath-taking Ceremony for the Third Session of the Transformation Elite Team, Huawei Executive Office Speech No. [2015] 078)*

A leader must have a sense of direction. The role of a leader is not to carry a hoe or dig a trench. It's about leading the team out of difficulty and finding the right direction forward. A sense of direction is about making a definite judgment on the way forward out of uncertainties, especially when resources are limited. Of course, a sense of direction can also involve making a vague judgment that somehow helps to lead the team out of chaos. We used to follow others in the world; but in the future, we will take the lead. What should we do? Years ago, the Personal Handy-phone System (PHS) and TD-SCDMA almost killed me. Why? Because of the tough decisions I had to make. When PHS was really hot in the market, our teams said they could develop similar products within three months, and I had to decide whether to do it or not. TD-SCDMA was a similar story. That kind of anguish lasted eight years, and sometimes I wonder how I made it; it was so hard to be a leader. If I said no, what if I was wrong? If I said yes, we might waste our strategic resources on non-strategic opportunities. If that happened, would we still have become what we are today? Now it is your turn to lead the world, you will then feel what it's like to be raked over hot coals. *(Ren Zhengfei: Scale New Heights and Forge Ahead into Uncharted Territory Along Multiple Paths in Multiple Waves—Key Messages of Discussions at Mobile World Congress and in Ukraine, Huawei Executive Office Speech No. [2016] 068)*

3.3.2 In Field Offices Are Highly Competent Lean Teams Dealing With Uncertainties; In Back Offices Are Functional Departments and Shared Services Centers Dealing with Certainties

In the future, the company will become an organization composed of highly competent lean teams. We should focus on building such teams in field offices to deal with the uncertainties of technology, customer needs, transaction terms, and delivery terms. Operations with certainty should be handled by functional departments in regions. *(Ren Zhengfei: Speech at the Briefing on the Progress of the Transformation Elite Team, Huawei Executive Office Speech No. [2015] 029)*

When our field offices become light and agile, we won't have to pour our energy into routine matters any more, and our key operating teams can focus on their primary work. Our key operating teams must clearly describe needs. First, they must spell out customer needs so that our R&D team can help meet them. Second, they must clearly state their needs for supply so that our back offices can provide support. Once these needs are clarified, everyone will know their own responsibilities, and it will be easy to measure performance. *(Ren Zhengfei: Speech at the Briefing on the Progress of the Transformation Elite Team, Huawei Executive Office Speech No. [2015] 029)*

Over the past two decades, IBM has helped us connect the dots, establish multiple platforms, and achieve rigorous, well-ordered development. In the next decade, we will need to change our operating model from large teams to highly competent lean teams to enhance the effectiveness, timeliness, and accuracy of our organization. We should allow such lean teams to deal with uncertainties and have our functional departments or shared services centers deal with certainties. When assessing the performance of departments that deal with uncertainties, we should focus on their ability to control risk. When assessing the performance of departments that deal with certainties, we should focus on their efficiency and results. During the transformation, we should place some command centers in field offices to enable those who are closest to customers to call for support. The purpose of this is to prevent our organization from growing too big and too bureaucratic. The LTC[10] process has enabled us to identify customer needs. Back offices will become more capable in providing professional services and support. *(Ren Zhengfei: Speech at the Meeting with Accenture Chairman Pierre Nanterme, Huawei Executive Office Speech No. [2015] 040)*

In the future, our field offices will be made up of lean teams that deal with uncertainties, and our back offices will be made up of shared platforms that deal with certainties. We need to create certainty out of uncertainty and build a rational authority delegation and oversight mechanism, enabling those who are closest to customers to call for support. This will boost our overall operating capabilities and efficiency. *(Ren Zhengfei: Speech at the Oath-taking and Awards Ceremony of the Transformation Elite Team, Huawei Executive Office Speech No. [2015] 047)*

Lean teams are intended to deal with all kinds of uncertainties, including changing customer needs, transaction terms, and business environments. The key is to reduce our operating risks. Uncertainty in customer needs is primarily about marketing and R&D. We spend so much money on them ever year, but much is uncertain. Uncertainty in transaction terms means our contractual situations are uncertain. At the moment, we can't even get our contract estimations straight. There are very few projects in which we submit bids based on clear estimations. For businesses of certainty, like delivery, service, finance, and supply chain management, we need to set up shared platforms. The key is to boost efficiency. When assessing our work in areas of certainty, we should focus on efficiency and results. *(Ren Zhengfei: Speech at the Oath-taking and Awards Ceremony of the Transformation Elite Team, Huawei Executive Office Speech No. [2015] 047)*

---

[10] LTC: Lead to Cash. It is a main business process at Huawei that spans from leads, sales, and delivery to payment collection.

3.4 Success Is Not a Reliable Guide to Future Development

3.4.1 The Only Thing that Is Constant Is Change

We are now in an era of rapid change in the IT industry. The only thing that is constant is change. If we hesitate to change, we will fall far behind. If we are happy with the status quo, and refuse to make progress or listen to criticism, it will be even worse. Should we head towards failure or even death to avoid losing face? Or should we correct our mistakes – without being scared of losing face – in order to catch up? To survive, we have to excel, and to excel, we have to move beyond our own limits, which requires promptly correcting all our mistakes. To achieve this, we need to be self-reflective. As Confucius said, "In a group of three people, there is always someone I can learn from." For Huawei, our competitor is one of these three people. The other two are our customer who speaks frankly about the issues of our products, and our subordinate who is frank and candid. We can correct any mistake we may have as long as we remain humble and open to criticism. *(Ren Zhengfei: Why Do We Need Self-reflection?, 2000)*

Greek philosopher Heraclitus said, "The only thing that is constant is change". Change is not terrible. It won't necessarily harm us if we keep working hard. This is a relative truth that we have always believed in and worked for. That's why Huawei has become what it is today. If our value assessment system – which advocates customer centricity, dedication, and perseverance – continues to function and refine its own structure and form over time, it will gradually become less dependent on human intervention and will evolve into a new model – and an enduring system. No matter who leaves, our system will remain and evolve to an extent where it will no longer depend on human intervention. While people come and go, our system will persist. Relative truth continues to exist because of our tolerance towards it. *(Ren Zhengfei: From "Philosophy" to Practice—Speech at Huawei Annual Management Conference 2011, Huawei Executive Office Speech No. [2011] 016)*

Great changes have taken place in the business environment. We must think about how to adapt to these changes and promote transformations accordingly. Technology has changed significantly as well, from the era of voice to the era of broadband and on to the era of information. The size of the future market that these changes will create is beyond our imagination. Take cloud computing as an example. We have no idea how broad and deep its impact will be, nor can we foresee clearly what the future has in store. What will the future information society look like? It is impossible to design a perfect business model for this. *(Ren Zhengfei: Success Is Not a Reliable Guide to Future Development, Huawei Executive Office Speech No. [2011] 004)*

3.4.2 We Are the Only Ones Who Can Defeat Ourselves

Crises always lurk behind prosperity. But a crisis is not an inherent part of prosperity; it is something people feel in a booming environment. Hard work will eventually lead to prosperity. However, as soon as people are no longer dedicated, prosperity will inevitably fade. History is full of rises and falls. It is a mirror from which we can learn everything. If we forget the hardships we have been through, we are abandoning Huawei's culture. *(Ren Zhengfei: Standing Against Pride and Complacency and Being Mentally Dedicated, 1996)*

Who is likely to defeat us? Not others, but ourselves. If we fail to evolve, improve our management, and carry on our tradition of dedication, we will be defeated by ourselves. History is rife with examples of companies that succeeded for a time but failed to sustain their success. The DNA of failure is often embedded in success. We can set the pace only when we maintain a sense of urgency and create a drive for proactive innovation and adaptation to the future. *(Ren Zhengfei: Toasting Those Who Succeed and Offering a Helping Hand to Those Who Fail, 1997)*

A long, peaceful time and too many promotions may turn out to be a disaster for Huawei. The Titanic set off with a fanfare of hurrahs, didn't it? *(Ren Zhengfei: Spring of Northern Country, 2001)*

The past successes of hi-tech companies are often the mother of their failure. In this rapidly changing information society, only those who remain vigilant can survive. *(Ren Zhengfei: Spring of Northern Country, 2001)*

A group of Executive Master of Business Administration (EMBA) students from the School of Business at Renmin University of China visited Lancaster University in the UK. They were deeply impressed by the glories of Britain's industrial revolution and the UK's current development. One of them mentioned Huawei and some other leading Chinese companies to a British professor. The professor said, "Huawei is walking on a road which some famous companies in the world have once traveled. They were glorious at one time. Before reaching their peak, they stayed customer-centric and worked hard. However, when they reached the top, they started to become conservative and refused to listen to customers. As a result, they declined." I think this professor made the right historical observation: He foresaw what a company would eventually become if it evolved on its own. I once recommended an article listing defectors who had once been loyal to a certain undertaking. And where are the big fish who were once heavyweight players in the 1980s when China was reforming and opening up with vitality? Everything in the world is changing. And we are already left behind even without our awareness of it. *(Ren Zhengfei: From "Philosophy" to Practice—Speech at Huawei Annual Management Conference 2011, Huawei Executive Office Speech No. [2011] 016)*

Recently, we have been encouraging middle and senior managers and manager candidates to study the company's management culture outline, which summarizes the elements that have inspired us to remain dedicated over the past two decades. This outline was put together by the editorial board and other relevant personnel. It will be the eternal beacon that forever illuminates our path forward. But we need to understand our culture correctly; otherwise, overreliance on our past successes will cause us to go down the wrong path. *(Ren Zhengfei: Success Is Not a Reliable Guide to Future Development, Huawei Executive Office Speech No. [2011] 004)*

Are we going to be left behind by the times? Can we afford to be left behind? These are important questions. Many great inventors failed to expand on their initial successes. These include Marconi, who was the first to use radio waves for wireless telegraphy; Motorola, a pioneer in cellular communications; Lucent, inventor of optical transmissions; and Kodak, creator of the world's first digital camera. They failed because they didn't see the future clearly, or because they didn't have the courage to reinvent themselves or give up their vested interests when they did. Large companies have their advantages, but if they fail to keep pace with the times, they will vanish in the blink of an eye. The way forward in this new era may not be a straight path. Even light bends. Some long-standing theories in economics may be upturned in the new era. Previously successful methods may not work anymore when applied in the new era. How can we adapt to the rapidly changing era? We made several mistakes in the past regarding major strategies, including in broadband and softswitching. We later had to play catch-up in these two areas. Given Huawei's size, it will be very dangerous if we don't have the courage to embrace the future in this fast-changing era. The future is full of uncertainty, and we might even need to overturn our own advantages accumulated over the years. Where will we end up if we refuse to embrace this future? The extent to which we understand and envision the future information world is too small. That's why I'm encouraging senior managers to attend more international conferences, drink a cup of coffee with others, and have idle chats with others. Through today's idle chats, we have come up with many good ideas, right? Google is a visionary company. Can Huawei look as far into the future as Google does? But I think this degree of foresight is not enough. We need to look much further than Google, in order to adapt to this era of change. We need to predict what the future will be like, catch up, lead the way, and avoid being left behind. Through adaptation, openness, gradual restructuring, and effective handling of customer needs – initiatives similar to what IBM has done – even a large company can be revived, and it won't necessarily fade away. *(Ren Zhengfei: Speech and Comments at the Carrier Network BG's Strategy Retreat in Huizhou, Huawei Executive Office Speech No. [2012] 010)*

3.4.3 The Best Defense Is a Good Offense; Moving beyond Existing Advantages to Create New Ones

China's "reform and opening-up" policy has delivered remarkable results, and a large part of this success is attributable to those who have frequently criticized the policy. These critics watched us in China closely and found fault with everything we did, urging us to do even better. What has enabled Huawei to become what it is today is continuous improvement. We criticize ourselves day after day and expose our own faults. In doing so, we become stronger. In the future, we must strengthen our continuous improvement and establish a Blue Team that is dedicated to challenging Huawei. Every department should have a Blue Team to challenge themselves. As it meets these challenges, our Red Team will become stronger. If the leader of the Blue Team is unable to challenge Huawei, he or she must not remain in the position. The reason is simple. A leader who is unable to challenge Huawei does not know its potential for development. Such a leader is incompetent and will not move forward if he sticks to what he already has. Managers who are unable to criticize Huawei have reached their ceilings and will no longer be promoted. In contrast, those who can criticize Huawei have broad vision and unique opinions, and only such people should be promoted. *(Ren Zhengfei: Speech and Comments at the Strategy Retreat of the Business Process & IT Management Department, Huawei Executive Office Speech No. [2012] 026)*

The best defense is a good offense. We need to move beyond existing advantages to create new ones. If we fail to do so, sooner or later other companies will surpass us. We should communicate more with our competitors (e.g., Ericsson, Alcatel Lucent, and Nokia Siemens) at academic conferences, and form strategic partnerships with them in relation to industry standards and policies. This will enable us to adapt to the fast-changing world. *(Ren Zhengfei: Speech at a Meeting with the GTS Network Planning and Optimization Team, Huawei Executive Office Speech No. [2014] 012)*

In the past, we moved up the value chain by offering quality products at low costs. This was the only approach we could take. It strangled our Western peers and also dealt a heavy blow to ourselves. However, our American peers, like Google and Facebook, have always moved down the value chain with strategic innovations. Wi-Fi is in direct competition with LTE. Who knows what tricks our American peers will have up their sleeves? We need to play it by ear. There's no way we can work out tactics in advance to guard against our competitors. We have made all our strategies open. We can't succeed with defense only. We need to remain open, as this is the foundation for our future success. *(Ren Zhengfei: Speech at a Meeting with the GTS Network Planning and Optimization Team, Huawei Executive Office Speech No. [2014] 012)*

We need to keep our feet on the ground and engage in hands-on practice. We won't know which one of us will stand out from the crowd. We are a team of some 150,000 people, and I think someone will step up and lead us to success, though I don't know who he or she is right now. I place my hope in you, and I expect you to take on your responsibility. *(Ren Zhengfei: Speech at a Meeting with the GTS Network Planning and Optimization Team, Huawei Executive Office Speech No. [2014] 012)*

Open Access This chapter is licensed under the terms of the Creative Commons Attribution-NonCommercial-NoDerivatives 4.0 International License (http://creativecommons.org/licenses/by-nc-nd/4.0/), which permits any noncommercial use, sharing, distribution and reproduction in any medium or format, as long as you give appropriate credit to the original author(s) and the source, provide a link to the Creative Commons licence and indicate if you modified the licensed material. You do not have permission under this license to share adapted material derived from this chapter or parts of it.

The images or other third party material in this chapter are included in the chapter's Creative Commons licence, unless indicated otherwise in a credit line to the material. If material is not included in the chapter's Creative Commons licence and your intended use is not permitted by statutory regulation or exceeds the permitted use, you will need to obtain permission directly from the copyright holder.

CHAPTER 4

Enhancing Core Competencies through Strategic Mergers and Acquisitions and Corporate Venture Capital Investment

Corporate venture capital (CVC) and independent venture capital (IVC) differ in their objectives. CVC is more about its own strategic intent and strategic alignment with the parent company, than direct financial returns from the entity receiving investment. In contrast, IVC pursues financial returns; its strategic intent is usually absent or vague.

Trying to achieve both the strategic intent and financial returns presents a dilemma for CVC. Equal emphasis on both usually leads to success in one but failure in the other. If CVC deviates from its strategic intent, it will be no different from IVC. Large companies that expect their CVC initiatives to gain financial returns are putting the cart before the horse.

At Huawei, the strategic intent of CVC is clear: to enhance the core competencies and overall value of the parent company through its strategic and business alignment with the parent company. The goal of CVC is not to solely focus on maximizing the returns of any individual entity that makes investment. Huawei strictly controls the objectives and boundaries of its CVC projects, and prohibits unfocused investment, with the intention of achieving big profits in core business rather than smaller wins across a wider area.

This chapter gives concise and to-the-point explanations about the strategic intent and investment principles of Huawei's CVC.

4.1 Bridging Gaps in Core Competencies Through Strategic Mergers and Acquisitions

4.1.1 Capital Investment Should Serve the Strategic Purpose and Help Huawei Acquire Key Technologies and Capabilities

Meeting attendees agreed on a set of capital investment policies which include four key points. First, growing from within is the core and major driving force behind Huawei's future development, whereas capital investment is an alternative that can be used in certain circumstances. Second, capital investment must serve the strategic purpose, which is to help Huawei acquire key technologies and capabilities, or grow market share. Third, mergers and acquisitions (M&As) must be confined to domains closely related to our core business. Joint venture initiatives may be carried out in domains that slightly deviate from our core business, but must be managed by specific business unit owners. CVC must focus on opportunities that allow us to grow our business ecosystem, stimulate market demand, fill technological gaps, and acquire cutting-edge technologies. Fourth, capital investment is very risky and must thus be treated with caution. Oversight and management are crucial to attaining the objectives of capital investment and reducing associated risks. *(Source: Resolution on Proposals for Capital Investment Policies and Decision-making Systems, Finance Committee Resolution No. [2011] 038)*

The Corporate Development Department must focus on supporting Huawei's core business. Through capital investment, the department helps business departments rapidly acquire new products and capabilities, address areas of weaknesses, control strategic resources, complement internal innovation, and conduct research through external parties. The department must also actively acquire patents in alignment with Huawei's patent strategy. Capital investment in our core business should be an ongoing effort. *(Source: Minutes of the Report on the Results of Operations Management of Capital Investment Projects, EMT Meeting Minutes No. [2014] 001)*

4.1.2 Focusing CVC Investments on Developing Cutting-Edge Technologies, Preventing Technological Risks, and Supporting Development Strategies in Our Core Business

The Corporate Development Department needs to prioritize and proactively work on technology-related VC. It must do this regularly, with the company's future goals in mind and a focus on key technologies for Huawei's core business. *(Source: Minutes of the Report on Principal Investment and Venture Capital, Finance Committee Meeting Minutes No. [2012] 046)*

CVC is a vital means for Huawei to complement internal innovation, understand and develop cutting-edge technologies, prevent technological risks, and cope with future uncertainties. CVC must be confined to strategic projects that support our core business in ICT and aim to achieve the following goals: create channels for Huawei to access innovation resources and gain insights into innovation trends in the industry; develop cutting-edge technologies and innovate with third parties; control key resources, promote strategic cooperation, and ensure supply security; build a healthy ecosystem for our core business; develop data pipe capabilities, expand pipe traffic, and increase the coverage and volume of connections. *(Source: Resolution on Proposals for Optimizing the Venture Capital Decision-making Process and Delegation of Authority, EMT Resolution No. [2015] 006)*

The objective of CVC at Huawei is to support the development of our core business. The significance of CVC needs to be clarified, and its boundaries need to be clearly defined. *(Source: Minutes of the Discussion on Proposals for Optimizing the Venture Capital Decision-making Process and Delegation of Authority, Finance Committee Meeting Minutes No. [2015] 018)*

In principle, we don't invest outside of Huawei. Investing in a company means that we have to buy from them for the rest of our lives. Our approach is this: We buy from whoever provides high-quality products and services. We always look for the best option. We also establish strategic partnerships with our suppliers, but we require that they not lag behind. If they do, we will buy from others. We aim to make the world's best products, rather than just assembling what our partners produce. *(Ren Zhengfei: Minutes of a Meeting with Employees of the Japan Representative Office and the Japan Research Center, Huawei Executive Office Speech No. [2016] 080)*

4.1.3 The Purpose of Acquisitions Is to Make Up for Weaknesses in Our Core Business Rather Than Diversifying Our Business

Since June 2011, the company has stopped investing in non-core business. This ban will remain in force moving forward and all existing investments in non-core businesses will be discontinued. *(Source: Minutes of the Report on the Results of Operations Management of Capital Investment Projects, EMT Meeting Minutes No. [2014] 001)*

As our future direction indicates, our strategic goal is all about vertical development in our data pipe business, instead of horizontal expansion. The amount that we invest in the data pipe business is higher than any other company. It is a well-known fact that every year we invest about 8 billion US dollars in R&D, and we can do this without any difficulty. Our capital structure supports this investment strategy, without the need for new capital from outside investors. Huawei is not likely to become an investment company that answers to investors. Huawei answers only to employees who have put their own efforts into the company. *(Ren Zhengfei: Speech at a Meeting with Employees of the Legal Affairs Department, Secretariat Office of the Board of Directors, and Wireless Network Product Line, Huawei Executive Office Speech No. [2015] 015)*

Huawei sticks to its core business. All acquisitions aim to make up for weaknesses in our data pipe business, not to diversify our business. Huawei has never ceased acquisition efforts. Acquisitions valued below 10 million US dollars don't need my approval, so the number of our acquisition projects should not be insignificant. At Huawei, the purpose of acquisitions is to make up for what we lack in our data pipe business, not to further diversify our business. If we acquire a ton of companies doing other businesses, what if they're just shells? Or what if they're poorly run? Such companies will only hasten our demise. The most profitable business in the world is printing money. But this isn't practical, so we need to be selective about what we do and what we don't do. *(Ren Zhengfei: Speech at a Meeting with Employees of the Legal Affairs Department, Secretariat Office of the Board of Directors, and Wireless Network Product Line, Huawei Executive Office Speech No. [2015] 015)*

4.2 Principles for External Investments and M&As

4.2.1 Never Making Principal Investments Aimed Solely at Achieving Financial Returns

The company reaffirms the prohibition of principal investments that only seek financial returns. *(Source: Minutes of the Report on Principal Investment and Venture Capital, Finance Committee Meeting Minutes No. [2012] 046)*

Moving forward, all investments, mergers, and acquisitions must be centrally managed and reported by the Corporate Development Department to company management. This department must ensure the scope of our investment remains focused on our core business. Projects that are not included in the project pipeline of the department are "illegal", and will not have the support or approval of the company. Over the next two years, our company will strengthen the management of these projects and keep a tight rein on M&A-driven business development. *(Source: Recommendations on Investment and M&A Management, EMT Resolution No. [2011] 041)*

When there is a new project request, the Corporate Development Department must carefully assess whether it falls within the scope of our core business. When assessing investments and doing project initiation verification, the department must approach its work in an objective, neutral, and professional manner. The goal is to ensure the quality of the project from the very beginning. *(Source: Minutes of the Report on the Results of Operations Management of Capital Investment Projects, EMT Meeting Minutes No. [2014] 001)*

4.2.2 Strengthening Post-Investment Management to Ensure Investment Goals Are Achieved

Expenses on capital investment projects, including investment funds, M&A funds, and project operating costs, must be borne by the departments that benefit from such projects. According to this principle, the investments or M&A funds for these projects need to be budgeted and accounted for under the "investment centers" (such as BGs and product lines), rather than under the "non-investment centers" (such as regional offices, representative offices, or key account departments). *(Source: Regulations on Budgeting and Accounting of Expenses on Capital Investment Projects, Finance Committee Doc. No. [2012] 001)*

The Corporate Development Department needs to strengthen post-investment integration and management to ensure investment goals are achieved. Incubating a potential investment project and managing it in the post-investment stage are crucial tasks for this department. *(Source: Minutes of the Report on the Results of Operations Management of Capital Investment Projects, EMT Meeting Minutes No. [2014] 001)*

4.2.3 No Support for Employees Starting a Business: No Investing or Engaging in Such Activities

The cost of any failed investment must be borne by the organization that made the decision to invest. Huawei forbids the sale of any business to external parties. If a business losses momentum or does not align with the company's strategic demand, it must be directly closed, rather than sold. Huawei does not support employees starting a business; nor does it invest or engage in these activities itself. *(Source: Resolution on Forbidding Internal Start-ups and Sale of Any Business, EMT Resolution No. [2015] 012)*

Open Access This chapter is licensed under the terms of the Creative Commons Attribution-NonCommercial-NoDerivatives 4.0 International License (http://creativecommons.org/licenses/by-nc-nd/4.0/), which permits any noncommercial use, sharing, distribution and reproduction in any medium or format, as long as you give appropriate credit to the original author(s) and the source, provide a link to the Creative Commons licence and indicate if you modified the licensed material. You do not have permission under this license to share adapted material derived from this chapter or parts of it.

The images or other third party material in this chapter are included in the chapter's Creative Commons licence, unless indicated otherwise in a credit line to the material. If material is not included in the chapter's Creative Commons licence and your intended use is not permitted by statutory regulation or exceeds the permitted use, you will need to obtain permission directly from the copyright holder.

CHAPTER 5

Strengthening Risk Control and Compliance Management

As the company goes global, Huawei faces many risks both externally and internally. External risks involve geopolitics, financial crises, unstable economic growth, shrinking investment, fluctuating exchange rates, strict controls over foreign exchange, anti-globalization, protectionism, anti-dumping, labor disputes, changes in customer business models, and other challenges. Internal risks include risks associated with blind expansion, product quality, business continuity, supply, long overdue inventory, long overdue accounts receivable, cyber security, user privacy protection, taxation, trade compliance, legal compliance, and corruption. All of these risks pose tremendous challenges to Huawei's growth in the global market. When the world is in an imbalanced state, will Huawei keep its balance? How will it do so?

In a complex and nonlinear world, there is no guaranteed correlation between the strength of a cause and its result. Likewise, the potential impact of a local problem is not determined by how big the problem is. As Huawei grows in scale, network coverage increases, and network architecture becomes increasingly complicated, a butterfly effect has been observed. This means that changes in one area can spread and cause severe losses across the whole company, and a small problem can evolve into a larger one and explode.

Despite this, risks are accompanied by opportunities. Huawei does not stop progressing because of risks, nor does it ignore risks as it moves ahead. Huawei's approach to future risks is to use the certainty of rules to

© The Author(s) 2019
W. Huang, *Built on Value*,
https://doi.org/10.1007/978-981-13-7507-1_5

deal with the uncertainty of results and use the certainty of legal compliance to deal with the uncertainty of international politics. The company must strictly monitor internal and external compliance, and strictly operate within the boundaries of its business. It must identify and control risks while harvesting more crops, because the latter is the purpose of the former. The company must keep improving its risk control system to ensure that it operates in compliance with rules and gain freedom in the course of development.

This chapter discusses the rules for managing the internal and external risks that Huawei faces. Detailed rules on oversight, internal controls, and internal audit will be explained in the corresponding chapters in Part II of the book.

5.1 Controlling Risks During Expansion: The Purpose of Control Is to Ensure Sustainable and Profitable Growth

5.1.1 Can Huawei Keep Its Balance in an Unbalanced World? How Can It Do So?

As our company grows in scale and our business becomes increasingly complicated, we also face more internal and external risks. *(Ren Zhengfei: Wearing American Shoes and Starting from Scratch to Build Huawei's Internal Control System—An Introduction to IBM's Internal Control Practices and EMT's Guidelines for Building Huawei's Internal Control System, Huawei Executive Office Speech No. [2007] 032)*

Over the next five to ten years, the world will become increasingly complicated. When the world is imbalanced, can we keep our balance? How can we do so? In such a complex external environment, we also face significant pressure from risks such as shrinking investment, great fluctuations in exchange rates, protectionism, rising wages, labor disputes, and large-scale demonstrations. These are all serious challenges that we face in this era. *(Ren Zhengfei: Speech at the Meeting of the New Board of Directors and the New Supervisory Board, Huawei Executive Office Speech No. [2011] 001)*

Externally, the global financial environment is still turbulent and there are no signs of recovery from the European sovereign debt crisis, making consumers less willing to buy, governments reluctant to invest in infrastructure, and carriers more cautious about capital expenditure (CAPEX). Exchange rates are fluctuating wildly, exposing Huawei to a greater risk of exchange losses. In addition, inflation in emerging markets has not been effectively controlled, driving up operating costs and squeezing the company's profitability. Political turmoil in some countries and regions has affected the continuity and security of Huawei's business operations. There are also significant operating risks caused by geopolitical issues. Trade barriers caused by political maneuvering between large nations, protectionism, cyber security issues, and other factors make our business environment more challenging as well. Weak global demand, the bursting of asset bubbles, and financial deleveraging are likely to occur simultaneously, thus increasing uncertainty in the global economy. *(Ren Zhengfei: Guidelines on the Analysis of the Business Environment and Key Business Strategies, Corp. Doc. No. [2012] 081)*

More than a decade ago, former Nortel CEO William Owens suggested that we work together to develop low-orbit satellites, similar to the solutions that Facebook and Google actually deploy today. We didn't do that, because satellites might have involved military projects. We committed ourselves to never developing equipment for military purposes, or touching the confidential information of others. As a private company, we honor this commitment. So, is it possible that something will emerge to reshape today's telecom networks? I believe so. Motorola's Iridium satellite initiative was indeed very good, but unfortunately, fiber optics appeared, and turned the initiative upside down. Who's to say that telecom networks will not be reshaped? *(Ren Zhengfei: Remarks at Meetings with Huawei Fellows, Huawei Executive Office Speech No. [2016] 069)*

5.1.2 Do Not Focus Exclusively on Opportunities Without Considering Risks

We must ensure trade compliance and pay attention to anti-dumping. In some places we set our prices very low in an effort to compete. We must stop doing this in some contracts because we will suffer huge losses if anti-dumping measures are taken against us. *(Ren Zhengfei: Implementing Oversight with Care, Huawei Executive Office Speech No. [2011] 013)*

In terms of investment strategy, although we have numerous opportunities in the industry, we should not focus exclusively on opportunities without considering risks. We should guard against having ambitious strategic pursuits but lacking the commercial operations capabilities to convert them into financial results. Currently, most business departments follow a V-shaped path when formulating business and strategic plans, claiming that they have not reached the break-even point. They all hope for a better tomorrow in spite of the difficulties today. They all ask for more resources from HQ, but stick to an unrealistic vision with respect to future business results. We need to consider what to invest in, what to give up, and what investment pace to adopt. We also need to decide whether to invest before making profit, or whether to invest while making profit and then increase investment. *(Ren Zhengfei: Guidelines on the Analysis of the Business Environment and Key Business Strategies, Corp. Doc. No. [2012] 081)*

The Consumer BG must remain profit-centric and strictly control inventory risks. Survival is the first step to the future. We must change our value assessment system from one that is technology-oriented to one that is oriented towards business success. The Consumer BG has become part of Huawei's core business and a core business must create value. Value here does not just mean leading technology. *(Ren Zhengfei: Avoiding Opportunism in the Era of Big Opportunities—Speech at the Luncheon with the Administrative Team of the Consumer BG, Huawei Executive Office Speech No. [2014] 025)*

The Consumer BG must enhance strategic partnerships with suppliers. If we keep forcing down their prices, we will face risks. A problem with a single component could cause a whole batch of phones to malfunction. If the batch is very large, the Consumer BG might face a disaster. So first, we need to control inventory, and second, we need to improve our relationships with suppliers. We must use high-quality components to make high-quality phones. *(Ren Zhengfei: Speech at the EMT ST Meeting on August 28, 2015, Huawei Executive Office Speech No. [2015] 132)*

As the capacity and transmission speed of our products increase, we will face greater risks. Any small problem can evolve into a big one and explode. To make our products more reliable, we have to depend on the meticulous German and Japanese people, and on designers in China to improve quality. *(Ren Zhengfei: Minutes of a Meeting with Employees of the Japan Representative Office and the Japan Research Center, Huawei Executive Office Speech No. [2016] 080)*

The year 2016 has seen a flock of black swans – both political and economic – sweep across the globe. Nevertheless, we have remained focused on our strategy and have patiently applied ourselves to making breakthroughs and creating real value for our customers. The macro environment is full of risks: the ongoing transformation of the ICT industry, mounting business pressures faced by our customers, and escalating economic uncertainty around the globe. As we aim to seize new opportunities, we must be better prepared for risks. *(Xu Zhijun: Focusing on Creating Value for Customers, Achieving Sustainable Growth, Huawei Executive Office Speech No. [2016] 099)*

5.1.3 Pursuing Sustainable and Profitable Growth and Curbing Blind Expansion

Over the past two decades, Huawei has been an opportunity-driven company. This has enabled us to become what we are today. In the next two decades, Huawei should be a profit-driven company. We should not seek to become a company with the largest scale; instead, we should pursue more profits and stable growth. *(Source: Positioning and Responsibilities of the Finance Committee Under the Board of Directors [Provisional], Board of Directors Doc. No. [2012] 002)*

The SDC and the Human Resources Committee (HRC) must work hard to drive growth, but they are constrained by the Finance Committee (FC). What sort of constraints are they subject to? First, they can only spend money within their budgets; second, they must ensure that profit targets are hit. *(Source: Positioning and Responsibilities of the Finance Committee Under the Board of Directors [Provisional], Board of Directors Doc. No. [2012] 002)*

Opportunities do not necessarily emerge from new industries. We must have controls and constraints in place for entry into new industries. There are also opportunities in our strategic businesses. The FC decides on the resources allocated to different opportunities and set different profit targets for them. *(Ren Zhengfei: Using Budgeting and Accounting to Drive Sustainable and Profitable Growth in Huawei's Core Business—Speech at the Retreat on the Positioning and Responsibilities of the Finance Committee, 2012)*

Pursuing a diversified business portfolio presents a big challenge to us. We need to determine our direction, pace, and priority, to ensure that we are growing stably with risks under control. *(Guo Ping[1]: Effectively Managing Corporate Value to Pursue Sustainable and Profitable Growth, Huawei Executive Office Speech No. [2012] 005)*

Every business unit needs to set higher profit targets, and curb their desire to expand blindly. The company asks each business unit to turn in a profit. Strategically, this is to prevent blind expansion of new business and

---

[1] Guo Ping was the Rotating CEO of Huawei at the time.

to crack down on irrational expansion. If a new business turns out to be worth expansion and is part of our core business, we can give it space to grow. Otherwise, the business needs to turn in more profits if it wants to grow. We have a plan in place that helps to prevent blind expansion by asking for higher profits from new projects. If every business unit focuses on scaling out and becomes bloated like they used to, but contribute no profit to the company, then our company will be ultimately dragged down. *(Guo Ping: Effectively Managing Corporate Value to Pursue Sustainable and Profitable Growth, Huawei Executive Office Speech No. [2012] 005)*

The economic prospects don't look good. We don't allow blind development. When talking about market space, we must be realistic and emphasize the contributions being made right now. We are in a period of big risks. We must be clear about our strategy and make full use of our strengths, as this is necessary to generate enough profits to ensure our survival. Departments that do not generate profits must be downsized. If a product doesn't generate any profits, then don't develop it blindly. Don't say that it will make contributions in the future. If we cannot survive, then future contributions are meaningless. No one should build their success on the backs of others. Don't be overly optimistic when making estimations; be more conservative. *(Ren Zhengfei: Speech at a Work Report of the Network Energy Product Line, Huawei Executive Office Speech No. [2012] 043)*

We should take a pragmatic approach to countries that we predict we won't have big opportunities when looking at their future economic growth. If we don't have big opportunities in a war-torn country, we should not maintain large teams there. In the future, we need to downsize local offices in countries where we don't see large growth potential. We only need to engage in sales activities, with a focus on services. For these countries, we only look at their profits, not sales revenue. *(Ren Zhengfei: Minutes of the Report on the Opportunity to Order for 2017, EMT Meeting Minutes No. [2016] 021)*

5.1.4 Balancing Expansion and Control

We have a team of more than 80,000 employees. Such a large team losing momentum would be disastrous. So we must continue to forge ahead. No team can afford to fail, as this could cause a chain reaction. We must remain prepared to fight hard battles and make improvements during this process. We cannot afford to stop to make improvements. We have already assigned a larger weight to positive cash flow and positive profit margins during performance appraisals. This acts as a tight band around the head of our staff on the front line, and we should not place any more shackles on them. Otherwise, the whole company will have to stop to make improvements. This is too risky. In performance appraisals, we have shifted our focus to profitable and self-sustaining growth. This change has already begun and will not progress too quickly. As long as we move in the right direction, we will achieve the desired results. *(Ren Zhengfei: Speech at a Meeting with the IFS Project Team and Staff from Finance, Huawei Executive Office Speech No. [2009] 004)*

We must strike a balance between expansion and control and strengthen our strategic focus. We must be selective about what we do and what we don't. Only in this way can we seize the strategic high ground. We must continue to focus on our core business. Then in three to five years, we can find a way out. *(Ren Zhengfei: Guidelines on the Key Points of Huawei's 2012 Business Management)*

We must improve operations quality and drive sustainable and profitable growth. As we increase investment, we must better incorporate the company's strategic pursuits into business goal setting and closed-loop performance appraisals. We need to improve the way we manage risks, maintain robust, standardized operations, and use the certainty of rules to deal with the uncertainty of the global economy. *(Ren Zhengfei: Guidelines on the Key Points of Huawei's 2012 Business Management)*

A global business presence will lay a foundation for our survival in the global market. We must increase investment and build a corporate culture that allows effective deployment of talent, capabilities, experience, and resources around the world. This will enable us to forge extensive partnerships with our stakeholders in countries and regions where we operate, helping create a harmonious ecosystem and avoid possible strategic risks in the future. *(Ren Zhengfei: Guidelines on the Key Points of Huawei's 2012 Business Management)*

5.2 A MULTI-FACETED SYSTEM FOR CONTROLLING FINANCIAL RISKS AT HUAWEI

5.2.1 The "Four Threes" System for Risk Control

From a financial perspective, we have established a system of "Four Threes" to manage the company's risks. The "Four Threes" are the three categories of risks, which are strategic risks, operational risks, and financial risks; the three lines of defense built into every business activity; the three blue teams established in London, New York, and Tokyo that operate independently to challenge red teams; and the three layers of review established by three independent organizations, which are CFOs, Accounting, and Treasury. *(Meng Wanzhou: Outline of the Report on the Operations of the Financial Risk Control Center in London, 2017)*

Three Categories of Risks We have defined risks by category. For example, in the strategic risk category, we know that our company will surely face technical risks: Will a disruptive technology emerge to challenge our technological model? For operational risks, we can look at supply. The recent problem with the flash memory of our P10 series smartphones is a typical supply risk. The upstream supplier controlled the number of parts supplied to Huawei. The third risk category is financial risks, which include foreign exchange risks and tax risks. We assign a single individual to be responsible for each category of risks, and they manage risks throughout the company by dismantling department silos and dissolving organizational boundaries. This individual identifies, assesses, responds to, monitors, and reports risks to minimize their impact. This is how we manage the three categories of risks. *(Meng Wanzhou: Outline of the Report on the Operations of the Financial Risk Control Center in London, 2017)*

Three Lines of Defense In all circumstances, the first line of defense is business managers. They naturally assume process responsibilities and incorporate risk management and control activities into their everyday work. The second line of defense is the internal control and inspection teams that provide support to business managers. The internal control team develops an internal control methodology, similar to a physical examination checklist, to help business managers perform self-checks. With this checklist, business managers can review and identify areas for improvement. The inspection team identifies major risks and most likely problems in processes and focuses on major conflicts and major risks. These two teams are assistants to business managers, reporting to business managers and helping them control 90% of operational risks. The third line of defense is the audit team. They report independently to top management. This team conducts random checks on specific activities to establish deterrence across the whole organization. This is how we build three lines of defense into every business activity. *(Meng Wanzhou: Outline of the Report on the Operations of the Financial Risk Control Center in London, 2017)*

Three Financial Risk Control Centers (FRCCs) In 2013, we established an FRCC in London. We chose this city because British people respect rules, especially in the financial sector. We appreciate their conservative approach, not their proactive approach to innovation. We hope to bring a large number of high-end British financial professionals into our company. We expect them to independently assess the financial strategies and architecture that we are working on. We aim to establish rules for everything. Even if something uncertain happens, we have rules to follow. We established an FRCC in Tokyo because Japanese people are meticulous and always dive deep into details. This center helps us better manage our contracts and projects because our end-to-end delivery usually lasts about two to three years. They will check whether something is poorly managed during this period, whether there are embedded contracts, and whether there has been any violation of rules. If yes, they will produce an independent audit report to inform the relevant staff, such as finance staff, project engineers, and project designers, telling them in which areas they need to improve. The FRCC in New York focuses on studying the macro economy. Huawei can't survive in its own world. At this center, we have a team dedicated to researching oil prices. They monitor the trends of exchange rates and foreign exchange reserves in OPEC countries and predict how their exchange rates will change and whether they will impose controls on foreign exchange. We want to figure out how we can improve today from the standpoint of tomorrow. *(Meng Wanzhou: Outline of the Report on the Operations of the Financial Risk Control Center in London, 2017)*

Three Layers of Review This is a special system. In many companies, CFOs are independent, but Treasury and Accounting may not. At Huawei, we assign a CFO to each business manager. In addition to the CFOs we have deployed in countries and regions, and for customers, we also assign a CFO for each large contract and each project. The Human Resource Management Department and the General Procurement Department also have their own CFOs. What do these CFOs do? First, they offer specialist support, helping business teams to make better-informed decisions. Second, they identify risk items during their independent reporting, and escalate the issues to upper-level management, reminding them to intervene and resolve the issues. *(Meng Wanzhou: Outline of the Report on the Operations of the Financial Risk Control Center in London, 2017)*

5.2.2 Two Perspectives of Financial Risk Control

Huawei implements its financial risk control system from two perspectives: The first is from an external perspective. The three centers in London, Tokyo, and New York work together to create synergies. The center in London aims to use the certainty of rules to deal with future uncertainty. The center in Tokyo looks at the smallest unit of operations. And the center in New York looks at how we can improve today from the standpoint of tomorrow.

The other perspective is an internal one. In addition to the three centers, we also have three layers of review. The first layer is daily reconciliation. The Treasury Management Department completes bank reconciliation on a daily basis to ensure that every cash flow comes from accounting treatment. The second layer is accounting. This function ensures that processes are followed, authority is properly exercised, and accounting is accurately handled. The third layer is independent CFOs, who establish onsite checks and balances for business decisions. *(Meng Wanzhou: Key Points of the Report on Risk Monitoring, 2017)*

5.2.3 Three Financial Risk Control Centers

Now we need to determine the different focuses of the three FRCCs. British people respect rules and are good at setting rules, so the FRCC in London is responsible for setting rules for each country and each industry. Japanese people are down-to-earth. They are good at doing projects, so the center in Tokyo should focus on project risk management. Americans have a global view, so the center in New York focuses on macroeconomic research. Leveraging the different strengths of the three nations, we can establish three pillars to support our operations. *(Ren Zhengfei: Speech at the Meeting with the Finance Management Philosophy Editorial Board, 2017)*

The FRCC in London provides guidelines on financial policies, tax policies, and implementation rules for Huawei

Why did Huawei choose to establish an FRCC in London? It's because the UK has mature rules and institutions. The legal, financial, and tax frameworks in the UK are widely applied by other countries. This unique strength enabled the UK to be the first country to move beyond the 2008 financial crisis. And following the crisis, London has further consolidated its position as a global financial center. Specifically, there are three reasons:

5 STRENGTHENING RISK CONTROL AND COMPLIANCE MANAGEMENT   123

First, timing. Since the seventeenth century, London has been a world economic and trade center. Today the city is home to the world's largest financial derivative market and 49% of global financial derivative deals take place there.

Second, location. London is an inclusive financial center and can easily cover regions like Europe, Africa, the Middle East, and Central Asia. It is the first city that has launched a prudent oversight plan for the financial sector.

Third, talent. London has more than one million financial professionals, far exceeding Frankfurt and Paris. And the pay of senior financial professionals is lower than in China.

Huawei's FRCC in London is specialized in three key areas: accounting, tax, and treasury. It manages process design, financial strategies, operations quality, and compliance risks from end to end. This center aims to use the certainty of rules to deal with the uncertainty of results and provide guidelines on financial policies, tax policies, and implantation rules for Huawei globally. The center also sets country-specific policies to deal with tax risks. Here is an example of how the FRCC has played its role. Before the crises in Russia and Greece broke out, the center identified the risks and transferred funds out of these countries to secure our assets. The center systematically manages the settlement of transactions worth US$1.2 trillion and the associated liquidity risks, covering more than 180 countries and regions and over 145 currencies. *(Meng Wanzhou: Key Points of the Report on Risk Monitoring, 2017)*

The FRCC in Tokyo focuses on project risk control

The FRCC in Tokyo focuses on project management. Japanese people are willing to focus on details. They are good at turning complicated things into simpler ones and doing simple things right the first time. They are meticulous in project baseline and budget management. They even have the courage to halt projects if risks are detected. Their philosophy of project risk management is that exceptions are allowed, but accidents are not.

The meticulousness and craftsmanship of Japanese people – always seeking to do things even better – have enabled the country to establish the highest-standard benchmark in project management around the world. This is why we have established an FRCC in Tokyo, focusing on project operations. Project operations are about examining our management opportunities and making improvements through business case design, negotiations, risk estimation, project execution monitoring, and final accounting upon project completion. We can identify areas for systematic improvement from the details of our project operations, which will drive more thorough improvements in these areas. In terms of project operations, we can prepare a guide like the pilot manual and promote it globally. Our ultimate goal is to fuel project operations, increase soil fertility, and harvest more crops. *(Meng Wanzhou: Key Points of the Report on Risk Monitoring, 2017)*

The FRCC in New York helps the company judge and deal with risks in the macro economy

The US's economic cycle and dollar trends directly affect the global economy, and decisions of the US also directly influence geopolitics and national risks. New York is where the decisions are made. It marks the trail that the rest of the US economy and financial sector will follow. As a financial center, New York has a broad horizon, enabling the city to forecast long-term trends, seize the high ground in policy development, and wield global influence.

We established an FRCC in New York so that we can leverage its vision and global, broad horizon, and absorb the energy of the universe. We hope to cooperate with leading financing institutions and think tanks on Wall Street to obtain first-hand information, helping our company to make better-informed decisions and respond to risks in the macro economy. We also want to help avoid negative impacts on Huawei caused by black swan events, including political uncertainty and uncertainty caused by trade wars like punitive tariffs on a certain industry. We must also watch out for economic uncertainty, such as global economic trends and uncertainty in exchange rates (e.g. when will the USD reach an inflection point?). We need to take a fine-grained approach to all these issues. *(Meng Wanzhou: Key Points of the Report on Risk Monitoring, 2017)*

5.3 FINANCIAL RISK PREVENTION AND CONTROL

5.3.1 We Need to Have Contingency Plans to Deal with Financial Crises, But the Key Is Improving Contract Quality

First, what was most affected by financial crises? The bubble economy. Companies that had the biggest bubbles, such as those in the financial and real estate sectors, suffered most in financial crises. Second, telecommunication services cost small amounts of money and don't fluctuate significantly with the changes in the financial sector. Third, as the digital deluge approaches, demand for network bandwidth will increase. *(Ren Zhengfei: Comments at a Meeting with Sales Financing Experts, Huawei Executive Office Speech No. [2012] 025)*

We face different risks in different countries, at different times, and under different scenarios. We must have a contingency plan for each specific risk to minimize losses and avoid a conservative approach to our business. *(Ren Zhengfei: Remarks at Meetings with the UK R&D Center, Beijing Research Center, and Financial Risk Control Center in London, Huawei Executive Office Speech No. [2015] 075)*

Due to an unfavorable global economic environment, credit risks may arise among our key customers, which may result in their inability to make payments on time. For example, in the first half of the year, Brazil's Oi applied for bankruptcy, and India's Reliance faced debt risks. This situation placed clear requirements on us: Huawei's growth must be built on high-quality contracts. If an international political crisis arises, we will survive if we still have money to buy bread. If we don't have money, what should we do? We must not do things randomly. Instead, we must strengthen contract management, and focus on increasing efficiency and profitability in the marketplace. In particular, we must strengthen contract management in countries where there are higher risks related to payment collection. We need to increase the proportion of advance payments, and decrease the proportion of payment upon receipt of the Final Acceptance Certificate (FAC), so as to ensure quality growth this year. *(Ren Zhengfei: There Will Not Always Be Flowers Along the Road Ahead—Speech at the H1 Huawei Market Conference, Huawei Executive Office Speech No. [2016] 079)*

We must have contingency plans in place to deal with financial crises, and we must improve our risk control and operational compliance oversight through organizational building and manager deployment. *(Xu Zhijun: Focusing on Creating Value for Customers, Achieving Sustainable Growth, Huawei Executive Office Speech No. [2016] 099)*

When our revenue reaches US$200 billion, the FRCC in London alone will not be enough to support our operations. We must develop our FRCCs in Japan and New York to better control financial risks associated with projects and the macro economy. *(Source: Minutes of the Work Summary During the Rotating Period [April to September 2015] and Relevant Discussions, BOD Executive Committee Meeting Minutes. No. [2016] 004)*

5.3.2 Taking Diversified Approaches to Financing and Settlement

To disperse financial risks, we must become less reliant on loans from Chinese banks, pay more attention to local financing, and build a stronger local financing team. *(Source: Minutes of the Report on the 2012 Group Budget Review, EMT Meeting Minutes No. [2012] 012)*

We need to take diversified approaches to financing and settlement, and reduce foreign exchange losses by spending local currency locally as much as possible. In Japan and Europe, a good proportion of local settlements are done in local currencies, which partially hedges our foreign exchange position. In these countries and regions, we don't need to convert local currencies into USD. In countries where local currencies have no way to be used, we assume exchange risks. *(Ren Zhengfei: Speech at the EMT ST Meeting, March 30, 2012)*

The more rapidly we develop, the higher the risks we will encounter. We face great risks in our operations. In the 170-plus countries and regions where we operate, we face all kinds of risks, including war, disease, and currency-related issues. We have set up an FRCC in London. Last year, this center effectively controlled risks concerning the settlement of over CNY5 trillion in 145 currencies from 178 countries, and managed to minimize financial losses to our company. We will also establish FRCCs in Tokyo and New York, where we can leverage excellent global talent to manage and control risks with the company's funds, contracts, and project management. Great achievements have been made in this area, laying a solid foundation for the company to go global. *(Ren Zhengfei: Dedicated to China's Century-old Dream of Revitalizing Science and Technology, Huawei Executive Office Speech No. [2016] 067)*

5.3.3 Do Not Stop Progressing Because of Risks or Ignore Risks in Order to Progress

The company must establish an early warning and rapid response system to predict and sense any subtle but major changes in the external environment caused by competitors, customers, suppliers, and policies and regulations. *(Source: The Huawei Charter, 1998)*

Risk management involves resolving problems immediately after they occur and taking measures beforehand to foresee and prevent risks. But this does not mean that we need to build huge organizations or processes.

Instead, we need to gradually improve our risk management framework on the basis of existing processes and management systems. *(Source: Minutes of the Work Report on Risk Management, EMT Meeting Minutes No. [2005] 059)*

We do not stop progressing because of risks, or ignore risks in order to progress. We have strict rules: Making opportunistic financial investments and using financial leverage are both forbidden. We cannot afford to run risks on two fronts at the same time. *(Ren Zhengfei: Remarks at Meetings with the UK R&D Center, Beijing Research Center, and Financial Risk Control Center in London, Huawei Executive Office Speech No. [2015] 075)*

5.4 Business Continuity Management

5.4.1 Huawei's Primary Obligation: Maintaining Stable Network Operations

Our business is to construct networks. Networks with global coverage must be stable at all times. Our products and services are now found everywhere: plateaus where there is a lack of oxygen, scorching hot deserts, the frozen Arctic Ocean, dangerous areas full of land mines, forests, rivers, oceans, and more. Wherever there are people, there are our products and services. *(Ren Zhengfei: Speech on Cherishing Life and Assuming Professional Responsibilities, Huawei Executive Office Speech No. [2011] 009)*

Our obligation is to maintain stable network operations. This is different from stores that sell tofu and fried dough, because they can be closed whenever their owners like. We can never do this. When there is a disaster or a war, we have to do everything we can to maintain basic network stability. *(Ren Zhengfei: Speech on Cherishing Life and Assuming Professional Responsibilities, Huawei Executive Office Speech No. [2011] 009)*

Turmoil may occur at any time. Wherever we are and at whatever time, our responsibility is to maintain basic network stability and never get involved in the politics of any country. *(Ren Zhengfei: Speech on Cherishing Life and Assuming Professional Responsibilities, Huawei Executive Office Speech No. [2011] 009)*

Our managers and administrative departments must develop contingency plans for possible emergencies. While the company is implementing a contingency plan to respond to a crisis, all departments must take their due share of responsibility to ensure that the company's business continues to operate normally. *(Ren Zhengfei: Speech on Cherishing Life and*

Assuming Professional Responsibilities, Huawei Executive Office Speech No. [2011] 009)

Business continuity is a guarantee of our customer services and our survival, so we must not leave it to luck. To ensure supply security and business continuity, we must boldly make strategic investments, embrace open innovation, draw on the achievements and strengths of others, and make strategic breakthroughs in key technologies, basic software platforms, key chips, and key components. *(Source: Overtaking the United States and Enjoying the Ride—Speech by Xu Zhijun at Huawei Annual Management Conference 2013, Huawei Executive Office Speech No. [2013] 244)*

5.4.2 Building Strategic Reserves to Prevent Supply Risks

In the current economic environment, some of our suppliers may face business problems and may be unable to supply the raw materials we need. To prevent such risks, we can consider taking part of the savings from raw material price cuts as reserve funds to fight against risks. We can use the money to buy extra materials, which can serve as reserve inventory to ensure our normal production and supply security. We can also use this money to reward outstanding suppliers and those who have demonstrated outstanding performance, which will in turn bring Huawei more benefits. *(Ren Zhengfei: Speech at the Report on the 2009 Business Strategy by the Procurement Qualification Management Department, EMT Meeting Minutes No. [2009] 013)*

We must maintain the right level of inventory to ensure our survival. We allow no risk to this part of inventory. We must take various measures, such as adopting strategic initiatives to ensure availability of key items, sourcing from multiple regions, and building strategic reserves, to ensure the business continuity of our major network products. *(Source: EMT Meeting Minutes No. [2012] 004)*

We have two goals in making strategic breakthroughs: Internally, we must survive; externally, we must overtake our competitors. If we are unable to achieve these goals, all our efforts will become meaningless. We must not seek to become a weak company that relies on certain big countries; instead, we must be determined to overtake our competitors and become an industry leader. Since we are several years behind those with advanced technology, we must aim to make strategic and technological breakthroughs, have "spare tires" in place, and overtake our competitors. *(Ren Zhengfei: Minutes of the Annual Work Report on Business Continuity and Strategic Breakthroughs, EMT Meeting Minutes No. [2013] 005)*

We need to have a red team and a blue team in our product development division. The red team focuses on honing our competitive edge and the blue team focuses on ensuring that we have "spare tires". Members of the two teams can rotate regularly or move between product releases. Product architecture must be flexible and boards must be interchangeable. *(Ren Zhengfei: Minutes of the Annual Work Report on Business Continuity and Strategic Breakthroughs, EMT Meeting Minutes No. [2013] 005)*

For strategic reserves, we must follow the "first in, first out" principle and ensure that there is no shortage of supply during replenishment of inventory. During emergencies, we can use the reserved materials to support ongoing sales of spare parts and services. *(Ren Zhengfei: Minutes of the Annual Work Report on Business Continuity and Strategic Breakthroughs, EMT Meeting Minutes No. [2013] 005)*

5.4.3 Avoiding the Inclusion of Countries and Regions Affected by War, Civil Unrest, or Epidemics into Emergency-Triggered Management Cycles

Countries and regions affected by war, civil unrest, or epidemics must be managed differently from those where our business operates normally. These hardship countries must be treated fairly and their emergency response assurance, organizational evaluations, performance appraisals, talent management, incentives, and organizational climate need to be revisited systematically. The Hardship Areas and Position Management Department must provide emergency response assurance for these countries and systematically review their management frameworks and rules to avoid including these countries into emergency-triggered management cycles. *(Source: Minutes of the Work Report by the Hardship Areas and Position Management Department, BOD Executive Committee Meeting Minutes No. [2014] 012)*

We have eight employees in Yemen. The Hardship Areas and Position Management Department must figure out how to create a better living environment for them. For example, we don't need to change the exteriors of their houses, but we can install steel plates on the interiors, replace window glass with laminated glass, and introduce mechanical ventilation systems. You can go and talk to the Capital Construction Management Department about this. The windows and steel plates for the Yemen office can be bought in China and delivered by air. HQ can bear the expense. The Yemen office only needs to pay installation costs. A report on what was done in Afghanistan can also be published for people to read. None of our staff there have been injured despite the ongoing war. In these countries, we need to build a caring environment where everyone feels safe and united. There is nothing more important than the lives of our employees. We must do everything we can to keep them safe and avoid doing anything too risky. When we risk our lives to provide products or services in the face of war or violence, then the price of our products should go up. We're not trying to extort anyone, but we need to let carriers understand our situation. That way, we can break even in small countries. Turning in profits to the company is not important here. *(Ren Zhengfei: Minutes of the Briefing on the Progress of Differentiated Appraisals for Regions, Huawei Executive Office Speech No. [2015] 050)*

During administrative services management, we must look at more than just the size of a country. We must also consider how tough it is to work and live in that country. We need to make all this very clear, because it is not easy to provide a comfortable environment in hardship regions. *(Ren Zhengfei: Improving the Working Environments in Hardship Countries—Speech at the EMT ST Meeting on March 7, 2016, Huawei Executive Office Speech No. [2016] 037)*

5.5 Using the Certainty of Legal Compliance to Deal with the Uncertainty of International Politics

5.5.1 Legal Compliance Is the Most Important Basis on Which We Survive, Provide Services, and Contribute Worldwide

Individual income tax risks are mainly faced overseas. The purpose of complying with applicable laws in countries outside China is to ensure our operational security there. In China, our principle in complying with individual income tax laws is to be a follower; innovation is not encouraged. *(Ren Zhengfei: Minutes of the Meeting on Individual Income Tax Related Problems, 2011)*

All employees must respect and strictly observe laws and regulations. No one should think they are above the law. *(Source: Employees Must Comply with Laws, EMT Resolution No. [2015] 016)*

Huawei is obliged to comply with all applicable laws and regulations, including Chinese laws about managing the information on content operations platforms. *(Source: Employees Must Comply with Laws, EMT Resolution No. [2015] 016)*

The primary goal of the Legal Affairs Department is not to put out fires or win lawsuits, but to prevent fires. *(Ren Zhengfei: Speech at a Meeting with Employees of the Legal Affairs Department, Secretariat Office of the Board of Directors, and Wireless Network Product Line, Huawei Executive Office Speech No. [2015] 015)*

Guo Ping has said that we must use the certainty of legal compliance to tackle the uncertainty of international politics. He has shown us where we should be heading as we deal with international relations. *(Ren Zhengfei: Be First to Know When Springtime Comes. Vow Not to Return Till We Reach Our Goals—Speech at an Oath-taking Rally for Reassigned Senior R&D Experts and Managers, Huawei Executive Office Speech No. [2016] 093)*

As we face an increasingly complicated business environment, we must leverage the certainty of legal compliance to tackle the uncertainty of international politics, to bridge discontinuity in the macro environment. *(Xu Zhijun: Focusing on Creating Value for Customers, Achieving Sustainable Growth, Huawei Executive Office Speech No. [2016] 099)*

As long as China continues with its reform towards the rule of law and the market economy, it will be a more powerful country and will make greater contributions to the world in the coming decades. Huawei has a business presence in over 170 countries and regions. Legal compliance is the most important basis on which we survive, provide services, and contribute worldwide. We abide by laws of the countries and regions where we operate, and by United Nations resolutions. In sensitive regions, we regard the laws of the US as international laws. If we didn't do so, it would be impossible for us to go global. *(Ren Zhengfei: Dedicated to China's Century-old Dream of Revitalizing Science and Technology, Huawei Executive Office Speech No. [2016] 067)*

The world today is full of uncertainty and crises. We must strictly abide by rules and laws, and use the certainty of legal compliance to tackle the uncertainty of international politics. We must strictly monitor internal and external compliance, and operate within the boundaries of our business. *(Ren Zhengfei: Dedicated to China's Century-old Dream of Revitalizing Science and Technology, Huawei Executive Office Speech No. [2016] 067)*

Over the next three to five years, our company may face huge risks, so we must abide by the law and use the certainty of legal compliance to tackle the uncertainty of international politics. The world is undergoing tremendous changes. The only thing we can do is to ensure legal compliance in the countries and regions where we operate. *(Ren Zhengfei: There

Will Not Always Be Flowers Along the Road Ahead—Speech at the 2016 H1 Huawei Market Conference, Huawei Executive Office Speech No. [2016] 079)

First, Huawei is a company. We must not engage in politics, as that is the job of politicians. And we are not familiar with politics. We must serve our customers in a down-to-earth manner. That is how we can achieve success. *(Ren Zhengfei: Minutes of a Meeting with Employees of the Japan Representative Office and the Japan Research Center, Huawei Executive Office Speech No. [2016] 080)*

5.5.2 Focusing on Protecting User Privacy in the Same Way We Have Done in Cyber Security

The public, governments, and customers are increasingly concerned about user privacy protection. Therefore, to develop our consumer and enterprise businesses, we need to enhance user privacy protection. Just as what we have done in cyber security, we will make important commitments to the public, governments, and customers on user privacy protection to fulfill our corporate responsibilities. We will take all possible measures to enhance user privacy protection. *(Source: Resolution on Enhancing User Privacy Protection, EMT Resolution No. [2014] 031)*

Business managers take full responsibility for cyber security and user privacy protection within their own business domains. Process owners take full responsibility for cyber security and user privacy protection within their respective processes. Managers in BGs and BUs are responsible for all operating results, including technological competitiveness, market share, profit and loss, as well as for cyber security and user privacy protection. *(Source: Resolution on Enhancing User Privacy Protection, EMT Resolution No. [2014] 031)*

5.6 Compliance Management and Subsidiary Boards' Oversight Responsibilities

5.6.1 Strengthening Compliance Management to Harvest More Crops

We must ensure the operational compliance of overseas representative offices, subsidiaries, and research institutes to avoid negative incidents. *(Source: 2010 Key Work Requirements, EMT Resolution No. [2010] 007)*

Any non-compliance may have major impact or even cause fatal damage to our company's reputation and our continued, stable development around the world. *(Ren Zhengfei: Promoting Operational Compliance of Subsidiaries to Support the Company's Robust Growth, Huawei Executive Office Speech No. [2015] 012)*
Principles for managing compliance risks:

1. We must set a clear goal and plan for compliance management. We then need to classify countries into different categories based on the stringency of their compliance requirements, their population, and our in-country business volume. We need to set and implement a compliance plan for the next three years to ensure that our core business complies with all applicable laws before the end of that period.

Compliance risks are dynamic and relative, not absolute. If the company does not give a risk a green light, we must ensure compliance unconditionally. For high-level risks that may have severe impacts on the company's major business, reputation, and brand image, we must set red lines and ensure that these basic requirements are met first.

2. For all compliance risks, we must achieve pre-set compliance goals within the required timeframes. For individual risks for which we cannot ensure 100% compliance for the moment, we must monitor them in real time, manage the progress of improvement, and monitor the status of the risks. *(Source: Minutes of the Report on the Work Priority "Building and Improving the Overseas Operational Compliance Management Mechanism, Regulating Subsidiary Management Operations, and Establishing Oversight-oriented Boards at All Overseas Subsidiaries", BOD Executive Committee Meeting Minutes No. [2014] 017)*

Don't be afraid during the compliance management process. We must move forward cautiously and ensure we do not cross any red lines. In the future, we will accept fines if they come as a result of crossing a red line due to a lack of capabilities despite a collective decision. What we will not accept is paying the price for ignorance. *(Ren Zhengfei: Remarks During Visits to Countries Where Cash Is Trapped, Huawei Executive Office Speech No. [2015] 023)*

Subsidiary boards oversee compliance to make sure we comply with laws and regulations while harvesting more crops. This is also our long-term goal. Any short-term dip in revenue must be in the service of that long-term goal. Compliance isn't an excuse for harvesting less crops. That is an outdated, false understanding of what compliance means. *(Ren Zhengfei: Speech at the Mid-year Workshop on the Enablement of Subsidiary Board Directors, Huawei Executive Office Speech No. [2014] 074)*

We must enhance compliance management and improve our related capabilities. In the future, we will boost our capability to manage compliance by training managers or through lectures and self-learning sessions, much like those given in Egypt. *(Ren Zhengfei: Remarks During Visits to Countries Where Cash Is Trapped, Huawei Executive Office Speech No. [2015] 023)*

The goals of our oversight-oriented subsidiary boards are the same as those of our operating teams, which are to harvest more crops and increase soil fertility. Here crops not only include sales revenue, but also profits and cash flow. By harvesting more crops, we aim for profitable revenue and healthy cash flow. Currently, our oversight-oriented subsidiary boards are responsible for overseeing subsidiaries' internal and external compliance, managers, accounting compliance, and operating results. In the future, they may also act as a platform for public relations, legal affairs, and logistics support. The boards and operating teams will each play their own roles, and operating teams can move forward nimbly while complying with relevant laws and rules. *(Ren Zhengfei: Speech at the Meeting on Extension of the Company's Oversight and Management Control System, Huawei Executive Office Speech No. [2017] 041)*

5.6.2 Subsidiary Boards: Performing Integrated Oversight in the Field on Behalf of the Company Without Interfering in Business Operations

We must delegate more authority to field offices, allowing those who are closest to customers to make business decisions. At the same time, we must strengthen oversight and management. *(Ren Zhengfei: Success Is Not a Reliable Guide to Future Development—Speech at the Huawei Market Conference on January 17, 2011, Huawei Executive Office Speech No. [2011] 004)*

Our policies are clear: We must establish only one platform and have only one controlling entity in every country. We must not register multiple companies in one city. This can help improve our governance structure, regulate the establishment of legal entities in countries, and ensure operational and legal compliance. *(Ren Zhengfei: Speech at a Workshop on Europe's Business Environment, Huawei Executive Office Speech No. [2013] 054)*

Let's allow people who can hear the gunfire to call for artillery. It's important that we promptly delegate decision-making authority to the field and at the same time prevent the field from acting randomly. As such, our oversight system must also be moved to the field by leveraging the power of the company's capital. Capital management is not a part of our normal processes. As our forces quickly advance, it's the job of subsidiary board directors to sit and observe. If they spot a problem, they need to take a helicopter to get to the heart of the problem. This is not a process-based action. On behalf of the company, our subsidiary boards leverage the power of capital to provide oversight. International laws support such capital management. But remember not to interfere in business operations. *(Ren Zhengfei: Speech at the Mid-year Workshop on the Enablement of Subsidiary Board Directors, 2014)*

Why should subsidiary boards become an integrated governance platform? In the future, our revenue will be far more than 70 billion US dollars and may reach 100 or even 200 billion US dollars. We are not sure how large data traffic will become. We must have an integrated management platform in place. Only in this way can we promptly satisfy customer needs and delegate authority to operating teams. If we don't do this, it will be impossible for us to scale out. We now have one platform. In the future, we will have an integrated management platform consisting of more than 100 subsidiary boards, enabling us to promptly respond to and satisfy customer needs. Over the past two years, we have followed the needle-tip strategy and have become very likely to be the industry leader in terms of technology. Our talent pyramid was stable in the past, but to inspire passion across the company, we need to further optimize the pyramid. Within three to five years, we will implement all our management transformations and reach the same management standards as Western companies. In five to ten years, we will delegate business decision-making authority to teams that are closest to customers. After that, the integrated platform will play an important role. We must pay attention to this. We also need to strengthen financial management and integrated management. We need to readily recognize staffing of the finance division. *(Ren Zhengfei: Speech at the Briefing on the Deployment of Subsidiary Boards of Directors Outside China, Huawei Executive Office Speech No. [2014] 048)*

Subsidiary boards are currently focusing on compliance oversight, and have identified a number of pressing problems relating to labor, taxation, and permanent establishment. These problems are the same ones we have seen in field offices. Most managers focus more on business management and strategic operations, and pay less attention to these problems. We're currently stepping up efforts to develop our enterprise and consumer businesses, so our problems are now more exposed to public scrutiny than in the past. By establishing subsidiary boards at this time and by using oversight to bridge the gaps I mentioned, our operations will be more robust, which will be conducive to our future growth. *(Ren Zhengfei: Speech at the Mid-year Workshop on the Enablement of Subsidiary Board Directors, Huawei Executive Office Speech No. [2014] 074)*

We must enhance our legal entity management capabilities in overseas subsidiaries.

1. The Investments Management Department has launched a series of projects to build legal entity management capabilities in overseas subsidiaries. They have developed subsidiary entity management processes, improved the processes of determining specific functions undertaken by subsidiaries, refined subsidiary management policies, and improved subsidiary compliance capabilities. Relevant policies and plans need to be completed by the end of 2014 and implemented in 2015.
2. In the legal entity management of overseas subsidiaries, we must focus on major subsidiaries, especially entities responsible for a wide range of functions, such as the subsidiaries in the UK, France, Germany, and Malaysia. We need to optimize their governance structure and pilot appointing subsidiary general managers to manage all entities at the subsidiary level. We must effectively manage subsidiary legal entities and build a platform to support business development and resource allocation.
3. We must focus on countries where compliance risks are high, especially the US. Have we bought insurance for subsidiary board directors? We must enhance our risk prevention measures for individual directors. *(Source: Minutes of the Report on the Work Priority "Building and Improving the Overseas Operational Compliance Management Mechanism, Regulating Subsidiary Management Operations, and Establishing Oversight-oriented Boards at All Overseas Subsidiaries", BOD Executive Committee Meeting Minutes No. [2014] 017)*

Over the next five years, our annual revenue will top US$100 billion. We will definitely delegate authority to the very front line. That means we will no longer have one, centralized management platform, but several decentralized ones. So we will need a neutral organization to oversee our field operations on behalf of the company. That will be the mission of our subsidiary boards. *(Ren Zhengfei: Speech at a Briefing on the Solution for Management Oversight by Oversight-oriented Subsidiary Boards and the Pilot Results, Huawei Executive Office Speech No. [2015] 072)*

Subsidiary boards are authorized to exercise onsite oversight on subsidiary operations on behalf of the company and are organizations with their own inherent authority. Auditing, inspection, internal controls, offices of ethics and compliance (OECs), legal affairs, and other departments are organizations responsible for execution. They need to support subsidiary boards in exercising their oversight authority. Subsidiary boards must show the value of authority and must not try to grab or take over the work of these supporting departments. These departments will ultimately report to the subsidiary boards. *(Ren Zhengfei: Speech at a Briefing on the Solution for Management Oversight by Oversight-oriented Subsidiary Boards and the Pilot Results, Huawei Executive Office Speech No. [2015] 072)*

Today, the Legal Affairs Department manages compliance on behalf of the company and implements rules and systems, including programs. This is a highly centralized approach where the Legal Affairs Department reports directly to the corporate Board of Directors. In the future, we will change this centralized governance approach by delegating authority to the field, with the local legal and oversight functions in place reporting to subsidiary boards and higher-level business departments. Without this change, HQ will become bloated. In the future, we will gradually delegate more authority to field offices because they know the most about the business and are closest to customers. Despite this, people who are delegated authority must be subject to oversight, so our oversight teams must also be moved forward into the field. That does not mean that HQ will no longer play any oversight role. Instead, HQ will become more specialized, and will use its expertise to support oversight in field operations. Local legal affairs teams will report compliance statuses to subsidiary boards, local business management teams, and the President of the Legal Affairs Department at HQ. Local legal affairs teams also play their part in building compliance capabilities. *(Ren Zhengfei: Speech at a Meeting with the Managerial Control Elite Team, Huawei Executive Office Speech No. [2015] 060)*

The company's Supervisory Board will assist the Subsidiary Board Directors Resources Bureau and the Investments Management Department in setting up subsidiary boards, which in turn will be managed directly by the Supervisory Board in the future. The Subsidiary Board Directors Resources Bureau and the Investments Management Department must focus on training subsidiary board directors and increasing the number of full-time directors at the Subsidiary Board Directors Resources Bureau. Any manager reassigned to another position must receive training in the Managerial Control Elite Team before being appointed to another managerial position, or they may spend some time as a director on a subsidiary board. There must be a two-way flow between the two. *(Ren Zhengfei: Speech at a Briefing on the Solution for Management Oversight by Oversight-oriented Subsidiary Boards and the Pilot Results, Huawei Executive Office Speech No. [2015] 072)*

Subsidiary boards are responsible for operational compliance as we go global. Because each board member was previously a trusted senior staff member who held a managerial position at Huawei for many years, we can consider granting them the authority to approve operational matters (but not approving decisions) in the IT system. In this way, the Chinese members of subsidiary boards can be authorized at the operational level under a given framework so that both business decision-making and oversight authority can be moved to the field. This can also place constraints upon solution design departments. *(Ren Zhengfei: Remarks During Visits to Countries Where Cash Is Trapped, Huawei Executive Office Speech No. [2015] 023)*

Our subsidiary boards oversee subsidiary operations on behalf of the company. They must be good at identifying and exposing problems. Their role is not to interfere in field operations or to help field offices cover up problems. Subsidiary boards may sometimes take steps to smooth ruffled feathers, but that is not their goal. Their ultimate goal is still to help win hard battles and to harvest more crops. *(Ren Zhengfei: Speech at a Briefing on the Solution for Management Oversight by Oversight-oriented Subsidiary Boards and the Pilot Results, Huawei Executive Office Speech No. [2015] 072)*

Rather than be merely limited to external compliance, subsidiary boards need to extend their responsibilities to also include internal compliance. Both areas are vital, and subsidiary boards must fulfill their oversight responsibilities by paying attention to both risks and risk control mechanisms.

First, risks. The first thing is to scan for high-risk areas. Subsidiary boards can obtain information from sources including (a) audit, internal control, HR, and legal affairs departments; (b) past cases of incompliance in the region, indicating which issues have recurred multiple times; and (c) by identifying high-risk areas and analyzing high-risk scenarios within these areas.

Second, systems. Look at the risks and management blind spots that you've discovered, and check whether the subsidiary management team is effectively implementing Huawei's policies. Have they put in place effective processes and oversight measures? Have they effectively organized employee education, management, investigation, disciplinary, and legal efforts? Are there significant gaps in their systems? Subsidiary boards must remind the management team to make improvements as needed. *(Ren Zhengfei: Speech at a Briefing on the Solution for Management Oversight by Oversight-oriented Subsidiary Boards and the Pilot Results, Huawei Executive Office Speech No. [2015] 072)*

We have established multiple subsidiary boards staffed by former regional presidents and former senior representative office general managers. These subsidiary boards are in charge of internal and external compliance, and are accountable for overseeing operations in subsidiaries. Members of these subsidiary boards are independent. They don't have to have group discussion. Group discussion is only necessary when there is a major issue. Without group discussion, board members can look into any issue that may lead to a major crisis. This shows their loyalty. The company will not intervene in their commendations, promotions, or rewards. However, their removal from positions or criticism directed against them must be approved by the company's top management. This mechanism is able to properly constrain a huge sales team that is made up of inexperienced young people, and develop them into an effective team that is well-organized, well-disciplined, courageous, and dedicated. *(Ren Zhengfei: Dedicated to China's Century-old Dream of Revitalizing Science and Technology, Huawei Executive Office Speech No. [2016] 067)*

Our subsidiary board members must have the courage to expose problems and effectively manage the boundary between internal and external compliance. They must not break rules, or give or accept bribes. We don't want to see corruption at Huawei. And we don't want to see our employees break the laws of the countries where they work or even the laws of the United Nations. We must not break US laws, either. Everything we do must be within the bounds of law. We are just businesspeople and our job is to do business. *(Ren Zhengfei: There Will Not Always Be Flowers Along the Road Ahead—Speech at the H1 Huawei Market Conference, Huawei Executive Office Speech No. [2016] 079)*

Compliance-oriented subsidiary boards will continue to serve as a rubber stamp. Our current focus is to establish oversight-oriented subsidiary boards. When we make some progress, we can combine compliance- and oversight-oriented subsidiary boards, and create a true authority. If they are only compliance-oriented, they will need to dive into too many details, which may make it difficult for them to focus. *(Ren Zhengfei: Speech at the Meeting on Extension of the Company's Oversight and Management Control System, Huawei Executive Office Speech No. [2017] 041)*

Open Access This chapter is licensed under the terms of the Creative Commons Attribution-NonCommercial-NoDerivatives 4.0 International License (http://creativecommons.org/licenses/by-nc-nd/4.0/), which permits any noncommercial use, sharing, distribution and reproduction in any medium or format, as long as you give appropriate credit to the original author(s) and the source, provide a link to the Creative Commons licence and indicate if you modified the licensed material. You do not have permission under this license to share adapted material derived from this chapter or parts of it.

The images or other third party material in this chapter are included in the chapter's Creative Commons licence, unless indicated otherwise in a credit line to the material. If material is not included in the chapter's Creative Commons licence and your intended use is not permitted by statutory regulation or exceeds the permitted use, you will need to obtain permission directly from the copyright holder.

CHAPTER 6

Finding the Right Amount of Openness, Compromise, and *Huidu*, and Properly Balancing Expansion and Control

According to Huawei's management philosophy, a company is an open system filled with contradictions. All contradictions co-exist, interacting with, standing against, and changing into each other. This upward reinforcing spiral creates the momentum that propels the company forward. Properly handling contradictions requires the right amount of openness, compromise, and *huidu*, and is a key part of the art of leadership.

Lao Tzu, the ancient Chinese philosopher and the founder of Taoism, said, "If you want to fold something, you must first unfold it. If you want to weaken something, you must first make it strong. If you want to let something decay, you must first let it prosper. If you want to have something, you need to first set it free. This is the plain truth." He further states, "The guiding principle behind Taoism is that everything can be its own opposite. Taoism advocates adaptation rather than change." This philosophy of opposites complementing each other is a dialectical approach that can be used to observe things and promote their development by leveraging contradictions.

Control and expansion are at odds with each other. The need to exert control is a natural result of expansion as it can cause risks. The purpose of control, however, is to expand more effectively.

The most notable aspect of Huawei's management philosophy is the idea of "creating order out of chaos and creating chaos out of order", as proposed by Huawei CEO Ren Zhengfei. IBM's consultants said that Huawei "didn't have time to do things right the first time, but did have time to do the same thing over and over again" with its own self-developed management system. Under the guidance of consultants from IBM and other renowned consulting firms, Huawei has successfully implemented five major process transformation programs and established an advanced, modern management system. The five transformation programs are Integrated Product Development (IPD), Integrated Supply Chain (ISC), Integrated Financial Services (IFS), Customer Relationship Management (CRM), and IT Strategy & Planning (IT S&P). These transformations have dramatically changed the company's processes, improved operating efficiency and business performance, and have allowed the company to "create order out of chaos". However, Ren Zhengfei soon after proposed another concept, which was to "create chaos out of order, disrupt balance, and continue to expand". This can be seen as the largest defining feature of Huawei's management philosophy.

This chapter elaborates on six contradictions that arise from expansion and control. Other contradictions are integrated into other chapters of this book.

6.1 Opportunity-Driven Versus Resource-Driven

6.1.1 More Emphasis on Opportunity-Driven Resource Allocation

Large companies usually invest about 10% of their sales in R&D to create opportunities. China lags far behind in this regard. We identify opportunities only after they emerge and seize them to achieve success. This is what happens at Huawei. However, the world's leading companies create opportunities through R&D to shape consumption. They quickly gather up all profits within a short window of opportunity and then reinvest the profits to create even greater opportunities. That is why these companies develop faster than we do. *(Ren Zhengfei: What Can We Learn from the American People?, Improvement Issue No. 63, 1998)*

Opportunities are the driving force behind company growth. *(Ren Zhengfei: What Can We Learn from the American People?, Improvement Issue No. 63, 1998)*

Western companies drive company development with resources. At Huawei, we emphasize that opportunities drive company development. *(Ren Zhengfei: Timely, Accurate, High Quality, and Low Cost Delivery Calls for Professional Process-compliant CFOs—Minutes of a Meeting with*

Trainees of the CFO Session of the Reserve Pool, Huawei Executive Office Speech No. [2009] 021)

We must leverage our core resources to identify new targets and opportunities, and then turn those opportunities into business results. Advanced equipment and high-quality resources in our back offices should be utilized promptly once field offices identify targets and opportunities. In other words, back offices shouldn't try to command operations just because they own resources; instead, they should support field operations. Who should call for support? Those closest to customers. They are the people who should make decisions. *(Ren Zhengfei: Who Calls for Artillery and How Do We Provide Timely Artillery Support?—Speech at the Awards Ceremony of Sales & Services, Huawei Executive Office Speech No. [2009] 001)*

I think cost and quality are the product and soul of the industrial economy. We are no longer in the industrial age, but we still haven't changed our mindset. Value creation doesn't completely rely on cutting costs and improving quality. We must maintain a strategic focus and leverage our resources to develop features that can help us hone our competitive edge. *(Ren Zhengfei: Working Together Towards the Same Goal, Concentrating Advantageous Resources on Our Core Business, and Having the Courage to Seek Greater Opportunities and Further Widen the Gap—Minutes of the Work Report on the Wireless Business, Huawei Executive Office Speech No. [2011] 039)*

We must seize opportunities created by industry transformation and dare to increase investment to seize strategic opportunities. We need to narrow our strategic focus, seize the strategic high ground, and ultimately achieve sustainable and profitable growth, thus laying the foundation for survival and long-term development. *(Ren Zhengfei: Guidelines on the Analysis of the Business Environment and Key Business Strategies, Corp. Doc. No. [2012] 081)*

Humanity is at a turning point. In the next two to three decades, we will enter an intelligent world, where we will see an information explosion. This will present us with huge opportunities, but without a direction or strength, we will not be able to create value. Without making correct assumptions, there will be no correct direction. Without a correct direction, there will be no correct ideas. Without correct ideas, there will be no correct theories. Without correct theories, there will be no correct strategies. *(Ren Zhengfei: Remarks at Meetings with Huawei Fellows, Huawei Executive Office Speech No. [2016] 069)*

6.1.2 Channeling High-Quality Resources to Valued Customers, Valued Countries, and Mainstream Products

We need to be clear about who our primary strategic partners are in each region and what their relationships with us are. We will then serve them with our best resources, such as our best service managers and sales managers. *(Ren Zhengfei: Eight Points Made After Receiving the "2008 Business Plan and Budget" Report at the EMT ST Meeting on January 31, EMT Meeting Minutes No. [2008] 009)*

As we build strategic partnerships with customers, we should not confine ourselves to just sales and delivery. We should open our minds and think carefully about what value we bring to customers. We need to make customers fully aware of what we do as their strategic partner during the joint development process and how our strategies align and how much extra value we can create. *(Source: Guidelines on Sales Priorities, EMT Meeting Minutes No. [2008] 014)*

The most crucial factor in achieving our sustainable growth is establishing a favorable presence in three areas: valued customers, valued countries, and mainstream products. Therefore, product lines and regions must reasonably allocate human resources; priority should be given to these three areas, rather than to products and regions with weak growth momentum. We must expand our competitive presence in these three areas in order to support our sustainable growth. *(Source: Issues and Principles That Require Attention During Near-term HR Management, EMT Resolution No. [2009] 002)*

We must use practical principles and methods to prioritize markets. We should adopt Tian Ji's[1] horse racing strategy and prioritize markets based on our strategic advantages and previously secured opportunities. We need to allocate resources based on feasibility. We must avoid prioritizing markets based on our supposed share in markets around the world. This doesn't mean we will give up markets that are not on our priority list. We still need to pursue potential opportunities. *(Ren Zhengfei: Minutes of the*

---

[1] Tian Ji (田忌; c. 340 CE) was a military general of the Qi state during the early Chinese Warring States period (fourth century BC). At a horse-racing event hosted by the king, an acquaintance recommended Tian Ji follow a specific strategy to win. Tian used his inferior horse to race with the king's best horse, his average horse to race with the king's inferior horse, and his best horse to race with the king's average horse, winning two out of three races.

Report on the Company's 2010 Business Plans and Budgets, EMT Meeting Minutes No. [2010] 006)
We should boldly change our business models, shut down operations in unprofitable countries, and walk away from certain customers. Fewer countries mean lower costs, so we can focus on delivering good services. Why do we have to cover 170 different countries and regions? If we are to ensure a reasonable level of profits in software, then we need to shift from "meeting the needs of every customer" to "serving valued customers". We also need to reorganize the geographic layout of our software organizations. Not every representative office needs a software department; only large carriers and large representative offices should have one. We do not have to let ourselves be dragged around by the nose by small carriers. Software sales departments should be relatively independent. If you are not independent, then the core business will pin you down and treat you like a free giveaway used to secure customers' contracts. So you have to be bold enough to end business with some customers, and just serve valued ones. *(Ren Zhengfei: Focusing on the Core Business and Seizing Strategic Opportunities—Speech at the Product Investment Strategy Review Meeting, Huawei Executive Office Speech No. [2015] 123)*

Don't give up any country. Every market is critical to Huawei. At the same time, we must make strategic choices and focus on valued customers. If you give up one small country, you will then give up a second one, a third one, and eventually all of them. You will be pushed steadily back into China. If you continue to give up Tibet, Yunnan, and Guizhou, then Xinjiang, and Qinghai, then only Beijing and Shanghai will be left for us. These two markets are the most profitable, but can we retain them? Once we are surrounded, we will be doomed. To survive, we must value each and every market. Every region is important, but we should select our customers carefully. Not everyone who has demand will become our customer. If they don't pay, how can they be called a customer? Only those who pay for what they demand and allow us to make profits are our customers. Those who pay more than others are valued customers. We need to change our understanding of who our customers should be. It's a big world; we cannot meet all customer needs. *(Ren Zhengfei: Speech at a Meeting with Employees of the Central Asia & Caucasia Region, Huawei Executive Office Speech No. [2016] 063)*

6.1.3 Managing Investment Portfolios and the Pace of Investment Based on Corporate Strategy, Investment Capacity, and Business Opportunities

We need to strengthen product and business portfolio management, steadily promote diversification in certain domains, and explore more flexible ways to duplicate our advantages in the marketplace, technology, and management, including through capital investment. This will shorten the time needed to enter new domains and help us achieve greater synergy. *(Ren Zhengfei: Work Report to the Board of Directors on the Completion of the 2003 Business and Budget Goals, 2004)*

For a single product line, optical transmission, for example, we can further lower gross profit margins for low-end products in order to outperform our strategic competitors. At the same time, we need to continuously improve our profitability in high-end products where our competitors lack a competitive edge. We must not ignore low-end products as we strive to succeed in high-end products; otherwise, we will be handing opportunities to our strategic competitors. *(Source: Guidelines on Sales Priorities, EMT Meeting Minutes No. [2008] 014)*

We need to separate mature and emerging industries during our appraisals. The company can strategically subsidize newly emerging industries during their first three to five years, and those industries can repay the company later on after they have grown. We shouldn't use a mature industry to subsidize an immature one. This support should be provided by the company, not by a product line. *(Ren Zhengfei: Speech at the EMT ST Meeting on April 29, 2010)*

How exactly should we assess opportunities and decide which to seize? What should we do and what should we not do? Should we do things for strategic purposes or just make normal deals? By strategic purposes, I mean we allow short-term losses; by normal deals, I mean we should shut a business down if it loses money. *(Source: Minutes of the Report on the 2012 Group Budget Review, EMT Meeting Minutes No. [2012] 012)*

Our corporate strategy should focus on our core business of massive data traffic. First, we must boldly seize the strategic high ground with our high-end products and must not sell them too cheaply. We can then duplicate our advantages in high-end products among mid-range and low-end products. Second, we must ensure high quality and low costs for our mid-range and low-end products. We must increase our scale in these two market segments. Our mid-range and low-end products must be maintenance-free throughout their lifecycle. *(Ren Zhengfei: Speech at a Meeting with Elite Teams at the Training Camp on July 23, 2013, Huawei Executive Office Speech No. [2013] 174)*

We must keep our pace of market investment under control and have the courage to give up some regions where we are not achieving the value we expected. You need to focus on regions with potential, and fully share resources with local account departments and representative offices to improve business results. For actual market investment strategies, you can learn from how we handled the carrier market in our early years, assigning a small team to a new market at the beginning and then expanding the team after the market had grown. *(Source: Minutes of the Report on the Progress of the Enterprise BG's Focus Strategy, EMT Meeting Minutes No. [2012] 018)*

As we compete for the high-end market, we must not lose our grip on the low-end. Today we are adopting a "needle-tip" strategy and maintaining a tight focus as we move forward. What I'm worried about is that we may dive head first into a new target market, but leave our backs exposed. If we leave the low-end market open to others, we may just be nurturing potential competitors. Ultimately, our high-end market will be affected as well. Huawei has drawn energy from the low-end market to enter the high-end. Why wouldn't other companies follow our example? *(Ren Zhengfei: Innovating to Create Global Value—Speech at the Corporate Strategy Retreat, Huawei Executive Office Speech No. [2015] 006)*

Our low-end products must be standardized, streamlined, and maintenance-free during their entire lifecycle. We are not walking the path of low price and low quality. That would undercut our ability to make strategic moves. In terms of technology and service models, we must become highly competitive through mass production. If customers want more functionality, they can buy our high-end products. This is the "mile-a-minute weed"[2] theory, and we now have this advantage. *(Ren Zhengfei: Innovating to Create Global Value—Speech at the Corporate Strategy Retreat, Huawei Executive Office Speech No. [2015] 006)*

We are still engineers with business acumen. In fact, our innovation is still limited to engineering; it does not have much to do with technological theories. We have not been sufficiently engaged in technological innovation, but we already have access to scientists and professors from

---

[2] "Mile-a-minute weed" is an extremely vigorous plant that can survive and grow quickly even in harsh conditions.

technological domains. This is one direction in which we're heading, and so we should begin to develop a culture of scientists. Just as you have said, we haven't reached this level yet. And I hope we will place emphasis on this in the future. *(Ren Zhengfei: Remarks at Meetings with Huawei Fellows, Huawei Executive Office Speech No. [2016] 069)*

6.1.4 Keeping the Costs of Resources in Mind and Acquiring Resources to Achieve Growth Goals

We must introduce the concept of cost management to our work. We need to manage cost and forbid extravagance and waste. We can't do this simply by looking at money or performance indicators. We need to analyze many things. For example, what has caused an increase in cost? How much of this increase is truly necessary? How much have we invested in R&D? How many opportunities has this investment created? How much of our investment has failed? What percentage is it of our total R&D investment? Is this percentage reasonable? *(Ren Zhengfei: Speech at a Meeting with Commodity Experts Groups, 2000)*

We must improve the quality of our operations and drive sustainable and profitable growth. We must better incorporate the company's strategic pursuits into our business goals and closed-loop performance appraisals. We need to improve the way we manage risks, maintain robust, standardized operations, and remain calm in the face of uncertainties in the global economy. We should boldly invest in strategic opportunities to pursue growth. However, the resources we acquire must be used to achieve our committed goals for business growth. We must manage planning, budgeting, and accounting in a closed loop, and directly link business results to the performance ratings and incentives of those responsible for decision making and execution. *(Ren Zhengfei: Guidelines on the Analysis of the Business Environment and Key Business Strategies, Corp. Doc. No. [2012] 081)*

Field teams will have the authority to directly call for support within their scope of authorization. This means that during project management, authority will be delegated according to the authorization documentation provided by IBM consultants that cover contract terms, contract signing, and pricing, as well as based on gross profit margins and cash flows. Within their scope of authorization, field teams can directly command operations. But matters beyond the scope of authorization need to be approved. Of course, calling for support incurs costs, which need to be borne by those who have called for the support. They also need to be held accountable for the decisions they make. *(Ren Zhengfei: Who Calls for Artillery and How Do We Provide Timely Artillery Support?—Speech at the Awards Ceremony of Sales & Services, Huawei Executive Office Speech No. [2009] 001)*

Additional resources we invest need to be ultimately reflected in ambitious business goals. We need to assess whether resource investment is reasonable using clear and measurable business performance indicators. *(Source: Minutes of the Report on Business Forecasts and Compensation Package Baseline Calculations for the Next Three Years, EMT Meeting Minutes No. [2011] 002)*

Our Human Resource Management Dept needs to develop policies that specify the relationship between budgets and value distribution. Some business units are wasting too much money, and are exceeding budgets before completing their plans. We have to deduct some of their bonuses. In contrast, some other business units have saved money but didn't miss any strategic opportunities, so their current business performance is also good. Should we give back some of the money they saved? This should be reflected in our HR policies. Closed-loop management will absolutely affect value distribution. Both budgeting and accounting should be managed in a closed loop. If you use the budget we give you to hire more people, acquire more resources, and invest them in strategy execution, we will see what business results you have achieved during accounting. The value you share will be based on the business results you have achieved. If we establish a link between budgets, accounting, and headcount, constraints will be automatically in place. *(Ren Zhengfei: Using Budgeting and Accounting to Drive Sustainable and Profitable Growth in Huawei's Core Business—Speech at the Retreat on the Positioning and Responsibilities of the Finance Committee, 2012)*

6.1.5 Guiding Resource Allocation with Differentiated Value Assessments

Our market investment budgets should continue to be based on relative numbers. We can gradually align budgets with business targets based on the historical patterns of change in our expense/revenue ratios so that increases in business expenses, especially customer-facing expenses, align with sales growth. We need to use different expense/revenue ratios for emerging and mature markets. In terms of R&D investment, we must not simply calculate decreases in R&D expense/revenue ratios. We need to set different expense/revenue ratio targets for different product lines. It is okay for the expense/revenue ratios of mature product lines to decrease by 1 percentage point. For immature product lines though, whether we need to decrease the ratios, or how much we need to decrease them, has to be discussed at length. Don't use a single percentage for all product lines when decreasing R&D expense/revenue ratios. You just need to calculate how much the overall R&D expense/revenue ratio is lowered based on data from each product line. You shouldn't be overly focused on performance indicators. *(Ren Zhengfei: Comments at the Meeting Regarding the Planning and Budgeting Work for 2005, 2004)*

We need to channel high-quality resources to markets that contribute more value to our company. Identifying and managing regional markets based on their differences in terms of value and development is important. *(Source: Minutes of the Report on Differentiated Management Plans for Regional Markets, EMT Meeting Minutes No. [2008] 039)*

The Finance Committee (FC) is the company's overall enterprise value integrator. The FC operates under the Board of Directors and uses budgeting and accounting to exercise macro control over business operations, investment activities, and enterprise risks. Ultimately, this helps strike a dynamic balance between opportunities and resources, the two drivers that facilitate sustainable and profitable growth. The FC should focus on the company's key strategy while conducting macro control, decision making, and oversight activities. Through management processes like resource allocation, budgeting, and accounting, the FC guides the company to improve efficiency and business performance, and facilitate sustainable and profitable development for the company. *(Source: Positioning and Responsibilities of the Finance Committee Under the Board of Directors [Provisional], Board of Directors Doc. No. [2012] 002)*

We will allocate resources from a value management perspective. The FC is responsible for the company's overall macro controls. It uses budgeting and targeted accounting to generate opportunities and control our pace of development. The FC also oversees the pace, direction, and structure of resource investment, channels more resources into high-value domains, and focuses on business results in low-value domains. The FC's ultimate goal is to meet the entire company's profit requirements. *(Guo Ping: Effectively Managing Corporate Value to Pursue Sustainable and Profitable Growth, Huawei Executive Office Speech No. [2012] 005)*

6.2 Growth Versus Profits

6.2.1 Focusing on Long-Term Strategic Development to Turn Today's Cash into Tomorrow's Profits

The overall objective of our company is to increase sales and profits. We must increase R&D investment. If the investment turns out to be worthwhile, it will bring us more opportunities, and we must cherish these opportunities. We must also increase investment in marketing and sales, as this can help us obtain new opportunities. We must seize these opportunities, as the value they bring will be higher than their costs. When there are conflicts between opportunities and costs in the company, which is more important? Our answer is opportunities. I always believe that, in the tech industry, the value opportunities bring is higher than their costs. As long as opportunities bring value, an increase in costs is acceptable. *(Ren Zhengfei: Minutes of a Work Report on Annual Taxes and Budgets, 2001)*

Huawei has been built on waste. Over the years, Huawei has wasted a lot of money, but the lessons we have learned in doing so will pay off eventually. Integrating all of our processes will unleash great energy and we will finally have a highly effective team. Once that happens, we will no longer rely on huge numbers of people to succeed, and the compensation of our remaining people will increase accordingly. *(Ren Zhengfei: Speech and Comments at the Strategy Retreat of the Business Process & IT Management Department, Huawei Executive Office Speech No. [2012] 026)*

We now need to make heavy, focused investment in our strategic areas. Once we seize the strategic high ground, we can sell our products at higher prices and generate more profits, which can then be invested in advanced research. *(Ren Zhengfei: Comments to Staff of the Enterprise BG, Huawei Executive Office Speech No. [2014] 006)*

6.2.2 Focusing on Both Opportunity-Driven Scaled Growth and Profit-Driven Sustainable Growth

We have already assigned a weight to positive profits, positive cash flow, and per-capita efficiency improvements during performance appraisals. In fact, we have made a big shift in the direction of our appraisals. This shift though, has occurred very slowly. I am not saying that you no longer need to focus on sales. Instead, I am asking you to focus hard on these three indicators. We have a team of more than 80,000 employees. Such a large team losing momentum would be disastrous. So we must continue to forge ahead. This change has already begun and will not progress too quickly. As long as we move in the right direction, we will achieve the desired results. *(Ren Zhengfei: Speech at a Meeting with the IFS Project Team and Staff from Finance, Huawei Executive Office Speech No. [2009] 004)*

Investment in and subsidies for emerging growth opportunities may increase the company's overall expenses, but this is positive growth. We need to take a positive attitude toward this. The company doesn't pursue excessively high profits; rather, we strive to turn excessively high profits into momentum for future growth. *(Ren Zhengfei: Minutes of the Report on the Company's 2010 Business Plans and Budgets, EMT Meeting Minutes No. [2010] 006)*

You need to figure out what strategies you should adopt. I will not tell you whether you should increase scale or profits first. This must be your decision. If you can't make a decision on this, you, as country CEOs, are not worth the compensation the company pays you. *(Ren Zhengfei: Be Bold at Work, Be a Humble Person, and Follow the Patterns of Consumer Products in the Pursuit of Maximum Growth and Success—Speech at a Meeting with the Key Employees of the Consumer BG, Huawei Executive Office Speech No. [2011] 014)*

Many of our offices in small countries have made good profits, and so we need to consolidate our position in these countries. We need to be selective about what we do and what we don't do in small countries. Our goal is to earn profits. A portion of our profits can be given back to regions and representative offices so that they can improve the quality of services they provide to customers. *(Ren Zhengfei: Minutes of the Report on the 809 Strategic Guidelines, EMT Meeting Minutes No. [2012] 016)*

We need to maintain a steady profit flow and a robust financial position. This is necessary for Huawei to continuously invest in the future and for the industry to maintain a reasonable level of profits. This is also conducive to building a long-term and stable environment for market competition. *(Ren Zhengfei: Speech and Comments at the Carrier Network BG's Strategy Retreat in Huizhou, Huawei Executive Office Speech No. [2012] 010)*

Our growth must be sustainable and profitable. Our warehouses should hold food instead of dust and mice. The management teams and heads of departments that are talking about various types of innovations or models should rein in their impulses, carefully analyze the costs and benefits of their projects, and align their personal financial interests with their commitments. They need to share both benefits and losses. *(Guo Ping: Effectively Managing Corporate Value to Pursue Sustainable and Profitable Growth, Huawei Executive Office Speech No. [2012] 005)*

Our employees in the Consumer and Enterprise BGs must not rush to catch up with Apple or Cisco. No matter how high the Himalayas are, there is still only a single summit. It is very cold at the top, and you can't stay there for 20 years. When you collapse, where will you deploy your extra people? I can't fix that for you. When I say not to rush to catch up, I mean hold back from scaling up too quickly. We should still aim to increase profits. Currently neither the Consumer BG nor the Enterprise BG is convinced. So you adopt a betting mindset, and one "general" will be made at the sacrifice of numerous "foot soldiers". I think you need to adopt a mindset of long-term survival, be practical, and gradually improve profitability. *(Ren Zhengfei: Speech at the EMT ST Meeting on March 29, 2013)*

We need to shift our operational focus from the blind pursuit of scale to long-term, sustainable growth – profitability, efficiency, and quality. Product lines and business units in non-strategic domains need to set high profit targets. This is to inhibit their expansion and avoid spreading our human resources too thin. *(Ren Zhengfei: Building a Highly Competitive Team—Speech at the Q3 Regional Presidents' Meeting, Huawei Executive Office Speech No. [2013] 093)*

6.2.3 Company Operations: A Dissipative Structure

What is a dissipative structure? If you exercise every day, you are in a dissipative state. Why? Because you dissipate energy, turning it into muscle and increasing blood flow. If you dissipate all latent energy, you can avoid obesity and diabetes, and instead remain fit and attractive. This is the simplest example of dissipative structure that I can think of. Then why do we need this dissipative structure? If everyone says that they are loyal to the company, that is because the company pays them too much and such loyalty may not last long. Therefore, we need to dissipate this love for the company and instead rely on dedicated employees and processes to make the company stronger. Dedicated employees work hard first before they get paid. Their loyalty is different from that of those who get paid well first. Knowing the difference is a kind of progress for us. We need to dissipate our potential energy to create new momentum. *(Ren Zhengfei: Success Is Not a Reliable Guide to Future Development—Speech at the*

Huawei Market Conference on January 17, 2011, Huawei Executive Office Speech No. [2011] 004)
We have been embracing changes, alternating between stability and instability and between balance and imbalance. The purpose of this is to maintain the company's vitality. If you eat too much beef and don't exercise, you may become obese; but if you eat a lot of beef and exercise hard enough, you could become the next Liu Xiang.[3] In both cases you are eating beef, but you end up in completely different places by the end; it all depends on whether you dissipate energy or not. *(Ren Zhengfei: Success Is Not a Reliable Guide to Future Development—Speech at the Huawei Market Conference on January 17, 2011, Huawei Executive Office Speech No. [2011] 004)*

During our first 20 years, we focused more on internal balance to create synergies and be more effective. Over the next 20 years, we hope to disrupt balance to generate greater energy and achieve greater success. *(Ren Zhengfei: Speech at the Meeting of the New Board of Directors and the New Supervisory Board, Huawei Executive Office Speech No. [2011] 001)*

Huawei is doing quite well in its current stage. We should increase investment to dissipate our current advantages and create new ones. The entirety of society is going through a rough patch, and the global economy might be about to enter a cyclical downturn. Our numbers show that our growth is slowing, but we're still in relatively good shape compared with other companies. We must not hesitate to invest in our future. It is a lack of leaders, generals, and long-term strategies that has made us hesitate in making investments. *(Ren Zhengfei: Speech at the Meeting with Staff from the 2012 Laboratories, Huawei Executive Office Speech No. [2012] 035)*

6.2.4 Pursuing Rapid Growth on the Basis of a Reasonable Profit Margin

Opportunities and market share are always the most important things for companies to consider when developing in a high-tech industry. But sometimes you have to sacrifice hefty profits to gain market share. *(Ren Zhengfei: Speech at a Meeting with Financial Staff, 1997)*

Our aim is to maximize growth while ensuring a certain profit margin. We need to maintain a growth rate that is higher than the industry average and our major competitors' growth rates, all to bring new life to the

---
[3] Liu Xiang: China's former Olympic 110-meter hurdles champion.

company, attract the best people, and best allocate our operating resources. *(Source: The Huawei Charter, 1998)*

We need to maintain a growth rate that is higher than the industry average and our major competitors' growth rates. Over the years, our annual growth rate has remained at 100%. In the future, our growth rate will inevitably slow as the baseline for further development goes up. It will be a huge challenge for us to find the right pace to maintain a relatively solid position in the industry. *(Ren Zhengfei: How Long Can Huawei Survive?, 1998)*

Rather than seeking maximum profits, we will set profitability targets that are sufficiently high, but reasonably tailored to different stages of development, to address our need for sustainable growth. *(Source: The Huawei Charter, 1998)*

Maximizing profits for us often means squeezing the profits of our customers and partners. Why should they tolerate this? *(Ren Zhengfei: Managers Should Live and Pass on Huawei's Core Values—Speech at the First Workshop on Human Resource Management Outline, Huawei Executive Office Speech No. [2010] 009)*

We need to separate mature and emerging industries during our appraisals. The company can strategically subsidize newly emerging industries during their first three to five years, and those industries can repay the company later on after they have grown. We shouldn't use a mature industry to subsidize an immature one. This support should be provided by the company, not by a product line. *(Ren Zhengfei: Speech at the EMT ST Meeting on April 29, 2010)*

6.3 Long-Term Versus Short-Term Interests

6.3.1 Short-Term Interests Ensure Survival

As long as we have a clear long-term goal, we should seize opportunities the moment when the window of opportunity opens and make profits. This can help us ensure that our long-term strategic products can survive and thrive. *(Ren Zhengfei: Speech at the Dedication Conference of the Wireless Network Product Line, Huawei Executive Office Speech No. [2008] 007)*

We can see the value of our long-term strategy only when we actually survive. Without short-term success though, there will be no basis on which to consider our longer-term strategy. Without a strategic vision and a clear view of the future, our short-term efforts will be no different than what Chinese peasants did for thousands years: working day in and day out with no innovation or change. To achieve sustainable and profitable growth, we need to consider financial indicators in the short term; in the medium term, we need to look at capability improvement; in the long term, we need to focus on the industry landscape, business ecosystem robustness, and industry sustainability. Business success will always be a concern for our company throughout its lifecycle. Management is about weighing the present against the future and balancing the short term and the long term. If short-term interests are gained at the cost of long-term interests, or even worse, at the cost of the company's survival, then it's clear that management has not made the right trade-off. This type of decision is irresponsible. *(Ren Zhengfei: Our Transformation Goals Are to Harvest More Crops and Increase Soil Fertility—Speech at the 2015 Huawei Market Conference, Huawei Executive Office Speech No. [2015] 016)*

A basic rule of business is equivalent exchange. If we can promptly and accurately provide high-quality and cost-effective services to our customers, we will naturally receive reasonable rewards in return. Some of these rewards will be in the form of short-term business interests, some in the form of mid-to-long-term business interests, but ultimately, they must all be reflected in the company's financial results: revenue, profits, and cash flow. Any business activity that results in ongoing losses has deviated from or misinterpreted our core value of customer centricity. *(Ren Zhengfei: Our Transformation Goals Are to Harvest More Crops and Increase Soil Fertility—Speech at the 2015 Huawei Market Conference, Huawei Executive Office Speech No. [2015] 016)*

6.3.2 Striking a Balance Between Long-Term and Short-Term Interests

We must enable our employees to fully recognize the relationship between short-term and long-term interests, and the significance of long-term investment. We must avoid short-termism, because it essentially kills the goose that lays golden eggs. We entered the communications industry out of naivety, not realizing that our competitors were global leaders. In the company's early years, driven by a sense of urgency, we had invested heavily in R&D, market expansion, and talent development every year, even though 95% of our employees didn't own their own apartments. Thanks to this huge pressure, we became a strongly united company. The spirit of remaining dedicated and prioritizing work over life was internalized by all Huawei employees. *(Ren Zhengfei: Characteristics of Huawei's Development, 1996)*

Huawei as a company is most concerned about its long-term interests and how to constantly hone its long-term competitive edge. However, our employees are most concerned about their short-term interests, because they do not know whether they will continue to work for Huawei in the future. To resolve this contradiction, we need to strike a balance between long-term and short-term interests. *(Ren Zhengfei: How Long Can Huawei Survive?, 1998)*

Our core strategy should be future-oriented, with a clear execution roadmap. When strategic investment is required, we need to assess the value the investments have for the company using a long-term roadmap. For non-strategic investment, we need to look at the roadmap for short-term improvement and profitability. *(Ren Zhengfei: Speech and Comments at the Carrier BG's 2013 Strategy Retreat, Huawei Executive Office Speech No. [2014] 016)*

Question: How can we balance long- and short-term goals? It will take a long time to turn research and algorithms into commercial products. Sometimes, this will cause conflict. **Ren Zhengfei:** This is why China hasn't made significant contributions to humanity over the past 5000 years. Archimedes was not from China, and Arabic numerals were not invented by the Chinese. There have been many great civilizations to stand beside the Chinese. A Chinese mindset often seeks to solve problems, whereas a Western mindset often seeks to find logic. This is why the ancient Chinese classic, *The Nine Chapters on the Mathematical Art*, is different from Euclid's geometry. How can you strike a balance between long-term and short-term goals? First, you should remain dedicated despite what others say about you. As long as not everyone is saying bad things about you, and as long as you have an opportunity to work, then things will be fine. You might say, "It's okay if you don't give me a pay raise. As long as I have got enough to eat, I think that will be okay." But if you succeed in 10 or 20 years' time, you will be a great PhD or scientist. Then you will have everything. Second, our organization should be lenient to such people. If Ludwig van Beethoven came to us to seek a job right now, I think he would definitely not get one. He was a deaf musician. Recruit him? Are you kidding me? Just think about it. So our organization must be lenient to scientific researchers. I welcome more people with great aspirations, but our culture is not yet inclusive enough. *(Ren Zhengfei:*

Speech at a Meeting with Employees of the Noah's Ark Laboratory, Huawei Executive Office Speech No. [2016] 083)

Enterprises that last follow different principles than those that don't to balance short-term and long-term interests. These principles stem from how they understand their purpose – to create value for customers. *(Ren Zhengfei: Our Transformation Goals Are to Harvest More Crops and Increase Soil Fertility—Speech at the 2015 Huawei Market Conference, Huawei Executive Office Speech No. [2015] 016)*

6.4 CENTRALIZATION VERSUS DECENTRALIZATION

6.4.1 Development: Staying Focused, Involving Little Uncertainty, and Supporting Business Success

We first need to think carefully about what we do and what we don't do. We need to center our thinking on a number of general principles. Take high-speed network chips as an example. If we don't use many, why are we making them on our own? If we don't have to make them on our own, we can choose to collaborate with others for the time being. We will then free up some resources and invest them in our core products. We have a broader product portfolio than Lucent, Nokia, Ericsson, and Cisco. With such a wide line, how many resources do we need to get us ahead of the pack on all our products? This is the most pressing issue we face right now. *(Ren Zhengfei: Speech at the Work Report of the Product Line Management Office, 2000)*

We should not be too idealistic when it comes to product development. If a product fails, just close the project and quickly reassign its people. We shouldn't always strive for unreachable goals. Heroes should not spend too much time chasing perfection. By the time we achieve perfection, we may not exist any longer. We cannot wait for perfection to come, and we don't have the ability to make it happen ourselves. So we have to close failed projects. This does not mean that a failed project has no heroes. People from failed projects are also assets, because their wrong turns have brought us valuable experience. We need to have people circulating more quickly around the company. *(Ren Zhengfei: Focusing on the Core Business and Seizing Strategic Opportunities—Speech at the Product Investment Strategy Review Meeting, Huawei Executive Office Speech No. [2015] 123)*

Objectively, R&D employees have made great contributions to the company's development. They need to explore new technologies. More importantly, they need to be sensitive to and integrate customer needs. They must develop products and services that meet customer needs. The R&D's goal is to shift from developing products to supporting business success. Customers don't need products, they need services and operations. To achieve business success, we need to turn products into operation and service enablers. We cannot simply aim to hit our KPIs. Instead, we need to consider actual user experiences on our networks. Our products must be competitive, and must support business success. *(Ren Zhengfei: There Will Not Always Be Flowers Along the Road Ahead—Speech at the H1 Huawei Market Conference, Huawei Executive Office Speech No. [2016] 079)*

Development is a project of special certainty, and should be well-planned, with well-managed budgets and accounting. Its finances should be transparent, not only in terms of investment, but also in terms of process management and accounting. We should develop a stronger finance team in R&D. We should gradually work towards effective management. The reason why development projects have special certainty is that you can reapply for budgets if you fail. *(Ren Zhengfei: The Essence of IPD: From Opportunity to Commercial Success—Speech at an Awards Ceremony for IPD Whiz Kids and Outstanding XDTs, Huawei Executive Office Speech No. [2016] 084)*

During this year's budgeting process, we won't earmark much money for product development, since it is a job of certainty and needs to focus on targets and efficiency. Our budgets must be primarily allocated for future growth and breakthroughs in uncharted territory. We must not randomly take an investment-intensive approach. We need to review this approach carefully. Research and innovation on uncertainties must also have boundaries and serve our core business. We need to limit research and innovation initiatives that don't serve our core business. *(Ren Zhengfei: Speech at the EMT ST Meeting on January 25, 2016, Huawei Executive Office Speech No. [2016] 054)*

To break down management barriers, we ask that Products & Solutions not initiate projects for small products. If they do, front-end management will become increasingly complex. Maybe we can talk about developing small products again after our processes are integrated. We must not randomly create small products, and we must use budgeting to make changes. We must close small products that can be closed. We can only shrink and simplify things to overcome management barriers. The simpler things are, the easier it will be for us to break down barriers. It is acceptable if you make things complex again after barriers are removed, but right now we can't break down barriers because we have taken on too much. *(Ren Zhengfei: Speech at the EMT ST Meeting on January 25, 2016, Huawei Executive Office Speech No. [2016] 054)*

6.4.2 Research and Explore Across a Wide Scope

Huawei is a company that deals with engineering, not one of basic scientific research. So, why are we entering the field of basic scientific research? Because electronics and information technologies are developing too rapidly. We cannot just sit around and wait until scientists complete their research and release their scientific papers. If we only begin to do engineering experiments based on our understanding of current scientific papers, and then use the results of those experiments to guide our engineering work, the cycle will be too long. We should thus start experimenting with engineering methods as soon as scientists raise questions during their basic research. This approach will enable us to respond to social development needs more rapidly and thus survive. Therefore, we need to enter the field of basic research in thermophysics. *(Ren Zhengfei: Remarks at a Meeting at the National Academy of Sciences of Belarus, Huawei Executive Office Speech No. [2016] 087)*

We should open our technology "bell mouth" wider to allow sufficient open cooperation and greater global collaboration. Our company has two strategies for the future: One is the customer strategy and the other is the technology strategy. Our technology "bell mouth" should be big enough to include all technologies, development paths, and directions – even less advanced technologies. They might lag behind for the time being, but this will not last forever. They will likely become more advanced than other technologies in the future. We can invest consistently in the same direction in different locations. Previously, we had red teams and blue teams.[4] Now we all belong to blue teams. Whoever wins will be our red team. We are open to collaboration. We sponsor scientists, but we don't seek to own their scientific papers or patents. Instead, we just want to be informed of their research and how they solve specific problems and then learn from their failures. If we just wait until they release their research results, the

---

[4] As part of its ongoing effort to identify potential weaknesses, Huawei employs a "Red Team and Blue Team" method of self-reflection. The Blue Team plays the role of a competitor, always challenging the Red Team and exposing its faults to help the Red Team improve.

cycle will be too long. We should thus begin to consider engineering application during scientists' theoretical explorations. Our partners do not necessarily need to succeed. Lessons learned from failures are also a kind of success. Scientists can illuminate us – and others – like beacons. However, we don't seek to own these *beacons* or interfere in how their research results are applied. *(Ren Zhengfei: Remarks at a Meeting at the National Academy of Sciences of Belarus, Huawei Executive Office Speech No. [2016] 087)*

Huawei's innovation is now mainly centered on engineering sciences, such as engineering-related mathematics and physical algorithms. We haven't truly begun researching in basic theories. We are gradually reaching the limits defined in Shannon's Theorem and Moore's Law, but theories that can tackle issues concerning massive amounts of data traffic and low latency have not yet emerged. The road ahead is full of uncertainties, and we don't know exactly where we are heading. Major innovations are key for survival in uncharted territory. Without theoretical breakthroughs, technological breakthroughs, and a solid technological foundation, explosive innovation would be impossible. *(Ren Zhengfei: Dedicated to China's Century-old Dream of Revitalizing Science and Technology, Huawei Executive Office Speech No. [2016] 067)*

At Huawei, we should stay focused on our core business. At the same time, we should "absorb the energy of the universe over a cup of coffee" to keep our wheels rolling ahead. We should resolutely forge ahead into uncharted territory where we will have no conflicts of interests with others. We are expanding in a fair and equitable manner. "Borrowing" energy from others is conducive to the development of the world as a whole. Large companies will not go against us. And smaller ones will be unable to keep up with us, so it would be pointless for them to talk against us. We can only fly freely once we get to uncharted territory, because we won't have competitors there. How do we define uncharted territory? First, there must be no one to tell us which path to take or which direction to go. Second, there must be no rules there, so we won't know where the traps might be. This is a completely new territory. Huawei used to follow others, and thus saved a great deal of money which should have been used for exploration. Today, we have to blaze a trail ourselves. Inevitably, we will make mistakes. *(Ren Zhengfei: Remarks at Meetings with Huawei Fellows, Huawei Executive Office Speech No. [2016] 069)*

We must not randomly use the word "failure" in the future. Instead, we should use "exploration", because heroes arise from both successes and failures. In any closed project, you should analyze its reasons for success or failure. Even if it fails, it was an exploration. *(Ren Zhengfei: Remarks at Meetings with Huawei Fellows, Huawei Executive Office Speech No. [2016] 069)*

Therefore, we should adjust how we view success and failure, as failure is also a treasure for us. We can also learn from failure, and it is the most precious learning experiences. How many times can we fail in our lives? We cannot repeat anything. We will retain dedicated employees from failed projects, so that they will not fail again in the future. Our HR team should reconsider this issue. Our appraisal system must not be rigid, and we should adopt flexible appraisal methods. *(Ren Zhengfei: Remarks at Meetings with Huawei Fellows, Huawei Executive Office Speech No. [2016] 069)*

We should embrace challenges and disruptions. We should not be afraid of disruptions. When real challenges emerge, we should meet them head on. Society is going to change. Dedication without a direction or sufficient strength would be meaningless. Small companies are not strong. Some big companies are strong, but have no direction. Huawei is a strong company, and is exploring its future direction. Why wouldn't we lead the future? *(Ren Zhengfei: Remarks at Meetings with Huawei Fellows, Huawei Executive Office Speech No. [2016] 069)*

The "Van Fleet Load" type of heavy investment along multiple paths and in multiple waves mainly focuses on research and innovation. The "bell mouth" at the upper end of our "de Laval nozzle" must be made wider. Our proportion of annual revenue invested in R&D and our investment in management improvement are among the highest in the industry. In the past, we invested 20% of our R&D budgets directly in research. We now plan to increase that to a higher ratio, say, 30% or a percentage that is reasonable; we need to do this step by step. Of course, the proportion of annual revenue invested in R&D should also increase. *(Ren Zhengfei: Scale New Heights and Forge Ahead into Uncharted Territory Along Multiple Paths in Multiple Waves—Key Messages of Discussions at Mobile World Congress and in Ukraine, Huawei Executive Office Speech No. [2016] 068)*

In the future, our "Van Fleet Load" type of heavy investment will not be made in product development. We should not try to develop small products. Any such attempt will be strictly controlled. There has to be discipline in how we spend money in product development. Product development is part of delivery and a task of certainty. Planning, budgeting, accounting, and delivery management processes must be put in place.

(Ren Zhengfei: Scale New Heights and Forge Ahead into Uncharted Territory Along Multiple Paths in Multiple Waves—Key Messages of Discussions at Mobile World Congress and in Ukraine, Huawei Executive Office Speech No. [2016] 068)

We can spend more on research and innovation. Our "Van Fleet Load" type of heavy investment should be used for future endeavors, but our exploration must have boundaries. We won't bring people outside these boundaries into our company, but I would welcome exceptional scientists who are willing to perform research within our scope of focus. They don't have to become Huawei staff; collaboration is also welcome. This way we can bring on board scientists from all over the world. But they don't have to join Huawei. As Ken Hu[5] said, we need to weaken our "staff badge culture" over time. As long as scientists or talented people who may seem eccentric move in the same direction as us, we should sponsor them and create the future together. We should be more open-minded and share what we have achieved. For the upward facing "bell mouth" of the "de Laval nozzle", we will bring in a large number of like-minded partners to allow multiple paths for our research and innovation. With the "bell mouth" facing downward, we will communicate our core values to future generations and inspire them to join us. Development is a special project of certainty, and it should be well-planned, with well-managed budgets and accounting. If people doing development work make mistakes, they can reapply for budgets. *(Ren Zhengfei: Scale New Heights and Forge Ahead into Uncharted Territory Along Multiple Paths in Multiple Waves— Key Messages of Discussions at Mobile World Congress and in Ukraine, Huawei Executive Office Speech No. [2016] 068)*

We should change the R&D budget mix to increase our percentage of investment in research and innovation. We need to change the way we distribute our capabilities. Everything used to be stacked in Shenzhen, but in the future our centers of expertise will all be located wherever we can find the right resources. Some high-end, high-precision, and cutting-edge components can be manufactured in Germany or Japan, and then shipped to China. At the workshop to be held in Japan at the end of March, we can add a topic: Japanese craftsmanship. We can invite Japanese scientists to talk about the characteristics of Japanese craftsmanship, and we will pay them consulting fees. *(Ren Zhengfei: Scale New Heights and Forge Ahead into Uncharted Territory Along Multiple Paths in Multiple Waves—Key*

---

[5] Ken Hu: Rotating Chairman of Huawei.

Messages of Discussions at Mobile World Congress and in Ukraine, Huawei Executive Office Speech No. [2016] 068)
We are willing to set up a Thought Research Center at the top of our organization. Our senior experts and senior managers can have brainstorming sessions at this research center and explore what direction the world may be heading. Our 2012 Laboratories can verify our ideas. We must be open-minded to embrace the world. The Thought Research Center should have a boundary, within which we will allow innovation by either our own staff or scientists outside Huawei. This will ensure that, if black swans appear, they will fly out of our coffee cups. We will be able to turn them into white swans. You are asking about a possible change in our organizational structure. We are now thinking about this change. *(Ren Zhengfei: Minutes of a Meeting with Employees of the Japan Representative Office and the Japan Research Center, Huawei Executive Office Speech No. [2016] 080)*

6.4.3 Narrowing Our Strategic Focus and Setting Ourselves Apart from Competitors in Our Core Business

When making major investment decisions, we don't necessarily have to pursue today's highly profitable projects. We also should pay attention to emerging markets with huge potential and growth opportunities in new products. We will not diversify our operations, as doing so would distract company resources and the energy of our top management away from what's important. *(Source: The Huawei Charter, 1998)*

To become a leader, we must narrow our strategic focus. We must focus our energy on our core business and strategic markets to seize the strategic high ground. Today I talked about bandwidth and an operating system for networks. If we can overtake all other players, we will very likely hold the future in our hands. *(Ren Zhengfei: Speech and Comments at the Carrier Network BG's Strategy Retreat in Huizhou, Huawei Executive Office Speech No. [2012] 010)*

We must focus on valued customers and valued regions. We must technologically integrate our R&D, the macro pipe, the micro pipe, and the tap along our pipe strategy. Businesses that are not included in the above list should be generating large profits to support the company's strategy. The company should not scatter its investments just to realize scientists' dreams. Rather, scientists should dedicate themselves to the company's strategy. *(Ren Zhengfei: Focusing on Strategy and Streamlining Management, Huawei Executive Office Speech No. [2012] 041)*

We think that broadband will be front and center in the future. As we move toward ultra-broadband, Huawei has the advantage to stay ahead of all other companies. Within the next three to five years, Huawei will have the capacity to seize this market segment. Information that flows through big data pipes will then flow to thinner pipes – enterprise networks. This will allow us to extend data flows to enterprises. We compare devices to water taps, through which data flows run. *(Ren Zhengfei: Comments at a Meeting with Sales Financing Experts, Huawei Executive Office Speech No. [2012] 025)*

As per our needle-tip strategy, we have entered uncharted territory where we have no competitors, won't step on the feet of others, and can improve the business ecosystem. This will give us greater bargaining power in product pricing. Haven't you noticed this effect during the last couple of years? Our products have been selling well, while still yielding higher profits. *(Ren Zhengfei: Speech at a Meeting with Trainees at the First Training Session for the Sales Project Management Resource Pool, Huawei Executive Office Speech No. [2014] 066)*

6.5 Opportunities Versus Risks

6.5.1 Managing Both Opportunities and Risks, with More Attention Paid to Risks

We need to look at risks from a value management perspective. Internal potential risks can be divided into three categories: First are implicit risks that have existed throughout our 20-plus years of rapid growth. Such risks may begin to surface when the external economic environment deteriorates or business growth slows down. These risks include long overdue accounts receivable, loss-bearing contracts, high-risk contracts, over-commitment, and unapproved vouchers in the hands of customers. We need to quantify, measure, and handle these risks, and gradually eliminate them. Second are the risks that arise from a slowdown of business growth. Huawei used to be a fast growing company. As long as revenue grew, profits grew as well. Our value assessment and distribution systems were also designed using a model founded on rapid growth. In 2011, the company's financial performance made this model ineffective. We saw revenue growth but profits declined sharply, and our growth rate was lower than that of our major competitors. A decline in growth could also cause a decline in our profitability and financial performance. This means we need to take operating efficiency very seriously, and guard against problems associated with contract quality, new business models, and special transaction models. We need to clarify issues surrounding authorization and approval, and ask boastful management teams to generate more profits. At the same time, we need to establish a mechanism that links budgeting and accounting to headcount, using value distribution to guide resource allocation and improve efficiency. The third category is risks that arise from uncertainty in investing in multi-core businesses. When developing our consumer and enterprise businesses, we must pay attention to the ratio, structure, and pace of our investments in people, capital, and materials. We need to ensure our investments are in line with the company's resource and business strategies. We should also pay special attention to a series of new problems with the Consumer BG's inventory and product quality as well as with the Enterprise BG's channel partners. And we need to develop solutions and capabilities to address these problems. *(Guo Ping: Effectively Managing Corporate Value to Pursue Sustainable and Profitable Growth, Huawei Executive Office Speech No. [2012] 005)*

The financial crisis is not over yet. Perhaps it hasn't even truly started yet, and we just can't predict its full impact yet. Huawei faces many challenges connected to the financial crisis. To evade the crisis and prevent our company's collapse, we must comply with the laws of the countries in which we operate, and follow established international practices. At present, we are strengthening our sales revenue management, and have developed accounting principles specifically for sales revenue. Our goal is to prevent any kind of "bubble effect" that will drive us into the financial crisis. We stand firm in our fight against accounting fraud, and will severely penalize anyone involved in it. *(Ren Zhengfei: Speech at the Work Briefing of the West European Region, Huawei Executive Office Speech No. [2014] 073)*

We are facing both opportunities and risks, and we should give greater weight to risks than sales. We should reduce expenses in countries where we cannot see opportunities and transfer employees there to our strategic reserves. *(Ren Zhengfei: There Will Not Always Be Flowers Along the Road Ahead—Speech at the H1 Huawei Market Conference, Huawei Executive Office Speech No. [2016] 079)*

6.5.2 Inaction Has No Risk, But Will Leave Us Behind

Of course, if we do nothing, we will face no risks. But we will definitely be overtaken. In the future, we are likely to attract more attention as we become stronger. If we want to do something great, we must manage our compliance risks more effectively. Wherever risks and challenges are discovered, we must be honest about them. No cover-ups, no hiding. *(Ren Zhengfei: Remarks During Visits to Countries Where Cash Is Trapped, Huawei Executive Office Speech No. [2015] 023)*

We have spent 25 years building high-quality platforms and have managed to gather resources. These resources are valuable assets that came after much money was wasted by our senior managers and experts. Failed projects and products wasted money. Of course the money wasted was money you earned in the first place. We would not be where we are today without such waste. We value the success that we have achieved by learning from our failures. So long as we refuse to be complacent, boldly walk away from what we have, and have the courage to embrace new things, Huawei may not necessarily fall behind. *(Ren Zhengfei: Applying the Spirit of the Tortoise to Catch up with the Dragon Spacecraft—Speech at Huawei Annual Management Conference 2013, Huawei Executive Office Speech No. [2013] 255)*

6.5.3 Promoting Sales Growth While Effectively Managing Risks

We must assess risks based on facts. Just as the Yangtze River needs to keep flowing, we must not discontinue our business flows just to play it safe. *(Source: Minutes of the Work Report on Risk Management, EMT Meeting Minutes No. [2005] 059)*

The company's goal is to promote sales growth while effectively managing risks. During contract terms reviews, some functional departments simply say "No" without proposing any feasible solutions. They do this because these departments don't have to meet sales targets. We must establish a management mechanism that changes this lack of alignment between responsibility and authority. *(Source: Minutes of the Report on the 2009 H1 Performance Review, EMT Meeting Minutes No. [2009] 038)*

We must be fully aware that, in the face of the risks ahead, we can only use the certainty of rules to deal with the uncertainty of results. This is how we can follow our heart without breaking rules and gain greater freedom through development. There are two sides to every coin. *Huidu* in our management allows us to survive and thrive. We must thoroughly understand openness, compromise, and *huidu*, and the company's philosophy of "Digging In and Widening Out". The light of wisdom will never fade away. *(Ren Zhengfei: Digging In, Widening Out—Speech at the Commendation Meeting of the Operations and Delivery Division, Huawei Executive Office Speech No. [2009] 009)*

Representative offices need to agree with BGs on their annual business goals, and be responsible for attaining these goals. Low-profit and high-risk projects should be subsidized by BGs. If they aren't, then representative offices need to have the authority to veto such projects. However, when exercising veto authority, representative offices should also be responsible in part for BGs' business goals, and avoid sacrificing growth opportunities as a result of an excessive focus on profits and risks. *(Source: Resolution on Piloting Organizational Design and Authorization Management Principles in the Guangzhou Representative Office, EMT Resolution No. [2012] 033)*

We should pay more attention to risks when managing our opportunities and risks. This means that we should have a rational strategic presence. It is not that risks are greater than opportunities in all the countries where we operate. We divide these countries into two categories. One is countries where risks are being controlled, and where managing risks is more important than managing opportunities. The other is countries where risks are not a major focus. In these countries, we need to be opportunity-driven and strive to identify and seize opportunities. *(Ren Zhengfei: Minutes of the Report on the Opportunity to Order for 2017, EMT Meeting Minutes No. [2016] 021)*

The purpose of managing risks is to help create value, effectively balance business expansion and risk control, and avoid leaning towards either extreme of ignoring risks or being excessively conservative. Representative offices should be profit-centered and must ensure they always comply with trade rules and regulations. When striking a balance between expansion and control, business commanders might approach or even cross the red line. When this happens, subsidiary board directors must ensure business compliance, but they are not there to control business. Instead, they need to charge forward along with business commanders, and help them succeed and achieve internal and external compliance during the journey. The responsibility of business commanders is to succeed and the responsibility of subsidiary board directors is to ensure compliance while helping achieve success. Although these responsibilities are different, they have the same goal, which is to succeed, rather than to exercise strict control or micromanage people like they are toddlers. If no crops are harvested, what's the point of implementing management and control? *(Ren Zhengfei: Speech at the Meeting on Extension of the Company's Oversight and Management Control System, Huawei Executive Office Speech No. [2017] 041)*

6.6 Creating Order Out of Chaos Versus Creating Chaos Out of Order

6.6.1 Purpose of Fine-Grained Management: Preventing Chaos During Business Expansion

Willingness to improve management is not enough. We also need to improve how the company approaches management. Otherwise, we will never be efficient and will eventually meet our demise. The per-capita efficiency of Huawei is at least three times lower than that of our Western peers. So what is being wasted? Resources and time. This is a result of ineffective management. *(Ren Zhengfei: Do Not Be a Temporary Hero, 1998)*

Fine-grained management represents planning, budgeting, and accounting, all of which need to be based on reliable data. Representative offices manage their operations based on plans and financial data. Only when financial data is clear will financial analysis be clear. Clear financial analysis is the basis for setting clear management KPIs. These, in turn, will tell us what areas need to improve and how, guide future business development, and help develop reasonable and feasible business strategies and action plans. How can we achieve fine-grained management? The key is to have a reasonable plan and avoid being blind. Planning is critical because it is the basis for budgeting. Plans and budgets can then be corrected and measured through accounting. Fine-grained management, as I mentioned, is not about pursuing a low cost strategy; instead, it is about how to make more contributions to the company with the same budget. These two strategies are different. Fine-grained management is an open strategy while pursuing a low cost strategy is a closed one. *(Ren Zhengfei: Speech at the Report by the BT Account Department and the UK Representative Office, Huawei Executive Office Speech No. [2007] 015)*

Representative offices need to use financial data to guide people to specify and clarify business strategies and measures, and use report templates to implement fine-grained management. These goals are particularly critical during planning, budgeting, and accounting. Fine-grained management that focuses on planning and operations is the core basis of profit-centered performance appraisals, and is also the direction of the company's business center development. Fine-grained management is a prerequisite for implementing profit-centered performance appraisals and ensuring accurate and reliable profit data. *(Ren Zhengfei: Speech at the Report by the BT Account Department and the UK Representative Office, Huawei Executive Office Speech No. [2007] 015)*

For fast-growing markets and products, our main objective is to win strategic projects, more customers, and more market share. At the same time, we should carry out fine-grained management to prevent chaos caused by blind expansion. When appraising growth, we need to look at sales revenue, sales growth potential, and breakthroughs with tier-1 carriers. When I say we should win more customers, I do not only mean geographically, but also from product and carrier perspectives. Doing that is like shaping the market landscape. When it comes to mature markets where we are growing steadily but have limited potential for growth and to products in the final stage of their lifecycles, we need to focus on fine-grained management while exploring new opportunities. We have clear appraisal criteria for such markets and products: generating cash flow and profits for the company. *(Source: Guidelines on Sales Priorities, EMT Meeting Minutes No. [2008] 014)*

We don't focus too much on growth. Regions that are growing slowly now might have been growing rapidly a couple years earlier. In such regions, we want to focus on effective, fine-grained management. Eventually, the managers and management approaches of these regions should be transferred to expansion teams. All departments will at some point struggle with further expansion and will need to implement fine-grained management. This doesn't mean teams that are still advancing don't need this type of management though. Therefore, I think that our planning system should be used to facilitate operations, not to report to HQ. You must keep this in mind. If you ignore this, our company will gradually shrink. *(Ren Zhengfei: Remarks After Watching the Battle of Moscow—Speech at the Egypt Representative Office, Huawei Executive Office Speech No. [2008] 004)*

Our profits now come from growth rather than management. With this model, if the company stops growing, we will have negative profits and cash flows. So we need to increase internal efficiency before we stop growing. *(Ren Zhengfei: Speech at the EMT ST Meeting in May, 2009)*

When we were growing rapidly, we focused too much on sales. This was because more contracts meant more profits. As the market becomes saturated, there are fewer and fewer opportunities for us to seize and make profits on. To survive, we need to implement fine-grained management.

(Ren Zhengfei: Remarks at a Meeting with Senior Managers at a Project Management Summit, Huawei Executive Office Speech No. [2009] 007)
Huawei is a company that has developed out of chaos. If we didn't use processes or appraisals to drive high performance, we will be slaves to Brownian motion, where each molecule acts on its own and momentum for growth cannot be achieved. After standardization, everything works well according to processes, just like gas flows through the "de Laval nozzle". When compressed gas reaches the velocity of sound, it continuously expands, creating an extremely fast jet engine. This is how rockets work. Rocket engines are based on the "de Laval nozzle". We at Huawei have followed a path of "standardization first, and then less control". *(Ren Zhengfei: Remarks at Meetings with Huawei Fellows, Huawei Executive Office Speech No. [2016] 069)*

6.6.2 Striking and Disrupting a Balance

When I last spoke at our UK Representative Office, I emphasized fine-grained management. By that, I meant we must create order out of chaos. What I didn't mention was the need to seek to create chaos out of order, or to disrupt balance to expand further. During actual work, some representative offices are deviating from what I said. During my recent visit to the Mexico Representative Office, I said that doing business is not like painting or embroidery, and we need more than just fine-grained management. We must have clear goals, and focus on the most important issue in the market and the key factors that influence the issue. If we only emphasize fine-grained management, we will shrink. The purpose of fine-grained management is to prevent chaos during expansion, not to seal our doors closed. Fine-grained management doesn't mean we stop expanding. We must stand up to face the competition, and we must have the courage to win. This is necessary to become skilled at achieving success. Fine-grained management doesn't conflict with expansion, so we just have to effectively combine them. *(Ren Zhengfei: Speech at the UK Representative Office, Huawei Executive Office Speech No. [2007] 027)*

We need to change from one-size-fits-all management approaches to more scenario-specific approaches. These appraisals should guide the balanced development of our company. Over the years, we have moved away from chaos and gradually standardized our operations. We have made significant advancements in our management systems and established a large platform. This is a great accomplishment. I think that our overall HR policy of first establishing a large platform is correct. However, our performance appraisal approach is too rigid. The next time we transform our incentive systems, we should continue to emphasize different incentive models for different products, regions, and types of work. *(Ren Zhengfei: Speech at the 2008 Mid-year Report by Regions to the EMT, EMT Meeting Minutes No. [2008] 028)*

There is an old Chinese saying to the effect that the Yellow River changes course every 30 years. Huawei has survived for nearly 30 years, and is thus approaching an age when many companies falter and fail. To continue to survive, we must change everything from our organizational structure to our talent management approaches. If we don't change, we will not be able to survive. If we discard this generation of our existing employees and replace it with a completely new generation, there will be discontinuity. History proves that this approach is not feasible. Thus, what we can do is to reinvent our experienced employees. Through change, we will inject new energy into our existing workforce. This generation of employees can bridge the past and the future, and grow by inheriting knowledge and experience from the previous generation. *(Ren Zhengfei: Speech at a Briefing on Strategic Reserve Development, Huawei Executive Office Speech No. [2016] 085)*

We must not confine ourselves to our own circles, and must be open-minded. In the field of machine learning, there must be a lot of software that is far better than ours out there. There must be many people who will launch amazing things. We need to cooperate with the best companies in this field. As we build our own Great Wall, we should use American bricks here, European bricks there, and also Japanese bricks. It doesn't matter where the bricks come from. We will use them as long as they help us win. We don't need to make every brick ourselves. On this big platform or "stage", our own Great Wall, we allow all sorts of people to give great performances like Riverdance. We will also allow the eccentric to dance on our "stage". They will not overwhelm the platform; instead, they will revitalize it. We will focus on our core business and at the same time leverage other people's advantages. This is what I just said about GTS, and our efforts in AI should focus on the several areas I just mentioned. *(Ren Zhengfei: Speech at a Meeting with Employees of the Noah's Ark Laboratory, Huawei Executive Office Speech No. [2016] 083)*

We are now in an age of innovation. After much of our work with certainty and uncertainty are integrated into processes, the emergence of new things will be inhibited. Japan is a great country, as it standardizes everything, even the simplest things, including how screwdrivers, components, and tissue paper are stored in workshops. Young workers have to strictly follow these standards, and as a result, they don't want to create new things. The UK is also a great country. One of its most notable cultural products that it exports is its system of rules. The UK has rules for every part of a process, even at the end. In contrast, the US is a country set up by all sorts of European immigrants. They tore apart the UK's system, and instead only standardized their overall legal framework. They didn't over-standardize the details. In this way, the US reshaped British culture, creating a prosperous country within only 200 years. *(Ren Zhengfei: Remarks at Meetings with Huawei Fellows, Huawei Executive Office Speech No. [2016] 069)*

Open Access This chapter is licensed under the terms of the Creative Commons Attribution-NonCommercial-NoDerivatives 4.0 International License (http://creativecommons.org/licenses/by-nc-nd/4.0/), which permits any noncommercial use, sharing, distribution and reproduction in any medium or format, as long as you give appropriate credit to the original author(s) and the source, provide a link to the Creative Commons licence and indicate if you modified the licensed material. You do not have permission under this license to share adapted material derived from this chapter or parts of it.

The images or other third party material in this chapter are included in the chapter's Creative Commons licence, unless indicated otherwise in a credit line to the material. If material is not included in the chapter's Creative Commons licence and your intended use is not permitted by statutory regulation or exceeds the permitted use, you will need to obtain permission directly from the copyright holder.

PART II

Value Management

Three elements are necessary to guarantee Huawei's future success. First, we must have a strong leadership team that is open to criticism. Second, we should have stringent and well-established rules and systems that evolve over time. What are rules? Rules are about certainty, which we can use to tackle uncertainty and define the boundaries for our development. Third, we need to have a large, hard-working, courageous, and dedicated team that is adept at learning. – Ren Zhengfei

CHAPTER 7

Guidelines for Value Management

To ensure long-term survival and development, Huawei must first go international, then go global. It must explore new domains and expand its development space. Expansion requires the support of a proper management system. Without such a system, expansion would end in vain and could also be very dangerous. If that is the case, it would be better not to expand at all.

As Huawei creates value for its customers, Finance plays the role of a value integrator. It turns the value created by capital, technology, and talent into the company's revenue, profits, and cash flow. It also performs the task of turning the effort of the entire workforce into hard cash. To fulfill its mission as a value integrator, Finance must establish a scientific, standardized, and highly efficient management system that is able to keep risks under control. Since 2007, under the guidance of IBM consultants, Huawei spent seven years successfully implementing its Integrated Financial Services (IFS) program. This transformation has reinvented Huawei's financial management system, making it on-par with those of world-class companies and effectively supporting Huawei's rapid business growth worldwide.

Research on theories and new sciences shows that all systems exist and develop on the basis of several major principles. These principles define the overall characteristics and paths of evolution for these systems. Similarly, Huawei's financial management system also evolves, transforms, and improves according to some basic principles. Summarizing and distilling

© The Author(s) 2019
W. Huang, *Built on Value*,
https://doi.org/10.1007/978-981-13-7507-1_7

these basic principles will help people gain a deeper understanding of the essence and rules of financial management. They will also help improve the initiative of management, reduce passiveness and blindness, and move the company from the realm of necessity to the realm of freedom.

This chapter elaborates on the guidelines and basic principles that Huawei's Finance uses for value management. These guidelines and principles are not doctrines, but a road map for financial management. What is important is that they provide the methodologies for understanding Huawei's value management.

7.1 Huawei's Most Valuable Asset: An Enduring Management System

7.1.1 Management Is Key to Ending Reliance on Talent, Technology, and Capital, and Enabling the Company to Evolve from the Realm of Necessity to the Realm of Freedom

Management is key to ending our reliance on talent, technology, and capital, and enabling the company to evolve from the realm of necessity to the realm of freedom. Effective management can enable us to build a platform that helps unleash the biggest potential of talent, technology, and capital. Talent is our most valuable asset, but when we still rely on talent, technology, and capital, our value assessment system is, to some extent, distorted. When this happens, we can't say we are free. Only when we no longer rely on these three elements can we make scientific decisions. The reason we drafted *The Huawei Charter* was to build a platform and a framework to unleash the potential of our talent, technology, and capital. *(Ren Zhengfei: How Long Can Huawei Survive?, 1998)*

We need to establish a sound system of management controls and the right policies to ensure our corporate strategy, policy, and culture are well-aligned. Built on this, we can fully delegate authority to managers at all levels, and create a vibrant, efficient, and stable environment where the company is both goal-oriented and value-driven, and at the same time have processes and policies to follow. *(Source: The Huawei Charter, 1998)*

Management and services are what concern Huawei's life and death. Talent, capital, and technology are not, as they can be acquired from outside sources. Management and services though cannot simply be copied.

Only by relying on the joint effort of all our employees can we identify advanced management and service theories and apply them to our practices. Based on this, we need to build our own effective management and service system, and ensure that the system runs smoothly across the company and throughout our business processes. *(Ren Zhengfei: Do Not Be a Temporary Hero, 1998)*

The challenges we face in the future will not be related to technologies or products. Instead, they will likely be in basic research and innovation. The key to overcoming these challenges lies in our management. The biggest challenge we face right now is internal management – to build organizations, processes, and IT systems that can promptly adapt to market demands and meet customer needs. If such a management system is not in place, problems will arise as our company continues to grow. To avoid a decline and slackoff, we must constantly motivate our organization and maintain its vitality. While we should keep our organization under control at all times, we must not control it to the point that it loses vitality. What matters is a balance between motivation and control, and this balance must be constantly adapted according to changing dynamics. *(Ren Zhengfei: Huawei's Opportunities and Challenges, 2000)*

Huawei must go global. We can't remain content with just being a Chinese company forever. Staying this way will cause problems for us. What if the Chinese market becomes saturated in a few years? Our R&D has been providing content services, exploring new fields, and developing new software to create more space for development. To increase our likelihood of survival, we must expand into overseas markets, and this process must be governed by a solid management system. Growth without the support of a solid management system can be very dangerous. If that is the case, it would be better not to expand at all. *(Ren Zhengfei: Speech at the Training Session for Marketing Managers, 2002)*

First, we need to manage employee conduct. Second, we need to implement an ownership system for processes at all levels. We also need to develop a code of conduct and rules for discipline and rewards, and define positional responsibilities. With these in place, process owners won't dare to slack off. Approaches, methodologies, and templates are what our oversight department needs to develop in order to provide professional and standardized guidelines. You can send them to business departments and allow them to establish their own oversight systems, but you need to assess and approve them. This approach is how we can truly link oversight and business operations. *(Ren Zhengfei: Speech at a Briefing on Regional Oversight, 2007)*

Western companies have developed their modern business management systems by fine-tuning approaches to scientific management over the last century. Built on the trial and error of countless companies, these systems are precious embodiments of human wisdom and represent a wealth for humanity. Huawei must be humble and systematically learn these management systems. Only with a modern business management system can our large-scale product innovation lead to business success. It is with this system that we are able to deliver results, accumulate and transfer knowledge and experience, and advance by stepping on the shoulders of giants. *(Ren Zhengfei: Speech at the Awards Ceremony for Whiz Kids, Huawei Executive Office Speech No. [2014] 039)*

Huawei's most valuable asset is its enduring management system, which uses the certainty of rules and systems to deal with uncertainty and help us succeed in this era of massive data traffic. *(Ren Zhengfei: Speech at a Work Report on Corporate Quality, Huawei Executive Office Speech No. [2015] 067)*

7.1.2 Goal of Transformation: To Harvest More Crops and Increase Soil Fertility

We adopt a committee-based decision-making mechanism on major issues. For execution- or project-level issues, we allow department heads or project leaders to make decisions. That's why we can make decisions quickly. *(Ren Zhengfei: Speech at a Meeting with Trainees of the 10th Senior Management Seminar at Huawei University, Huawei Executive Office Speech No. [2011] 031)*

We should constantly optimize our corporate governance structure and clearly define the company's authority delegation and oversight mechanism for each BG. This will ensure that BGs do not deviate from the company's overall strategy or operational rules as they forge ahead. We should improve our performance appraisal and incentivization mechanisms to better motivate BGs to expand effectively and ensure sustainable and profitable growth for the company. In this new era, we should establish more scientific management approaches by truly living our corporate values and implementing good policies and processes. In addition, we should strengthen oversight while gradually delegating authority, so as to move forward on both of these wheels. *(Ren Zhengfei: Guidelines on the Analysis of the Business Environment and Key Business Strategies, Corp. Doc. No. [2012] 081)*

We can only leave behind two types of legacies for our company: One is a management system supported by our management architecture, processes, and IT systems. The other is an employee management and incentivization mechanism. No one stays at a company forever. Even if someone stays with a company their whole life, they will eventually pass away, but management systems won't expire. A management system is enormously valuable and can exist for hundreds or even thousands of years. If it is being continuously improved by our managers, how much will our management system eventually be worth? So long as we survive in the marketplace, this system will play its role. If we go public one day, the value of the company will completely depend on the value of these two legacies. We therefore highly prioritize our processes. *(Ren Zhengfei: Speech and Comments at the Strategy Retreat of the Business Process & IT Management Department, Huawei Executive Office Speech No. [2012] 026)*

Over the next five to ten years, the company will focus on logistical service transformation. We must strive to change our centralized management approach and give both responsibility and authority to field offices so that those closest to customers can call for support. Our goal is to change HQ's role from management and control to service and support, and build a modern company that meets modern needs. *(Ren Zhengfei: Speech at a Meeting with the Representatives' Commission, Huawei Executive Office Speech No. [2013] 056)*

During our future transformation, we need to emphasize that our goals are what matter most. Our goals are to *harvest more crops, make strategic contributions,* and *increase soil fertility.* We should cut back on anything that doesn't serve these goals. Our transformation is primarily intended to establish processes and systems that help create value for customers. Anything that does not serve this primary purpose should be streamlined. Our current processes are overly complex because we haven't fully understood our goals. A clear understanding of our goals will help us improve efficiency and develop outstanding people who are both diligent and courageous. Then over the next three to five years, we will make some progress in our management. *(Ren Zhengfei: Heroes Are All Around Us—Speech at the Q4 Regional Presidents' Meeting, Huawei Executive Office Speech No. [2014] 086)*

We must have a yardstick in place to measure our management progress. Our goal is to *harvest more crops*. Representative offices that are seeing little growth in customer orders but are experiencing profit growth are making management progress. We need to examine what contributions they can make to the company and ask whether these contributions are random or sustainable. This will provide us with rough baselines that we can use to measure our management progress. *(Ren Zhengfei: Speech at the Briefing on the Transformation Elite Team and Related Progress, Huawei Executive Office Speech No. [2015] 026)*

Based on the integration of the LTC process, we determine that our goals are to achieve the consistency of inventory accounts and goods (CIAG) in stage one and the Five Ones[1] in stage two of our transformation. Of course, we shouldn't limit our objective to the Five Ones – Five Twos are also fine. Why do we strive for *one second*? One minute, one hour, or one day would all be fine, as they are all *ones*. Our ultimate goal is to *harvest more crops and increase soil fertility*. We will discard anything redundant during our transformation process. *(Ren Zhengfei: Speech at the Briefing on the Transformation Elite Team and Related Progress, Huawei Executive Office Speech No. [2015] 026)*

Huawei has passed its chaotic period and is now moving towards standardized operations. We must learn to use new approaches, improve our understanding of strategies and tactics, and increase our capabilities in specific operations. This is our mission for this new era. Without the support of IT systems, we would become an organization without a history. If we rely only on people to remember what we have done, they may forget what they have done as soon as they get up from their desks. Now, with the support of both processes and IT systems, we will improve step by step. In part, we use the certainty of rules and systems to deal with any uncertainty to continue down the right path. In truth, we are already on the right path. We just need to keep pushing on. *(Ren Zhengfei: Speech at a Work Report on Corporate Quality, Huawei Executive Office Speech No. [2015] 067)*

---

[1] "Five Ones": any PO from receiving to order generation in One day, any shipment preparation in One week, any product delivered at agreed location in One month, any software ready for download in One minute, and any site from delivery to customer acceptance in One month.

7.2 Business Plays a Leading Role and Accounting Plays an Oversight Role

7.2.1 When We Say That "Business Plays a Leading Role and Accounting Plays an Oversight Role", We Mean That We Do Not Focus Solely on Financial Returns on Investment

We must stick firmly to our macro management approaches and systems, under which business plays a leading role and accounting plays an oversight role. When we say that "business plays a leading role", we mean that we optimally develop our business based on our goals and needs. When we say that "accounting plays an oversight role", we mean that managers at all levels must fulfill their financial management responsibility, implement effective project management, and enhance accounting and cost control. This is how we can strike a balance between development and control. *(Ren Zhengfei: Key Points for Management, 1999)*

When we say that "accounting plays an oversight role", we mean that Finance provides standardized services. During this process, accountants exercise oversight. Services need to be standardized based on plans, budgets, and costs. At the current stage, the internal audit team mainly manages exceptions, but they also manage daily routine. After that stage, processes must not be changed and the sole task of the internal audit team is to manage exceptions. Our internal audit team also needs to oversee our accounting team outside China. *(Ren Zhengfei: Speech at a Briefing on Four Unifications and 2000 Work Plan of Finance, 1999)*

When we say that "business plays a leading role and accounting plays an oversight role", we mean that business managers have decision-making authority and are responsible for their own decisions. They are also responsible for the growth and financial robustness of the regions within their purview. Finance needs to serve and oversee business. By fulfilling their oversight responsibility, Finance will ensure that financial data truly reflects actual business activities and will help business managers make correct choices and decisions. *(Ren Zhengfei: Speech at a Briefing on Methods and Results of CFO Appraisals, 2011)*

Business managers are the primary owners of operating risks and internal controls within their purview. Financial personnel are assistants to business managers at all levels. You're there to give advice and disclose risks. You are part of their team and must play your role. Finance and business are highly interdependent, so you can only achieve shared success when you grow together. If Finance does a poor job, business will suffer. *(Ren Zhengfei: Speech at a Meeting with Financial Staff, Huawei Executive Office Speech No. [2011] 032)*

Business plays a leading role and accounting plays an oversight role. I said this over a decade ago to criticize those who were driven only by financial returns on investment. By saying "business plays a leading role", I meant we need to earn profits through technological innovation, talent introduction, and market expansion. Accounting, as I see it, does not simply keep our books. It also carries out project accounting and other financial management activities. By saying "accounting plays an oversight role", I mean Finance provides services and support while fulfilling management and oversight responsibilities. *(Ren Zhengfei: Speech at a Meeting with Financial Managers, Huawei Executive Office Speech No. [2012] 029)*

7.2.2 Accurately Recognizing Revenue, Accelerating Cash Inflows, Ensuring Visibility of Project Profits and Losses, and Managing Business Risks

Accurately recognizing revenue based on actual business activities is the basis for robust business operations

Currently, IFS is the most important business transformation at Huawei. Its critical value to the company can be described as "accurately recognizing revenue, accelerating cash inflows, ensuring visibility of project profits and losses, and managing business risks". *(Guo Ping: Respecting Professionalism and Doing Financial Work Well in 2009—Speech at the Annual Meeting of Finance on January 17, 2009, Improvement Issue No. 327, 2009)*

We need to link customer contract information to procurement contract information to support the company's fine-grained management. Our IDS1[2] focuses on transactions, which has streamlined the Opportunity to Cash (OTC) and Procure-to-Pay (PTP) processes from end to end, optimized and delivered a series of processes and rules, built integrated IT systems, and integrated customer contract information with procurement contract information. These results have helped achieve business goals like fast and accurate billing and accurate revenue recognition. Based on this, we are now able to access data on financial performance, operating efficiency, and operating quality like order, shipment, revenue, and payment

---

[2] IDS: Integrated Deployment Solution.

collection on our business fulfillment monitoring platform iSee. This has helped us accurately locate problems, take effective business management actions, and enable fine-grained management in business units at all levels. *(Meng Wanzhou: IFS: Working with Business Teams to Comprehensively Improve the Capabilities of Financial Staff, Improvement Issue No. 407, 2012)*

Sales revenue is one of the most important financial indicators that are used to measure the company's business operations and quality. Objective, accurate, and prompt revenue recognition is crucial for robust operations. All business units must strictly observe the company's policies, rules, and processes for sales revenue recognition to ensure company operations are compliant and robust. Those who falsely recognize revenue will be held accountable. The following are all punishable offences: Recognizing revenue in advance or postponing revenue recognition by falsifying delivery progress information or delivery documents, and hiding true business information. These are all serious violations of *Huawei's Business Conduct Guidelines (BCGs)* and may have a material impact on the company's financial statements. The company has zero tolerance towards such misconduct and will immediately handle any such cases that are discovered. Extra bonuses granted because of inflated revenue must be returned and employees and managers directly responsible for these intentional violations will be disciplined according to the *BCGs*. *(Source: Resolution on Disciplining Those Who Have Falsely Recognized Sales Revenue, Finance Committee Resolution No. [2014] 016)*

We must strengthen our control and management of cash flow

Emphasizing both sales revenue and profits is not enough. We also need to strengthen cash flow management. We may have good contract terms, high prices, and high profits on our books, but if customers make payments years later, we may run short of cash and drive the company into the ground. Therefore, it is critical to control and manage cash flow. *(Ren Zhengfei: Speech at the Mid-year Market Conference, Huawei Executive Office Speech No. [2006] 036)*

The purpose of sales is not only to secure orders or sign contracts. "Any order, no matter how exciting it is, must generate revenue. All revenue, no matter how large it is, must bring profits and cash flow." Otherwise, we will just be quenching our thirst with poison and will ultimately be walking towards our company's demise. *(Source: Resolution on Designating Team Members of the Joint Committee of Regions for Promoting Contract Quality Improvement, EMT Resolution No. [2011] 029)*

Cash flow is a major issue, and is our life line. If we don't have money to pay salaries, employees will leave and we will lose the strategic accomplishments made over the past two decades. We have managed to build an organization through hard work. Once it collapses, what can we do then? We must pay attention to local financing and further develop our local financing team to disperse financing risks. *(Ren Zhengfei: Speech at the EMT ST Meeting, 2012)*

Project management is the basis for the company's business management

We must remain project-centered and improve our project operations management. This is how we will increase efficiency and profits over the next couple of years. We need to focus on three types of projects: customer, R&D, and transformation projects, and establish a project operations management framework that includes projects, programs, and project portfolios. We need to develop a complete system that runs from "doing the right things" to "doing things right" to drive the company's organizational change from a pyramid, function-centered structure to a project-centered structure with functional departments playing an auxiliary role. *(Guo Ping: Transform Continuously and Improve Field Operating Capabilities to Ensure the Company's Sustainable and Profitable Growth—Speech at Huawei Annual Management Conference 2013, Huawei Executive Office Speech No. [2014] 020)*

In the future, we will implement a project-based total budget system. Under this system, we will first deduct the company-borne expenses from project budgets, because the company spends money transferring resources to projects. The remaining budget will be given to projects, and with the money, project managers can buy resources from Supply Chain and services from HQ. Project managers do not have to buy unnecessary resources. Functional departments do not have any budget pressure right now. As a result, they are not motivated to sell resources to projects. That is why we have a bloated organization at HQ. We must manage project plans and budgets. When a project is completed, we need to do project accounting to see if it has made or lost money. Project profitability is a key criterion for assessing a project manager's performance. *(Ren Zhengfei: Remarks at a Meeting with Members of the Project & Financial Management Enablement Program for High Potentials, Huawei Executive Office Speech No. [2014] 054)*

Over the next five to ten years, we will gradually shift from a centralized management model to one that allows employees closest to customers to call for backup. Currently, we are tentatively shifting from function-centered to project-centered operations. If we can truly delegate managerial authority to field offices and if back offices can provide better support services in five to ten years, we will be able to increase our response speed and our ability to meet customer needs. We will then survive the surging waves of massive data traffic. *(Ren Zhengfei: Our Transformation Goals Are to Harvest More Crops and Increase Soil Fertility—Speech at the 2015 Huawei Market Conference, Huawei Executive Office Speech No. [2015] 016)*

While shifting from a function-centered structure to a project-centered structure, we need to clearly specify how projects should operate and what management systems we should adopt, so that our project line is separate from our resource line. For sales and delivery projects on the front line, SDTs at all levels are our decision-making teams, and physical organizations at representative offices, regions, and HQ are our resource departments. Projects have budgets and resource departments provide resources, so that project teams can deliver to customers what contracts require. Under this operations management system, project operations, budget management, resource management, and project teams will all need to change to support the shift from a function-centered model to a project-centered model. *(Source: Minutes of the Work Report on the Project for Changing Function-centered Operations into Project-centered Operations, BOD Executive Committee Meeting Minutes No. [2015] 020)*

Controlling risks from a perspective of value management

We need to guard against the operating risks arising from some possible high-risk customers, for example, carriers that may be acquired. We also need to strengthen our internal controls and auditing processes and systems, and conscientiously implement them to fend off corruption. We also need to pay attention to the possible impact of protectionism and further plan for and meet local manufacturing requirements. *(Source: 2010 Key Work Requirements, EMT Resolution No. [2010] 007)*

Corruption and overstocking are the two biggest challenges the Consumer BG faces. I won't compromise on these two things. Overstocking even only once or twice may lead to our demise. I would rather take a longer time to meet consumer needs, rather than engage in overstocking. As consumer products become increasingly customized, overstocking will pose ever greater risks. *(Ren Zhengfei: Be Bold at Work, Be a Humble Person, and Follow the Patterns of Consumer Products in the Pursuit of Maximum Growth and Success—Speech at a Meeting with the Key Employees of the Consumer BG, Huawei Executive Office Speech No. [2011] 014)*

Adopting a new business model is always risky. This requires us to establish a stringent control mechanism. *(Ren Zhengfei: Guidelines on the Analysis of the Business Environment and Key Business Strategies, Corp. Doc. No. [2012] 081)*

We need to summarize our past experience and determine our strategic goals for tomorrow based on where we are today. Over the past 25 years, Huawei has generally adopted a correct strategy. When the global economy was growing, we emphasized growth through economies of scale. As long as we operated at a large scale and won lots of contracts, we were able to dilute our fixed costs and generate profits. If our products were expensive at that time, would customers buy them? Of course not. Now though, our people are still doing the same thing. They focus too much on getting orders and contracts without considering their quality. They win contracts blindly as long as they can drive up sales. If we hadn't strengthened contract quality management, resolutely changed our strategic goals, and emphasized that we must be profit-oriented during the past two years, we would have been unable to have a meeting here today and most of you would probably have already been sent home. That's why over the past couple of years, we have emphasized that we focus on profits for managed services and consumer products and don't measure their sales revenue. This shift in KPIs is a kind of transformation. Of course, we still need to further transform our budgeting. Over time, we will see more change. *(Ren Zhengfei: Why Can't Water from the Himalayas Flow to the Amazon River?—Remarks at the Work Conferences of the Latin America Region, Key Account Departments, and Carrier BG, Huawei Executive Office Speech No. [2014] 044)*

A financial crisis could arise any time now. We must reduce long overdue inventories and long overdue accounts receivable (AR). *(Ren Zhengfei: Speech at a Meeting with Employees of the Quality, Business Process & IT Management Department, Huawei Executive Office Speech No. [2016] 094)*

7.2.3 How Can Financial Personnel Effectively Serve and Oversee Business If They Do Not Understand It?

Financial personnel are not decision makers. Rather, you are there to give advice and oversee business. If you don't understand business, how can you effectively serve and oversee it? You need to meet reasonable business needs and provide valuable financial services. You should be able to identify whether business needs are real and reasonable. You need to effectively oversee business operations and help business managers grow. You must have your own judgment and cannot just blindly rely on what others are saying. *(Ren Zhengfei: Speech at a Meeting with Financial Staff, Huawei Executive Office Speech No. [2011] 032)*

Business departments take responsibility for all risks. Finance analyzes and reminds business departments of the risks. Business departments are responsible for growth, profits, and most importantly, for legal compliance. *(Ren Zhengfei: Minutes of the Meeting with Staff of the Romania Accounting SSC, Huawei Executive Office Speech No. [2011] 021)*

Regional and representative office CFOs are responsible for overseeing the quality of contracts in regions within their purview. They must dare to veto poor-quality contracts. This can help establish checks and balances between regional CEOs and CFOs. CFOs at all levels must participate in pre-sales contract reviews and must have the courage to veto poor-quality contracts. Contracts vetoed by CFOs must be escalated to a higher-level contract review team. The contract review team of the same level will no longer have the decision-making authority over the vetoed contracts. CFOs that can't handle this work must be replaced promptly. *(Source: Minutes of the Report on the 2011 H1 Performance Review, EMT Meeting Minutes No. [2011] 011)*

CFO authority to veto contracts is primarily the authority to escalate contracts to an upper-level decision-making team. When CFOs voice a differing opinion about contract terms or business models, the contract decision-making team of their same level can no longer make decisions on the contract. In such cases, a decision needs to be made by a higher-level team. *(Source: Minutes of the Report on Improving Contract Quality, EMT Meeting Minutes No. [2011] 012)*

Our management must respect facts. Those who manipulate business data and commit fraud will be held accountable. *(Ren Zhengfei: Minutes of the Report on the Opportunity to Order for 2017, EMT Meeting Minutes No. [2016] 021)*

7.2.4 Oversight Means Firm Commitment to Process Management

Modern management systems are actually founded on distrust. If they weren't, we would not need process-based operations, authentication, or enhanced oversight. It's just that no one says this openly in the books. Although systems do not place trust in people, we are people-friendly when implementing these systems. There are always risks out there, but we cannot stop our processes for the sake of guarding against risks. Such a system at Huawei will help us constantly improve ourselves. *(Ren Zhengfei: Remarks at a Meeting with Procurement Managers, 2000)*

Financial policies must be developed centrally by the Finance Management Department. Regional offices cannot develop them. If regional offices want to add some additional provisions or notes, they must obtain approval from the Finance Management Department. *(Ren Zhengfei: Speech at the Briefing by the Audit Department on Audit Projects in Latin America and South Africa, 2004)*

Finance must oversee business operations while providing fast, accurate, secure, and standardized services to business departments. Standardized management is the basis for providing fast, accurate, and secure services to business departments. This is precisely the value that Finance can bring to business. *(Ren Zhengfei: Building Finance into an Invincible Organization That Adapts Quickly to Our Business Development—Speech at the Training Class for Financial Managers in the European Region, 2005)*

Huawei's management philosophy is like a cloud in the sky. Both internal and external factors, such as management philosophy, strategic requirements, and the industry environment, are the forces that push the company's operations forward. *Rainwater* from the *cloud* needs to be properly channeled to ensure accurate execution. The *cloud* must turn into *rain*, and *rainwater* must flow along the proper *channels*, eventually reaching the sea. That's the water cycle. At Huawei, *rainwater* is our business activities, including financial activities. Financial oversight must be in place at key *channel* nodes, in order to ensure *rainwater* flows in the *channels* at a proper speed and with the desired quality. *(Ren Zhengfei: Remarks at the Briefing on Finance Process Building, Huawei Executive Office Speech No. [2013] 091)*

Financial oversight means firm commitments to process management. We must build oversight into every part of our processes. We must dare to expose problems and push for improvement. *(Ren Zhengfei: Speech at a Meeting with Staff in Mauritius, Huawei Executive Office Speech No. [2013] 016)*

Oversight is part of business. It is based on processes and realized in business practice. The majority of our oversight will be built into processes. Processes themselves are lines of defense, so if we have well-designed processes, we will already have an effective oversight system. *(Source: Huawei's Oversight Philosophy, 2015)*

7.2.5 Everything We Do Must Support Field Operations, Serve Business, and Contribute to Business Success

The primary goal of establishing a management system is to increase operating capabilities of field teams. We need to learn from the US military's practices in the twenty-first century: On the front line are highly competent units that focus on goals and pursue success. At the back office is the decision-making center that sets the direction, develops strategy, and fully delegates authority. All competence centers have clear responsibilities, are targeted at operations, and form a joint support platform. This system is like a dragon, whose head moves flexibly to look for food or attack a target. Its highly developed bone systems are well-coordinated to ensure that the whole body moves to support any attack the head may start. *(Guo Ping: Transform Continuously and Improve Field Operating Capabilities to Ensure the Company's Sustainable and Profitable Growth—Speech at Huawei Annual Management Conference 2013, Huawei Executive Office Speech No. [2014] 020)*

"Everything we do must support field operations, serve business, and contribute to business success." This could become the slogan for our era of transformation. Within the next decade, we will implement a strategy of deploying highly competent elite teams with the support of a large platform and gradually separate resource management authority from command authority. The latter authority should be further delegated to field offices, which will allow for more flexible decision making and encourage more outstanding leaders to work in the field. Representative offices serve as profit centers and are responsible for results. Our command and decision-making authority should first be delegated to representative offices. Likewise, oversight authority should move to field offices as well. After several years of exploration and development in field offices, our subsidiary boards of directors have gradually matured in terms of compliance management, both internally and externally. These efforts have started to pay off, so we can begin piloting authority delegation to field business departments in certain countries. We need to allow representative offices to approve more contracts. This is what authority delegation is all about. Our workflows should be linked both vertically and horizontally. We must allow those who are closest to customers to call for support and ensure that the support they request will be provided. We must strive to improve contract quality, so that we can earn money promptly. Each project should have a CFO, who must participate in the end-to-end process from contract planning to contract closure. *(Ren Zhengfei: Firm Belief and*

Strong Focus Lead to Greater Success—Speech at the 2016 Huawei Market Conference, Huawei Executive Office Speech No. [2016] 007)
All managers in field offices must focus on achieving success, giving functional departments the authority to manage things that are certain. All managers in functional departments should keep a close eye on field offices and urge their own departments to provide prompt and accurate services. Your appraisals will be based on the services you have provided to field offices. If field offices fail, you will have also failed. We must learn to find faults in success and identify the root causes of failure. People in ancient China had ritual rooms for self-reflection. Why can't we learn to reflect on our failure? Heroes can also emerge from failures. The faults of managers should not overshadow the efforts of their subordinates, as some of them might have done things that deserve praise. *(Ren Zhengfei: Firm Belief and Strong Focus Lead to Greater Success—Speech at the 2016 Huawei Market Conference, Huawei Executive Office Speech No. [2016] 007)*

7.3 Using the Certainty of Rules to Deal with the Uncertainty of Results

7.3.1 Setting Rules to Prevent Chaos

Why did we implement the IFS Program in the first place? We hoped to use the certainty of rules to deal with the uncertainty of results. We are not sure about our company's future direction. It's impossible for us to know exactly where the company will be heading in the future. It's the entire society and our business environment – not we ourselves – that will shape the future of our company. We can't be too idealistic in deciding what our future will be like, but we can set rules that will help us prevent chaos as we move ahead. Therefore, the reason we implement IFS is to use the certainty of rules to deal with the uncertainty of results. Do we have to find an optimal form for the IFS program? I cannot bring everything good from other companies into Huawei. Even if I could, we may not be able to integrate those elements into Huawei. Can't we just learn from a good teacher? Even things we introduce from IBM may not be used directly. What is the best in the industry? I don't know what the best is. In fact, I don't think there is something that can be called the best. The thing that best suits our needs is the best for us. *(Ren Zhengfei: Speech at a Meeting with the IFS Project Team and Staff from Finance, Huawei Executive Office Speech No. [2009] 004)*

We must set rules. If we use the certainty of rules to deal with the uncertainty of results, we will move forward faster. Take for example the Tokyo station. Although traffic volume there is huge, things are going fast, and both business management and oversight are extremely effective. The Tokyo station is seven storeys tall, with five for metro lines and two for high-speed trains. On each storey, dozens of trains are running. Escalators and lifts are used to connect different storeys. Trains are running at high speeds, but I have never seen people directly oversee them, and there are no collisions. This shows an ideal relationship between oversight and business. The high-speed trains and all the conveniences modern transportation brings are examples to be followed for business and internal controls. *(Ren Zhengfei: Speech at a Meeting with the IFS Project Team and Staff from Finance, Huawei Executive Office Speech No. [2009] 004)*

7.3.2 Using the Certainty of Rules to Deal with the Uncertainty of Results for Major Processes, Allowing Flexibility at the Endpoints

When it comes to major processes, we need to use the certainty of rules to deal with the uncertainty of results. However, we must have common interfaces for different processes and workflows. We need standardization at higher levels of the organization; otherwise, confusion could occur at lower levels. At the lower levels or endpoints, we can allow some flexibility. By endpoints, I mean our field teams. Things are changing fast out there, so we must allow flexibility and avoid being rigid. During transformations, we must emphasize that the interfaces of all outputs at representative offices must be absolutely standardized. However, representative offices can also have their own operations models and differences are acceptable. I think it is understandable to allow some flexibility at the endpoints. The bottom line is we must operate based on business needs. *(Ren Zhengfei: Speech at a Meeting with the IFS Project Team and Staff from Finance, Huawei Executive Office Speech No. [2009] 004)*

We should have stringent and well-established rules and systems that evolve over time. An important feature of these rules and systems is certainty. This is our understanding of the rules of the market and corporate operations. Rules change slowly. Therefore, we should use their certainty to tackle any uncertainty. *(Ren Zhengfei: Our Transformation Goals Are to Harvest More Crops and Increase Soil Fertility—Speech at the 2015 Huawei Market Conference, Huawei Executive Office Speech No. [2015] 016)*

I think the most important part of our transformation is to establish rules for unified logistical services. We need to set standards for basic needs of different teams, and establish a platform that supports self-service at the front line. Doing so will enable field teams to self-manage, self-oversee, and self-improve themselves, thus forming a positive cycle. Based on such small management cycles at representative offices, logistical services for some general-purpose products can cycle through at the regional or corporate level, so that self-decision-making and self-oversight can be achieved. We also need to properly leverage contractors and reasonably assess and oversee them, to ensure our own capabilities are properly supplemented. *(Ren Zhengfei: Speech at a Meeting with BCG Consultants, Huawei Executive Office Speech No. [2015] 039)*

Three elements are necessary to guarantee Huawei's future success. First, we must have a strong leadership team that is open to criticism. Second, we should have stringent and well-established rules and systems that evolve over time. What are rules? Rules are about certainty, which we can use to tackle any uncertainty and define the boundaries for our development. Third, we need to have a large, hard-working, courageous, and dedicated team that is adept at learning. *(Ren Zhengfei: Heroes Are All Around Us—Speech at the Q4 Regional Presidents' Meeting, Huawei Executive Office Speech No. [2014] 086)*

7.3.3 Using the Certainty of Rules to Deal with the Uncertainty of Execution

The point of inviting consultants to Huawei is to help us establish rules and standards. The purpose of establishing a logistical service platform is to better support and serve the front line during their decision making. We need to use the certainty of rules to deal with the uncertainty of execution. In doing so, we will have clear rules and allow flexibility during execution, with oversight later on. *(Ren Zhengfei: Speech at a Meeting with BCG Consultants, Huawei Executive Office Speech No. [2015] 039)*

Contract managers mainly deal with certainties. They are responsible for efficiency and effectiveness following existing processes. Contract scenario experts deal with uncertainties. Their job is to minimize risks and gradually turn uncertainties into certainties. *(Ren Zhengfei: Speech at the Report on How to Develop Contract Scenario Experts, Huawei Executive Office Speech No. [2015] 071)*

At the moment, some certainties are still managed as uncertainties, resulting in too much discussion, low efficiency, and wasted energy, and leaving too little time to deal with true uncertainties. *(Ren Zhengfei: Speech at the Report on How to Develop Contract Scenario Experts, Huawei Executive Office Speech No. [2015] 071)*

7.4 EFFECTIVELY CONDUCTING OVERSIGHT WHILE FURTHER DELEGATING AUTHORITY TO THE FIELD

7.4.1 Centralized Authority Over Treasury, Accounting, and Auditing Management

In the future, we will delegate authority to the field in every business. However, we retain treasury, accounting, and auditing management authority at HQ. The Consumer BG was set up not long ago but has developed into what it is today. It is a great accomplishment. In the future, these centralized platforms will contribute significantly to you, but of course, they will also restrict you in some ways. The Consumer BG has to generate profits and cash flow. It needs to grow as well. Don't pass this profit pressure down to lower-level departments, as that will result in fraud and lies, or people might press customers for money. We must respect facts. If you can't generate as much profit as expected, you can reduce your headcount. That will lower your costs. You can transfer your extra people to the Strategic Reserve, who can go to work in the field again after updating their skills. This is actually a scientific approach to development. *(Ren Zhengfei: Speech at Consumer BG's Annual Meeting, Huawei Executive Office Speech No. [2017] 024)*

The company has centralized authority over three lines of oversight: treasury, accounting, and auditing management. These three lines directly penetrate into every level of our organization and are transparent at every level. Members of our subsidiary board of directors need to develop integrated compliance oversight platforms at the subsidiary level so that risks can be identified and managed in business activities. For example, our understanding of market demand must not be one-sided. We must link market demand to customers' capacity to pay. Our public relations personnel must be sensitive to politics, promptly and correctly make overall assessments of the regions where business environments are deteriorating, and incorporate these assessments into market operations principles.

Today, we haven't set ourselves apart from others in products, management, and business positioning. In countries where we should have made profits, we haven't achieved our profit goals and we are investing too much in high-risk regions. During performance appraisals, we need to separately look at the lawfulness of our financial reports and the reasonableness of our operations and incentive reports. This can help us truly turn our representative offices into profit centers. *(Ren Zhengfei: Speech at the Meeting on Extension of the Company's Oversight and Management Control System, Huawei Executive Office Speech No. [2017] 041)*

7.4.2 Delegating Command Authority to the Field and Giving Field Commanders the Final Decision-Making Authority

Huawei's governance model is not individual-centered, but team-centered. In general, authority should be delegated based on our business environment to cross-department committees or departments so that collective decision making and coordinated execution will be possible and accountability for decisions made will be shared. Currently, it is difficult to accurately delegate authority to particular positions, roles, or individuals. In addition, due to one-sidedness of individual decision making, role-based delegation will expose our organization to risks and cause conflicts and friction between different roles. *(Ren Zhengfei: Speech at the Report on IBM's Authorization Practices and Huawei's Direction for Improvement, EMT Meeting Minutes No. [2008] 004)*

At Huawei, we delegate decision-making authority over gross profits and cash flow to field operating teams. Within the scope of authorization, things can be done even without approval by representative offices. The goal of the military is to defeat enemies and our goal is to earn profits. Our Customer Centric 3 (CC3) face customers and aim to earn profits. Otherwise, all our management activities will be meaningless. *(Ren Zhengfei: Who Calls for Artillery and How Do We Provide Timely Artillery Support?—Speech at the Awards Ceremony of Sales & Services, Huawei Executive Office Speech No. [2009] 001)*

We will delegate authority, exercise authority, and conduct oversight based on processes. This will help us break free of low efficiency and overstaffing caused by centralized governance and become a process-based organization driven by customer needs. *(Ren Zhengfei: Who Calls for Artillery and How Do We Provide Timely Artillery Support?—Speech at the Awards Ceremony of Sales & Services, Huawei Executive Office Speech No. [2009] 001)*

Our entire organization needs to be restructured to make mission command effective. The "Squad Leaders' Fight" does not mean that we leave squad leaders to fight alone. Rather, this model requires the support of the following:

- Division of responsibilities: Give tactical command authority to field operating teams. Executives and HQ should focus on developing corporate strategies, setting the company's direction, and allocating resources.
- Authority delegation: Separate administrative management authority from operations command authority, and properly delegate authority based on clearly defined rules and the preparedness of subordinates.
- Organizational structure: Remove or restructure field teams by function based on business needs.
- Resource distribution: Deploy tactical resources close to field operating teams and centrally allocate strategic resources to ensure rapid and effective response.
- Capability development: Comprehensively develop capabilities based on strategic needs.
- Processes: Business operations processes should focus on improving operating capabilities to adapt to a complex, volatile environment. Administrative management processes need to be rigorous and comprehensive.
- Information systems: Build an interconnected information environment to allow commanders at all levels to get whatever information they need anytime and anywhere to complete a task and develop a common understanding of the operating environment.

(Ren Zhengfei: Speech at a Briefing on the Takeaways and Challenges for Huawei Relating to the "Squad Leaders' Fight", Huawei Executive Office Speech No. [2014] 078)

As a traditional saying in China says, people are born good. Some say this theoretically is the reason there is often a lack of authority delegation and oversight in China. In the West, however, systems are used to keep people under control. The weakness of such systems is that they are too standardized, even at their most basic levels. At Huawei, we need to have less stringent decision-making processes at our most basic level and avoid the rigidity of Western systems. How? Where do we intend to tighten our control? We need to identify the critical points. Below these points, the field will be allowed to command operations. Above these points, reporting must be standardized. I think that we need to give our field teams more authority to decide on how they operate and how they deal with the results of operations. *(Ren Zhengfei: Rigorous, Well-ordered, and Simple Management Is Crucial for Huawei to Scale New Heights, Huawei Executive Office Speech No. [2014] 028)*

During organizational transformation, the ultimate command or decision-making authority needs to be clearly delegated. I agree that there can be many different types of decision-making authority, but what I mean here is the "ultimate" decision-making authority. BGs are sales-revenue-oriented, while regional offices are profit-oriented. I believe that business decision-making authority should be given to regional offices. BGs should focus their efforts on building up resources, developing strategies, and taking part in operations. In order to increase sales revenue, BGs should find ways to persuade field commanders to adopt their points of view. I tend to agree that the Consumer BG holds the decision-making authority over its own business. For all other businesses, however, decision-making authority rests with regional offices. *(Ren Zhengfei: Speech at a Briefing on the Takeaways and Challenges for Huawei Relating to the "Squad Leaders' Fight", Huawei Executive Office Speech No. [2014] 078)*

When giving the ultimate decision-making authority to field commanders, it is important that we do not allow BGs or the Strategic Reserve to do what field commanders are supposed to do. If you do not think field commanders are up to the job, you can redeploy them and appoint new ones. However, the command authority should still remain with the field. In addition, I think we should delegate the decision-making authority on operational matters to subsidiary boards of directors. In the past, approval was made by HQ. But HQ cannot handle all approval requests. What kind of decision-making authority HQ should have? Decisions on solutions. Our experts have decision-making authority over solutions. When it comes to execution, however, the decision-making authority should rest with the field. Regarding the oversight over decisions made in the field, subsidiary boards of directors have a role to play. *(Ren Zhengfei: Speech at a Briefing on the Takeaways and Challenges for Huawei Relating to the "Squad Leaders' Fight", Huawei Executive Office Speech No. [2014] 078)*

This is what our transformation is about: laying the foundation for delegating more authority to the field. That is why we aim to streamline our LTC process over the next three to five years, and are striving to achieve the CIAG and Five Ones. Our subsidiary boards of directors are the oversight system of the company in the field. When they have the required oversight capabilities, we can delegate authority to our field command centers. *(Ren Zhengfei: Speech at the Oath-taking and Awards Ceremony of the Transformation Elite Team, Huawei Executive Office Speech No. [2015] 047)*

7.4.3 Moving Oversight to the Field While Delegating Authority to the Field

At HQ, we should streamline our organization and keep our processes simple. We should reduce direct command and remote control from HQ, move command centers to field offices, and give field teams the authority to perform their own planning, budgeting, and accounting. This means we are delegating the management and sales decision-making authority to field offices. Field offices need to have more tactical mobility to flexibly deal with changes in actual situations. Back offices need to step up their efforts to provide services based on plans and budgets and oversee the exercise of delegated authority through accounting. This can make sure field teams have the authority they need to get the job done and HQ doesn't need to worry about the authority being abused. *(Ren Zhengfei: Speech at the UK Representative Office, Huawei Executive Office Speech No. [2007] 027)*

We need to quickly establish a top-down oversight system that is independent of local offices. We can add independent directors or supervisors to our subsidiary boards of directors as oversight personnel. They can be non-Chinese. We need to optimize the governance structure of our subsidiaries and strengthen our oversight mechanism as we delegate authority to the field. *(Source: Resolution on Setting Roles of General Managers and Board Directors in Subsidiaries Outside China, EMT Resolution No. [2008] 004)*

Heads of business departments are the owners of oversight. We first need to make it clear that process owners are responsible for business self-checks, internal controls checks and assessments, and delegation system building. The Business Controls Department must not take the job of business departments. We must avoid such a situation where business owners don't care about oversight but oversight personnel are very active. This won't resolve issues. As business departments are not doing their job in a standardized manner, the Business Controls Department is there to help them standardize, ask process owners to fulfill oversight responsibilities, and through internal controls checks and assessments, encourage heads of business departments to be responsible for business within their own purview. The Business Controls Department has the authority to assess business departments, evaluate their managers, and even demand the removal of managers from their positions when necessary. *(Ren Zhengfei: Speech at a Briefing on Regional Oversight, 2007)*

It is necessary to build an effective auditing and oversight system during our transformation from a centralized governance model to a decentralized governance model in which authority is fully delegated and checks and balances are in place. *(Ren Zhengfei: Staying Customer-centric, Inspiring Dedication, and Persevering Are Key to Our Success—Speech at the 2010 Huawei Market Conference, Huawei Executive Office Speech No. [2010] 002)*

Oversight naturally conflicts with efficiency. We could let things pass quickly and examine what happens afterwards. We could also exert controls before things happen and ask business departments to explain them clearly before they can be passed. The approach we choose depends on our own judgment and understanding of the risks we face. *(Ren Zhengfei: Minutes of the Meeting with Staff of the Romania Accounting SSC, Huawei Executive Office Speech No. [2011] 021)*

We need to give more authority to the teams working closely with customers. Only such flexible strategies and tactics can increase customer satisfaction, help us succeed, develop managers, and improve business performance. When we delegate authority to the field, we also need to move our oversight to the field. *(Ren Zhengfei: Building a Highly Competitive Team—Speech at the Q3 Regional Presidents' Meeting, Huawei Executive Office Speech No. [2013] 093)*

Business departments oversee their own exercise of authority throughout business processes, whereas auditing personnel oversee process activities. This can ensure that exercise of authority is meaningful and reliable. *(Ren Zhengfei: Building a Highly Competitive Team—Speech at the Q3 Regional Presidents' Meeting, Huawei Executive Office Speech No. [2013] 093)*

Business managers are fully responsible for employee education and internal controls. Those who are not comfortable fulfilling these responsibilities will have to be transferred to operational positions. Business managers should perform well in employee education. This includes local managers educating local employees. We need to ensure managers fulfill their responsibilities of managing themselves, their subordinates, and their internal controls, and properly match authority with responsibilities for typical high-risk positions. We also need to implement key internal controls in our consumer business, delivery, sales, and enterprise business to effectively increase internal controls maturity. *(Ren Zhengfei: Speech at a Briefing on the Progress of Large-scale Elimination of Corruption, Huawei Executive Office Speech No. [2014] 010)*

7.4.4   Oversight Is the Means to Our End Goal: Business Success

We will focus on profits during our performance appraisals. Representative office managers should understand management, finance, and operations. They should also continuously improve internal management and reduce operating costs. We aim to establish a management model under which business plays a leading role and finance plays an oversight role at account departments and representative offices. While focusing on profit-centered performance appraisals and fine-grained management, our financial reports must be fact-based and must not be overly optimistic or pessimistic. Finance must provide support to business. *(Ren Zhengfei: Speech at the Report by the BT Account Department and the UK Representative Office, Huawei Executive Office Speech No. [2007] 015)*

We must gradually change HQ from a management and control center to a support and service center that also performs oversight functions. We need to develop capabilities that enable the front line to drive back offices. We need to plan and make a shift from centralized management and control to delegation of operations authority to entry-level operating teams, ensuring our command centers are as close to our customers as possible. We need to help organizations at all levels become profit centers that reflect their own business characteristics. *(Source: Resolution on the EMT's Priorities and Management Approaches from 2007 to 2009, EMT Resolution No. [2007] 012)*

We will continue delegating authority to managers at all levels. What are the primary responsibilities for all managers at Huawei? The first responsibility is to create value. The second responsibility is to implement effective oversight. We have delegated authority to you, so you must help us manage the business that is in your charge. If you simply let corruption occur or turn a blind eye to it, we will consider you unqualified for your job, and you will no longer be allowed to serve as a manager. If you exercise strict controls against corruption, your people will work hard with you to earn and share more bonuses. You, as a manager, will grow from this and your team will grow too. If you fail to conduct oversight, we cannot delegate authority to you, and you will be replaced by someone else. *(Ren Zhengfei: Speech at a Meeting with Trainees of the 10th Senior Management Seminar at Huawei University, Huawei Executive Office Speech No. [2011] 031)*

We need to further delegate authority to the field, as this can help us seize opportunities. Our HQ should mainly play service, support, and oversight roles to better support the field in serving customers and controlling risks. *(Ren Zhengfei: Focusing on Strategy and Streamlining Management, Huawei Executive Office Speech No. [2012] 041)*

Internal controls teams need to go out to the field and work closely with field teams to ensure efficient operations and appropriate oversight. Engineering inspection teams are currently tasked with combating widespread corruption. Internal controls teams need to work with engineering inspection teams to develop policies and methods that ensure scientific oversight. The purpose of oversight is to ensure smooth business operations. Oversight is the means to our end goal – business success. *(Ren Zhengfei: Speech at a Meeting with Financial Managers, Huawei Executive Office Speech No. [2012] 029)*

Trusting employees doesn't mean we don't need oversight. Oversight doesn't mean we don't trust employees. *(Ren Zhengfei: Building a Highly Competitive Team—Speech at the Q3 Regional Presidents' Meeting, Huawei Executive Office Speech No. [2013] 093)*

The ultimate purpose of establishing an oversight and accountability mechanism is to prevent corruption, support effective business operations, and achieve business success. *(Source: Minutes of the Report on the Charter for Building an Oversight and Accountability System, EMT Meeting Minutes No. [2014] 023)*

Oversight personnel should be well aware that we have been solving problems as we move forward, rather than stopping to solve all our problems before moving on. Huawei would have stopped moving forward a long time ago if we did that. Therefore, we still emphasize solving problems as we move forward. We must not stop moving on because of corruption or ignore corruption in order to develop. The purpose of establishing an oversight system is to ensure the company's long-term development. *(Xu Zhijun: "Cure the Disease and Save the Patient": Let Our People Start Afresh and Do Their Jobs Without the Weight of the Past on Their Shoulders, Huawei Executive Office Speech No. [2015] 064)*

7.5 STREAMLINING OUR ORGANIZATIONS AND PROCESSES TO CREATE VALUE FOR CUSTOMERS

7.5.1 Simplicity Is Key: Standardizing and Streamlining Routine Management

To ensure Huawei's long-term survival and development, we must standardize our procedures. Foreign companies have scientific procedures in place for every payment they make. Why don't we learn from them? When standardized procedures are running smoothly, our finance system will become an open system and you will have more freedom rather than more constraints. *(Ren Zhengfei: Speech at a Meeting with Financial Managers, 1995)*

The primary goal of our management transformations is to increase efficiency and *harvest more crops*. During this process, we must also integrate our processes from end to end to streamline management. So long as our 150,000 employees stay united, our value management system is basically correct, and we continue to optimize and streamline our management, we will be a highly competent company. I believe that in five years, we will catch up with today's Ericsson in terms of management. What do we need to do right now? We need to implement management transformations to mobilize our employees. *(Ren Zhengfei: Speech at the Report on the Integrated Management Transformation in Small Countries, Huawei Executive Office Speech No. [2014] 062)*

We need to establish standardized and simplified shared services centers. How can our IT systems support our strategic command and delegation system? How can we implement a process ownership system? It's harder than just pressing a button and giving orders. We have to think about who will be responsible for oversight, statistics, and testing. The purpose of transforming our shared services centers is to make them simpler and more standard and their services easier to use. Personnel in our Quality, Business Process & IT Management Department must not always pursue innovation. They must not make our processes too complicated. The purpose of any of our transformations is to *harvest more crops and increase soil fertility*. Transformations that do not serve this purpose are redundant and should be stopped. *(Ren Zhengfei: Building High-Quality IT Systems Using Advanced Software Packages from Europe and the US—Speech at a Work Report by the Quality, Business Process & IT Management Department, Huawei Executive Office Speech No. [2015] 010)*

We should allow those who are closest to customers to call for support. Simplicity is key. Our authority must be delegated level by level, and our management must be standardized and streamlined. We should spend less time on meetings, simplify our appraisals, and have fewer examinations. We should not manage our employees as if they were students, let alone allow examination scores to impact their compensation. Our energy should mainly be focused on *harvesting more crops* and our appraisals should be based on contributions. *(Ren Zhengfei: Our Transformation Goals Are to Harvest More Crops and Increase Soil Fertility—Speech at the 2015 Huawei Market Conference, Huawei Executive Office Speech No. [2015] 016)*

Stable processes should be gradually standardized and streamlined. This can increase our capability to provide services promptly, and cut period and management costs. Issues of uncertainty should be transferred to departments responsible for miscellaneous issues. *(Ren Zhengfei: Our Transformation Goals Are to Harvest More Crops and Increase Soil Fertility—Speech at the 2015 Huawei Market Conference, Huawei Executive Office Speech No. [2015] 016)*

Strategic Reserve training needs to be scenario-based and focus on practice. The Transformation Project Team and Huawei University must collaborate to rotate golden seeds and let them unleash their potential. Both are required to identify several scenario types and develop tailored templates and case studies. This will provide representative offices with a full set of standardized methods to handle any scenario they may encounter. Strategic Reserve training needs to be scenario-based. There is no urgent need to train people for all scenarios. If someone understands one scenario, they will likely be able to understand others more easily. *(Ren Zhengfei: Speech at the Briefing on the Transformation Elite Team and Related Progress, Huawei Executive Office Speech No. [2015] 026)*

Our management needs to be standardized and streamlined in order to increase efficiency. Process owners need to promptly and accurately provide services, and quickly check relevant issues based on simple and standard processes without exercising excessive oversight. We have told the Consumer BG repeatedly that they need to make simple and standardized products that are maintenance-free during their lifecycles. Our aim should be to make the device manufacturing process similar to printing money. Similarly, their management needs to be standardized and streamlined with clear instructions like a high-speed railway. Why do we need to have so many checkpoints? It's really unnecessary. We must increase efficiency. HQ must provide services to field offices, and slash the number of meaningless checks. Our accounting system is like a sieve that allows most grains to pass through unhindered. Only one or two grains are caught by the sieve. Those grains represent issues that need to be reported and addressed. Currently, in some parts of our processes, information is flowing even more slowly than physical goods, which indicates that there are a lot of internal obstacles. If a manager is incapable of doing their job well, we should replace them with someone more capable as soon as possible. This is what the process ownership system is all about. *(Ren Zhengfei: Speech at a Meeting with the Managerial Control Elite Team, Huawei Executive Office Speech No. [2015] 060)*

In the future, we will set standard prices for standard products, beginning with boxes. Things that are uncertain – including customs clearance, engineering, and delivery – should be taken care of by representative offices. Land and sea shipment expenses will be allocated to beneficiary departments based on the amounts shipped. This mechanism will simplify appraisals, help people in remote markets, and allow the company to have less intermediate links. We currently have hundreds of different prices for the same equipment, because we factor expenses such as shipment and customs clearance into the prices. The pricing is so complex that representative offices cannot do it. As a result, the job has to be shifted back to HQ. We should continue to simplify the process. We will reduce headcount in field offices and at the same time streamline management at functional departments in back offices. *(Ren Zhengfei: Speech at the EMT ST Meeting on January 25, 2016, Huawei Executive Office Speech No. [2016] 054)*

Our business is growing, and our global presence is expanding. In spite of established processes and systems, our oversight still cannot be perfect all the time. Therefore, we still require self-discipline from our managers and employees to lower management costs. We also need to identify, select, and develop new managers in great numbers. To become outstanding managers, you need to create value and prevent problems through effective management, governance, and internal controls. The more systematic and process-driven we are, the more conscientious we need to be. This is similar to the relationship between the rule of law and religious belief in Western countries. We have established systems, but faithful adherence is necessary to ensure compliance. Can you imagine how much it would cost if we had to establish different layers of oversight for every single possibility? *(Ren Zhengfei: Speech at the Huawei Market Conference on January 11, 2017, Huawei Executive Office Speech No. [2017] 007)*

Functional departments at back offices should provide capabilities that are specialized enough to satisfy different needs. These capabilities should also be made easily accessible to field offices. Field offices should be given the authority to orchestrate these capabilities. This is similar to the Chinese online doctor consultation platform "Hao Yisheng" ("Good-Doctor"), which uses utilization rates (like data traffic) as a standard for assessing departments that provide services. If the capabilities of certain departments are not utilized often, it may mean that they are not urgently needed. If this happens, we will first enhance departments who face greater demand, the same way we deal with spikes in data traffic. Then we should look at the workload of each employee and determine promotions accordingly. If a department's capabilities are rarely used, its headcount should be reduced. *(Ren Zhengfei: Speech at a Carrier BG Briefing on the Progress of Three Cloud 2.0, Huawei Executive Office Speech No. [2017] 018)*

To streamline processes and make them transparent, you need to begin with their source. If the source data is not accurate, data in the downstream may not be accurate, either. We must have standards in place for the introduction of new products. We need to consider whether products are manufacturable, deliverable, easy to maintain, or even maintenance-free before we begin developing them. How can we ensure that the new products we introduce meet our standards? The product acceptance template is like a sieve. Our R&D has to test things through the sieve. Things that can't pass through the sieve must not be produced. This will force our R&D to improve. Our R&D personnel need to learn these standards well and early on, so more of their work will pass through the sieve. They have to standardize their own work using your template. If they think there are issues with your template, they can discuss with you and together you can make improvements. *(Ren Zhengfei: Our Aim Is to Achieve High Quality—Speech at a Tour to the Songshan Lake Factory, Huawei Executive Office Speech No. [2017] 036)*

7.5.2 *Any Department or Process That Doesn't Create Value for Customers Is Redundant*

Managers at all levels must focus their efforts on creating value and improving business. They should continuously improve their business capabilities, increase service quality, reduce operating costs, streamline processes, optimize organizations, and reasonably reduce headcount. These initiatives will allow our company to hone our competitive edge and improve our extensive relationships with customers. *(Ren Zhengfei: Minutes of a Talk at the Xinsheng Building, 2012)*

One goal of our transformation is to *harvest more crops*, including sales revenue, profits, high-quality delivery, efficiency improvements, the CIAG, and the "Five Ones". The other goal is to *increase soil fertility*, which includes strategic contributions, customer satisfaction, and effective risk management. Processes and systems that cannot directly or indirectly contribute to these two goals should gradually be streamlined. Only by doing so can we maintain our competitive advantages while remaining customer-centric. *(Ren Zhengfei: Our Transformation Goals Are to Harvest More Crops and Increase Soil Fertility—Speech at the 2015 Huawei Market Conference, Huawei Executive Office Speech No. [2015] 016)*

We must learn a lesson from the sinking of the Vasa warship.[3] Warships are intended for battle, so any ornamentation is unnecessary. During our transformation, we must avoid taking unnecessary actions and making processes complex. The purpose of our transformation is to create value for customers. Departments, processes, and personnel that cannot directly or indirectly create customer value are redundant. We must keep this purpose in mind while streamlining our organizations and processes. *(Ren Zhengfei: Our Transformation Goals Are to Harvest More Crops and Increase Soil Fertility—Speech at the 2015 Huawei Market Conference, Huawei Executive Office Speech No. [2015] 016)*

The Regions Management Department should arrange for employees to study Huawei Executive Office E-mail Speech No. [2015] 016 Our Transformation Goals Are to Harvest More Crops and Increase Soil Fertility. Managers are required to write takeaways from this speech, list the problems that exist in their departments, and formulate plans on how they can solve them. They must avoid empty talk. Processes that don't help us harvest more crops or increase soil fertility are redundant, and must be eliminated. In some parts of our processes, information is flowing even more slowly than physical goods, indicating there are too many check points and our HQ is too bloated. So we need to reduce the number of managers and increase the number of experts. HQ managers who don't have much work to do can be transferred to the Strategic Reserve and gain field experience. Managers at HQ must have field experience and must

---

[3] The Vasa is a retired Swedish warship built during the early seventeenth century. The ship was richly decorated, a symbol of Sweden's "great power period", but was also unstable and top-heavy. This lack of stability resulted in the Vasa sinking minutes into its maiden voyage.

have served as project managers. As our organization gradually matures, we must remove duplicate processes and work, minimize the amount of work that creates no real value, and streamline our processes. In the next couple of years, we should fast-track the promotions of hundreds of outstanding project managers. They will serve as role models for other managers. *(Ren Zhengfei: Minutes of the Briefing on the Progress of Differentiated Appraisals for Regions, Huawei Executive Office Speech No. [2015] 050)*

Due to a lack of clear transformation goals, we made our management system over-complicated, added many unnecessary procedures, and employed tens of thousands of new staff. Now we need to make things simpler and gradually downsize. We have set a goal for our transformation, which is to *harvest more crops*. Anything that doesn't help us *harvest more crops* is meaningless. Any process, department, or employee that doesn't help us *harvest more crops* is redundant. That's the principle we should follow when we seek to streamline management. Of course, strategic investment in projects that *increase our soil fertility* will also enable us to *harvest more crops*. As we follow that principle, there'll be fewer loopholes in our system, our processes will run faster, and we'll be able to reduce our headcount more rapidly. We shouldn't overemphasize risks or set up too many risk control points for our processes. One representative office once held quite a few meetings over a matter worth 10 yuan. How much did these meetings cost? *(Ren Zhengfei: Speech at a Meeting with the Managerial Control Elite Team, Huawei Executive Office Speech No. [2015] 060)*

When we sent out the article *Is the US Military Still Capable of Fighting a War* as a Huawei Executive Office E-mail, I wrote a little introduction, where I said, "A soldier's responsibility is to achieve victory. Making sacrifices is simply a mindset." Becoming a general is not just about enduring hardships. You also have to contribute. Learning must be well-targeted as well. What is the use of a bellyful of knowledge without the ability to create value? A process, department, or person that puts no food on the table is redundant. They should all be cut. *(Ren Zhengfei: Generals Are Born of Battle—Speech at the 2015 Project Management Summit, Huawei Executive Office Speech No. [2015] 118)*

We should stay focused during our transformation and IT system development. This means that we should reduce the number of our transformations and must not have too many IT systems. For every new segment or checkpoint we add to our processes, we must eliminate two existing ones. Processes should serve our operations and help us *harvest more crops*. Are underused processes redundant? If a process is streamlined day by day, some people might complain. You should go and talk with them and check whether their requirements can be integrated into other processes. Of course, we can't simply eliminate individual processes, as that might result in breakpoints and conflicts, and eventually failure. *(Ren Zhengfei: Speech at a Meeting with Employees of the Quality, Business Process & IT Management Department, Huawei Executive Office Speech No. [2016] 094)*

Open Access This chapter is licensed under the terms of the Creative Commons Attribution-NonCommercial-NoDerivatives 4.0 International License (http://creativecommons.org/licenses/by-nc-nd/4.0/), which permits any noncommercial use, sharing, distribution and reproduction in any medium or format, as long as you give appropriate credit to the original author(s) and the source, provide a link to the Creative Commons licence and indicate if you modified the licensed material. You do not have permission under this license to share adapted material derived from this chapter or parts of it.

The images or other third party material in this chapter are included in the chapter's Creative Commons licence, unless indicated otherwise in a credit line to the material. If material is not included in the chapter's Creative Commons licence and your intended use is not permitted by statutory regulation or exceeds the permitted use, you will need to obtain permission directly from the copyright holder.

CHAPTER 8

Financial Management Throughout End-to-End Business Processes

At Huawei, business plays a leading role and accounting plays an oversight role. Finance is positioned to serve business and create value, with its oversight role integrated into processes. The goals for the first phase of the Integrated Financial Services (IFS) program are: accurately recognizing revenue, accelerating cash inflows, ensuring visibility of project profits and losses, and managing business risks. These goals are set to address weak links of the company's end-to-end business processes for value creation. It is a long-term task for Huawei to build and continuously improve its process-based organization and management systems for major business processes.

Opportunity to Cash (OTC) is a major business process that defines how Huawei does business with its customers. It carries the company's major flows of physical goods, money, and working capital. To ensure the process runs smoothly, Huawei must first improve contract quality at the very beginning to control contract risks. Second, the company must go back over the entire OTC process, with a focus on billing, to review and streamline all activities and work requirements as necessary. Third, to make the process run faster, the company must keep customer PO information transparent throughout the process and transform related business processes in an integrated manner.

Integrated Product Development (IPD) is a major process for market-oriented innovation. In this process, Finance manages product development as an investment. Finance needs to focus on how to monetize

© The Author(s) 2019
W. Huang, *Built on Value*,
https://doi.org/10.1007/978-981-13-7507-1_8

opportunities and plays an active role in IPD's cross-departmental decision making, decision checkpoint (DCP) reviews, and product portfolio management. Finance can make the product development process visible and support the commercial success of product development through planning, budgeting, and accounting.

Benchmarked against IBM's procurement process, Huawei's Procure-to-Pay (PTP) process includes a clear matrix of separation of duties (SOD) and assessment mechanisms. To ensure payment security, key control points (KCPs) are set at all stages of the process, including invoice receiving and processing, invoice matching, duplicate payment checking, and payment. To ensure project operations responsibilities are properly fulfilled, the company takes a methodical approach to project-driven procurement and stretches procurement cost accounting down to the project level. This way, procurement processes are integrated with financial processes.

Clouds, *rainwater*, and *channels* are how Huawei describes its approach to management transformation. Huawei's management philosophy is like a *cloud*; *rainwater* is Huawei's business activities; and *channels* are processes and rules established through systematic transformation after Huawei's operations were benchmarked against the best practices of Western companies. *Clouds* are valuable only when they turn into *rainwater*. And the *rainwater* needs to be channeled properly in order to generate electricity. Without the right *channels* to guide the *rainwater*, it will flow anywhere, and its energy will dissipate.

This chapter describes how financial management is integrated into Huawei's three major end-to-end business processes and how Finance provides effective oversight while serving business.

8.1 Financial Management Throughout the OTC Process

8.1.1 KCPs Throughout the OTC Process

Building a process-based organization and management system that suits the OTC process is a long-term task for Huawei

Bidding, contract signing, delivery, billing, and payment collection are the key stages of one of our company's major business processes. They largely determine the flow of our physical goods and cash. One of our long-term tasks is to build a process-based organization and management system tailored to this major business process. Growing from a small company, we've always operated less efficiently than our Western peers. We have serious overlapping, disconnection, duplication, low efficiency, and segmented processes in operations and delivery. We lag far behind our peers when it comes to Days Sales Outstanding (DSO) and Inventory Turnover (ITO). There is still much we can do to improve inventory and cash turnover, and reduce end-to-end costs. This is a key battlefield on which we should implement our "Dig In and Widen Out" strategy. IPD, another major business process, is another area where we can build cost advantages into product design. *(Ren Zhengfei: Digging In, Widening Out—Speech at the Commendation Meeting of the Operations and Delivery Division, Huawei Executive Office Speech No. [2009] 009)*

Net cash inflow is the lifeline of our company

Without water and food, you would burn to death in a desert. Whether or not our company can maintain steady growth depends on whether we have enough food. Winter is coming. We must prepare enough clothing. What exactly is our company's clothing though? Internally, it is cash flow; externally, it is market size and market space. *(Ren Zhengfei: Corporate Development Should Focus on Meeting the Current Needs of Customers—Speech at a Meeting with Key Employees of the Optical Network Product Line on April 18, 2002)*

Maintaining sufficient cash flow is the only way for us to survive. Our biggest risk is cash flow, not anything else. *(Ren Zhengfei: Strengthening Payment Collection and Improving Cash Flow—Speech at the EMT ST Meeting on February 28, 2006, Huawei Executive Office Speech No. [2006] 007)*

Net cash inflow is the lifeline of our company. We must place more emphasis on net cash flow during performance appraisals. And now we must assign a proper weight to net cash flow during representative office performance appraisals. During this process, we must avoid being too radical as this may make us unable to incentivize or push the offices to maintain a proper net cash flow. *(Source: Minutes of the Report on the Performance Appraisal and Incentivization Plan for Frontline BUs, EMT Meeting Minutes No. [2009] 006)*

We can conduct more business in countries with strict foreign exchange controls if we can repatriate more money. We need to adopt a pragmatic approach in these countries. What are real customer needs? Those are the needs of customers that can pay. In these countries, payment collection is our biggest difficulty. If we can collect payments, we won't worry about sales; we may even raise prices. *(Ren Zhengfei: Minutes of the Work Report by the Algeria Representative Office, Huawei Executive Office Speech No. [2014] 070)*

In countries with strict foreign exchange controls, we should base our investment on how much money we can collect. We decide to take contracts based on how much money we can repatriate back to China. The value of a contract can be 10% or 20% higher than the amount that can be repatriated. Our only way to weather the current financial crisis is to boost efficiency and profitability as much as we can. If we can do that, then the financial crisis will not affect us. The crisis is not over and will last a long time. *(Ren Zhengfei: Comments to Staff of the Brazil Representative Office and Brazil Supply Center, Huawei Executive Office Speech No. [2014] 050)*

Accurately recognizing revenue based on contract terms and project delivery status

Since 2009, we have recognized revenue upon receipt of preliminary acceptance certificates (PACs). This way we can appropriately match revenue recognition with cash inflows. However, we should not simply recognize revenue upon the receipt of a single document. We must also look at project delivery status to match revenue recognition with actual business progress. Project financial controllers (PFCs) must assume this responsibility. *(Ren Zhengfei: Keeping Customer PO Information Transparent to Support Payment Collection, Revenue Recognition, and Project Budgeting and Accounting—Speech at a Work Report by the IFS Project Team on December 29, Huawei Executive Office Speech No. [2009] 002)*

We cannot take a one-size-fits-all approach to revenue recognition. Business departments are the owners of revenue recognition. They must promptly provide Finance with the key information that supports revenue recognition. Finance then needs to carefully check the information and determine an appropriate method and timing for revenue recognition based on contract terms. *(Ren Zhengfei: Keeping Customer PO Information Transparent to Support Payment Collection, Revenue Recognition, and Project Budgeting and Accounting—Speech at a Work Report by the IFS Project Team on December 29, Huawei Executive Office Speech No. [2009] 002)*

Setting up a joint liability system for billing; the purpose of delivery is to collect payments

We must create a solid "Iron Triangle" team for billing and payment collection. In this team, the sales financing and payment collection manager must collaborate closely with both the front-end contract manager and the back-end delivery manager. This creates a robust triangle. We must also develop a joint liability system for billing, under which the three managers will be jointly responsible. In fact, these three roles constitute a billing team. *(Ren Zhengfei: Keeping Customer PO Information Transparent to Support Payment Collection, Revenue Recognition, and Project Budgeting and Accounting—Speech at a Work Report by the IFS Project Team on December 29, Huawei Executive Office Speech No. [2009] 002)*

We must deliver projects and collect payments according to visible progress, or delivery milestones. For example, we can collect partial payment after we finish laying the foundation of a house, even though we have not finished building the entire house. *(Ren Zhengfei: Keeping Customer PO Information Transparent to Support Payment Collection, Revenue Recognition, and Project Budgeting and Accounting—Speech at a Work Report by the IFS Project Team on December 29, Huawei Executive Office Speech No. [2009] 002)*

We must build a mechanism for regular customer communication to ensure payments are collected based on delivery milestones and to make billing more accurate and effective. The Accounting Management Department is responsible for exercising internal controls over invoices. *(Ren Zhengfei: Keeping Customer PO Information Transparent to Support Payment Collection, Revenue Recognition, and Project Budgeting and Accounting—Speech at a Work Report by the IFS Project Team on December 29, Huawei Executive Office Speech No. [2009] 002)*

We must systematically manage billed and unbilled accounts receivable (AR). We must also establish a responsibility matrix for handling AR disputes and clearly identify who is responsible for dispute management. These individuals are usually representative office deputy general managers or regional vice presidents in charge of sales. *(Ren Zhengfei: Keeping Customer PO Information Transparent to Support Payment Collection, Revenue Recognition, and Project Budgeting and Accounting—Speech at a Work Report by the IFS Project Team on December 29, Huawei Executive Office Speech No. [2009] 002)*

The purpose of managing credit is to drive healthy, sustainable growth in sales and allocate resources to more valuable projects. The job of the credit management team is to disclose risks. Sales teams make decisions on these risks within the scope of their authority. *(Ren Zhengfei: Keeping Customer PO Information Transparent to Support Payment Collection,*

Revenue Recognition, and Project Budgeting and Accounting—Speech at a Work Report by the IFS Project Team on December 29, Huawei Executive Office Speech No. [2009] 002)

The sales department must provide complete and correct contract information to downstream departments

We only have two stages: securing a contract and fulfilling a contract. What matters during these two stages are implementation costs and final profits. The core terms of a contract like delivery and payment are very important. The sales department must provide complete and correct contract information to downstream departments. *(Ren Zhengfei: Keeping Customer PO Information Transparent to Support Payment Collection, Revenue Recognition, and Project Budgeting and Accounting—Speech at a Work Report by the IFS Project Team on December 29, Huawei Executive Office Speech No. [2009] 002)*

Making changes to a contract is inevitable during sales. The key to contract changes is not the changes themselves. What actually matters is ensuring that the contract management and delivery teams are accurately informed of the changes. *(Ren Zhengfei: Keeping Customer PO Information Transparent to Support Payment Collection, Revenue Recognition, and Project Budgeting and Accounting—Speech at a Work Report by the IFS Project Team on December 29, Huawei Executive Office Speech No. [2009] 002)*

Better managing the end-to-end delivery process

We must gradually integrate project delivery plans with manufacturing and shipment plans. We must manage shipment, delivery, acceptance, and payment collection on a site-by-site basis. Site-based shipment and management is an important way to increase the efficiency of working capital and achieve rapid and low-cost delivery. *(Source: Resolution on Enhancing Working Capital Management and Achieving Site-based Shipment by Managers at All Levels, EMT Resolution No. [2007] 040)*

We must better manage the end-to-end delivery process. During current contract execution, functional departments are only responsible for specific segments of the process from bidding to payment collection. An individual or a team must be designated to monitor and coordinate the entire process and be accountable for its final results. The IPD management system already ensures that the IPD process flows smoothly from end to end. The next step is to establish a department responsible for delivery from end to end and to develop an operational mechanism. We must shorten days in inventory and the acceptance cycle by improving contract quality, project delivery, and acceptance, and providing timely and whole-set shipments to sites. It's important to remain realistic when we set improvement targets. Our targets must be objective and measurable. *(Source: Guidelines for Delivery, Working Capital Management, and Team Building, EMT Meeting Minutes No. [2008] 013)*

We must streamline cost management from end to end and avoid fragmented cost management. By relying on its cost committee, each product line needs to coordinate the cost management efforts of all relevant functions like manufacturing, logistics, project delivery, maintenance, R&D, and technical sales. All the costs must be reflected in product package requirements. This way, we can build our cost competitiveness into the design and R&D stages of our process. We don't want to play whack-a-mole or do meaningless work. *(Source: Minutes of the Report on the 2009 H1 Performance Review, EMT Meeting Minutes No. [2009] 038)*

We must take an end-to-end approach to the transformation of our supply chain, which means we should aim to be the best in every link of our chain. First, we need to make our R&D the best in the world. This does not just mean that our R&D personnel feel that we are the best. Our customers must also feel the same way. Second, we need to make our manufacturing the best in the world. Since we are an industry leader in R&D, our manufacturing must also be industry-leading. Third, we must make sure our shipments are done right. We must have correct contracts and deliver on the contracts, covering all supply chain and contract acquisition activities. Fourth, we must provide the best services. Since we earn money from customers, we need to serve them well, no matter how difficult it is. Customers are always there and we need to make them happy. Otherwise, we will not be able to survive. *(Ren Zhengfei: Doing It Right the First Time—Speech at the Global Warehouse Meeting, Huawei Executive Office Speech No. [2014] 060)*

8.1.2 Controlling Contract Quality at the Very Beginning

We need to improve our contract quality and reduce contract risks and gradually move from massive, low-margin growth to more profitable growth. We will gradually strengthen the assessment and control of contract risks to gradually improve contract quality. We must focus on target carriers and further standardize business activities such as financing and payment collection. *(Ren Zhengfei: Speech at a Meeting with Members of the Financing Team, 2005)*

We will gradually strengthen the assessment and control of contract risks to gradually improve contract quality. The Treasury Management Department must get closer to financial resources and the Market Finance Department must get closer to customers. No matter how tough a project is, the Market Finance Department must learn how to understand customer needs, provide guidance for financing, avoid major risks, and facilitate project success. Since the Market Finance Department takes different approaches in different circumstances, their job is difficult and they must be good strategists when on the front line. *(Ren Zhengfei: Speech at a Meeting with Members of the Financing Team, 2005)*

A good contract lays the foundation for high-quality delivery and profitability. We must stick to our principles during contract negotiations, fight for favorable contract terms, and avoid making unprincipled concessions. *(Source: Guidelines for Delivery, Working Capital Management, and Team Building, EMT Meeting Minutes No. [2008] 013)*

We don't encourage last-minute rushes to get sales orders, because that sacrifices contract quality and compromises the company's future development. Financial analysis must provide both positive and negative feedback on the company's operations management to truly reflect performance. Finance must have checks and balances in place to control last-minute rushes. It must also continue to step up efforts to audit business data, ensuring that financial data correctly mirrors company performance. *(Source: Minutes of the Report on the 2011 H1 Performance Review, EMT Meeting Minutes No. [2011] 011)*

Regional and representative office CFOs are responsible for overseeing the quality of contracts in regions within their purview. They must dare to veto poor-quality contracts. This can help establish checks and balances between regional CEOs and CFOs. CFOs at all levels must participate in pre-sales contract reviews and must have the courage to veto poor-quality contracts. Contracts vetoed by CFOs must be escalated to a higher-level contract review team. The contract review team of the same level will no longer have the decision-making authority over the vetoed contracts. CFOs that can't handle this work must be replaced promptly. *(Source: Minutes of the Report on the 2011 H1 Performance Review, EMT Meeting Minutes No. [2011] 011)*

Transaction quality is not the same as contract quality. Contract quality is not the same as contract terms. Our ultimate goal is to improve transaction quality and achieve our expected operating results, rather than to simply improve the quality of contract terms. We must not forget that we are building a church when moving bricks. A good contract is made in the initial phases of project operations, and is not the result of contract review. To improve contract quality, we need to do more in initial project phases and in building customer relationships. We can't just focus on contract terms. More importantly, we can't simply compromise our profits or overpromise during contract negotiations. *(Source: Minutes of the Report on Improving Contract Quality, EMT Meeting Minutes No. [2011] 012)*

We are overly random in our contract terms, which creates huge risk. At the moment, a contract takes effect as soon as it is signed by a frontline manager. We must change this practice. We need to build a centralized transaction management center and a mechanism for contract approval. A contract must be signed by those with the authority to do so. Not everyone has the authority to sign a contract. All contractual documents need to be signed by authorized staff. Contractual documents include but are not limited to bids, quotations, clarification letters, contracts, appendixes, PowerPoint presentations, and emails that could be viewed as elements of a contract by local law. *(Ren Zhengfei: Speech at the EMT ST Meeting, August 31, 2012)*

We must establish approaches, management systems, and associated performance appraisal systems to improve contract quality from end to end. Improvements in contract quality must be given full consideration in performance appraisals and incentive mechanisms. Performance appraisals must be closely linked to sales revenue, profits, and cash flow. Incentive mechanisms should give higher bonuses to operating units that have better contract quality, and those with poor contract quality must bear the losses. *(Ren Zhengfei: Guidelines on the Analysis of the Business Environment and Key Business Strategies, Corp. Doc. No. [2012] 081)*

Customers need advanced, high-quality, and cost-effective products, along with good services. We want market success and profits. In addition, we need to address the conflict between increasing compensation requirements of our excellent employees and the company's necessity of investing more in cutting-edge technologies. Therefore, when we negotiate on prices and commercial contract terms, it doesn't mean we are not humble. *(Ren Zhengfei: Being a Humble Leader—Speech at the 2014 Huawei Market Conference, Huawei Executive Office Speech No. [2014] 014)*

When we say "from end to end", both ends are customer needs. For Huawei, starting and ending with customer needs is currently unrealistic and difficult. So we must make this process shorter: from the company to representative offices and from representative offices to sites. We must start with signing high-quality contracts and accurately understanding customer needs. We must better understand customer needs and improve our execution skills to ensure that everything at the source is accurate. We have come this far, but just think about how much money we have wasted along the way. We have launched the Five Ones and CIAG projects, but no matter how important they are, ensuring the accuracy of customer needs – the source of everything we do – is still the most important. We are still unclear about many contract scenarios, so we need to gradually standardize them as this will help increase efficiency. This is the first point I want to make. The second point is that we must have accurate contract estimation. These are our two weaknesses in customer engagement. Right now, our delivery is only confined to project delivery, but this does not mean this is our sole goal. We must also accurately understand customer needs and improve contract quality as this is the source of everything we do. *(Ren Zhengfei: Speech at a Meeting with Employees of the Peru Representative Office, Huawei Executive Office Speech No. [2014] 040)*

We used to focus on sales. Now, we have shifted our focus to developing representative offices in an all-round manner. Representative office profit growth must be built on high-quality contracts. Our contracts must undergo two approvals. First, configuration and price clauses must be approved, and second, contractual commitments must be approved. The Regions Management Department needs to develop a guide for this, stipulating which clauses cannot be skipped during the collective review of contracts. What caused the Central Bank of Bahrain to collapse? It was the bank's unclear authorization system. During the second collective contract review, you first need to check whether all products to be sold are on the approved list of sellable products. You must not make a commitment on products not on the list. Second, you must review and check items like whether there are clauses stipulating the beginning and ending years of a contract, whether fees and interests are claimed for delayed payments, and whether legal compliance is ensured. *(Ren Zhengfei: There Will Not Always Be Flowers Along the Road Ahead—Speech at the H1 Huawei Market Conference, Huawei Executive Office Speech No. [2016] 079)*

Sales people need to thoroughly analyze and understand many scenarios. There is a wide range of expertise that sales people can study. Where should they start? The company emphasizes two things. One is contract quality improvement. Managers cannot improve contract quality by being overconfident or making rash decisions. Contract quality involves a lot of scenario design. Contract scenario experts play a very important role in this process. The other thing is scenario-targeted improvement during contract execution. Contract scenario experts can play a role in improving both contract quality and delivery quality. I hope that our contract scenario experts will be able to take up these meaningful responsibilities in sales. You can envision future trends with the big picture in mind. You have to shoulder greater responsibility to grow, to play a truly meaningful role, and to advance your position in the company. The role of contract scenario expert is something new. You can discuss and decide what responsibilities this role should assume. You need to know what the top priorities are in the eyes of regional presidents. You should think about how you can become a Liu Yalou,[1] and the chief-of-staff to your commander! *(Ren Zhengfei: Speech at a Meeting with Contract Scenario Experts, Huawei Executive Office Speech No. [2017] 020)*

8.1.3 Integrating Payment Collection, Revenue Recognition, and Project Budgeting and Accounting Based on Customer Contracts/POs

Reviewing and streamlining activities and work requirements, with a focus on billing

Billing means we issue a customer-accepted invoice based on a contract. As long as we complete billing, it means the customer has formally accepted the project delivered by Huawei, and is obligated to make payment. It also means that all barriers of payment collection on the Huawei side have been removed. Therefore, we must look back over the OTC process, with a focus on billing, and review and streamline activities and work requirements as necessary. In other words, we must coordinate all our efforts based on billing requirements and analyze how we should sign contracts and deliver projects by looking back over the process. *(Source: Resolution on Process Optimization at Representative Offices, EMT Resolution No. [2009] 003)*

Delivery project managers must develop delivery plans based on the delivery units and billing schedules stipulated in contracts, deliver projects as stipulated, and promptly trigger billing. Effectively triggering billing is an important responsibility for delivery project managers and as such is

---

[1] General Liu Yalou (April 1910–May 1965) was the first commander-in-chief of the People's Liberation Army Air Force, known for his victories in Manchuria during the Chinese Civil War.

one of their KPIs. Only when a project is successfully delivered and a customer-accepted invoice is issued can we say that delivery project managers have effectively fulfilled their responsibilities. Delivery project managers are responsible for the effectiveness and authenticity of billing, or customer-accepted invoices. They must properly manage their projects' contracts and POs, and completely and accurately record any configuration information or changes about sites delivered. The contract managers of the Contract Support Office (CSO) are responsible for triggering and managing billing. Business personnel must ensure business authenticity while financial personnel must faithfully keep accounts and play an auditing role. *(Source: Resolution on Process Optimization at Representative Offices, EMT Resolution No. [2009] 003)*

Keeping PO information transparent throughout the OTC process

Customers are placing a greater number of small POs under framework contracts. This trend will continue. As customer needs become increasingly diverse, customization will become a trend in the industry. Our competitiveness will then rely more on management than on technology. The biggest issue we have in keeping customer PO information transparent throughout the OTC process lies in the inconsistencies between our POs and customers'. As a result, customer PO information is missing during fulfillment within Huawei. Additionally, our IT systems cannot process POs in an automated and integrated manner. We need to integrate both data flows and business flows. An IT system has no value unless it actually helps with business operations. *(Ren Zhengfei: Keeping Customer PO Information Transparent to Support Payment Collection, Revenue Recognition, and Project Budgeting and Accounting—Speech at a Work Report by the IFS Project Team on December 29, Huawei Executive Office Speech No. [2009] 002)*

PO bundling is forbidden because it makes it harder for downstream departments to understand the PO and increases fulfillment costs. We must forbid PO bundling and encourage large framework contracts under which small POs can be placed. The company must make it very clear that POs cannot be bundled and contracts must be separately signed for different types of business. Supply chain and GTS departments must manage their work by customer PO. *(Ren Zhengfei: Keeping Customer PO Information Transparent to Support Payment Collection, Revenue Recognition, and Project Budgeting and Accounting—Speech at a Work Report by the IFS Project Team on December 29, Huawei Executive Office Speech No. [2009] 002)*

To address pain points relating to the OTC process, the IFS project team has developed a solution for integrating payment collection, revenue recognition, and project budgeting and accounting based on customer contracts and POs. This solution addresses problems that have plagued the company for years, effectively integrating transaction processes with financial processes, clarifying operational requirements, and improving data quality. Over the past few years, the company has seen an increase in its operating efficiency. This would have been impossible without the efficient collaboration between different departments. *(Meng Wanzhou: Growing amid Transformation—Thoughts at the Closing of the IFS Program, Improvement Issue No. 463, 2014)*

We must stay focused on our core business and integrate processes based on contract information flows. Contract information includes information about contract generation, project delivery, and payment collection. We can put other information aside for the time being. I previously said at a Lead to Cash (LTC) meeting that we aim to integrate contract information flows, and can put other modules aside, including optimization and capability modules. The GTS process has been basically integrated, and Yan Lida[2] has managed to basically integrate the Enterprise BG's processes. The remaining systems that cannot be integrated are those we have been using for many years. Why have they become so entangled? Because we haven't focused on our core business and have incorporated all messes into these systems. Our processes must support the major systems of our core business. We need to promote more people working on these systems, so outstanding talent will be drawn to integrate these systems. After we integrate our major processes, we can continue to dig small ditches or channels. How could Yu the Great[3] prevent disaster just by digging small ditches and not dredging big rivers? Why does our Quality, Business Process & IT Management Department face such great difficulties? Because processes for our core business haven't been integrated. As a result, many resources have been wasted in developing hundreds of useless IT systems. *(Ren Zhengfei: Speech at a Meeting with Employees of the Quality, Business Process & IT Management Department, Huawei Executive Office Speech No. [2016] 094)*

---

[2] Yan Lida currently serves as President of the Enterprise Business Group of Huawei.
[3] Yu the Great (c. 2200 – 2100 BC) was a legendary ruler in ancient China famed for his introduction of flood control.

Keeping contract configuration information transparent is key to improving the operating efficiency of major business processes

Increasing PO processing efficiency, keeping contract configuration information transparent, and calculating billing amounts are the three hurdles field offices must overcome to increase operating efficiency in major business processes. At their core, these three issues all need transparent contract configuration information. We need to consider converting our customer bill of materials (CBOM) into a customized sales bill of materials (SBOM), which is easy to be converted into a build bill of materials (BBOM). This may increase HQ's maintenance workload but it can reduce the number of manual conversions needed to go between CBOMs, SBOMs, and BBOMs during the seven stages of our process and thus will benefit field offices. *(Ren Zhengfei: Keeping Customer PO Information Transparent to Support Payment Collection, Revenue Recognition, and Project Budgeting and Accounting—Speech at a Work Report by the IFS Project Team on December 29, Huawei Executive Office Speech No. [2009] 002)*

Product departments need to address the problem with integrated product configuration. They must work together with the Quality, Business Process & IT Management Department to solve this problem and deliver a report to company management as soon as possible. This problem has limited our ability to grow our business and seize the strategic high ground. With regard to interconnecting PO information in our and customers' IT systems, we can begin with tier-1 carriers first. *(Ren Zhengfei: Keeping Customer PO Information Transparent to Support Payment Collection, Revenue Recognition, and Project Budgeting and Accounting—Speech at a Work Report by the IFS Project Team on December 29, Huawei Executive Office Speech No. [2009] 002)*

Payment collection is not the sole responsibility of Finance; all departments involved share this responsibility

Payment collection is the last activity of sales and is the most difficult. Quality of contractual payment terms, equipment delivery, installation, and acceptance all have a direct impact on payment collection. Therefore, payment collection is not the sole responsibility of the Market Finance Department; all departments involved need to share the responsibility. *(Ren Zhengfei: Speech at the Annual Meeting of the Market Finance Department, 2005)*

We must work out a better approach to collecting overdue receivables. We cannot take a radical approach; otherwise, we may kill our golden goose. We must not press for payment at the expense of long-term interests. If payment collection problems are caused by transaction models, we need to improve our models. Every year we need to make some improvements over the previous year so that we can gradually improve our AR management. *(Source: Requirements for Huawei's Business Management Strategy in the Current Period, EMT Meeting Minutes No. [2008] 035)*

We must take a more scientific approach to payment collection. Moving future receivables forward will not be good for the company in the long run. *(Source: Minutes of the Report on the 2011 H1 Performance Review, EMT Meeting Minutes No. [2011] 011)*

8.1.4 Setting Up a Contract Support Office That Offers One-Stop-Shop Services to Support Contract Fulfillment

Streamlining sales management, clarifying contract authorization, and establishing global contract centers

Can we have frontline sales people focus on key terms, like those that differ from standard contract terms or require extra negotiation, while following IBM's authorization and credit management framework? In my opinion, we can establish one or more contract guiding centers worldwide, like the bidding center in Pakistan. Contracts will no longer be prepared onsite; they will be airmailed to wherever they are needed. We currently have approximately 120 contract preparation centers, with employees working overtime to prepare contracts. We don't have many lawyers or credit managers so it's impossible to have both roles in each of these 120 countries. We certainly make mistakes because of this. I had an idea after listening to a presentation from two experts. With standardized management, everyone just needs to focus on their own part. For example, if I negotiate with a customer on extra contract terms, I need to review the negotiated terms and send them to the contract center after the negotiation. We only need to establish a few contract guiding centers worldwide. This way, more employees can be freed up and contract quality will be improved. In Canada, for example, contracts are signed by the research center chief, who has no experience dealing with sales contracts. This is because the contract preparation centers don't really need to be close to customers; we only need to engage closely with customers on key contract terms, often only two pages. *(Ren Zhengfei: Speech at a Work Report by the IFS Project Team on October 16, 2007, ESC[4] Meeting Minutes)*

We must figure out a way for handling contract authorization and allocate experts and oversight personnel to establish a system for this. I think the first step is to streamline sales management. In the past, when something deviated from standards, I would say it was OK if something could not be streamlined. However, since we have started to work with IBM, our contracts need to be standardized. IBM may deliver us a standard template after working with us for one or two years. *(Ren Zhengfei: Keeping Customer PO Information Transparent to Support Payment Collection, Revenue Recognition, and Project Budgeting and Accounting—Speech at a Work Report by the IFS Project Team on December 29, Huawei Executive Office Speech No. [2009] 002)*

Establishing a comprehensive support platform to support and manage the end-to-end contract fulfillment process

Externally, CSO offers one-stop-shop services to customers; internally, it functions as a comprehensive support platform, responsible for managing contract handover, contract information entry and release, and order verification. It also provides the information and documents that are required for revenue recognition, issues invoices, monitors the end-to-end contract fulfillment process, and maintains contact with customers. *(Ren Zhengfei: Keeping Customer PO Information Transparent to Support Payment Collection, Revenue Recognition, and Project Budgeting and Accounting—Speech at a Work Report by the IFS Project Team on December 29, Huawei Executive Office Speech No. [2009] 002)*

CSO is responsible for managing basic contract information. All contract information is recorded by this department into the IT system. No other department is allowed to do this anymore. CSO is also responsible for contract management, goods preparation and shipment, delivery, revenue recognition, billing, and payment collection. Sales, delivery, and finance departments rely on CSO to complete billing and payment collection. *(Ren Zhengfei: Keeping Customer PO Information Transparent to Support Payment Collection, Revenue Recognition, and Project Budgeting and Accounting—Speech at a Work Report by the IFS Project Team on December 29, Huawei Executive Office Speech No. [2009] 002)*

---

[4] ESC stands for Executive Steering Committee, which oversees Huawei's transformation programs.

CSO staff should be experienced people who have worked hard in hardship regions. We can give more opportunities to these people. People who have a good attitude and are willing to learn will have job opportunities at Huawei. Wherever things are tough, we will develop resource pools and managers. We must establish a platform, build a resource pool, and organize training sessions as soon as possible. Every piece of information must only have one owner in the company and must be shared throughout the processes. Before contract information is released, the sales department must ensure its completeness and accuracy. *(Ren Zhengfei: Keeping Customer PO Information Transparent to Support Payment Collection, Revenue Recognition, and Project Budgeting and Accounting—Speech at a Work Report by the IFS Project Team on December 29, Huawei Executive Office Speech No. [2009] 002)*

8.2 Financial Management Throughout the IPD Process

8.2.1 The Essence of IPD: From Opportunity to Commercial Success

A management system is a set of frameworks and decision-making rules. It does not change when individuals or operations change

Leading global companies attach great importance to R&D, and their R&D personnel are also responsible for technical sales, technical support, cost, and quality. They rely on R&D to create opportunities and shape consumption. They quickly gather all profits within a short window of opportunity and then create even greater opportunities. This is why these companies develop faster than Huawei. This is why we went to the US to study management, to learn how a small company develops into a large one and evolves out of chaos. *(Ren Zhengfei: What Can We Learn from the American People?, Improvement Issue No. 63, 1998)*

If we don't have good management approaches during our large-scale operations, we may operate inefficiently and waste resources, and for that, we may pay the price of our lives. *(Ren Zhengfei: Learning the Essence of IPD to Ensure Successful Transformation—Speech at the IPD Mobilization Meeting, Improvement Issue No. 90, 1999)*

The IPD management system is our most important enabler of IPD. A management system is a set of frameworks and decision-making rules. It does not change when individuals or operations change. Here, the whole is greater than the sum of its parts. When a cross-department team acts as an integrated management and decision-making team, individuals and the organization play a much bigger role than they normally would. The IPD management system describes how different roles collaborate to ensure effective operations of the company. It is the internal gauge used to evaluate the value of IPD both inside and outside the company. *(Source: Lew Kimmel, IPD Management System—Paving the Way for Huawei's Sustainable Development, Huawei People Issue No. 128, 2000)*

The IPD management system describes how to manage relationships within a matrix organization. Every organization has its mission, role, and responsibilities, so the responsibility matrix is very clear and authority can be delegated to different teams as needed. These matrix organizations are often cross-department teams. Through flexible, effective communications, they focus on project goals and team management, and ensure that all relevant departments stay involved and collaborate. They also provide functional department inputs during each phase of product development. A team that runs effectively can help make the best decisions and take action based on facts. *(Source: End-to-End Guide to Huawei's IPD Management System, 2016)*

As long as we follow the IPD management system and process, our capabilities will improve and we will be able to develop high-quality products. We must change our past model that relied on individual heroes for success to a model where success is guaranteed through organizational effort. Any qualified Product Development Team (PDT) manager can develop successful products by leveraging their abilities and following the IPD management system and process. *(Xu Zhijun: Being Clear About Your Role, Following the IPD Process, and Ensuring Timely and High-quality Delivery—Speech at the Annual Wrap-up and Commendation Meeting of Outstanding PDTs and TDTs,[5] 2005)*

Before 1999, Huawei occasionally launched good products by relying on individual or collective efforts. After we implemented IPD, however, we could systematically launch competitive products and solutions. *(Guo Ping: 2011: Let's Start Anew—Speech at the Annual Meeting of Finance, Improvement Issue No. 376, 2011)*

---

[5] TDT: Technology Development Team.

Managing product development as an investment and pursuing business success

IPD looks at product development projects from a commercial perspective. One important consideration is finance. In other words, how should Finance work with IPD to measure the costs and benefits of a project? Before making an investment, an Integrated Portfolio Management Team (IPMT) must know how much money is available for investment. They need to know how many projects they can support given their current capabilities and how to assess a project from a commercial perspective. *(Source: Involvement of All Departments Ensures IPD Success—Speech by IBM Consultant Arleta Chen at the IPD Mobilization Meeting, Improvement Issue No. 90, 1999)*

Huawei has established an IPD process that focuses on customer needs. With this process, customer needs can be quickly and accurately incorporated into product release roadmaps. During this process, structured and standard parts are widely applied and technologies are fully shared. In the product development process, Huawei has established comprehensive advantages in speed, quality, and cost that have enabled the company to help customers gain a more competitive position. *(Source: Huawei 2007 Annual Report)*

According to Chinese-American scientist Li Kai, research is the process of converting money into knowledge, whereas development is a process of converting knowledge into money. Success represents premium customer experiences and highly competitive products. Therefore, technology is only a means to an end. It must align with customer needs, helping to deliver good user experiences and services and realize commercial value. *(Ren Zhengfei: The Essence of IPD: From Opportunity to Commercial Success—Speech at an Awards Ceremony for IPD Whiz Kids and Outstanding XDTs, Huawei Executive Office Speech No. [2016] 084)*

We must fully understand the core concepts surrounding IPD and follow processes in everything from reviewing opportunities to monetizing them. We must dare to take on difficult projects and achieve great success. We aim to establish a large system and a large platform. We must do some planning; otherwise, we will be unable to build our own Great Wall. China's Great Wall cannot change, but our Great Wall can, and we can rebuild parts of it at any time. If bricks in the groundwork of our own Great Wall are not replaced or optimized as time goes by, then our company will become rigid. *(Ren Zhengfei: The Essence of IPD: From*

Opportunity to Commercial Success—Speech at an Awards Ceremony for IPD Whiz Kids and Outstanding XDTs, Huawei Executive Office Speech No. [2016] 084)

Shifting the focus of R&D from technology to market-oriented innovation and becoming engineers with business acumen

We must think about everything we do with a commercial mindset, and look at problems from the perspective of the whole company, rather than the perspective of a department. When I visited the US, I asked people there what backgrounds or qualifications are required for IPD leaders? Their answer is: Don't see IPD as a task of R&D; look at problems from a commercial perspective. This answer was quite impressive. You must not look at problems merely from your own department's perspective, but from a commercial perspective. *(Source: Looking at Problems from a Commercial Perspective—Speech by Sun Yafang[6] at an IPD Training Session, Improvement Issue No. 90, 1999)*

Customers' business success is the ultimate measure of the value of any cutting-edge technology, product, or solution. When it comes to making decisions on product investment, we prioritize customer needs over technology. Our products and solutions can only remain competitive when we keep innovating in products and solutions based on our deep insights into customer needs. *(Ren Zhengfei: My Thoughts on a 100-Year-Old Church That Survived the Wenchuan Earthquake—Speech at the Commendation Meeting of the Central Research & Development Unit, Huawei Executive Office Speech No. [2008] 016)*

Most employees in our R&D team are engineers. They are eager to develop the best possible technology. They think that only by doing so can they prove their worth. In R&D, if you do something right in a simple way, you may not get a high performance rating; but if you do it in a complicated way and make it look difficult, you may get a higher rating. This is not customer-centric. Customers want us to achieve the same results and deliver the same services in the simplest way. We need to recognize engineers with business acumen who can develop functions in a simple way. In doing so, we can encourage customer centricity in R&D. I hope you can develop more business acumen rather than just being engineers. *(Ren Zhengfei: Customer Centricity, Increased Platform Investments, and Open Collaboration for Shared Success—Speech at the 2010 PSST Managers' Meeting, Huawei Executive Office Speech No. [2010] 010)*

---

[6] Sun Yafang: Chairwoman of the Board of Huawei from September 1999 to March 2018.

We must move beyond the notion that "IPD is an R&D process". In essence, it is a market-driven innovation process. As such, we must link product development to market analysis and segmentation, portfolio analysis, business strategy development, and planning. This means that we must rely on real, high-value customer needs to drive product development while fully considering needs such as manufacturability, installability, and serviceability. We need to complete business model designs and identify target users in the product development phase. *(Guo Ping: Transform Continuously and Improve Field Operating Capabilities to Ensure the Company's Sustainable and Profitable Growth—Speech at Huawei Annual Management Conference 2013, Huawei Executive Office Speech No. [2014] 020)*

8.2.2 Key Control Points Throughout the IPD Process

IPD can help Huawei establish a structured product development process and develop products according to a pre-set schedule. Cross-department teams made up of senior executives decide whether to continue with a product at specific decision checkpoints. This can help effectively manage company investment and product launches. *(Source: IPD and Huawei's Dream, IBM-Huawei IPD Core Team, Improvement Issue No. 127, 2000)*

Our R&D team has over 70,000 people and is operating highly effectively. This is all because of our IPD process, a product development transformation initiated by Huawei and IBM in 1998. Since then, we have never stopped optimizing our R&D processes, streamlining our organization, and improving R&D capabilities. From ideation to product launch, we have never ceased improving our management systems, processes, tools, and capabilities. No matter how many people are involved – whether it's 70,000 or double that number – our management systems can still operate robustly and ensure that stable and quality products are made. This is attributed to our efforts in optimizing our management systems and R&D processes over the years. *(Source: Presenting a True Huawei, an Exclusive Interview with Xu Zhijun by Fortune, 2012)*

With the IPD process, we no longer need to rely on "heroes" in product domains. Rather, we can develop products that meet customer needs and deliver an assured level of quality simply by relying on processes. *(Xu Zhijun: Streamlining and Integrating Processes for Operating Units, Realizing the "Five Ones" Target, and Achieving Consistency of Inventory Accounts and Goods—Speech at the Transformation and Management*

Improvement Session of the 2014 Huawei Market Conference, Huawei Executive Office Speech No. [2014] 018)

The key to the IPD management system is to manage the IPD process. The goal is to provide a management process and decision-making policy for company management so that they can monitor major business activities on an ongoing basis and make decisions to balance major businesses, achieve business goals, and take responsibility for performance and business results. *(Source: End-to-End Guide to Huawei's IPD Management System, 2016)*

The Finance Management Department of Products & Solutions is a reliable business partner for product line presidents. They share responsibility for investment, operations, and internal controls management, supporting sustainable and profitable business growth. Finance uses specialized investment assessment methodologies to support the execution of corporate investment strategies and drive improvements in investment efficiency and effectiveness. They manage financial operations to align macro and micro activities, and execute financial and other relevant processes to effectively manage risks and achieve secure, robust operations. *(Source: Notice on Positioning and Responsibilities of the Finance Management Department of Products & Solutions, Group Finance Notice No. [2016] 027)*

The Finance Management Department of Products & Solutions takes the following responsibilities in terms of investment management:

1. Build a full series of investment management rules and an associated data reporting system.
2. Fully engage in the Develop Strategy to Execute (DSTE) and IPD processes, produce product investment analysis reports, and support business departments in making investment decisions.
3. Monitor and drive proper use of resources based on the company's business and financial strategies. Establish a mechanism for investment risk warning and escalation to drive efficient use of resources.

(Source: Notice on Positioning and Responsibilities of the Finance Management Department of Products & Solutions, Group Finance Notice No. [2016] 027)

In an IPMT, responsibilities of finance members are as follows:

1. Give financial advice and identify opportunities from a financial perspective to ensure that the product line hits its revenue and expense

targets and executes its business strategies. Monitor and track product line and product costs to ensure that they are within expectations.
2. Provide financial guidance and expert advice when reviewing product investment portfolios and offering guidance to individual Business Management Teams (BMTs) and Super Product Development Teams (SPDTs). Review and sign off on financial information in business plans to ensure that the information is complete and accurate.
3. Review the consistency between suggestions on product development investment and investment baselines and ask relevant teams to explain when there are inconsistencies.
4. Ensure financial data of product lines and budgeting and accounting data of product releases are provided in a timely and accurate manner to support product line operations and fine-grained management.
5. Monitor and manage promised financial capability improvement activities and ensure that product lines have skilled financial personnel in place to provide the most competitive financial support for projects and investment portfolios. Maintain a list of financial resources (including people, expenses, and assets) and allocate necessary resources to PDTs at a certain DCP.
6. Hold regular meetings to guide BMT/SPDT finance members in fulfilling their responsibilities and providing feedback when it comes to a common business issue or an issue specific to a BMT/SPDT.
7. Implement IPMT resolutions and requirements for finance, monitor the performance of BMT/SPDT finance members, and provide inputs to their performance appraisals.

(Source: End-to-End Guide to Huawei's IPD Management System, 2016)

8.2.3 Industry Business Plans and Product Investment Portfolio Management

A company's ultimate goal is to earn profits. Product investment decisions are made based on product financial assessments. In the past, we decided whether to invest in a product's development after we roughly estimated its potential profit based on the estimated cost and sales price. However, questions that are commonly considered in a standard financial analysis were ignored in this process. In the IPD process, the product development team includes financial personnel who perform project cost and benefit analyses from a financial perspective and produce a comprehensive financial analysis report, informing investment decisions. We now have begun to make product investment decisions from a commercial perspective, marking a dramatic change in our approach. *(Source: Summary of the First Pilot of IPD in a PDT (II), Improvement Issue No. 161, 2001)*

We must enhance investment portfolio management, including investment allocation and the pace of investment. We need to pragmatically assess market size, profit models, and returns on investment. Based on these objective assessments, we can then determine the amount and pace of our investment. *(Source: Resolution on the Positioning and Business Development Strategy for the IT Product Line, SDC Resolution No. [2012] 006)*

Product and technology investment portfolios must be properly prioritized. Strategic plans (SPs) and business plans (BPs) for investment strategies and ROI must be closely linked. We need to specify the strategy for product and technology investment portfolios. We must have a clear strategic positioning and define investment priorities for every industry. And the strategies for product and technology investment portfolios of an industry must be prepared with SPDT as the basic unit. We need to set our three-year goals and the goals of year 2015 for returns from R&D investment, operating results, and product or technology competitiveness. Business units must invest enough to future-proof their core competencies. They should not pursue short-term performance at the expense of long-term investment. *(Source: Principles for R&D Investment Management and Budgeting Rules in 2015, SDC Business Directive No. [2014] 005)*

IPMTs must make investment decisions based on pre-defined industry SPs and think with a commercial mindset. They need to manage investment in a closed-loop manner by physical industry, not organization. This is because organizations may change, but physical industries will not. *(Source: Minutes of the Report to Xu Zhijun on the Project Charter of the Product Investment Portfolio Management Mechanism, 2014)*

According to SP and BP rules, Finance must formulate operations management rules based on a business department's long-term strategic pursuits and short-term business goals, and use these rules to guide business departments to self-balance their long-term strategies and short-term operations. Business departments must not cut long-term strategic investment due to short-term performance pressures, or tolerate long-term losses to preserve strategic investment. Our ideal operations management should be: *Having rice in our bowls, paddies in our fields, and rice in our warehouses.* (Meng Wanzhou: Using Budgets to Drive Resource Allocation and Aligning Resource Allocation with Strategies, Huawei Executive Office Speech No. [2014] 001)

Industries vary greatly, so R&D investment must be managed on an industry-by-industry basis. BUs must determine how to allocate their resources based on the revenue from target customers of a product. A BU's revenue refers to the total revenue from all of its global customers. *(Source: Principles for R&D Investment Management and Budgeting Rules in 2015, SDC Business Directive No. [2014] 005)*

We can allocate R&D resources using three approaches: ratios, amounts, and amounts plus ratios. Strategy, ROI, and product lifecycles are considered during this process. For products in the investment or decline periods, investment is managed based on amounts. For products in the growth or maturity periods, investment is managed based on pre-set ratios. Strategic investment made by the 2012 Laboratories is managed based on amounts and constrained by the R&D expense ratio set by the company. *(Source: Principles for R&D Investment Management and Budgeting Rules in 2015, SDC Business Directive No. [2014] 005)*

8.2.4 Integrating IPD and Other Business Processes

For years, Huawei has been learning and introducing management systems and processes, such as IPD, ISC, IFS, and CRM, from Western companies. When we introduced these processes, we gave up some parts of them due to our lack of knowledge and capabilities, and their suitability at that time. Currently, the problems we are facing in management, such as breakpoints, low efficiency, and process congestion, are to a large extent attributable to our failure to make full use of these management systems in the first place. During our management transformation, the biggest challenge is integration across functional departments. We need to systematically manage the interconnections and relationships between different transformation programs to create the end-to-end *backbone* of our management system. *(Source: Minutes of the Report on Initial Findings from the Review of Corporate Transformation Programs and Suggestions on ESC/PO[7] Restructuring, EMT Meeting Minutes No. [2014] 005)*

---

[7] PO: Project Office, supporting ESC operations.

Huawei's approach to management transformation can be compared to *clouds, rainwater*, and *channels*. (The *cloud* is Huawei's management philosophy. The *rainwater* is our business activities. And *channels* are the processes and theories that summarize the best practices of Western companies.) We must have the right *channels* in place to gather our *rainwater* together and generate electricity. We need to integrate our IFS, IPD, ISC, and LTC processes to form the right *channels*. Huawei's management philosophy is like a *cloud*, which is valuable only when it turns into *rainwater*. And the *rainwater* needs to be channeled properly. Without the right *channels* to guide the *rainwater*, it will flow anywhere, and its energy will dissipate. *(Ren Zhengfei: Rigorous, Well-ordered, and Simple Management Is Crucial for Huawei to Scale New Heights, Huawei Executive Office Speech No. [2014] 028)*

Last year, we proposed a new concept: object-oriented process integration. This means we must check whether our processes are truly streamlined and integrated for representative offices, regional offices, BUs, BGs, and other operating entities. We also need to check whether our processes can truly support our operating units' efforts to continuously improve operating efficiency, customer satisfaction, and profitability. The first transformation process we implemented at Huawei was IPD. The score of this process in the capability maturity assessment (CMA) has been around 3.2 points over the years. Why can't we hit our initial 3.5 point goal? Because we can only achieve 3.5 points when all relevant processes are integrated. That can't be achieved with the IPD process alone. Only when the IPD process is integrated with other processes in a way that focuses on objects can it achieve a score of 3.5 points in the CMA. To do this successfully, we must improve our overall efficiency. The same holds true for other processes. Every other process, including the LTC and the Issue to Resolution (ITR), must be integrated with other processes in a way that focuses on objects, and must support our operating units' efforts to continuously improve operating efficiency, customer satisfaction, and profitability. Only in this way can they achieve a 3.5 point CMA score. *(Xu Zhijun: Streamlining and Integrating Processes for Operating Units, Realizing the "Five Ones" Target, and Achieving Consistency of Inventory Accounts and Goods—Speech at the Transformation and Management Improvement Session of the 2014 Huawei Market Conference, Huawei Executive Office Speech No. [2014] 018)*

After many years of transformation, our vertical process design and development is essentially completed, except a few processes that still need time for deployment and optimization. Now we need to integrate processes to improve operating units' operating efficiency, customer satisfaction, and profitability. At this stage, representative offices and regional offices need to take more responsibility in process transformation and even become process deployment owners, because they are primarily the ones who will implement object-oriented process integration. *(Xu Zhijun: Streamlining and Integrating Processes for Operating Units, Realizing the "Five Ones" Target, and Achieving Consistency of Inventory Accounts and Goods—Speech at the Transformation and Management Improvement Session of the 2014 Huawei Market Conference, Huawei Executive Office Speech No. [2014] 018)*

8.3 Financial Management Throughout the PTP Process

8.3.1 KCPs Throughout the PTP Process

Reviewing the procurement process architecture, setting KCPs for payment security, and providing effective guidance to procurement

Huawei has seven procurement processes that are classified based on factors like business codability, IT system maturity, and procurement department involvement. This makes it difficult to modify and upgrade these processes. These processes were developed based on our business operation models and cannot support new business models like monthly payments for logistics service POs. In addition, since process classification criteria are not unified, processes become optional and users can bypass controls by choosing processes they like. Sometimes they even end up increasing operating costs by choosing a complex process for a business activity that is supposed to follow a simple process.

The PTP project team has come up with an approach to improving the existing seven procurement processes and will work with the ISC Business Process Executive (BPE) and the procurement department to implement it. Our current focus is on defining each of the seven processes' business scope and rules for use and setting KCPs for payment security. The purpose of these two actions is to allow our existing processes to provide a clearer guide for business operations. In the future, the seven processes will be gradually integrated into one common, modularized process as codes are applied to procurement activities and the ERP system is deployed for procurement. *(Source: Optimizing the Procure-to-Pay Process to Ensure*

Secure, Accurate, and Timely Payment, IFS-PTP Project Team, Improvement Issue No. 308, 2008)

Huawei has six accounts payable (AP) payment processes that are classified based on different standards, with complicated categories. The initial purpose of classifying them like this was to establish payment processes that are aligned with each procurement process. This makes payments inefficient and also makes it inconvenient to provide business support and centralize payment operations. For PO-based procurement, IBM has a common payment process. For procurement without a PO, IBM has a payment process called Invoice Only Invoice (IOI). Its payment process is divided into several activities including invoice receiving and processing, invoice matching, duplicate payment checking, and payment. The process architecture is very clear and can provide a useful guide for business operations. *(Source: Optimizing the Procure-to-Pay Process to Ensure Secure, Accurate, and Timely Payment, IFS-PTP Project Team, Improvement Issue No. 308, 2008)*

Establishing and optimizing the supplier invoice processing process and making invoice processing more efficient

Huawei has no clear guide for handling supplier-issued invoices. We have no way of ensuring suppliers issue correct invoices the first time. Our processes for collecting, transmitting, approving, entering, and querying invoice information are also not well-established and we have no process for handling problematic invoices. As a result, invoice processing is inefficient. The PTP project team plans to develop a guide for supplier invoice issuance and a process for handling problematic invoices. The team will also optimize our existing processes for collecting, transmitting, approving, entering, and querying invoice information to make invoice processing more efficient. *(Source: Optimizing the Procure-to-Pay Process to Ensure Secure, Accurate, and Timely Payment, IFS-PTP Project Team, Improvement Issue No. 308, 2008)*

Adding duplicate payment checking into the AP payment process and enabling the function in ERP

In Huawei's existing AP payment process, duplicate payment is checked by people without any clear process in place. The work is not done systematically or routinely. IBM's mechanism for duplicate payment checking includes both pre-payment and after-payment checks. A report is then sent to the AP and other relevant departments on a daily basis to ensure that only one payment is made to an external supplier for the same transaction. With this mechanism, duplicate payment can be prevented. Even if a problem is detected, it can be fixed immediately, reducing the company's financial losses. *(Source: Optimizing the Procure-to-Pay Process to Ensure Secure, Accurate, and Timely Payment, IFS-PTP Project Team, Improvement Issue No. 308, 2008)*

Optimizing the governance mechanism for the PTP process

The PTP project team plans to work with the Business Controls and Internal Audit (BC&IA) project team to build an SOD matrix and an assessment mechanism and further improve the risk acceptance mechanism. The team will also clearly define which procurement activities bypass the procurement department and establish a mechanism for identifying, recording, reporting, and assessing bypass activities. They will also set KCPs throughout the PTP process and perform process compliance testing to improve the PTP process's governance mechanism. *(Source: Optimizing the Procure-to-Pay Process to Ensure Secure, Accurate, and Timely Payment, IFS-PTP Project Team, Improvement Issue No. 308, 2008)*

Cleaning up supplier information, optimizing the mechanism for managing and maintaining supplier information, and ensuring that payment for one transaction is made securely and only once

Currently, Finance maintains our suppliers' bank information and Procurement manages all other supplier information. Poor coordination between these departments results in low efficiency and duplicate work. As supplier information is not updated or maintained as quickly as it should, our system is full of duplicate suppliers and suppliers who have not worked with us for a long time. This can cause payment delays and errors. By using IBM as a benchmark, our Procurement Operations Support Department has established a dedicated team to solve this problem. This team has cleaned up supplier information and will further improve our supplier information management policy based on the PTP project team's findings. The team will decide who will be responsible for entering and maintaining supplier information to ensure that the information is valid, complete, accurate, and unique and that payment for one transaction is made securely and only once. *(Source: Optimizing the Procure-to-Pay Process to Ensure Secure, Accurate, and Timely Payment, IFS-PTP Project Team, Improvement Issue No. 308, 2008)*

Pushing for the standardization of internal procurement requests, simplifying request approvals, and improving efficiency

The procurement team needs to ask requesting departments to streamline their request approval processes and standardize their procurement requests. Currently, the main pain points in procurement processes are bloated internal request approval processes and unclear request descriptions. Requesting departments need to clearly describe their requests and make continuous improvement. The procurement team should not assume responsibility for the quality of requests themselves. *(Ren Zhengfei: Minutes from a Procurement Work Report by Yao Fuhai, Huawei Executive Office Speech No. [2017] 048)*

Adhering to the principle of transparent procurement, and strengthening the management of supplier honesty and integrity

Suppliers that violate Huawei's *BCGs* are to be penalized according to the *Honesty and Integrity Agreement*. We need to prevent suppliers from doing things like bribing employees, including indirectly through family members. Procurement managers have to report all conflicts of interest. This isn't to say that procurement isn't possible when there are conflicts of interest. But these conflicts need to be reported for transparency. *(Ren Zhengfei: Minutes from a Procurement Work Report by Yao Fuhai, Huawei Executive Office Speech No. [2017] 048)*

8.3.2 Integrating Procurement and Financial Processes

Implementing the "Four Unifications" and benchmarking Huawei's procurement accounting against international practices

In September 1998, we hired KPMG to help us launch the "Four Unifications" project in Finance, which involved unifying policies, processes, codes, and tables. In the first half of 1999, KPMG began to help us design and improve our accounting system based on leading financial practices and proposed new processes and policies. As procurement was a relatively standard activity and most of our suppliers were large global companies, we applied these practices to procurement accounting first. With the joint effort of the KPMG consultants, the project team, and all involved employees, our "Four Unifications" solutions were applied to procurement accounting. We have seen tangible results from this. This has made us more determined to widely roll out the "Four Unifications" and has further encouraged us to benchmark our procurement accounting against international standards. *(Source: Implementing "Four Unifications" to Reach International Standards in Procurement Accounting, Improvement Issue No. 126, 2000)*

The procurement accounting section has developed or improved our regulations on procurement payment and made improvements to our processes, oversight, and tables. In October 1999, we successfully switched to the Chart of Accounts (COA). This has greatly improved the timeliness and accuracy of our accounting, as well as our fund security and work efficiency. *(Source: Implementing "Four Unifications" to Reach International Standards in Procurement Accounting, Improvement Issue No. 126, 2000)*

Optimizing the PTP process from a financial perspective and moving towards project-driven procurement

The reason procurement costs cannot be accounted for at a project level is that procurement is not project-driven. If procurement was already project-driven, wouldn't project-level procurement cost accounting already be implemented? We must now emphasize that procurement must be project-driven. This is consistent with our policy that says the front line must be allowed to ask for the resources they require. Our project management needs to take a longer-term view. We can develop our project procurement plans a few months in advance so that they can drive procurement. The centralized approach we adopted previously meant we didn't have a clear view of things. We must change this approach; otherwise, we will never achieve scientific, fine-grained project management. *(Ren Zhengfei: Speech at a Work Report by the IFS-PTP Project Team, 2010)*

Whoever makes a purchase must make the associated payment and bear the corresponding costs. All procurement costs must be charged to projects. Procurement personnel will be held accountable where this is not achieved. We don't need to seek globally unified cost baselines. Every country office, regional office, and project can have its own baselines. They can use these baselines to push themselves to do better. *(Ren Zhengfei: Speech at a Work Report by the IFS-PTP Project Team, 2010)*

Remaining user-centric, supporting frontline business, and making general procurement easier

General procurement involves a lot of small details, from stationery purchase to car or house rental. This is a part of our everyday work. After years of procurement transformation and the deployment of our AP process, we finally have a relatively unified and simplified AP process for general procurement. However, our business operations are still manual. Only part of HQ procurement is supported by IT systems and these systems are largely decentralized and not well integrated, making general procurement personnel in field offices very frustrated. How can we address these difficulties facing our field offices and make general procurement easier?

The General Procurement Department, the IFS-PTP Project Team, the Internal Service Management Department, the Accounting Management Department, and the Quality, Business Process & IT Management Department have established a joint work group to improve relevant processes and IT systems. After nearly a full year, starting in the second half of 2008, we have launched a web-based system called eGo globally to support general procurement. eGo is designed to be user-centric. Its purpose is to make our processes faster, internal controls more effective, and operations easier.

There is only one process and one point of entry and the entire process is visible. All general procurement will be done on this platform. Procurement requesters can find the items or services they want to purchase in the system catalog and both payments to suppliers and reimbursements to employees who make advance payments on behalf of the company will be done in this system. This will make procurement requests and expense analysis and management easier.

With this system, approvals are streamlined and real-time budgets are provided for reference. Only one approval is required after a procurement request is submitted. No further approval is required to make a payment. Approvers can approve requests anywhere and at any time. They can also delegate approval to others in the system. More importantly, managers can see how much of their department's budget has been used during approval and get detailed reports of purchased items. Thanks to this system, managers can have more information available so they can make informed approvals, reduce internal control risks, and trace issues when they occur.

In the eGo system, supplier qualification information is shown in catalogs. The system translates the qualification information into a catalog of items and services that can be purchased. This information includes supplier names, item and service descriptions, and prices. All the information is shown to users in the form of a catalog, like on an online shopping platform. Employees can find a wide variety of items and services to be purchased and complete their purchases themselves. Procurement qualification personnel can set up different catalogs to support different procurement models. This way, Huawei can make full use of qualified suppliers and procurement authorization can also be managed using the system.

In this system, documents can be automatically matched during accounting. No matter what type of business it is, the eGo system can generate PRs, POs, and acceptance information in a unified format. That PO and acceptance information can then be automatically imported into ERP. When Finance makes payments, they only need to input invoice information and the system will automatically match the invoice with the corresponding procurement, boosting efficiency and reducing manual errors. According to our estimations, Huawei may lead the industry in terms of annual invoice processing capacity once eGo is fully rolled out.

In addition, different requirements for internal controls are fully embedded and codified into this system, ensuring process compliance. *(Source: We Can Make General Procurement Easier, IFS-PTP Project Team, Improvement Issue No. 343, 2009)*

Simplifying the procurement process for low-value consumables and changing the way we offset the payment of low-value procurement

We must buy low-value consumables at supermarkets since most of these items are available there. We only need to qualify supermarkets and not the commodities sold at the supermarkets. We can use the rules that supermarkets already use to manage our procurement of low-value consumables. Low-value items can be purchased by employees directly. They can then get reimbursed by submitting an expense claim in the Self-service Expense (SSE) system. They don't need to follow the formal procurement process for these items. *(Ren Zhengfei: Speech at a Work Report by the IFS-PTP Project Team, 2010).*

We must do everything we can to streamline our processes. Complicated processes only make oversight more difficult and more costly. *(Ren Zhengfei: Speech at a Work Report by the IFS-PTP Project Team, 2010).*

8.3.3 *Automation and Payment Security of the PTP Process*

When implementing the PTP project, Huawei needs to focus on big issues. For items used in production lines, we must do exactly as our consultants say. For low-value office supplies, however, consultants can set less strict requirements. In the past, our offices had to use a very rigid system to procure the smaller items they needed. For example, suppliers had to be qualified for even just a pencil or a piece of paper. In some representative offices, a contract may be worth US$500 million; in some others, a contract may be worth only US$2 million. We used to be very rigid in this regard. That's why we had 300 people qualifying pencil and paper suppliers worldwide. Our final solution was to buy these items at big-name supermarkets. That way, we only need to qualify the supermarkets, rather than the items. You must use credit cards, not cash, when buying these items at supermarkets. What you have purchased must then be put in the system for everyone to see before you get them reimbursed online. Supermarket prices are fair, which helps us prevent internal problems in terms of inaccuracies and prices. With fair prices, we can set limits for the procurement of office necessities based on our pre-set budgets. Departments can then adjust the quantity of items they require based on the limits. In this regard, Huawei and IBM are a little different. In the PTP project, we need to focus on high-value, major items. For these items, we must do exactly as our IBM consultants say. For low-value items, we can consider their transformation in the future. *(Ren Zhengfei: Speech at a Work Report by the IFS Project Team on December 14, 2007, ESC Meeting Minutes)*

We must gradually implement AI-aided, standardized procurement of auxiliary engineering materials and allow each country office to make its own choices. Standard templates must also be used for engineering procurement. We need to build cost models for typical sites, but these models do not need to be overly detailed. We must be quality-centric, rather than price-centric in all procurement categories. We must work toward higher quality and higher quality will require higher costs. We need to drive higher quality among suppliers and offer them premium prices for higher quality items. *(Ren Zhengfei: Minutes from a Procurement Work Report by Yao Fuhai, Huawei Executive Office Speech No. [2017] 048)*

The department responsible for procuring auxiliary engineering materials can look to the successful use of AI in general procurement to gradually standardize operations. We must ensure normalization by category, and establish item codes and a shortlist of qualified suppliers. There must be globally unified guidelines and each country office must be given the freedom to make their own choices. Quality is the foundation of big data analytics. *(Ren Zhengfei: Minutes from a Procurement Work Report by Yao Fuhai, Huawei Executive Office Speech No. [2017] 048)*

Intelligence and automation are where we are all heading, but during this process, we should not overly simplify or marginalize human work.

1. Intelligence and automation are where we are heading. They will make payments more secure, but don't think they will replace people. That's a common misconception about how these tools work. The work done by machines is not always 100% accurate and machines are unable to flexibly respond to many changes. It's true that machines can do standardized work efficiently, but that doesn't mean that they don't make any errors. For some positions and industries, we just can't afford to have machines making errors. Today's flight technology relies on machines for many tasks, especially after planes reach a certain altitude and begin to cruise. Despite that, machines will never replace captains since they can never truly play the role of a captain. Would you dare to get on a plane that didn't have a captain?
2. Intelligence can help our payment personnel rapidly identify possible errors in massive amounts of data. Automation can help them find the right documents from huge amounts of files. But the "Go" button still needs to be pressed by people. Intelligence and automation can help payment personnel improve their work quality, rather than marginalizing and simplifying their work.
3. Automatic scanning can replace manual item-by-item checking. Payment personnel are supposed to focus their time and effort on key issues and maximize the value of their experiences, skills, comprehensive judgment, and analysis. I hope that automation and intelligence can encourage our payment personnel to proactively reflect on their operational skills and judgment to prevent future business problems.

(Ren Zhengfei: Speech at a Meeting with Payment Staff, Huawei Executive Office Speech No. [2017] 042)

Security, not innovation, is the most important consideration when we choose payment platforms and methods. We prefer using mature, traditional methods and channels rather than follow trends. We cannot innovate for the sake of innovation or become too focused on expanding or using new payment methods and channels. We must use secure, traditional payment methods, but we allow customers to use different payment methods. We must strictly assess, carefully analyze, and fully validate payment methods and channels before using them. Only when all its risks have been identified and eliminated can we try out a new payment method. We can formally introduce a payment platform only after it is proved to be secure and reliable through a long-time trial. *(Ren Zhengfei: Speech at a Meeting with Payment Staff, Huawei Executive Office Speech No. [2017] 042)*

Open Access This chapter is licensed under the terms of the Creative Commons Attribution-NonCommercial-NoDerivatives 4.0 International License (http://creativecommons.org/licenses/by-nc-nd/4.0/), which permits any noncommercial use, sharing, distribution and reproduction in any medium or format, as long as you give appropriate credit to the original author(s) and the source, provide a link to the Creative Commons licence and indicate if you modified the licensed material. You do not have permission under this license to share adapted material derived from this chapter or parts of it.

The images or other third party material in this chapter are included in the chapter's Creative Commons licence, unless indicated otherwise in a credit line to the material. If material is not included in the chapter's Creative Commons licence and your intended use is not permitted by statutory regulation or exceeds the permitted use, you will need to obtain permission directly from the copyright holder.

CHAPTER 9

Project Financial Management

Projects are the basic units and cells of business management at Huawei. There are different types of projects, including R&D, sales, delivery, and management transformation projects. If projects are not effectively managed, it will be impossible for a company to achieve robust operations. Huawei is working hard to shift its operating model from being function-centered to being project-centered. This is going to be a huge change. It means thousands of field teams will be mobilized. It also means that functional departments will no longer be centers of authority, but centers of expertise and resources. Huawei believes that a project-centered model will help reduce redundancy and avoid the pitfalls experienced by large companies that operate with a function-centered organizational structure. The project-centered model will also make the company more competitive and enable managers to develop rapidly.

To adopt a project-centered model, a company needs to establish a corporate-level project management system. Moving forward, Huawei aims to build a management system like a dragon, whose head moves flexibly to look for food or attack a target. Its bone systems are flexible and powerful to ensure that the whole body moves to support any attack the head may start. Our field project operations must be as flexible as a dragon's head and our back-office management support systems must be like a dragon's bone systems. This will make up the basic architecture of our future management system.

© The Author(s) 2019
W. Huang, *Built on Value*,
https://doi.org/10.1007/978-981-13-7507-1_9

When it comes to project financial management, we first need to improve the closed-loop management of project estimation, budgeting, accounting, and final accounting. For projects that can be measured by profits and losses, we should run them as profit centers, and establish project operations management, appraisal, and Contribute and Share systems based on revenue, profits, and cash flow. For delivery projects that are run as cost centers based on budget targets, we need to integrate pre-sales and post-sales activities, align accounting with budgeting and final accounting with estimation, and perform closed-loop management of assumptions and risks. We also need to establish an incentivization system based on the completion of budget targets to inspire passion across project teams.

This chapter discusses how Huawei manages project finances. Although financial management is only a sub-system of the project management system, it penetrates deep into all kinds of business activities and runs through the entire lifecycle of a project.

9.1 Shifting from Being Function-Centered to Being Project-Centered

9.1.1 Projects Are the Basic Units and Cells of Business Management

Huawei is gradually changing its corporate governance model from one that is centralized to one that enables field teams to call for support. Under this new model, field teams will have both responsibility and authority while back offices provide enablement training and take responsibility for oversight. Such a model is built on an effective management platform with elements such as processes, data, information, and authority. Over the past 20-plus years, with the help of Western consultants, we have established a relatively unified platform that provides guidance and support to field offices. In the next five to ten years, we will gradually delegate decision-making authority to the field and provide the right level of support to help them exercise authority. *(Ren Zhengfei: Applying the Spirit of the Tortoise to Catch up with the Dragon Spacecraft—Speech at Huawei Annual Management Conference 2013, Huawei Executive Office Speech No. [2013] 255)*

Only by being project-centered can we avoid the pitfalls experienced by large companies that operate with a function-centered organizational structure. The project-centered model can also make our company more competitive. We need to quickly change our operating model from being function-centered to being project-centered. Projects are the basic units and cells of business management. If projects are not effectively managed, it will be impossible for the company to achieve robust operations. Over the next two to three years, we will change the way we operate, from being function-centered to being project-centered. This is going to be a huge change. It means thousands of field teams will be mobilized. It also means that functional departments will no longer be centers of authority, but centers of expertise and resources. In 2014, we will further delegate budgeting, accounting, and incentivization authority to project teams, so that this most basic unit of business operations can be mobilized. *(Xu Zhijun: Focusing on Strategy, Streamlining Management, and Achieving Sustainable and Profitable Growth, Huawei Executive Office Speech No. [2013] 246)*

Project management is the basic cell that promotes improvements to company management. We must continue to improve project management as the most important type of management at Huawei. Project management training offered by Huawei University should be systematic. Projects are basic units of operations so we must continuously improve our project management. People who truly understand project management have the potential to be top leaders. Managers who fail to manage projects effectively won't be able to manage representative offices and regions effectively. *(Ren Zhengfei: Speech at a Work Report by the Huawei University Institute of Education, Huawei Executive Office Speech No. [2013] 242)*

Huawei's management improvement has to be built on project management improvement. People in the eight critical project roles[1] should be carefully selected and developed. Mature procedures and a large high-caliber management team have to be developed. We should build a pool of managers and experts on project management through the Strategic Reserve. We need to pass advanced methods and capabilities on to representative offices through employee rotation. We should be good at identifying "golden seeds" (people with high potential) and allocate them to different places to sprout and bloom. These transformations represent opportunities for departments at all levels to create value; they are also the

---

[1] The eight critical roles of a project include Project Manager (PM)/Project Control Manager (PCM), Technical Director (TD)/Technical Leader (TL), Project Financial Controller (PFC), Delivery Quality Assurance Engineer (DQA), Supply Chain Manager (SCM), Procurement Project Manager (PPM), Contract Manager (CM), and Project HR.

test beds that we can use to identify and develop managers. *(Ren Zhengfei: Applying the Spirit of the Tortoise to Catch up with the Dragon Spacecraft—Speech at Huawei Annual Management Conference 2013, Huawei Executive Office Speech No. [2013] 255)*

9.1.2 Establishing a Corporate-Level Project-Centered Management System

I think our future management system should consist of front, middle, and back ends. The front end is a project operations or action center that has clear targets. The middle end is an efficient platform from which the front end can call for support. It serves as a bridge between the front and back ends and streamlines both information and goods. It is an integrated service platform that consists of "satellites", "aircraft carriers", and communications systems. The back end is a decision-making and oversight center that has a clear view of front-end activities. This center is there to make sure that all front-end activities are transparent and comply with related business rules. *(Ren Zhengfei: Rigorous, Well-ordered, and Simple Management Is Crucial for Huawei to Scale New Heights, Huawei Executive Office Speech No. [2014] 028)*

A corporate-level project management system is needed to adopt a company-wide project-centered model. Moving forward, Huawei aims to build a management system like a dragon, whose head moves flexibly to look for food or attack a target. Its highly developed bone systems are well-coordinated to ensure that the whole body moves to support any attack the head may start. In the field, our project operations must be as flexible as a dragon's head and our back-office management support systems must be like a dragon's bone systems. This will make up the basic architecture of our future management system. *(Guo Ping: Becoming Project-centered to Support the Company's Sustainable and Profitable Growth—Speech at the 2014 Project Management Summit, 2014)*

Huawei is changing its operating model from one that is function-centered to one that is project-centered. In the future, customer, R&D, service, and transformation projects will be the primary building blocks of the company's operations. We will face numerous management problems. We need to ask ourselves many questions: How should we establish a three-level management system for project portfolios, programs, and projects? How should we streamline operations from end to end and make project operations a true reality by getting GTS and supply chain staff involved earlier in projects? How should we position various projects as responsibility centers and delegate authority appropriately based on their positioning? How should back-end support platforms respond to the call for resources by projects? How can we ensure effective resource allocation by combining our pull and push strategies with HQ being pulled by field offices? We need to delve deeper into these questions and explore ways to resolve them. The company's shift to a project-centered model will help reduce redundancy and avoid the pitfalls experienced by large companies that operate with a function-centered organizational structure. Such a model will also hone our competitive edge and enable managers to develop rapidly. *(Ren Zhengfei: Speech at the Awards Ceremony for Whiz Kids, Huawei Executive Office Speech No. [2014] 039)*

In the future, Huawei's model of operations should be integrated. This is known as the "Squad Leaders' Fight". After authority is delegated to field offices, we will make field operating teams leaner, downsize back offices, and step up efforts to build strategic mobile teams. The purpose of having smaller operating teams is not to further fine-tune the division of responsibilities. Instead, we are looking to significantly enhance their operating capabilities by equipping them with advanced tools and providing them with strong support. Of course, it is impossible to delegate authority overnight. Currently, there are still many management problems. Over the next three to five years, we will focus on streamlining LTC and achieving CIAG and Five Ones. Five years from now, we will resolutely allow field teams to gradually call for support, and resolutely remove redundant organizations at HQ. This way, our HQ will become less bureaucratic. *(Ren Zhengfei: Speech at the Briefing on HR Work, Huawei Executive Office Speech No. [2014] 057)*

Being project-centered is not just about running front-end business by projects. It also needs a management support system to provide full support for projects. In other words, we need to create a complete architecture to streamline both the front and back ends, involving people, processes, knowledge, strategies, and many other aspects. This is what the industry calls a corporate-level project management system. *(Guo Ping: Becoming Project-centered to Support the Company's Sustainable and Profitable Growth—Speech at the 2014 Project Management Summit, 2014)*

We will stay customer-centric and gradually change our centralized resource allocation model. In the future, our resource allocation will be aligned with strategy, enabling those in field offices to call for support. Under this new resource allocation model, field teams will have both responsibility and authority while back offices provide enablement training and take responsibility for oversight. This model will combine the "pull" and "push" strategies, with the "pull" strategy playing the leading role. Field operating units make every endeavor to seize opportunities for sustainable and profitable growth. The big platform at back offices not only needs to meet the support demand of field offices; but also needs to focus on our core business, and allocate strategic resources to create more demand and opportunities for our core business. This is the architecture of our future-oriented management system, and also an important means to ensure that we are able to scale new heights. *(Guo Ping: Transform Continuously and Improve Field Operating Capabilities to Ensure the Company's Sustainable and Profitable Growth—Speech at Huawei Annual Management Conference 2013, Huawei Executive Office Speech No. [2014] 020)*

Right now, our project management capabilities are still weak and there is still much waste. We need to equip our project teams with improved skills. Why was HQ so strong before? Because HQ controlled budgets: It approved its own bonuses, staffing, and job grades first. It would then send out employees with personal grades of 14 or 15 to field operating teams. Their personal grades were low and they still needed to figure out how to do their jobs. By the time they worked things out, large amounts of effort, time, and materials had already been wasted. Why couldn't we cultivate several generals with the money wasted? This was the problem with our function-centered model. In the future, we will adopt a project-centered model. We are already piloting it now. Going forward, we will gradually give more authority to our field operating teams and will also move oversight forward to the field to ensure better delegation and exercise of authority. Radical transformation, however, could be catastrophic to the organization. It takes time to transform a company's platform. We need to be patient and make concerted efforts to make it happen. During the process, a large number of outstanding managers will emerge. *(Ren Zhengfei: Heroes Are All Around Us—Speech at the Q4 Regional Presidents' Meeting, Huawei Executive Office Speech No. [2014] 086)*

The ultimate goal of our transformation is to change from being function-centered to being project-centered. Under the project-centered model, project managers will have planning, budgeting, and cross-charging authority, and will have control over project budgets. They can purchase resources based on project needs. Processes, departments, people, and actions that don't create value for customers are redundant.

When we remove such redundancy, Huawei's HQ will become less bloated. *(Ren Zhengfei: Generals Are Born of Battle—Speech at the 2015 Project Management Summit, Huawei Executive Office Speech No. [2015] 118)*

9.1.3 Back Offices Need to Collaborate to Provide Timely and Accurate Support for Field Operations

In the future, our organizational structure will look like a spindle – HQ departments are at the top; regions, product lines, and other execution departments in the middle; and representative offices and production lines at the bottom. Departments at HQ will be small in number and scale and will be composed of people with successful field experience. They understand the needs of field offices, have clear strategies and tactics, make correct decisions, respond quickly, and provide excellent services. Since functions will be integrated, the number of HQ departments will be reduced. The middle segment is responsible for numerous operating tasks. Since a lot of specific and specialized support needs to be provided, the middle segment has detailed division of responsibilities and a larger number of departments. Departments at the bottom are responsible for operations and execution. Functions of those departments need to be integrated, and don't need to be aligned with those of departments in the middle. Otherwise, there will be too much coordination and internal friction, which will lead to bureaucracy in field offices. That is why we have a smaller number of departments at the bottom. *(Ren Zhengfei: Speech at the UK Representative Office, Huawei Executive Office Speech No. [2007] 027)*

We have made it clear that our transformation should center on the actual needs of field offices. Back offices (including field teams that are not directly involved in project operations) should promptly and accurately address the needs of field operating teams. We establish departments to fight battles and we fight battles to make profits. Back offices should be established based on the needs of field teams, and must focus on supporting field teams. We should also further integrate business functions in back offices to reduce the number of functional departments and internal coordination, and thus provide timely and accurate services to field teams. *(Ren Zhengfei: Who Calls for Artillery and How Do We Provide Timely Artillery Support?—Speech at the Awards Ceremony of Sales & Services, Huawei Executive Office Speech No. [2009] 001)*

Field offices must provide accurate information about their needs, and back offices must accurately understand the needs and provide support as needed. *(Ren Zhengfei: Who Calls for Artillery and How Do We Provide Timely Artillery Support?—Speech at the Awards Ceremony of Sales & Services, Huawei Executive Office Speech No. [2009] 001)*

Back offices will become a systematic support force and must provide timely and effective support and services. They also need to be responsible for analysis and oversight. As a back-end organization, HQ does not represent the company. It must provide support and services to field offices and avoid being bossy and arrogant. *(Ren Zhengfei: Who Calls for Artillery and How Do We Provide Timely Artillery Support?—Speech at the Awards Ceremony of Sales & Services, Huawei Executive Office Speech No. [2009] 001)*

We are now engaged in too much internal coordination. I think we should have fewer teams in back offices; their functions can be integrated to reduce coordination. They need to coordinate efforts to provide integrated services. You need to take time to figure out what this means. Back offices must deal with difficulties themselves and should not bother field offices with this. For example, field offices make numerous calls to resolve conflicts between two managers from back offices. Why don't back offices integrate their functions into a unified administrative organization and deal with all difficulties internally? As company operations become more standardized and organized, we need to integrate business department functions as appropriate and reduce headcount, giving more responsibilities to employees in similar roles. This may help us work more efficiently. *(Ren Zhengfei: Speech at the EMT ST Meeting, April 2010)*

9.2 Key Activities for Project Financial Management

9.2.1 Closed Loop Operations: Project Estimation, Budgeting, Accounting, and Final Accounting

Perform accounting by project and customer

Projects and customers are basic units in business management. Representative offices should focus on projects and customers, and perform accounting by project and customer. Like a cell in an organism, a project is the most important building block of an organization. Without project accounting, it won't be possible for account departments and representative offices to effectively manage their business operations. Once we are clear about projects and customers, we will have a clear picture of our account departments. This will help us better measure what our representative offices and regions have done in the past. *(Ren Zhengfei: Integrating Project Estimation, Budgeting, Accounting, and Final Accounting to Support Project Operations—Speech at a Briefing on the IFS Project, Huawei Executive Office Speech No. [2010] 007)*

Project cost accounting is the basis for effective management in departments at all levels. *(Ren Zhengfei: Staying Customer-centric, Inspiring Dedication, and Persevering Are Key to Our Success—Speech at the 2010 Huawei Market Conference, Huawei Executive Office Speech No. [2010] 002)*

The company is now focused on developing profit-centric organizations. HQ must provide services to profit centers. In the future, profit centers will view project profits as a key factor in their decisions. Project managers must be project-centric and ensure profits. *(Ren Zhengfei: Remarks at a Meeting with Senior Managers at a Project Management Summit, Huawei Executive Office Speech No. [2009] 007)*

Project estimation, budgeting, accounting, and final accounting are key activities in project operations management. Project estimation is the process of planning project profits; budgeting and accounting involve managing revenue increases and cost savings; and final accounting is the process of passing on the experience and lessons learned in a project. The purpose of integrating these four activities is to serve account departments and project teams, and support business management at the project level. *(Ren Zhengfei: Integrating Project Estimation, Budgeting, Accounting, and Final Accounting to Support Project Operations—Speech at a Briefing on the IFS Project, Huawei Executive Office Speech No. [2010] 007)*

If we are not clear about planning, budgeting, and accounting, and what surrounds these three mechanisms, then our transformation will ultimately remain function-centered. That means we would still allocate resources and perform accounting based on functional departments. It would be impossible to streamline our management. We haven't touched upon the major issues during our transformation. *(Ren Zhengfei: Rigorous, Well-ordered, and Simple Management Is Crucial for Huawei to Scale New Heights, Huawei Executive Office Speech No. [2014] 028)*

When it comes to project operations, we first need to improve our budgeting and accounting capabilities. Project budgets must be reliable, clear, and executable. Project accounting must be accurate, complete, and measurable. We need to identify those who perform well in project budgeting and accounting and make fast-track promotion available to these employees. This can motivate employees and inspire passion across the entire organization. *(Ren Zhengfei Minutes of the Meeting on the Budgeting Work, Huawei Executive Office Speech No. [2014] 004)*

A project will become a command center once it has a budget. Our total budget system needs to provide support for this kind of operating mechanism. We must pay special attention to the cost of resources used in a project, and make all resources and their costs transparent. This will enable project teams to select the resources they need. *(Ren Zhengfei: Minutes of a Briefing on the Progress of the Project for Changing Function-centered Operations into Project-centered Operations, EMT Meeting Minutes No. [2014] 019)*

A project-centered budgeting system means that we need to manage planning, budgeting, accounting, and assessment in a closed-loop manner, linking the budgets of responsibility centers to project budgets. When preparing project budgets, we should go beyond sales projects and delivery projects, and also focus on leads and opportunities that are aligned with our customers' investment plans. This can ensure budgets are generated based on projects (Budgets for responsibility centers = $\sum$ Project budgets + Expenses funded by the company). Currently, the quality of our project estimation, budgeting, accounting, and final accounting is not high. About 65% of projects see a deviation of 15 percentage points in contribution gross profit rates between budgeted amount and actual figures. About 36% of projects witness a deviation of 15% between the rolling forecasts and actual figures. The GTS and Sales & Delivery Finance Management Department must analyze the root causes behind major issues in project estimation, budgeting, accounting, and final accounting, set clear goals for improvement, and make improvements as planned. *(Source: Minutes of the Work Report on the Project for Changing Function-centered Operations into Project-centered Operations, BOD Executive Committee Meeting Minutes No. [2015] 020)*

Over the entire project lifecycle, the project budget must be aligned with both our customer's and Huawei's annual budgets. Both we and our customers manage budgets on an annual basis, so the full lifecycle budget of the project must be broken down based on the customer's and Huawei's annual budgets. This supports operations management in representative offices and ensures our budget is reliable. *(Source: Minutes of the Meeting of the Finance Committee Office, July 2015)*

Project estimation, budgeting, accounting, and final accounting are key activities in project operations management. The following rules must be followed throughout the lifecycle of a project: Project estimation helps optimize solutions, make informed sales decisions, and set initial project goals. Project budgeting must align with project estimation. Resources are allocated based on project budgets to support the attainment of project goals. Comprehensive assessment of project operations must be based on project final accounting. A resource buy & sell mechanism needs to be established to improve efficiency. *(Source: Project Operations and Management Policy, Corp. Doc. No. [2013] 160)*

Project estimation is the basis for contract negotiation

Project quotations should be supported by cost baselines and should be used as budgets for project delivery throughout the project management process. Project managers should take care of both project delivery and project financial targets. The purpose of sales and delivery is to collect payments. *(Ren Zhengfei: Keeping Customer PO Information Transparent to Support Payment Collection, Revenue Recognition, and Project Budgeting and Accounting—Speech at a Work Report by the IFS Project Team, Huawei Executive Office Speech No. [2009] 002)*

The reason why we put project estimation and contract negotiation in the same COE is that contract negotiation is based on project estimation. We can't negotiate with customers before getting project estimation straight. We could select some outstanding employees in India and build a global COE for bidding, project estimation, and contract negotiation in order to integrate these activities. *(Ren Zhengfei: Keeping Customer PO Information Transparent to Support Payment Collection, Revenue Recognition, and Project Budgeting and Accounting—Speech at a Work Report by the IFS Project Team, Huawei Executive Office Speech No. [2009] 002)*

Project estimation must be performed by project operations managers. All managers are estimation managers. They should have a clear idea about estimation. If they do not have accurate profit estimations for this year, how can they make money? At the representative office level, representative office general managers and account department directors are estimation managers. Business financial controllers (BFCs) of account departments do the specific work. *(Ren Zhengfei: Integrating Project Estimation, Budgeting, Accounting, and Final Accounting to Support Project Operations—Speech at a Briefing on the IFS Project, Huawei Executive Office Speech No. [2010] 007)*

We do not know that much about estimation. What is the coefficient for the contract under this contract scenario? What is the standard coefficient? How many estimation models do we have? We do not know the answers. Instead, we just make guesses and give approximate numbers. If the CFO gets a number approximately the same as ours through actuarial work, we cannot just leave it alone. We need to analyze why there is a difference. We also need to assign people to check, as this can help us determine what the average number is and which one is more accurate. The purpose here is not to argue about who is right or wrong, but to figure out how to be more accurate. We need to strike a balance in our work. When our schedule is not that busy, we need to plan and check our contract scenarios efficiently and quickly. To thrive, our Latin America Region first needs to make profits. Even in strategic opportunities, we also need to turn a modest profit. The region is facing numerous issues, such as foreign exchange controls. Since you cannot grow your business right now, you should instead focus on seeking more profits. *(Ren Zhengfei: Speech at a Briefing of the Northern Latin America Region and Colombia Representative Office, Huawei Executive Office Speech No. [2014] 051)*

Resources incur costs – Those who call for resources should bear the costs

Field offices know best about what's going on in the field and can best assess project workload. While ensuring respect for the company's general principles and objectives, we need to allow autonomy in basic operating units, giving them the authority to decide on tactics and operations, staffing, and resource allocation. HR departments are mainly responsible for resource quality, while project managers determine resource allocation. There should be no bureaucratic restrictions or rigid execution. HR departments should not create barriers when project managers ask for resources. Field teams know the field and projects best, so we must give project managers more flexibility in resource allocation. *(Source: Remarks by Ren Zhengfei and Sun Yafang at a Briefing on Improving R&D Organization Operations, 2001)*

How do we coordinate resources? The key is to make it clear that resources incur costs and profit centers must bear the expenses and costs incurred for their own development. Only in this way can we say: the more opportunities, the better. When we find ourselves short of resources, it means we have too many profitable opportunities. We have people flying to different parts of the world all the time to provide services, and profit centers should bear the expenses incurred for this. What does calling for resources mean? It is actually about allocating the expenses incurred to profit centers. But I think there is still a problem. How can we ensure all expenses incurred by services for a project are allocated specifically to that project? We do not have a reasonable formula. This puts us at a disadvantage in terms of human resource management. Chen Yongzheng, a former Microsoft executive, said he did not have money and he couldn't understand why Huawei spent extravagantly. He also said that he needed to ask for money from project teams in representative offices. He would say to project teams, "I have provided you with services, so you have to pay me." At Microsoft, profit centers have the budget. In contrast, Huawei's HQ has a lot of money and has a large number of people, resulting in bloated functional departments. That's the problem with our accounting system. *(Ren Zhengfei: Speech at a Meeting with the IFS Project Team and Staff from Finance, Huawei Executive Office Speech No. [2009] 004)*

Representative offices need to ensure that their demand for goods is accurate. If goods are returned due to mistakes in your plan, the losses incurred will be deducted from your compensation packages. This is the only way for us to make sure that everyone at representative offices takes the accuracy of their goods demands seriously and prevent overstock. If we have too much overstock, costs and expenses will run out of control. Management savings of the company are directly reflected in our compensation packages. *(Ren Zhengfei: Comments to Staff of the Brazil Representative Office and Brazil Supply Center, Huawei Executive Office Speech No. [2014] 050)*

We need to gradually reduce how much secondary sorting we do in warehouses. Warehouse expenses and inventory costs must be allocated to beneficiary departments. But how can we truly reduce our secondary sorting? We need to make sure whoever benefits pays. First, all expenses, such as warehouse rent and labor expenses, should be allocated to those who benefit from them. Otherwise, we will still manufacture products blindly. Second, in the future, most expenses incurred during inventory, return, and scrapping, if not all expenses, should also be allocated to beneficiary departments. Third, supply center warehousing costs should also be allocated to beneficiary departments. If money is saved through direct shipment, rather than using supply center warehouses, we can take a portion from the saved money to reward the department involved. *(Ren Zhengfei: Doing It Right the First Time—Speech at the Global Warehouse Meeting, Huawei Executive Office Speech No. [2014] 060)*

What is the relationship between the financial budget and the headcount budget for delivery resources? Project teams must make plans and prepare budgets for their headcount. We have set clear rules for budget changes, which can flexibly adapt to business changes as needed. The company has formulated strict regulations on headcount control. Because of this, it is difficult for representative offices and resource pools to increase headcount to meet growing business needs. This is a systematic issue. We need to reveal the issue through this pilot project. We don't yet have a mechanism for adjusting project headcount, nor do we have trust-based headcount forecasting and approval. We need to work hard to resolve these issues. What resources do projects need? How do resource departments provide resources? We need to study our resource demand and supply mechanism and strike a balance in this regard. On one hand, we need to emphasize that project teams must develop accurate project resource plans. On the other hand, we must also make it clear that departments that supply resources must take primary responsibility for managing their entire resource plan and coordinating resources. If a project resource plan needs revision, the project team needs to apply for more resources or release resources in advance. The needed lead time can vary by resource level. If a project team fails to apply for more resources or release resources in advance, departments that supply resources can refer to the quotation approach adopted by the Translation Services Center and refund approach used in procurement. In this way, our project teams and departments that supply resources jointly bear costs. *(Source: Minutes of the Meeting of the Finance Committee Office, July 2015)*

Managing project profits and losses, cash flow, and working capital efficiency based on baselines

When assessing the value of a project, we need to assess the project's profits and losses, cash flow, and working capital efficiency, and manage them against baselines. We will continue to improve end-to-end transaction quality and manage it as a top priority of the company. During project execution, we need to closely follow the project plan, stay on budget, and effectively manage project costs, profits, and cash flow to ensure delivery quality. *(Source: 2010 Key Work Requirements, EMT Resolution No. [2010] 007)*

Each country office in the Northern Latin America Region needs to establish its own baseline. You can establish a baseline by analyzing data from the past three years and make improvements against the baseline. For example, you can compare data of this year with that of last year. You don't have to seek a unified baseline, as each country is very different. You should not aim for the best, optimal, or most scientific baseline. Instead, you should use a balanced scoreboard. If you find there are no improvements over the previous year in a given area, you should focus on improving this area next year. This can help improve your management over the long term. Under the Contribute and Share system, both improvements and waste are directly linked to your personal interests. In this way, our expense management will become more scientific. *(Ren Zhengfei: Speech at a Briefing of the Northern Latin America Region and Colombia Representative Office, Huawei Executive Office Speech No. [2014] 051)*

We need to keep optimizing baseline management for representative offices. Each country office should set its own baseline as appropriate. We will explore ways to further optimize baseline management with the help of IT systems and AI technology, which will make this work simpler. Though we do not have clear baselines now, I believe we will develop more scientific baselines. *(Ren Zhengfei: Speech at a Briefing on Improvements and Future Planning for Carrier and Enterprise Regional Organization Transformation, Huawei Executive Office Speech No. [2017] 030)*

9.2.2 Building an Awareness of Project Operations and a Project Operations Management Mechanism

(1) Projects are the basic units and cells of business management at Huawei. If projects are not effectively managed, it will be impossible for the company to achieve robust operations. (2) Project management teams are operating units. C&Q management should cover managers in both permanent and temporary project teams. We should select managers from amongst outstanding project management teams. (3) The annual budget needs to be prepared based on projects or opportunities. Resource allocation should also be based on projects. Project management teams need to buy resources from supporting departments according to their business plans and granted budgets. Supporting departments need to be responsible for resource efficiency. (4) Project management teams are the basic units that manage company operations. Representative offices, account departments, and product lines comprehensively manage project operations from three dimensions: product, customer, and region. The aim is to ensure balanced business development across the company. (5) Employee responsibilities in terms of project operations management must be clearly

defined. Only when responsibilities are assigned to individuals and only when managers are appraised based on the results they deliver, can our employees truly assume responsibilities, help streamline management, and ultimately improve efficiency. *(Ren Zhengfei: Speech at a Briefing on the IFS-PFM Project, Huawei Executive Office Speech No. [2013] 074)*

We need to change our project operations from relying on individual capabilities to relying on organizational capabilities. *(Ren Zhengfei: Speech at a Briefing on the IFS-PFM Project, Huawei Executive Office Speech No. [2013] 074)*

We attach great importance to field experience, which means experience in project operations management. Projects here include sales, delivery, and R&D projects. When selecting and deploying managers, we pay special attention to field and project experience. *(Ren Zhengfei: Speech at a Briefing on the IFS-PFM Project, Huawei Executive Office Speech No. [2013] 074)*

We should always select managers from outstanding project management teams. Project results should be linked to the removal of underperforming managers. We should let the top-performing 30% of project teams take over the bottom 30%. This move will help us constantly improve project operations management. Through this mechanism, we have improved the expertise of our managers, especially those at the junior and middle levels. *(Ren Zhengfei: Speech at a Briefing on the IFS-PFM Project, Huawei Executive Office Speech No. [2013] 074)*

Huawei's project operations are essentially about defining small operating units. Large companies need to be as dynamic and agile as small companies, but can our systems provide strong support in this regard? Large companies are afraid of rigidity, whereas small companies fear losing control. *(Ren Zhengfei: Rigorous, Well-ordered, and Simple Management Is Crucial for Huawei to Scale New Heights, Huawei Executive Office Speech No. [2014] 028)*

Guo Ping said our growth should no longer be driven by scale, but by efficiency and profits. Project operations management is an important way to get there. It is also a basic skill required of all managers. *(Ren Zhengfei: Applying the Spirit of the Tortoise to Catch up with the Dragon Spacecraft—Speech at Huawei Annual Management Conference 2013, Huawei Executive Office Speech No. [2013] 255)*

People in the eight critical roles of a project need to share the responsibility for high-quality project operations. The specifics of these responsibilities vary from role to role. In a project-centered operations pilot project, the Germany Representative Office can explore multiple approaches and ensure that all critical roles in the project assume common but differentiated responsibilities. For example, the PFC takes special responsibility for the accuracy of project budgets, forecasts, and accounting, and will be disciplined if any financial problems occur. If inaccurate financial data is produced during actual operations, the PFC needs to identify the root cause of the inaccuracy. This is also an opportunity for PFCs to get involved in business and continuously improve their project accounting skills. *(Source: Minutes of the Meeting of the Finance Committee Office, July 2015)*

Why do our projects fail to generate profits? The real reason is that our project managers do not conduct accounting properly in the first place. When you have too many resources, you get sloppy. Our project managers are focusing on delivering to customers, but they forget that they have another objective – to earn a profit. We stay customer-centric, but we also have to make profits. Our management at the moment is not effective: Project managers don't understand finances, and project CFOs don't understand business. So at one point we required some of our top project CFOs to serve as project managers in small projects, and some of our big project managers to be project CFOs on small projects. Project CFOs must understand the businesses they serve. On weekends, you can climb towers, or install a base station in a local city suburb. If you don't know how to configure it, you can still screw in the nuts and bolts. That way you'll at least know a little more than others, and you might be promoted faster. Project managers should also learn about finances: For this section of cable, how many man-hours are needed? What is the budget? Go through the calculations. I have approved fast-track promotions for 300 or 400 people in our latest round and some of them are jumping three grades. (*Ren Zhengfei: Generals Are Born of Battle—Speech at the 2015 Project Management Summit, Huawei Executive Office Speech No. [2015] 118*)

9.2.3 Integrating Pre-sales and Post-sales Activities

We must ensure that each large project is managed from end to end. Project estimation, budgeting, accounting, and final accounting span the entire process, from project initiation to payment collection. In reality, this process, which is supposed to be integrated from end to end, has been divided into two segments – sales and delivery. Our incentivization system is also fragmented. Incentives are provided in different phases and are not streamlined. This way, we don't know whether a project makes money or not. I think that bonuses for a sales project should be linked to project profitability. The ratio of timely incentive awards for orders needs to be adjusted based on their estimated profitability. This can drive employees to sign high-quality contracts and effectively manage contract terms. For delivery projects, any difference between project budgets and delivery costs is a key factor considered in bonus allocation. Of course, customer satisfaction is the most important factor. We must clearly understand our roles and responsibilities. *(Xu Zhijun: Building Capabilities Based on Processes to Realize Sustainable and Profitable Growth and Efficient Operations, SDC Office Doc. No. [2013] 011)*

Our management and operations should shift from being function-centered to being project-centered. Customer projects and product projects will be the primary building blocks of the company's operations. Therefore, improving project operations and management capabilities will be our key means of boosting efficiency and profitability over the next couple of years. In 2015, we will continue to promote project-centered operations and begin piloting the integration of pre-sales and post-sales activities at the project level. We aim to resolve issues in three key areas: delegation of authority to project managers, project resource assurance, and budget management. These initiatives will drive the company to change gradually from a weak matrix structure characterized by "function first, project second" to a strong one characterized by "project first, function second". Through the Strategic Reserve which is made up of elite teams, the Key Project Department, and the Project Management Resource Pool, Huawei aims to expedite the circulation of organizations, talent, technologies, management approaches, and experience during project operations. The purpose of this is to support the company's new operating model, enabling those in field offices to call for support. Under this new model, field teams will have both responsibility and authority while back offices provide enablement training and take responsibility for oversight. *(Hu Houkun: Embracing the Future and Building a Better Connected World, Huawei Executive Office Speech No. [2014] 087)*

I think project operations are an end-to-end process, involving pre-sales, post-sales, and collection activities. Delivery is only one part of the process. If regional presidents and representative office general managers only pay attention to profitability and ignore contract quality, the pressure of ensuring project profitability will be all passed on to delivery personnel.

This is unreasonable. *(Xu Zhijun: Developing Delivery into Huawei's Core Competencies, Huawei Executive Office Speech No. [2014] 024)*

Project owners must manage project operations from end to end, that is, from pre-sales to post-sales. In particular, project owners manage and use project budgets, approve applications for risk contingency, and ensure the attainment of project goals. In pre-sales projects, project directors (PDs) arrange for the signing of high-quality contracts, make estimations, identify major risks and assumptions, and ensure estimation quality. In delivery projects, PDs or project managers (PMs) deliver high quality projects efficiently at low costs based on contracts, ensure the attainment of project goals, and take responsibility for project KPIs such as delivery progress, quality, and customer satisfaction. As core members of project operations, project CFOs and PFCs help project owners and PDs/PMs with project operations. PDs/PMs should ensure process compliance and data accuracy during project operations management. PFCs participate in key operations activities throughout the project lifecycles, give early alerts for any potential risks, and support the attainment of project goals. The key operations activities include project estimation, budgeting, accounting, and final accounting, designing an integrated project financial solution, and developing or changing project plans. Project owners, PDs, PMs, and PFCs are all responsible for project results. *(Source: Project Operations and Management Policy, Corp. Doc. No. [2013] 160)*

9.2.4 Closed-Loop Management of Project Risks and Assumptions

Project estimation is based on a project's delivery solutions, baselines, risks, and assumptions. With quantitative analysis using the total cost model, project estimation can help make more informed sales decisions and optimize solutions, including contract terms, to deliver more competitive solutions. Approved project estimations are the initial goals of a project. Project estimations should include quantitative data, like profits, losses, and cash flow; risks and key business assumptions that have a great impact on estimations; and project sales decision making comments. *(Source: Project Operations and Management Policy, Corp. Doc. No. [2013] 160)*

The assumptions and risks described in project estimations reflect our expertise. We must make reasonable assumptions and avoid unrealistic risk assessments. When performing project final accounting, we should comprehensively assess the actual financial results while reviewing the risks and assumptions described in the estimation phase. If our assumptions and risk assessments deviate too much from actual results, our expertise needs to be improved. *(Ren Zhengfei: Speech at a Briefing on the IFS-PFM Project, Huawei Executive Office Speech No. [2013] 074)*

From an operations perspective, the IFS program has established a complete set of methodologies for project operations along the LTC process. As key activities of project operations management, our project estimation, budgeting, accounting, and final accounting are respected and implemented throughout the project lifecycle. Many key transformation points have been incorporated into our daily project management. These key points include "project estimation supporting decision making and solution optimization", "on-budget delivery", and "closed-loop management of risks and assumptions". Now, 99% of project estimations have been archived. Our percentage of budgeted projects has increased from 56% to 99%. A total of 56% of projects have identified and quantified potential risks. Through our High Potential Management Elite Team, reserve pools, and PFC Resource Pool, we are transforming from "operating a single project" to "operating batches of high-quality, replicable programs." *(Meng Wanzhou: Growing amid Transformation—Thoughts at the Closing of the IFS Program, Improvement Issue No. 463, 2014)*

9.3 Matching Project Managers and Project Management Teams' Authority with Their Responsibilities

9.3.1 Matching Project Managers' Authority with Their Responsibilities

To better serve our customers, we should set up our command centers in places that are closest to customers. We should also give field staff the authority to do planning, budgeting, and accounting and make sales decisions. Back offices will decide whether we should engage in a battle whereas field offices will decide how to fight that battle. Back offices should follow the instructions of field offices, rather than the other way around. HQ should be a support, service, and oversight center rather than a center of centralized governance. *(Ren Zhengfei: Speech at the UK Representative Office, Huawei Executive Office Speech No. [2007] 027)*

We should delegate business decision-making authority to field project teams and budgeting authority to project managers. We need to build a project-based incentivization system, and gradually develop a resource buy & sell mechanism. If representative offices are regarded as companies, they need to pay for all services they require from HQ and regions. We can view representative offices as sales and service companies and projects as independent profit centers. Only a clearly defined resource buy & sell mechanism can truly reflect project profits and losses. All of these are part of the most basic financial tools that the company is currently promoting: project estimation, budgeting, accounting, and final accounting. With these tools, we will be able to establish more accurate and clear baselines; have a clearer picture of how to continuously increase project profitability; and make our project-based value-sharing and incentivization systems more scientific and reasonable. *(Xu Zhijun: Building Capabilities Based on Processes to Realize Sustainable and Profitable Growth and Efficient Operations, SDC Office Doc. No. [2013] 011)*

This is going to be a huge change. That means we need to transfer authority from functional departments to project managers. In the future, functional departments will become centers of expertise and resources. Our focus will shift from functional departments to operating teams. Thousands of operating teams, including squads and companies, will be mobilized. *(Xu Zhijun: Building Capabilities Based on Processes to Realize Sustainable and Profitable Growth and Efficient Operations, SDC Office Doc. No. [2013] 011)*

Why do we delegate more authority to field offices? The reason is quite simple. We aim to give more opportunities to outstanding employees who can work independently and let them leverage their potential based on existing processes and policies. We expect our leaders in field offices to be proactive and creative in our core business and work together toward the same goal. *(Ren Zhengfei: Comments to Staff of the Guangzhou Representative Office, Huawei Executive Office Speech No. [2013] 057)*

Project owners should be hands-on, manage operations from end to end (from pre-sales to post-sales), and ensure the attainment of project goals. Project owners should be responsive and accountable, and selected from representative offices. *(Ren Zhengfei: Speech at a Briefing on the IFS-PFM Project, Huawei Executive Office Speech No. [2013] 074)*

We will further delegate authority to field offices, so that they can call for support when needed. Project teams are operating units. We are now setting up a large number of subsidiary boards of directors comprised of many veteran employees to oversee project implementation. *(Ren Zhengfei: Speech at a Meeting with Elite Teams at the Training Camp on July 23, 2013, Huawei Executive Office Speech No. [2013] 174)*

We need to transform how we assign responsibility and delegate authority. With effective oversight and proper checks and balances in place, we must fully trust and boldly delegate authority to qualified field commanders based on their job responsibilities, match their authority with their responsibilities, and get closer to our actual business. *(Hu Houkun: Correct Values and Strong Management Teams Will Lead Huawei to Long-term Success, Huawei Executive Office Speech No. [2013] 240)*

We will continue to drive organizational transformation, streamline management, get closer to our actual business, and give greater autonomy to field offices. The company can grow in size, but our management must not become increasingly complex. Rigorous, well-organized, and simple management is key to scaling new heights. Our efforts will continue to focus on changing HQ from a management and control function to a service and support function. We will give more authority to field offices, to commanders who know best what is going on in the field, so that our organization will be more responsive to opportunities and challenges. In addition, we will integrate all processes at the local and project levels to improve end-to-end efficiency and make it easier for customers to do business with us. *(Xu Zhijun: Focusing on Strategy, Streamlining Management, and Achieving Sustainable and Profitable Growth, Huawei Executive Office Speech No. [2013] 246)*

We must gradually change our top-down, level-by-level authority delegation model that is centered on functional departments. Instead, we need to give project and program managers the requisite authority to manage project operations based on project goals and budgets. Such authority includes authority related to human resources, finances, and daily operations. In this way, we will increase people's initiative in project and program operations management, and promote sustainable and profitable growth of the company. *(Guo Ping: Transform Continuously and Improve Field Operating Capabilities to Ensure the Company's Sustainable and Profitable Growth—Speech at Huawei Annual Management Conference 2013, Huawei Executive Office Speech No. [2014] 020)*

The company will gradually implement project-centered operations. All project managers will shoulder responsibilities related to resource usage, personnel appraisal, and financial approval. This is authority mainly relating to human resources, daily operations, and finances. In the past, project managers had little authority over human resources, as performance and people management were handled by functional departments. That's why we have added a training session on basics about people and performance management this time. (*Ren Zhengfei: Speech at a Meeting with Trainees at the First Training Session for the Global Solutions Elite Team, Huawei Executive Office Speech No. [2014] 064*)

The problem we face now is that collective decision making has gone too far. That's why we have placed greater emphasis on individual accountability. We call this the commander ownership system. We need to have control over our committee system. No committees should be set up in field offices. The closer to field offices, the more emphasis we should place on commander ownership; the closer to top management, the more emphasis we should place on collective decision making. Even in a collective decision-making system, committee or team directors should still assume responsibilities. Collective decision making should not be handled in a one-size-fits-all approach, as this will lead to high costs. We need to delegate more authority to lower levels. (*Ren Zhengfei: Minutes of a Briefing on the Progress of the Project for Changing Function-centered Operations into Project-centered Operations, EMT Meeting Minutes No. [2014] 019*)

9.3.2 Further Developing Project Management Teams and Inspiring Passion Across Field Operating Units

Sales decision-making teams (SDTs) are also project steering teams, responsible for winning contracts, ensuring contract-based delivery, and achieving project results. (*Ren Zhengfei: Speech at a Briefing on the IFS-PFM Project, Huawei Executive Office Speech No. [2013] 074*)

With proper checks and balances in place, we will delegate authority to field offices and increase the grades of frontline positions based on their responsibilities and contributions. This can make organizational operations more flexible and cost-effective. (*Hu Houkun: Correct Values and Strong Management Teams Will Lead Huawei to Long-term Success, Huawei Executive Office Speech No. [2013] 240*)

In terms of operations, we need to adopt a management system where projects are viewed as operating units. How do we define project-centered organizations? What is the role of managers in a project-centered organization? How do we delegate authority and ensure employees are properly incentivized? How do they acquire resources? How can they obtain the requisite authority based on budgets? We need to make changes and find answers to these questions. In the future, the management system should be able to cover all projects, be they R&D, delivery, transformation, or capital construction projects. A broad management system can cover the entire process from product development, to sales, supply, delivery, and finances. *(Ren Zhengfei: Rigorous, Well-ordered, and Simple Management Is Crucial for Huawei to Scale New Heights, Huawei Executive Office Speech No. [2014] 028)*

The fundamental reason we adopt a project-centered operating model is that we want to inspire passion across field operating units and improve operating efficiency. *(Guo Ping: Becoming Project-centered to Support the Company's Sustainable and Profitable Growth—Speech at the 2014 Project Management Summit, 2014)*

9.4 Project Appraisals and Incentives

9.4.1 Adopting an Appraisal and Incentivization Mechanism Based on Final Project Results

When it comes to authority delegation, value assessment, and incentivization for managers, we should move beyond a department-based mechanism and also establish a project-based mechanism. This will motivate all employees and experts in field offices, HQ, and functional departments to proactively participate in projects. They will work hard to make sure project teams are the most effective and agile operating units in the company that ensure project success. *(Ren Zhengfei: Do Not Expand Blindly and Do Not Assume That We Are Already Strong Enough, Huawei Executive Office Speech No. [2012] 006)*

We adhere to an appraisal and incentivization mechanism that is based on final project results. All appraisals and incentives must be based on results and responsibilities. Everyone involved in a project must be responsible for the results of their work. Appraisals based on processes rather than results will lead to buck-passing and fragmentation. Phase-by-phase appraisals can be implemented with the support of bonus points. The value of a bonus point must be ultimately determined by project results. *(Ren Zhengfei: Speech at a Briefing on the IFS-PFM Project, Huawei Executive Office Speech No. [2013] 074)*

Every department has its own unique value and role. Delivery is tasked with building deliverability into contracts; completing deliveries based on contract budgets, schedules, and quality requirements; and ensuring high levels of customer satisfaction. This is the primary value Delivery contributes. Delivery project managers may not necessarily participate in enhancing deliverability in front-end activities. Their primary value lies in supporting delivery based on contract budgets, schedules, and quality requirements, and ensuring high levels of customer satisfaction. Based on these considerations, it would be great if they could save some of their budgets. The performance appraisal of project managers at Siemens is very simple. Their budgets are always relatively accurate. Their project managers then can achieve a full appraisal score if they complete delivery according to schedules and quality requirements and come in at 5% below budget. This rule applies to both delivery and R&D projects. *(Xu Zhijun: Developing Delivery into Huawei's Core Competencies, Huawei Executive Office Speech No. [2014] 024)*

Projects are the basic unit of business management. People in the eight critical roles of a project need to assume the most fundamental management responsibilities for project operations. These people must be responsible for achieving project goals and help representative offices achieve their business goals through successful project operations. *(Ren Zhengfei: Speech at a Meeting with Trainees at the First Training Session for the Global Solutions Elite Team, Huawei Executive Office Speech No. [2014] 064)*

First, we should allow appraisal baselines to vary for different countries and regions. Work in developed regions is a little easier overall, so we should be setting the bar higher there. For example, the baselines for Beijing, Shanghai, and Guangzhou should be higher than those for Xinjiang. Adjusting baselines will encourage dedication in hardship regions and ensure people in these regions are rewarded fairly. *(Ren Zhengfei: Minutes of the Briefing on the Progress of Differentiated Appraisals for Regions, Huawei Executive Office Speech No. [2015] 050)*

9.4.2 Exploring Project Bonuses and Implementing the Contribute and Share System

Project budgets are based on field offices. Profit centers must pay for the services they enjoy, as services come at a cost. If field offices do not choose your services, that means your services are not competitive. In terms of financial resources, human resources, compensation, and bonuses, we need to shift from our current granting system to a Contribute and Share system. Finance needs to explore ways to establish a financial management system that runs representative offices as profit centers. *(Ren Zhengfei: Speech at a Meeting with Financial Managers, Huawei Executive Office Speech No. [2012] 029)*

Regarding incentives based on project results, can we just keep records, rather than require all incentive changes to get approval every time? We should trust in project managers' ability to distribute money fairly. Only by giving them this trust can the authority of project managers match their responsibilities and can they be motivated to effectively manage projects. *(Ren Zhengfei: Speech at a Briefing on the IFS-PFM Project, Huawei Executive Office Speech No. [2013] 074)*

We need to change our incentivization mechanism and adopt the Contribute and Share system whereby those who contribute more are rewarded more. This system will take root and bloom in a few years. *(Ren Zhengfei: Speech at a Meeting with Elite Teams at the Training Camp on July 23, 2013, Huawei Executive Office Speech No. [2013] 174)*

In 2012, I suggested that we implement a value-sharing mechanism for delivery projects to continuously reduce our delivery costs. What is a project value-sharing mechanism? For example, suppose the cost budget of a delivery project is US$1 million based on the capability baseline. However, the project manager motivates project team members to improve delivery efficiency and completes delivery at a cost of only US$900,000, saving US$100,000 for the company. To reward the delivery project team for its contribution, the company will take a portion of the US$100,000 that was saved to reward the delivery project team. This bonus is recognized as a cost in the books. Capability baselines will also be updated at the same time. In this way, every reward in cost saving will lead to a new delivery capability baseline. By sharing the costs saved, we can fully motivate all delivery employees to continuously improve delivery efficiency and reduce delivery costs. After repeated pushes from Dr. Howard Liang and myself, the value-sharing mechanism has been implemented for managed services projects. However, a consensus on the value-sharing mechanism for delivery projects has not been reached, mainly because the capability baseline for delivery projects has not been set and we cannot ensure accuracy or reliability of project budgets. *(Xu Zhijun: Developing Delivery into Huawei's Core Competencies, Huawei Executive Office Speech No. [2014] 024)*

We should implement the Contribute and Share system and effectively manage the structure of our value distribution. We need to pay attention to each part of the organization, and allow each and every employee to benefit from the company's growth. First, our analysis based on compensation benchmarks must be more reasonable. We need to effectively manage the ratio of how much is distributed to those pulling the cart and how much is distributed to those riding the cart. Pullers should get more than riders, and pullers should get the most when they are pulling the hardest. Second, we must not only widen the gap between the incomes of those at the top of our talent pyramid and top experts in the industry. We must also pay attention to those at the bottom of our pyramid, so we are effectively covering the entire organization. Non-monetary incentives should enable the majority of employees to see opportunities, and inspire them to work hard and strive for excellence. We must not depend solely on monetary incentives to seize strategic opportunities. More importantly, we must develop our strategic and systematic thinking. *(Ren Zhengfei: Speech at the Briefing on Recent Motivation Orientations and Principles, Huawei Executive Office Speech No. [2014] 079)*

The company has provided guidelines and a framework for project incentives, and regions have proactively implemented project bonuses. We have drawn two conclusions from this for future project incentives. First, project bonuses should come from project profits and should be part of a representative office's annual bonus packages. It has been proposed that bonuses for below-budget execution (also bonuses for project operations improvements) should be included in project costs. As we have not worked out a feasible solution for this, this proposal will not be considered for the time being. Second, the company has two key requirements for delivery projects. One is that delivery must be made on time and on budget, and to a high degree of quality to ensure customer satisfaction. The other is that revenue must increase and costs cut to improve project operations. We have implemented a value-sharing mechanism based on project operations improvements in the managed services projects of GTS and some regions. We encourage field offices to experiment with bonuses for project operations improvements. Regions and representative offices can develop their own solutions, but project bonuses must come from their annual bonus packages. *(Source: Minutes of the Work Report on the Project for Changing Function-centered Operations into Project-centered Operations, BOD Executive Committee Meeting Minutes No. [2015] 020)*

Project goals must include budget targets – on-budget execution and budget-based improvements. Additional rewards should be given for below-budget execution (i.e., generating more revenue, cutting costs). Project bonuses can be divided into two parts. The first part can be awarded for on-budget execution. A project team will receive this part as long as they complete the project on budget. The other part should be used to drive project operations improvements based on budget targets. *(Source: Minutes of the Meeting of the Finance Committee Office, July 2015)*

Open Access This chapter is licensed under the terms of the Creative Commons Attribution-NonCommercial-NoDerivatives 4.0 International License (http://creativecommons.org/licenses/by-nc-nd/4.0/), which permits any noncommercial use, sharing, distribution and reproduction in any medium or format, as long as you give appropriate credit to the original author(s) and the source, provide a link to the Creative Commons licence and indicate if you modified the licensed material. You do not have permission under this license to share adapted material derived from this chapter or parts of it.

The images or other third party material in this chapter are included in the chapter's Creative Commons licence, unless indicated otherwise in a credit line to the material. If material is not included in the chapter's Creative Commons licence and your intended use is not permitted by statutory regulation or exceeds the permitted use, you will need to obtain permission directly from the copyright holder.

CHAPTER 10

Optimizing the Management Control System for Responsibility Centers

Accurately defining what type of responsibility center (RC) a department will be is vital for a company's management control system to work effectively. Budgeting, appraisal, accounting, and incentivization all revolve around RCs. The purpose of defining RCs is to properly assign responsibilities, streamline management, and motivate the workforce. How do we define an RC? This is one of the major questions that a management control system must answer. Key considerations include the nature of the business and the type of operating mechanism. All in all, the operating mechanism must be value-driven.

RCs usually correlate to accounting granularity, or what order of magnitude their accounting deals with. Huawei's practices prove that granularity should be small and determined by actual circumstances. Otherwise, it will be difficult to properly assign business management responsibilities and determine how much value a team brings to the company. The inability to determine this value will make it difficult to tie incentives to contributions, causing organizational vitality to suffer. But this does not mean that smaller granularity is always better, because overly small granularity leads to more internal transaction interfaces and higher internal transaction costs. Therefore, a key consideration of management control is to define RCs from a strategic perspective to ensure cost effectiveness.

Huawei's experience has proven that a system of checks and balances must be in place between RCs. Profit centers, such as product lines and representative offices, must have their unique areas of focus. A product

© The Author(s) 2019
W. Huang, *Built on Value*,
https://doi.org/10.1007/978-981-13-7507-1_10

line – as a profit center – should prioritize revenue over profits, and maximize revenue with a more aggressive sales plan. A representative office, which is also a type of profit center, should focus on profits over revenue, so its sales plan tends to be more conservative. This arrangement enables us to strike a balance between being aggressive and being conservative, with checks and balances in place.

RC appraisal and incentive mechanisms must be designed in a way that ties incentives to results and encourages collective dedication. These mechanisms need to widen the gaps between incentives for different teams based on their results, or contributions. The mechanisms must also reinforce the company's customer-centric culture and fine tradition of "toasting those who succeed and offering a helping hand to those who fail". Huawei achieves these goals with multiple methods, including adjusted statistics and adjusted performance appraisals.

HQ must serve as a resource pool, and resources must be bought and sold according to market rules. Building HQ as a resource pool and field offices as profit centers is the direction in which Huawei is heading. Budgets for HQ are set at a baseline that is adequate to help maintain its normal operations. If HQ wants more money, it needs to provide resources and services to field offices and charge them for these resources and services. Field profit centers must bear the costs for these resources and services. This is the resource "buy & sell" model. It puts checks and balances between field and back offices to ensure that field offices don't become aimless and back offices have clearly defined capability requirements.

This chapter discusses in detail the above key points of management control systems for RCs.

10.1 Every Operating Mechanism Is Ultimately Value-Driven

10.1.1 Making Accounting Granularity Small as Needed

We need to transform field offices and product lines from revenue centers into profit centers. We have spent two decades of effort building up our organization and market presence. We did not do this just to bleed our capital or end up getting nowhere. The transformation of field offices into profit centers must gradually begin. When the marketing and sales team in China reported their work, they talked about how many contributions they had made and how great they were. But I just want to ask, "What contributions have you made to the company? Have you contributed enough profits to the company?" After being developed for 18 years, the Chinese market has matured. Currently, the marketing and sales team in China should earn enough profits for the company to support market development and product lines. This is how we should transform field offices into profit centers. *(Ren Zhengfei: Adapting the Manager Appraisal System to Challenges Facing the Transforming Industry, Huawei Executive Office Speech No. [2006] 036)*

Non-core business departments need to gradually shift towards independent accounting. They need to find their own way to make profits and survive, to use a market-driven approach to transact with core business departments. Smartcom (Huawei's subsidiary) and Staff Plaza (an arm of Smartcom) have both successfully rolled out independent accounting. Huawei University needs to do the same. You can scale up your business when profits grow, or scale it down if products and services are not selling well. *(Ren Zhengfei: Minutes of the Second Report on the 2012 Corporate Budget, EMT Meeting Minutes No. [2012] 010)*

We need to meaningfully restructure our organization to increase efficiency and reduce redundant workforce. Can field offices work normally if an entire HQ team takes a month of leave all together? If the answer is yes, then that HQ team is unnecessary. HQ must be downsized; otherwise, salary raises won't be allowed. If the downsizing of an HQ team negatively impacts the business of field offices, we need to figure out who really need to carry out their business. If field offices don't experience any pains after the downsizing, then that HQ team is simply redundant. If the team has no effect on field offices, it needs to be disbanded. It's like if you have a multi-horse wagon and the reins for one of the horses are always loose. This means the horse isn't running fast enough and is thus not necessary. It's better to cut these reins and let the horse go. Our organizational restructuring should follow the same approach. *(Ren Zhengfei: Speech at the EMT ST Meeting, 2012)*

A representative office's level depends on how much value it creates for the company, rather than the size of the country it represents. Every project must generate profits. Our best resources must be channeled to valued customers. We must first decide how many resources we invest in a customer based on the profit margin they can offer us, and then we work to improve customer satisfaction. We define "big project" as any project that earns us big money. Small projects are those that earn us small money. The size of a project must be determined by how much value it creates for the company, rather than its scale. A small project can become a big one, and the same principle applies to our representative offices. We won't see heroes emerge in great numbers if our managers' personal grades are determined only by how large their scope of management is, how high the level of their department is, or how many functional units they manage. *(Ren Zhengfei: Remarks at a Meeting with Members of the Project & Financial Management Enablement Program for High Potentials, Huawei Executive Office Speech No. [2014] 054)*

Our representative offices must be comprised of highly competent, lean teams, not large, cumbersome ones. This reflects our concept of "Squad Leaders' Fight". Where can these offices get the resources they lack? From mobile teams such as elite teams, the Key Project Department, and the Project Management Resource Pool. By utilizing mobile forces, we can downsize field command centers and manage them effectively to *harvest more crops*. *(Ren Zhengfei: Speech at the EMT ST Meeting on July 25, 2014, Huawei Executive Office Speech No. [2014] 059)*

The "Squad Leaders' Fight" is to make our operations flexible, agile, and efficient. At its core is the "mission command" approach, which, with the backing of the organization and systems, allows those who are closest to customers to call for support. By delegating authority and providing direction, mission command enables agile and adaptive lower-ranking commanders to carry out disciplined initiatives within the intents of their upper-level commanders. Mission command is the most effective way for lower-ranking commanders to realize the intents of their upper-level commanders. *(Ren Zhengfei: Speech at a Briefing on the Takeaways and Challenges for Huawei Relating to the "Squad Leaders' Fight", Huawei Executive Office Speech No. [2014] 078)*

Our entire organization needs to be restructured to make mission command effective. The "Squad Leaders' Fight" does not mean that we leave squad leaders to fight alone. Rather, this model requires the support of the following:

- Division of responsibilities: Give tactical command authority to field operating teams. Executives and HQ should focus on developing corporate strategies, setting the company's direction, and allocating resources.
- Authority delegation: Separate administrative management authority from operations command authority, and properly delegate authority based on clearly defined rules and the preparedness of subordinates.

- Organizational structure: Remove or restructure field teams by function based on business needs.
- Resource distribution: Deploy tactical resources close to field operating teams and centrally allocate strategic resources to ensure rapid and effective response.
- Capability development: Comprehensively develop capabilities based on strategic needs.
- Processes: Business operations processes should focus on improving operating capabilities to adapt to a complex, volatile environment. Administrative management processes need to be rigorous and comprehensive.
- Information systems: Build an interconnected information environment to allow commanders at all levels to get whatever information they need anytime and anywhere to complete a task and develop a common understanding of the operating environment.

(Ren Zhengfei: Speech at a Briefing on the Takeaways and Challenges for Huawei Relating to the "Squad Leaders' Fight", Huawei Executive Office Speech No. [2014] 078)

Our representative offices act like fortresses for our company, so we must consider how we should build them in the future. Current US military theory talks about direct command to the battalion, not just to the brigade. Direct command to the battalion places this unit as the operational base, and the US military can do this because it has powerful long-range firepower and clear processes. However, Huawei's country-level business performance baselines are far from clear. Each country office should establish baselines based on its average business performance from the past three years. If business performance in a country exceeds its baseline, we can say the managers in this country have done a good job. Otherwise, managers in Shanghai will certainly be promoted faster than those in Mozambique or Malawi because these two countries have less potential contracts to secure. The same can be said for Iraq and Libya. In my opinion, the Human Resource Management Department's most important role is to manage rules. This includes appraisal rules for business performance baselines, which should be reviewed each year. If there is a war, epidemic, or other challenge in a region and you still expect staff there to meet the previous business performance baseline – the unified, global baseline – then I would consider your appraisal method rather backward. In China, how can Shanghai and Xinjiang be measured on the same scale? In turn, the China region must establish different business performance baselines according to the specific circumstances of each location. I worry that no one will want to go to work in less developed regions like Xinjiang and Latin America, and that our operations in these locations will collapse. Therefore, I've recently made trips to some of these regions. I've just been to Xinjiang, where I told our local staff that they must become the first in China to achieve the "Five Ones". Why did I say this? For each process, we have a process owner. If inventory accounts are inconsistent with actual goods, then you cannot pass certain process checkpoints, which will force you to ensure the CIAG. This way, within six months, five exemplary process owners will emerge – let's call them "generals-to-be" for the time being. The following year, these five generals-to-be will be moved to Urumqi to ensure the CIAG there. Five successors – or deputy process owners – will be chosen to look after their processes. These successors must not only maintain the CIAG along these processes, but also review the accounts of previous periods. By doing this, another five "generals-to-be" will emerge. The combined efforts of these two groups of "generals-to-be" will lead to the CIAG in Xinjiang, two to three years ahead of the China region. Xinjiang is positioned to achieve these results first and become a hotbed for "generals". When heroes and managers emerge from such difficult regions, other people will want to go to work there. If we do not use this type of approach, who will want to go to work in challenging regions? *(Ren Zhengfei: Speech at a Briefing on the Takeaways and Challenges for Huawei Relating to the "Squad Leaders' Fight", Huawei Executive Office Speech No. [2014] 078)*

Representative offices should have the authority to select customers and products, and to make decisions on contracts. This will drive our back offices to transform. The decision-making authority of representative offices should be limited to businesses of uncertainty. Authority related to costs through the end-to-end process will not be delegated and these costs must follow pre-set baselines. *(Ren Zhengfei: There Will Not Always Be Flowers Along the Road Ahead—Speech at the H1 Huawei Market Conference, Huawei Executive Office Speech No. [2016] 079)*

Delegation of authority allows representative offices to approve more matters within a larger scope. Within our three-procedure loop, all business activities only need to go through three procedures – application, review, and approval. Achieving the three-procedure loop should be a goal that we pursue. This goal can only be attained if HQ can promptly provide the support and services that representative offices need to deliver results more easily and rapidly. *(Source: Minutes of a Report on Delegation of Authority, Three-procedure Loop, and Contract Approval by Representative Offices, EMT Meeting Minutes No. [2016] 007)*

All business domains are proactively delegating authority to field offices. The Executive Management Team (EMT) has approved three initiatives with regards to delegation, acquisition, and exercise of authority. First, regarding delegation of authority, we will review authority across processes in all domains, and delegate more authority to field offices from the top down. With a focus on field projects (known as the *cells* of business management), we must also holistically identify requests for authority from the bottom up while considering customer needs and business results, and then drive delegation of authority. Second, when it comes to acquisition of authority, our upper-level managers currently delegate authority on a level-by-level basis via delegation letters. Moving forward, authority will be directly assigned to field operating positions. Third, for exercise of authority, our existing processes cannot support diverse operating scenarios in the field, so we need to further clarify operating scenarios and optimize processes to ensure effective exercise of authority. *(Source: Minutes of a Report on Delegation of Authority, Three-procedure Loop, and Contract Approval by Representative Offices, EMT Meeting Minutes No. [2016] 007)*

Our appraisal policies need to vary by country, so that we can provide some support to hardship regions. Don't think that we just want to make money. After all, our mission is to serve humanity. We must take necessary measures to realize this mission. We might lose markets in some regions. That's okay. We must not allow them to drag our company down. *(Ren Zhengfei: There Will Not Always Be Flowers Along the Road Ahead—Speech at the H1 Huawei Market Conference, Huawei Executive Office Speech No. [2016] 079)*

10.1.2 Using the Value Distribution System to Drive Business Units to Operate on Their Own, Responsible for Profits and Losses, and Incentives and Constraints

Huawei has grown into what it is today because of its relatively balanced value distribution mechanism. Looking ahead, we must adopt diversified and multi-dimensional value distribution mechanisms. Support provided by different appraisal units must be reflected when we distribute value. We must ensure that the interests of all of our company stakeholders are balanced, and that all units across the company collaborate to achieve business success. We should also identify potential risks arising from delegation of the planning, budgeting, and accounting authority to business units, resolve the issue of value distribution across departments, and prevent the emergence of cliques with their own agendas. *(Source: EMT Meeting Minutes No. [2008] 014)*

We need to guide different business units through different performance indicator systems and appraisals. First, we need to examine market opportunities for the next two to three years, and identify which business units are becoming profit centers, which business units are in a transitional stage, and which business units are still in the growth stage. Second, we should fix the headcount and positions of business units that are built as profit centers. These business units will be appraised based on the profits they create for the company. When appraising business units that are built as sales centers, we should still focus on sales growth. Third, business units with a large revenue base and limited growth potential should be primarily appraised according to their absolute sales growth; business units with a small revenue base and large growth potential should primarily be appraised according to their relative sales growth. *(Source: Minutes of the Report on the Q1 Business Review, EMT Meeting Minutes No. [2009] 031)*

Our appraisal and incentive mechanisms are designed to encourage initiative. We need to gradually change from granting incentives from the top down to an approach that distributes value based on contribution. I expect to see a fundamental change in our appraisal and incentive mechanisms, moving from top-down value distribution, to performance-based value sharing. Once you have created value for the company, you can know roughly how much money you will get. This value sharing model will eliminate boss-centric behavior. In addition to sharing value with the company, you also need to share its risks, and accept the risk that you may earn less if you create less value for the company. Major risks faced by Huawei will be managed mainly through delegation of authority. *(Ren Zhengfei: Speech at the Self-reflection Session of the Executive Committee of the Board of Directors, 2012)*

Focusing on strategy and streamlining management are the key goals we must pursue. We need to delegate more authority and have fewer KPIs. We need to assess in-process work with fewer KPIs and eliminate KPIs intended for process segments. We need to gradually change our value distribution mechanism, from top-down granting to a Contribute and Share system. *(Ren Zhengfei: Focusing on Strategy and Streamlining Management, Huawei Executive Office Speech No. [2012] 041)*

The objectives of management are to improve efficiency and *harvest more crops*. The most important KPI should always be whether a business has *harvested more crops*. This is to discourage everyone from managing just for the sake of managing, doing unnecessary things, and ignoring the importance of *harvesting more crops*. *(Ren Zhengfei: Speech at the Report on the Integrated Management Transformation in Small Countries, Huawei Executive Office Speech No. [2014] 062)*

10.1.3 Leveraging the Value Sharing Mechanism and Strategic Investment to Reinforce Our Culture of "Toasting Those Who Succeed and Offering a Helping Hand to Those Who Fail"

We must encourage collective dedication. Our appraisal and incentive mechanisms should support both our customer-centric culture and our fine tradition of "toasting those who succeed and offering a helping hand to those who fail." Our incentive mechanisms, such as adjusted statistics and adjusted performance appraisals, will ensure that value is shared between field and back offices, and between operating and supporting teams. *(Source: EMT Meeting Minutes No. [2008] 021)*

To seize strategic opportunities, we may need to sacrifice some of the interests of shareholders temporarily and allow for a decline in our profits. We must first make our compensation structure more reasonable and formulate reasonable HR policies. During our pursuit of strategic opportunities, we may end up losing opportunities if we control compensation too tightly in order to maintain profits. *(Ren Zhengfei: Guidelines on the Analysis of the Business Environment and Key Business Strategies, Corp. Doc. No. [2012] 081)*

The Regions Management Department should review the appraisal baselines for countries with strict foreign exchange controls every year. We need to provide more timely incentives to teams in these countries so they will be motivated to make significant contributions. For these countries, we have always stressed that we sign contracts based on the amount of cash that can be repatriated to China. If the amount that can be repatriated in a given country is low, we need to reduce headcount there and transfer some employees elsewhere to seize strategic opportunities. When it comes to trapped cash, managers at all levels should study *Huawei Executive Office Speech No. [2014] 071 Remarks by Ren Zhengfei During Visits to Countries Where Cash Is Trapped.* In that speech, I gave clear instructions on how to deal with trapped cash. In the future, HQ will develop techniques for strategic decisions and function as an experts' team to make decisions on trapped cash issues. Project decision-making authority will be delegated to representative offices, regional offices, and subsidiary boards. This way, subsidiary boards will have both authority and responsibility, and authority will be moved closer to field offices. *(Ren Zhengfei: Minutes of the Briefing on the Progress of Differentiated Appraisals for Regions, Huawei Executive Office Speech No. [2015] 050)*

In countries affected by war, civil unrest, or epidemics, HQ can bear certain costs. This includes the cost of bottled water and dried food in desert areas, or face masks in polluted countries. Can HQ bear satellite rental costs to ensure Internet access in war-torn countries? Without network access, people cannot work. Remember, our employees are paid high wages. If such costs are paid by HQ, we would be able to develop reasonable appraisal baselines for different regions around the world. *(Ren Zhengfei: Minutes of the Briefing on the Progress of Differentiated Appraisals for Regions, Huawei Executive Office Speech No. [2015] 050)*

"Toasting those who succeed and offering a helping hand to those who fail." This is a slogan we coined in our early years, and it represented exactly what we did at work. But we have stopped following the spirit of this slogan. Why is that? It is because of our KPI-based appraisal system. When every representative office has their own sources of interests, they tend to work in isolation and hoard resources without considering the overall interests of the company. We need to revert to our original model that prioritizes the interests of the company as a whole. There needs to be major changes to our KPI-based appraisal system. Change is taking place gradually. Failure will be inevitable if field offices prioritize their own interests to the exclusion of all else. Through continuous improvement, we need to get rid of that mentality and adopt new work approaches. I see three operating scenarios for the future. First, there will be representative offices that are able to operate independently, without the support of our elite teams. Second, there will be representative offices that need the support of elite teams. They must pay for these elite team resources, and the company encourages them to seek support by giving them a budget for this purpose. When an elite team has helped a representative office secure a project, the costs of that elite team must be accounted for under the representative office. The costs must be recovered, because once the project is won, the representative office will have access to more opportunities. If the project fails, the company will bear the costs. In the third scenario, when there are huge changes in a hardship region, the local representative office can directly transfer its employees to the three elite teams of the

Strategic Reserve where they can rotate and receive training. True quality shines through, no matter where an employee works, be it the elite teams, the Key Project Department, or the Project Management Resource Pool. *(Ren Zhengfei: Speech at a Meeting with Trainees at the First Training Session for the Global Solutions Elite Team, Huawei Executive Office Speech No. [2014] 064)*

10.2 Methods for Managing Responsibility Centers

10.2.1 We Establish Responsibility Centers to Define Responsibilities, Streamline Management, and Motivate the Workforce

Just now, you said you wanted to adapt our processes to all three business groups (BGs). Then, what is the point of dividing our business into three BGs? At a previous briefing on financial budgeting, the presenter began the session by talking about adapting processes to support multi-BG expansion. I simply asked the presenter to stop talking and leave. Who says we will need multi-BG expansion? Our three-BG structure aims to streamline management, with each BG operating independently from each other. There is no need to adapt our processes to all three BGs. Resource sharing was important when the company was small, but this approach causes waste when the company is large. We have made our processes all-encompassing and excessively large, due to our overemphasis on process adaptation. When major processes are clean and transparent, we can streamline major sub-processes. After all unnecessary functions are removed, our sub-processes will become open and flexible. *(Ren Zhengfei: Speech and Comments at the Strategy Retreat of the Business Process & IT Management Department, Huawei Executive Office Speech No. [2012] 026)*

To reduce airfare costs, representative offices used to hire many people. This made it difficult for them to adapt to changes in business volume. Now, we have implemented a compensation package system, which has led to some changes. However, headcount in representative offices is still too high. Strategic mobile forces should be used to adjust this structure. *(Ren Zhengfei: Speech at a Briefing on the Takeaways and Challenges for Huawei Relating to the "Squad Leaders' Fight", Huawei Executive Office Speech No. [2014] 078)*

The purpose of transformation is to make operations easier, more prompt, and more accurate. *(Ren Zhengfei: The Purpose of Transformation Is to Make Operations Easier, More Prompt, and More Accurate—Speech at the Briefing on the ISC+ Transformation Program, Huawei Executive Office Speech No. [2016] 016)*

The goal of management is to effectively generate revenue. We must first streamline sales processes and then delivery processes, including our supply chain, allowing them to operate with agility. We should never accept processes that are not streamlined with the excuse that we are optimizing them. We must not invest huge amounts of resources in approving contracts level by level just to avoid shipping the wrong board. I would rather see such a mistake happen. We can analyze root causes later, but we need to streamline processes first. *(Ren Zhengfei: There Will Not Always Be Flowers Along the Road Ahead—Speech at the H1 Huawei Market Conference, Huawei Executive Office Speech No. [2016] 079)*

The purpose of management is to help the company succeed. We need to assign both responsibility and authority to managers at every control point of our processes, with appropriate oversight in place, of course. Many approvers sign their names without even looking at what they are signing. So why do we need such a control point? It's not necessary at all. We will gradually optimize our customer service process along two key lines. One is sales and the other is delivery. We must resolve customer problems quickly. We will also optimize our internal service processes, for example, finance. However, this optimization must not impact the sales process. *(Ren Zhengfei: There Will Not Always Be Flowers Along the Road Ahead—Speech at the H1 Huawei Market Conference, Huawei Executive Office Speech No. [2016] 079)*

The objectives and responsibilities of our managers at all levels must be clearly defined. Our appraisal system focuses on responsibilities and results. This system has created a simple and positive climate at Huawei, allowing more employees to fix their eyes on customers. Our focus on responsibilities and results will nurture many outstanding managers and discourage ingratiation and flattery at Huawei. *(Ren Zhengfei: Firm Belief and Strong Focus Lead to Greater Success—Speech at the 2016 Huawei Market Conference, Huawei Executive Office Speech No. [2016] 007)*

The Logistics Service Department should have the ability to provide professional services. The department should establish basic rules, and learn how to effectively leverage supplier resources to make up for its lack of capabilities. We should concentrate our supplier resources by reducing the number of suppliers, identifying suppliers that deliver high quality, and paying higher prices for their high-quality services. *(Ren Zhengfei: Speech on the Work of the Logistics Service Department and Smartcom, Huawei Executive Office Speech No. [2016] 086)*

Smartcom should try its best to outsource fragmented businesses, as this will streamline management and make it possible to provide high-quality, differentiated services. You might encounter problems early on in this process, but don't step back. You must be resolute. You should gradually outsource these businesses. If you open up to the outside world, your management abilities will mature and you will make our campus increasingly prosperous. When people make money, they become greatly motivated. Smartcom should only run a small part of businesses that are not yet ready for outsourcing. Outlets run by Smartcom should be appraised according to market rules. Don't turn Smartcom into a "group-owned company". You should establish a competition mechanism. The Employee Service Department is not the International Conference Center, so cost accounting needs to be performed. All costs for self-run outlets should be calculated, including rent, water, electricity bills, compensation, and dividends. All should be included in the virtual financial statement, which will be monitored and managed so that your business will continuously improve. *(Ren Zhengfei: Speech on the Work of the Logistics Service Department and Smartcom, Huawei Executive Office Speech No. [2016] 086)*

PO generation needs to be shifted forward. We must strive to generate POs correctly on the first try. If complaints about PO errors are filed after shipment, the back office should promptly review the rules that allowed the errors and make adjustments. They should not just examine and approve each PO. We will reduce the examination process from four steps to two. The first step should be easy, so people can do things right. During the second step, people with field experience should take charge of the examination, as they know where the errors are, and how to find and rectify them. Rules should only be changed after repeated reasoning. We should strive to reduce the original four levels of responsibility to two. The first level takes ultimate responsibility for the POs, whereas the second level takes responsibility for process rectification. *(Ren Zhengfei: Speech at the EMT ST Meeting on January 25, 2016, Huawei Executive Office Speech No. [2016] 054)*

Project-centered organizations and representative offices are the focuses of our organization transformation that involves our regional carrier and enterprise businesses. The aim of this transformation is to improve the decision-making capabilities of our field offices. We will give them responsibility, authority, and the corresponding interests. We will pilot a model where representative offices have the authority to approve contracts. The focus of our transformation over the next several years is to allow representative offices to make decisions on business operations, BGs to coordinate resources and develop capabilities, and HQ to provide service and support. We will use projects to guide representative offices, and use representative offices to guide Greater Regions and regional offices. Delegating authority is a means to an end. We also need to strengthen systematic training and oversight. We need to improve the decision-making capabilities of field offices, because making decisions is also fulfilling responsibilities. Moving forward, regional offices will have several layers of operational responsibility centers. The first layer will be project-centered organizations. The second layer will be key account departments of representative offices. The third layer will be representative offices. The company's Board of Directors assumes the ultimate responsibility for business operations, and HQ provides service and support to help fulfill this responsibility. Revolving around these layers of operational responsibility centers, we need to define responsibility, and design authority, oversight, and manager appraisal criteria. Greater Regions and regional offices above representative offices will not necessarily become operational responsibility centers. *(Ren Zhengfei: Speech at a Briefing on Improvements and Future Planning for Carrier and Enterprise Regional Organization Transformation, Huawei Executive Office Speech No. [2017] 030)*

10.2.2 Incorporating Checks and Balances into Responsibility Center Management

Over the years, the business relationship between BGs and regional offices has been unclear. Yesterday, the relationship was finally clarified. Regional offices are command centers that have the authority to command operations, select products, and make decisions on contracts. BGs provide necessary resources and collaborate with regional offices to secure contracts. The Joint Committee of Regions (JCR) will mainly drive the establishment of a manager rotation mechanism and create a favorable work environment. Its biggest decision-making authority relates to manager deployment, not business decisions. The JCR can't directly manage projects. The JCR, BGs, and regional offices need to work closely together towards the same goal and achieve business success. They should not operate independently from one another. Some people may ask, "Can BGs rotate their managers?" Yes, they can, but they should primarily rotate managers within their BGs. Cross-domain rotation may not be possible for them. The JCR can rotate outstanding managers across domains in different departments after conducting joint reviews. *(Ren Zhengfei: Speech at a Meeting with Trainees at the First Training Session for the Sales Project Management Resource Pool, Huawei Executive Office Speech No. [2014] 066)*

During organizational transformation, the ultimate command or decision-making authority needs to be clearly delegated. We first need to be clear about which types of authority should be delegated to regional offices, and which to BGs. I agree that there can be many different types of decision-making authority, but what I mean here is the "ultimate" decision-making authority. BGs are sales-revenue-oriented, while regional offices are profit-oriented. I believe that business decision-making authority should be given to regional offices. BGs should focus their efforts on building up resources, developing strategies, and taking part in operations. In order to increase sales revenue, BGs should find ways to persuade field commanders to adopt their points of view. I tend to agree that the Consumer BG holds the decision-making authority over its own business. For all other businesses, however, decision-making authority rests with regional offices. *(Ren Zhengfei: Speech at a Briefing on the Takeaways and Challenges for Huawei Relating to the "Squad Leaders' Fight", Huawei Executive Office Speech No. [2014] 078)*

To reduce airfare costs, representative offices used to hire many people. This made it difficult for them to adapt to changes in business volume. Now, we have implemented a compensation package system, which has led to some changes. However, headcount in representative offices is still too high. Strategic mobile forces should be used to adjust this structure. *(Ren Zhengfei: Speech at a Briefing on the Takeaways and Challenges for Huawei Relating to the "Squad Leaders' Fight", Huawei Executive Office Speech No. [2014] 078)*

When giving the ultimate decision-making authority to field commanders, it is important that we do not allow BGs or the Strategic Reserve to do what field commanders are supposed to do. If you do not think field commanders are up to the job, you can redeploy them and appoint new ones. However, the command authority should still remain with the field. We can take our recent meeting about how to address strict foreign exchange controls in Latin America as an example. The first point I would like to make in this respect is that the countries and personnel who are involved in addressing funds repatriation difficulties are the main operating teams. These people should be put ahead of even our sales teams in terms of opportunities to move higher up in the ranks, including manager selection. The reason is if they can find a way to repatriate 80 million dollars of foreign exchange, then achieving 80 million dollars in sales for that area will be a piece of cake. Despite this, we have treated these employees as low-ranking "aides" for too long. How does this help us solve our problems? Second, I think we should delegate the decision-making authority on operational matters to subsidiary boards of directors. In the past, approval was made by HQ. But HQ cannot handle all approval requests. What kind of decision-making authority should HQ have? Decisions on solutions. Our experts have decision-making authority over solutions. When it comes to execution, however, the decision-making authority should rest with the field. Regarding the oversight over decisions made in the field, subsidiary boards of directors have a role to play. I mention this point in the hopes that the Treasury Solution Department and the Finance Planning Department will step up to solve this problem. *(Ren Zhengfei: Speech at a Briefing on the Takeaways and Challenges for Huawei Relating to the "Squad Leaders' Fight", Huawei Executive Office Speech No. [2014] 078)*

We need to consolidate departments and reduce the review levels more rapidly, giving field offices the authority to approve more matters. Don't panic about authority delegation. We will still run audits on any exercise of authority. Representative offices will become profit centers and have certain command authority. As we continue to delegate more authority, representative office operating platforms will become larger for a period of time. This is because the shift of our HQ management platform forward to field offices is a process of gradual transformation. *(Ren Zhengfei: The Purpose of Transformation Is to Make Operations Easier, More Prompt, and More Accurate—Speech at the Briefing on the ISC+ Transformation Program, Huawei Executive Office Speech No. [2016] 016)*

There must be checks and balances between regional offices and BGs in terms of planning systems. BGs should have more ambitious sales plans, while regional offices should remain a little more conservative. You asked earlier about "deploying troops" and "maintaining troops", the project-based operations of marketing execution teams (METs). First, we need to change from unified planning to a more diversified approach to planning. This is something we've learned from the US military. US command centers have the authority to make battle decisions, but have no troops of their own. In contrast, its resource centers have troops, but don't have the authority to make battle decisions. Our BGs and product lines are our resource centers. They can see more opportunities, so their sales plans should be more ambitious. They should actively market their own products, and do not have to worry too much about project profits. Our regional offices are profit centers. Their sales plans should be more conservative, because they have to avoid locking themselves into situations that will bleed away their investment. Between the ambitious and the conservative, we have found a balance. Looking back at the system now, we see that it has helped boost the quality of our product lines even if it took time for us to understand the details. If BGs' sales plan targets are lower than regions', the BGs need to go back and rethink their plans. *(Ren Zhengfei: Building the Carrier BG's "Three-Cloud" Platform to Equip Field Offices with the Best Tools—Speech at the Carrier BG's Briefing on Developing Marketing Tools, Huawei Executive Office Speech No. [2015] 019)*

Regional offices have command authority and project decision-making authority, while BGs act as resource centers to support field operations. The goal of BGs is to increase sales while the goal of regional offices is to generate decent profits. Over the next five to ten years, regional offices will gradually change their function from maintaining large troops to building lean teams. If manpower is insufficient, the Strategic Reserve will act as a mobile force to provide support. In the future, our field offices will be made up of lean teams that deal with uncertainties, and our back offices will be made up of shared platforms that deal with certainties. This allows those closest to customers to call for support, and as a result, our overall operating capabilities will improve. In the future, the company's authority system will become a two-pole system. One pole will be regional offices. They are close to customers, and will command field operations. The other pole will be BGs. They will have the authority to provide support and services. BGs will focus on sales revenue, and regional offices on profits. That way, there will be checks and balances between the two poles. *(Ren Zhengfei: Speech at the Oath-taking and Awards Ceremony of the Transformation Elite Team, Huawei Executive Office Speech No. [2015] 047)*

Our incremental markets need to include countries with big opportunities. Small countries and hardship countries should be appraised against reasonable market share and reasonable profits. The "red dancing shoes" of sales revenue should be avoided. Having a high market share might not be a good thing. In some countries, we have landed contracts with local top three telecom carriers. Because the marketplace is often a zero-sum game, some of these carriers may collapse in the face of fierce competition. If you try to play the hero and rush in to save the day by cutting prices for the third-place carrier, you might end up dragging down the prices of the top two carriers as well. *(Ren Zhengfei: Our Human Resource Policy Should Develop in the Direction of Decreasing Entropy—Speech at a Report of the Strategic Reserve to Its Steering Committee, Huawei Executive Office Speech No. [2016] 098)*

We have established an accountability mechanism that promotes collaboration between different teams, allowing Sales to hold R&D accountable, R&D to be responsible for customers, and Marketing to serve as a bridge between Sales and R&D. Contributions to revenue should be included in the appraisal of product lines, so that they will be forced to deliver products and services that are needed by representative offices. Product R&D, Technical Sales, and Services must collaborate to develop solutions. Field personnel must not make commitments rashly, and must confine their commitments to the list of sellable products. New customer requirements must be discussed with Marketing, and product development can only begin after a resolution is reached. *(Ren Zhengfei: There Will Not Always Be Flowers Along the Road Ahead—Speech at the H1 Huawei Market Conference, Huawei Executive Office Speech No. [2016] 079)*

How can R&D ensure that they are customer-centric? R&D should organize meetings to develop appropriate measures. Marketing must serve as a bridge between Sales and R&D, and must dare to speak the truth. If no one intervenes in product line R&D, will the products they independently develop meet customer needs? Will these products be competitive? We stress that representative offices are profit-centered and product lines are revenue-centered. Representative offices have the authority to select which customers they serve, which products they sell, and which sales contracts they sign. Product lines must reach out to Technical Sales, Production, and Services. This will force our R&D to become customer-centric. Without sales revenue, life will be difficult for them. *(Ren Zhengfei: There Will Not Always Be Flowers Along the Road Ahead—Speech at the H1 Huawei Market Conference, Huawei Executive Office Speech No. [2016] 079)*

Expenses in small countries are high, so we must ensure that the expenses claimed in these countries are real. We don't worry too much about whether they are reasonable. We then compare real expenses with the profits these countries earn. Today network quality in small countries is not very good. Why? Employees in these countries are unable to obtain the resources needed to improve. There are very few base stations in small countries, and they don't have much money, so it is difficult for them to obtain the required resources. If they had the money to buy more resources, no one would hesitate to join them. Therefore, small countries need to have reasonable profits and a reasonable market share. As long as expenses in small countries are fact-based and free from corruption, they are understandable. Neither big countries nor small countries are allowed to falsify data. *(Ren Zhengfei: Internal and External Compliance to Generate More Revenue and Pave the Way for the Company's Future Success—Speech at a Meeting with the Oversight Team, Huawei Executive Office Speech No. [2017] 002)*

10.2.3 Responsibility Centers Must Adopt Different Approaches to Manage Certainties and Uncertainties

At the moment, some certainties are still managed as uncertainties, resulting in too much discussion, low efficiency, and wasted energy, and leaving too little time to deal with true uncertainties. Due to historical factors, HQ is filled with managers. In the future, we aim to equip HQ with a team of outstanding experts who are able to handle everything from Big Video, massive data traffic, big frameworks, and broad services to estimation and final accounting, system delivery, integrated maintenance, and transaction management. When field offices have a demand, these experts can provide support immediately. Every three to five years, these experts must rotate to the field to work on or run projects. We will also develop local experts' teams based on customer needs. *(Ren Zhengfei: Speech at the Report on How to Develop Contract Scenario Experts, Huawei Executive Office Speech No. [2015] 071)*

When I met with the Chairman of Accenture recently, I told him that Huawei had worked with IBM for over 20 years and had turned our fragmented processes and systems into a shared platform. Over the next 10 years, we will work with Accenture to change our organization from one of large teams into one of lean teams. We will deploy lean teams that deal with the uncertainties of transaction terms, customer needs, new technologies, and scenario management. The shared platform will deal with issues of certainty. In this way, we can reduce headcount while hitting the same sales targets. The increased profits can be distributed to these lean teams to boost their operating capabilities. This means that when we set different baselines for different countries and different industries, we are in fact stepping closer to building lean teams. *(Ren Zhengfei: Minutes of the Briefing on the Progress of Differentiated Appraisals for Regions, Huawei Executive Office Speech No. [2015] 050)*

At Huawei, if you want a high salary, you have to earn it. Those who put the most food on the table become our "generals". Generals are born of battle. So everyone must keep up the hard work, and keep making solid improvements in their ability to do their job. Delivery managers deal with certainties, so they should first increase efficiency and effectiveness. Service managers deal with uncertainties, so they should build up their overall ability to quickly deal with technical problems. Looking ahead, these two categories of managers should each be responsible for their own development. We should apply different performance appraisal criteria to these two categories. *(Ren Zhengfei: Generals Are Born of Battle—Speech at the 2015 Project Management Summit, Huawei Executive Office Speech No. [2015] 118)*

Commanders should focus on strategic goals and success, and deal with uncertainties. Daily matters of certainty should be handled by the General Manager's Office and the Quality Operations Department. The appraisal of matters of certainty should focus on the efficiency and quality of management, and process compliance is the best management approach for such matters. Of course, we can optimize our processes following specific procedures. There is much work of uncertainty in representative offices, so we are authorizing general managers to handle such work and asking them to be profit-centered. This means that representative offices have the authority to select which customers they serve, which products they sell, and which sales contracts they sign. The decision-making authority is not delegated based on the costs of the end-to-end process, but on the costs incurred by uncertainties. At the end of each year, we need to calculate how much profit each representative office earns. Their total profits will determine their performance rating and the amount of money they can distribute. *(Ren Zhengfei: Speech at a Meeting with Employees of the Central Asia & Caucasia Region, Huawei Executive Office Speech No. [2016] 063)*

10.3 Operating Mechanisms for Profit Centers

10.3.1 Focusing on Business Operations, Making Decisions Independently, and Never Rigidly Setting Job Grades Based on Scale and Levels

We must gradually change HQ from a management and control center to a support and service center that also performs oversight functions. We need to develop capabilities that enable the field to drive back offices. We need to plan and make a shift from centralized management and control to delegation of operations authority to entry-level operating teams, ensuring our command centers are as close to our customers as possible. We need to help organizations at all levels become profit centers that reflect their own business characteristics. *(Source: Resolution on the EMT's Priorities and Management Approaches from 2007 to 2009, EMT Resolution No. [2007] 012)*

The company is now focused on developing profit-centric organizations. HQ must provide services to profit centers. In the future, profit centers will view project profits as a key factor in their decisions. Project managers must be project-centric and ensure profits. *(Ren Zhengfei: Remarks at a Meeting with Senior Managers at a Project Management Summit, Huawei Executive Office Speech No. [2009] 007)*

As various transformations are implemented across the company over the next five to ten years, our representative offices will shift from maintaining large teams to building lean teams. Today, we have thousands of people in one representative office. Why do we need to maintain all these troops? If there is a sudden drop in a representative office's business, the office will not be able to feed them all. Representative offices are integrated units that are directly engaged in field operations. When a representative office selects the smallest possible team to engage in battle, that is a lean team. A representative office is commanded by its general manager, who has the ultimate authority over the entire office. If a representative office has multiple managers, there will be chaos and no battles can be fought. If there aren't enough personnel in representative offices, we can transfer some in from our strategic mobile forces. This is how we make our personnel mobile. Once we shift to open source code and open platforms, we can reduce duplicated development, and our R&D team will also become smaller. This is no longer a time in which we position ourselves by how many people we manage, how big our team is, or what level we are at. In the past, one could become a "platoon leader" only when he/she commanded dozens of people. Today, you can become a team leader, or even a "major general", with just three subordinates. As our organization gradually slims down, how are we going to deploy so many leaders? We need to change our approach. In battle, leaders still need to take on some of the work alongside their subordinates. Don't say that we cannot deploy a senior expert in a small team. We must have mechanisms to ensure that small teams can have senior experts, so that everyone can have confidence. Huawei's management system still needs to be improved. We can't rigidly set job grades based on job assessment results. Managers might have low job grades, but they should not have to worry about it – they still have the opportunity to become generals. Experts may be petty officers, but they can also enjoy special treatment. That's what creates the Huawei "can-do" spirit. In the US Department of Defense, a petty officer can effectively command a brigadier because he is in charge of global oil supplies. Often, what we need is an expert, not necessarily a general. That is something we need to consider during our management transformation. If we rigidly set job grades based on job assessment results, we will end up with no room for veteran experts, and our experts may choose to leave. *(Ren Zhengfei: Building the Carrier BG's "Three-Cloud" Platform to Equip Field Offices with the Best Tools—Speech at the Carrier BG's Briefing on Developing Marketing Tools, Huawei Executive Office Speech No. [2015] 019)*

We must allow those who are closest to our customers to call for support. This gives field offices the freedom to make decisions according to actual circumstances. Finance can then impose constraints based on how many resources were invested and how much revenue was generated. Our audit department will verify the facts and check where the resources have been deployed. If field offices don't generate any revenue, they will receive nothing according to our Contribute and Share system. This will be decided by our Human Resource Management Department and Corporate Leadership Management Department. As we link all costs, we will form a scientific operating model over the next few years. We will then transfer operating authority to field offices, and move our oversight teams forward by establishing subsidiary boards of directors. Together, all this will move field offices closer to our customers and increase our scope of engagement. Meanwhile, we will have the support of the Carrier BG as a center of expertise (COE) and a resource center. This will open the market to us. Therefore, I think regional offices should act as command centers and call for support. While they don't have operating teams, they do have operating authority. The Carrier BG should serve as a COE, a resource center, and a customer solution design center. The Carrier BG has operating teams but no operating authority. To deploy operating teams, you will need to receive approval from field command centers. Otherwise, you won't get a budget. We will spend ten years developing an operating system according to this concept. *(Ren Zhengfei: Building Advanced Tools and Enhancing Core Competencies to Achieve Success at a Higher Level—Speech at a Carrier BG Briefing on the Service Experience and Phased Acceptance of the "Three Cloud" Platform, Huawei Executive Office Speech No. [2015] 099)*

You have to allow those who are closest to our customers to call for support. That is how the US military operates, and we should learn from them, because the US military is the worlds' most powerful organization. The US is a country that values freedom, but the US military is extremely disciplined and is always improving itself. In that respect, it is exactly the same as Huawei. The Carrier BG currently advocates the "Three Cloud" strategy. This is actually its President's way of shaking up his organization and delegating authority to the field. In the future, this BG will be a resource center and a center of expertise. Our back office will become a team of elite experts who provide support to our field offices. Recently, President of the Regions Management Department was telling me that the department is also becoming a "commercial management cloud". This is what they are calling their experts' teams that mainly work on commercial management issues. These teams will enable us to speed up the delegation of authority to the field. So, where should we delegate authority first? Small countries. *(Ren Zhengfei: Building Lean Teams in Small Countries First; Allowing Field Teams to Call for Support—Speech at the Report of the JCR's Regions Management Department on Approaches to Small Country Operations, Huawei Executive Office Speech No. [2015] 126)*

10.3.2 Positioning HQ as a Resource Pool and Adopting a Resource Buy & Sell Mechanism

Delegating command authority to the field prevents HQ from becoming too bloated. If HQ keeps all command authority to itself, it will not generate new value despite the fact the organization will keep expanding and operating costs will continue to rise. Sooner or later, the company would collapse. We can see this happening throughout history with the decline of both big corporations and feudal dynasties. At this critical moment in our own history, we must be fully aware of the risks of an overly large HQ, and thus further delegate authority to field offices. We must streamline our Lead to Cash (LTC) process to achieve our CIAG and "Five Ones". Our subsidiary boards are taking on a historic mission during this period of transition. *(Ren Zhengfei: Speech at the Mid-year Workshop on the Enablement of Subsidiary Board Directors, Huawei Executive Office Speech No. [2014] 074)*

We will position our HQ as a resource pool and adopt a resource "buy & sell" mechanism, through which field offices can request resources and back offices can provide resources based on project budgets while also charging fees for the resources they provide. This mechanism will mean that those with money will have command authority, and approval by managers at HQ will no longer be required. This way, we can achieve checks and balances between field and back offices to ensure that field offices don't become aimless and back offices have clearly defined capability requirements. *(Ren Zhengfei: Speech at a Carrier BG Briefing on the Progress of Three Cloud 2.0, Huawei Executive Office Speech No. [2017] 018)*

Regional organization transformation aims to turn regional offices into COEs and resource centers. HQ is a resource pool, and resources must be bought and sold according to market rules. In addition, regional offices should guide the company's functional departments, R&D, and BGs. When field offices need to purchase resources, we will set prices using the Cost, Insurance, and Freight (CIF) model. We are now piloting this model. The company's fixed costs are added into the CIF-based prices, and we thus have globally standard prices prior to local customs clearance. Representative offices will be given the authority to make pricing decisions involving uncertain factors. Any additional profits obtained through CIF pricing will not be placed under HQ. After deducting the average salaries and bonuses that are allowed by HQ, these profits will be shared globally among all employees via a secondary profit distribution mechanism. The building of regional COEs and resource centers is not confined strictly to Greater Regions; regional offices can also be part of these efforts. The company's Board of Directors assumes the ultimate responsibility for business operations and ensures that COEs improve their capabilities and resource centers provide more support. *(Ren Zhengfei: Speech at a Briefing on Improvements and Future Planning for Carrier and Enterprise Regional Organization Transformation, Huawei Executive Office Speech No. [2017] 030)*

10.3.3 Authority Delegation and Responsibility for Profit Centers

Representative office general managers should be competent at running organizations, turning representative offices into profit centers, and taking responsibility for sustainable and profitable growth. *(Ren Zhengfei: Staying Customer-centric, Inspiring Dedication, and Persevering Are Key to Our Success—Speech at the 2010 Huawei Market Conference, Huawei Executive Office Speech No. [2010] 002)*

In the "Squad Leaders' Fight", the ultimate command and decision-making authority should be with regional offices. BGs and the Strategic Reserve are resource centers and mobile forces respectively, both of which provide operational assistance. *(Ren Zhengfei: Speech at a Briefing on the Takeaways and Challenges for Huawei Relating to the "Squad Leaders' Fight", Huawei Executive Office Speech No. [2014] 078)*

What does command authority mean? It is the actual ability to orchestrate capabilities. When it comes to authority delegation, we will give field offices the authority to select which customers they serve, which products they sell, and which sales contracts they sign. We will delegate authority to field offices, letting field commanders decide what capabilities they need and how to apply those capabilities to the opportunities they see. This way, field offices that are good at capability orchestration will make more money. If field offices don't know how to coordinate and utilize capabilities, our BGs can assign an experts' team to guide them to develop an operating solution. However, the experts' team should not interfere with business operations, and the decision-making authority still rests with field offices. *(Ren Zhengfei: Speech at a Carrier BG Briefing on the Progress of Three Cloud 2.0, Huawei Executive Office Speech No. [2017] 018)*

The military is made up of brigades, battalions, and companies. We will model our company on this structure and divide our departments into three types of units: brigades (large regional offices, resource centers, and HQ, which will sell resources to field offices), battalions (the operating platforms of representative offices), and companies (key account departments and project management centers of representative offices). We also need to use modern tools to reduce the number of layers in our management and improve the operating and decision-making capabilities of field offices. HQ will retain authority over treasury, accounting, and auditing and internal controls while delegating other authority to field offices. As long as data is transparent, the business decision-making authority will be delegated to field teams. As a result, these teams will have authority, responsibility, and interests, and will exert controls on themselves. *(Ren Zhengfei: Speech at a Meeting in Paraguay, Huawei Executive Office Speech No. [2017] 025)*

Our transformation should begin with projects and gradually progress into key account departments and representative offices. We will pilot delegating authority, and granting responsibility and interests to representative offices. Right now, some projects are recording huge waste of raw materials. This problem will be solved when interests are linked to representative offices, because they will proactively think about how to optimize their projects. In the future, representative offices will become profit centers. Key account departments will become coordinators and will have some decision-making authority. After the adoption of the CIF model, our product prices before local customs fees and expenses are added will be the same for all representative offices globally. However, costs related to customs clearance, engineering, and delivery are uncertain, because they differ by country. This means final sales prices will be different, and key account departments must not interfere with these final delivery prices. Assigning responsibility, authority, and interests to representative offices is a way to ask them to make decisions on local uncertainties. A price reference table for auxiliary materials will be released by our Procurement, and representative offices can choose whether to procure those materials from HQ or to procure them locally. Of course, allowing representative offices to approve contracts means we are giving them the leeway to also make mistakes (decisions that result in loss-bearing projects). However, they must assume responsibility for these mistakes and the losses must be made up in other projects. Subsidiary boards will oversee the internal and external compliance of representative offices, but will not interfere with their operations. Representative offices can be authorized to balance things out themselves. If we demand that everything must grow in value, we will only paralyze our workforce. *(Ren Zhengfei: Speech at a Briefing on Improvements and Future Planning for Carrier and Enterprise Regional Organization Transformation, Huawei Executive Office Speech No. [2017] 030)*

Open Access This chapter is licensed under the terms of the Creative Commons Attribution-NonCommercial-NoDerivatives 4.0 International License (http://creativecommons.org/licenses/by-nc-nd/4.0/), which permits any noncommercial use, sharing, distribution and reproduction in any medium or format, as long as you give appropriate credit to the original author(s) and the source, provide a link to the Creative Commons licence and indicate if you modified the licensed material. You do not have permission under this license to share adapted material derived from this chapter or parts of it.

The images or other third party material in this chapter are included in the chapter's Creative Commons licence, unless indicated otherwise in a credit line to the material. If material is not included in the chapter's Creative Commons licence and your intended use is not permitted by statutory regulation or exceeds the permitted use, you will need to obtain permission directly from the copyright holder.

CHAPTER 11

Developing a Better Planning, Budgeting, and Accounting System

The primary purpose of budget management is not to only determine what can be done with the resources available, but rather to push a company forward and help achieve goals. At Huawei, budgets are prepared in a way that encourages growth, and budget allocation is aligned with the company's strategy. Planning, budgeting, accounting, and appraisals at all levels of Huawei are managed in a closed loop. Specifically, planning and budgeting play a guiding role, and accounting is used to assess and oversee the execution of plans and budgets.

Huawei links budgets to a department's contributions and strategic importance. If a department belongs to a strategic domain, the company will grant a budget to this department. However, if it is not in a strategic domain, then that department must contribute profits to the company. Those who are in charge of strategic domains must be committed to achieving strategic goals.

Success is the result of proper planning. Huawei requires its planning staff to understand its business. Planning is critical because it is the basis for budgeting. The company aims to gradually shift the focus of its business management from business plans (BPs)[1] to strategic plans (SPs).[2]

---

[1] Business plans (BPs) are the company's one-year development plans.

[2] Strategic plans (SPs) are company-wide plans that look at mid- and long-term development.

At Huawei, there are two approaches to budgeting. For business departments that are responsible for expansion, including R&D, Sales, and Marketing, the company analyzes whether their detailed budgets are reasonable, rather than simply controlling their budget caps. Other departments are functional departments. Their expenses are fixed, and their total budgets are strictly controlled. The company approaches budgeting for business departments from the bottom up, and for functional departments from the top down.

Huawei plans to gradually put in place an outside-in, profit-center-based budgeting and final accounting system. Customers and projects are the focus of budgeting work. Operating departments in the field and functional departments at HQ both focus on the company's strategy when planning their own key customer, R&D, and transformation projects. This approach helps Huawei gradually establish a mechanism through which resources are channeled to strategic domains and valued customers.

Huawei separates functional department budgets from project budgets. Its annual budget is prepared based on projects or opportunities. The company has established a budget allocation system based on the "SP–project–budget" logic. Project teams buy resources from supporting departments according to their business plans and granted budgets. Supporting departments are responsible for resource efficiency. Huawei does everything it can to keep the expenses of functional departments as low as possible.

All budgets at Huawei are flexible, including the company's total budget and every individual department's budget. This flexibility aims to ensure field teams can obtain more resources after their business grows.

Accounting is an important indicator of management improvement. At Huawei, the rules for budgeting and accounting are the same. When a certain rule is used for budgeting, this same rule is also used for accounting. This is how the company achieves closed-loop budget management. Huawei focuses more on the most important points when it comes to cross charging for incentive purposes. The goal of this is to reduce the costs of internal transactions.

This chapter elaborates on the above management approaches and principles for planning, budgeting, and accounting.

11.1 Aligning Planning, Budgeting, and Accounting with Strategy and Business Operations

11.1.1 The Primary Purpose of Budget Management: Pushing the Company Forward Rather Than Only Determining What Can Be Done with the Resources Available

Our total budget is the basis for all of the company's business activities over the fiscal year. It is also an important way for us to manage the uncertainties of our external environment, make our decision-making process more methodical and less arbitrary, and improve the overall business performance and management of the company. *(Source: The Huawei Charter, 1998)*

The micro and macro are not completely disconnected. They are interconnected in one way or another. Budgeting is by no means just a financial, economic, or political issue. This is a very complicated management system. *(Ren Zhengfei: Speech at a Work Report on 1999 Budgets, 1999)*

The primary purpose of budget management is not to only determine what can be done with the resources available, but rather to push a company forward and help achieve goals. We should aim for sustainable revenue growth. We should constantly explore the rationality of flexible coefficients. These coefficients vary by region and by product domain. Flexible indicators are comprehensive. For example, we can assign different weights to indicators such as contribution gross margin, cash flow, and output, and put them together to obtain a set of flexible indicators. We need to create multiple types of flexible coefficients and gradually achieve scientific management. *(Source: Resolution on Strengthening Total Budgeting and Cost Management in the End-to-End Process, EMT Resolution No. [2016] 009)*

First, we need to be clear about our goals and responsibilities. After that, we should think about how to achieve these goals and fulfill these responsibilities through planning and budgeting. Budgeting ensures that resources are allocated in a way that supports strategy execution. Before getting started on planning and budgeting, we must know the general direction in which we are going and do the right thing following the direction. It is also important to understand the opportunities available to us and the things that need to be managed. Only then can we figure out how to get to where we want to go. Budgeting is very important, but it is not an easy job. It requires much more than working on one's own. Budgeting needs to be flexibly linked to goals and adjusted based on those same goals. Its contributions to results need to be determined through final accounting. *(Ren Zhengfei: Focusing on Strategy and Streamlining Management, Huawei Executive Office Speech No. [2012] 041)*

Budgets must be prepared in a way that encourages growth, enabling flexible resource allocation based on rolling business forecasts. Budgets should also encourage improvement and growth in individual departments. Huawei cannot adopt a one-size-fits-all approach to rigidly strike a balance among different departments. Planning, budgeting, accounting, and appraisals at all levels of the company should be managed in a closed loop. Specifically, planning and budgeting will play a guiding role, and accounting will be used to assess and oversee the execution of plans and budgets. At Huawei, operations management relies on a cycle of forecasting, planning, budgeting, and accounting. Managers who impede the company's ongoing improvements to data sharing, data transparency, and data quality should be transferred to the work group responsible for integrating data in their respective domains. *(Ren Zhengfei: Minutes of the Meeting on the Budgeting Work, Huawei Executive Office Speech No. [2014] 004)*

11.1.2 Establishing a Planning, Budgeting, and Accounting System to Support Business Success

At the corporate level, product lines represent a vertical line of planning, and regional offices represent a horizontal line of planning. Together, they form a matrix management system for planning, budgeting, and accounting. The purpose of establishing such a system is to support business success. The system should serve regional presidents, general managers of representative offices, and presidents of product lines, and should support their business success. The basic units of planning, budgeting, and accounting management are regional offices, representative offices, and product lines. Business planning authority should be delegated to these basic units. Managers of these basic units should use this methodology to direct business operations. *(Ren Zhengfei: Minutes of the Meeting on Developing a Planning, Budgeting, and Accounting System, EMT Meeting Minutes No. [2007] 024)*

Planning, budgeting, and accounting are not tasks performed solely by the planning, budgeting, and accounting departments. They are part of regional, representative office, and product line businesses. Planning and budgeting departments serve as the secretariat that helps regional offices, representative offices, and product lines put together plans and strike an overall balance to support their business operations. *(Ren Zhengfei: Minutes of the Meeting on Developing a Planning, Budgeting, and Accounting System, EMT Meeting Minutes No. [2007] 024)*

The plans for regional offices, representative offices, and product lines are used to facilitate business operations while the plans for HQ are used for macro forecasting and controls. *(Ren Zhengfei: Minutes of the Meeting on Developing a Planning, Budgeting, and Accounting System, EMT Meeting Minutes No. [2007] 024)*

When you work alone on a project without any instructions, staying profit-centered will always be the right thing to do. You have every right to work this way. If you don't receive any instructions for a project, you can certainly center your actions on profits. We think that regional offices have the authority to independently make decisions in such cases, as long as you stay profit-centered. However, when it comes to strategic issues, you need to report them to higher-level management and ask for instructions. Strategic issues often sacrifice short-term interests in exchange for long-term interests. If you do not ask higher-level management for instructions, who will subsidize your short-term losses? In addition, strategic issues are not that urgent, and you have plenty of time to report them, so you must follow certain procedures. *(Ren Zhengfei: Remarks After Watching the Battle of Moscow—Speech at the Egypt Representative Office, Huawei Executive Office Speech No. [2008] 004)*

I believe that good numbers are a result of good work; good numbers cannot be faked. We must focus our energy on analyzing the market and serving our customers. If we work hard to get our job done, I don't think we will get bad numbers. The planning system on the front lines is designed to facilitate business operations, not to report back to HQ. The regional office and product line plans have the same purpose. Frontline departments must have a clear direction and the right strategy for success. Regional offices that fail to reach the average compound annual growth rate of the company can focus more on fine-grained management. Departments that do not work on the front lines must provide high-quality services to the front lines by continuously improving themselves through fine-grained management. *(Ren Zhengfei: Speech at the EMT ST Meeting on January 31, EMT Meeting Minutes No. [2008] 009)*

We should first choose small countries to develop highly competent, lean teams. These countries are too small to maintain large teams anyway, so all of their resources have to come from back offices. That will make it easy for small countries to call for support. The key issues we need to address are: Who will provide the support? And how will it be accounted for? We should run a pilot program in small countries. We can correct any problems we might run into during the process of calling for support. Once the pilot program is successful, we can work out a model and apply it in medium-sized and then big countries. Whether big countries should have an independent platform can be talked about later. *(Ren Zhengfei: Building Lean Teams in Small Countries First; Allowing Field Teams to Call for Support—Speech at the Report of the JCR's Regions Management Department on Approaches to Small Country Operations, Huawei Executive Office Speech No. [2015] 126)*

11.1.3 Linking Budgets to Contributions and Strategies

Our market investment budgets should continue to be based on relative numbers. We can gradually align budgets with business targets based on the historical patterns of change in our expense/revenue ratios so that increases in business expenses, especially customer-facing expenses, align with sales growth. We need to use different expense/revenue ratios for emerging and mature markets. *(Ren Zhengfei: Comments at the Meeting Regarding the Planning and Budgeting Work for 2005, 2004)*

Business departments work hard to achieve their sales targets. We can therefore use these targets as a reference for resource allocation, but they should not be the sole basis. We should not rigidly allocate resources based on sales targets, as this may cause waste. Business departments should make commitments based on practical goals and get the resources needed to achieve those goals. Resources needed to achieve stretch goals should be allocated to business departments in phases rather than on a one-off basis. Otherwise, business departments will set lower targets for their KPIs. Reserve resources in the company must be covered with the company's overall budget, and their budgets will not be allocated to business departments. Otherwise, things will get complicated. The budgets for all flexible items will be listed separately and covered in the company's overall budget. *(Ren Zhengfei: Comments at the Meeting Regarding the Planning and Budgeting Work for 2005, 2004)*

Budgets must be linked to a department's contributions and strategic importance. If your department is in a strategic domain, we will grant a budget to you. However, if it is not in a strategic domain, then you've got to contribute profits to the company. Those who are in charge of strategic domains have to take an oath, pledging to achieve strategic goals. They should have a timetable for everything they do. Any modifications to business plans should be clearly explained, and money should be well spent. When a department applies for a budget, they must clarify their responsibilities and contributions. After approval is obtained, the results they deliver and the responsibilities they assume will be used as the most important basis for performance appraisals. *(Ren Zhengfei: Focusing on Strategy and Streamlining Management, Huawei Executive Office Speech No. [2012] 041)*

We should gradually put in place an outside-in, profit-center-based budgeting and final accounting system. Investments in BGs and SBGs[3] are determined by their output, and investments in functional departments at HQ are determined by the total output of the company. HQ's authority and size should be adapted to the company's organizational transformation in which those closest to customers can call for support. Representative offices should be our accounting centers. All expenses must come from representative offices. The authority to prepare and approve budgets cannot both be in the hands of HQ. Otherwise, HQ will become increasingly bloated. When we shift our focus to representative offices, HQ should help representative offices win key projects. They can even send people over to representative offices. In this way, they can earn money from representative offices, and the extra labor hours claimed by representative offices will come back to HQ. Budget committees must comprise of people from both business and finance departments. Our current problem is that tasks often cannot be completed even though we are spending money on them. We must clarify how compensation packages are generated. For example, how much should packages be based on where we are in executing a plan? Compensation packages should be based on business results, and then HR can further divide the packages. *(Source: Requirements for Continuing to Streamline the Organization to Improve Efficiency and Productivity, EMT Resolution No. [2012] 026)*

---

[3] Service Business Groups (SBGs) are business operations centers that provide services.

During total budget management, we must be very clear about our stance against the following conduct: making irrational final sprints to achieve KPIs, intentionally covering up business results for accounting or incentive purposes, and voluntarily giving up opportunities to achieve better results. We must create the right values and encourage teams to work hard and forge ahead. Business resources are primarily allocated and managed in two ways. First, we have a resource allocation plan. The total resources of the company are fixed. Those who contribute more will receive more resources. Second, resources will be allocated based on profits. We have different profit requirements for different businesses. If we want a business to develop faster, we will reduce its burden by setting lower profit requirements. If a business is too risky and inflated, the profit requirements will be higher. We will calculate the business results of profit centers based on the profit and cash flow requirements set for each BG and BU, and strike an overall balance between collecting profits and investing resources within the company. The Finance Committee will manage the end-to-end process in a closed loop by focusing on the total amount of investment, the opportunities created by such investment, and the results achieved. *(Guo Ping: Effectively Managing Corporate Value to Pursue Sustainable and Profitable Growth, Huawei Executive Office Speech No. [2012] 005)*

When we build our business strategic reserve pools, we should develop vertically rather than horizontally. Otherwise, we will have to cut projects and waste money. As for the HR reserve pool, we can set aside a budget provided by HQ to develop the elite teams, the Key Project Department, and the Project Management Resource Pool. Elite teams should participate in global projects to seize the strategic high ground. If they win, their costs can be charged to projects. If they lose, they have to take care of the costs themselves, with the budgets provided by HQ. This approach will allow the company to reinforce the fine tradition of "toasting those who succeed and offering a helping hand to those who fail". *(Ren Zhengfei: Speech and Comments at the Carrier BG's 2013 Strategy Retreat, Huawei Executive Office Speech No. [2014] 016)*

11.1.4 Shifting the Focus of Business Management from BPs to SPs

We will implement a new management system to delegate more authority to field offices. The purpose of this is to greatly increase our work efficiency and make sure field offices command back offices. We now make it clear that executives should command field teams when it comes to strategic issues; for tactical issues, field offices should command back offices, and back offices should provide full support to field offices. If back offices cannot provide services to field offices, they have no reason to exist in the first place. Strategic issues should be decided upon by executives at HQ because these issues normally involve sacrificing short-term interests in exchange for long-term interests. Such sacrifices should be reflected in the financial statements of the beneficiaries and be backed up by executives. *(Ren Zhengfei: Speech at the 2008 Mid-year Report by Regions to the EMT, EMT Meeting Minutes No. [2008] 028)*

If an overly rigid approach is adopted in performance appraisals, strategic goals will be affected. In the future, we will specify our strategic positioning in our general principles. We must plan and set strategic goals, which should be assessed in phases. *(Ren Zhengfei: Speech at the EMT ST Meeting on April 29, 2010)*

We should improve our capabilities in mid- and long-term strategic planning and strategy management at the company level as well as in BUs, marketing units (MUs),[4] and functional units (FUs).[5] We should shift the focus of our business management from BPs to SPs. This will better guide executives to focus on long-term strategies, perform regular strategy reviews, and arrange for work reports. It will also help regional offices, product lines, and other departments better collaborate with each other to ensure that strategies are well aligned and actions are consistent with strategies. Closed-loop management for SPs and BPs should be linked to performance appraisals of executives and financial planning of the company to ensure that the SPs and BPs are executed. *(Source: Huawei's 2011 Work Priorities, EMT Resolution No. [2011] 019)*

We must adopt different budgeting models for product investment to support strategic products and control products that are not in the core business. For strategic products, five-year R&D budgets will be approved on a one-off basis based on the company's SP cycle and will be granted on an annual basis. For products that are not in the core business, we will adopt Smartcom's model, whereby the profit goals are higher, and the profit that is above the average product profit can be allocated to R&D

---

[4] Marketing units (MUs) are regional or customer-facing departments.
[5] Functional units (FUs) are departments that provide specialized support for business operations.

investments. For non-strategic products in our core business, resources will be allocated based on annual budgets. *(Ren Zhengfei: Minutes of the Meeting on the Budgeting Work, Huawei Executive Office Speech No. [2014] 004)*

11.1.5 Establishing a Budget Allocation Mechanism Based on the "SP–Project–Budget" Logic

HQ does not have its own budget, as all resource budgets are in projects. Once the field calls for resources, we will deploy resources there, whose costs will be charged to the field. We need to change the current budget allocation method by granting the budget to the field. HQ has to get the budget it needs from projects by providing services. This is the only way we can downsize HQ. *(Ren Zhengfei: Integrating Project Estimation, Budgeting, Accounting, and Final Accounting to Support Project Operations—Speech at a Briefing on the IFS Project, Huawei Executive Office Speech No. [2010] 007)*

We need to separate functional department budgets from project budgets, and keep the expenses of functional departments as low as possible. The goal of functional department operations is to ensure that we promptly deliver high-quality products and services to customers at affordable prices. When functional departments support a project, they need to ask the project manager to pay for their work, and this payment can be deducted from the project budget. By taking this approach, functional departments will try to have the project manager pay for expenses, and the project manager will try their best to control project expenses through the efficient use of resources from functional departments. This will result in conflicts, but a balance will be achieved in the end. The purpose of establishing such a mechanism is to make sure HQ provides services to the field and charges them for these services. *(Ren Zhengfei: Integrating Project Estimation, Budgeting, Accounting, and Final Accounting to Support Project Operations—Speech at a Briefing on the IFS Project, Huawei Executive Office Speech No. [2010] 007)*

Currently, our budgeting is about granting funds to functional departments. It's a process of distributing authority among departments at various levels. Those who have budgets have authority. We will not be able to change our current situation if we don't change the owner of authority and the way budgets are generated. We must be clear about the sources and recipients of budgets and how budgets can be used to support strategy execution. *(Ren Zhengfei: Rigorous, Well-ordered, and Simple Management Is Crucial for Huawei to Scale New Heights, Huawei Executive Office Speech No. [2014] 028)*

Departments have always believed that, for their budgets, "what is in place is rational". They think if they had a budget the previous year, they should have one this year too. Now both resources and money are in the hands of functional departments. However, departments that fight on the front line do not have money, and they have to ask functional departments for budgets. We started to change this practice last year. Our R&D budgets are no longer granted to product lines. Instead, they will first be granted to the IRB[6] and IPMT so that budgets can be allocated to projects that can create value and execute strategy. As for accounting, we have to define our accounting units first, as that will make many things clear. *(Ren Zhengfei: Rigorous, Well-ordered, and Simple Management Is Crucial for Huawei to Scale New Heights, Huawei Executive Office Speech No. [2014] 028)*

We must transform our budget management system based on responsibility centers. Customers and projects must be the focus of our budgeting work, and our budgets should also be prepared in a way that helps create sustainable value and make contributions. By preparing budgets, we aim to execute business strategy and achieve business goals while aligning authority and interests with responsibilities. Budgets must be prepared in a way that encourages growth, and budget allocation must be aligned with our company's strategy. We must establish a budget allocation system based on the "SP–project–budget" logic. With this system, operating departments in the field and functional departments at HQ will both focus on the company's strategy when planning their own key customer, R&D, and transformation projects. This approach will help us gradually establish a mechanism through which resources are channeled to strategic domains and valued customers. *(Guo Ping: Transform Continuously and Improve Field Operating Capabilities to Ensure the Company's Sustainable and Profitable Growth—Speech at Huawei Annual Management Conference 2013, Huawei Executive Office Speech No. [2014] 020)*

We will optimize our rules for managing resource department budgets so that they only have budgets given by HQ. Other resource department

---

[6] The Investment Review Board (IRB), formerly known as the Product Investment Review Board, is a team that manages Huawei's investment portfolios, decision making, and end-to-end collaboration involving products and solutions for different industries.

budgets must be earned by supporting projects that request their resources. In this way, budgets will be used to facilitate business operations. These decisions only need to be approved by those who have budgets. Adopting this approach will allow our operations to shift from being function-centered to being project-centered. *(Guo Ping: Transform Continuously and Improve Field Operating Capabilities to Ensure the Company's Sustainable and Profitable Growth—Speech at Huawei Annual Management Conference 2013, Huawei Executive Office Speech No. [2014] 020)*

We stress that projects should have management authority and that resources come with a cost. *(Ren Zhengfei: Focusing on Strategy and Streamlining Management, Huawei Executive Office Speech No. [2012] 041)*

11.2 Preparing Plans and Budgets from the Bottom Up

11.2.1 Projects and Customers: The Focus of Planning, Budgeting, and Accounting

When preparing plans and budgets, we must prioritize field teams and projects. Project planning, budgeting, and accounting must be accurate. All project managers must take planning, budgeting, and accounting seriously. Effectively using projects as the basic unit to manage planning, budgeting, and accounting is the foundation of managing and appraising regional offices as profit centers. *(Ren Zhengfei: Minutes of the Meeting on Developing a Planning, Budgeting, and Accounting System, EMT Meeting Minutes No. [2007] 024)*

Project accounting units can be broken down into regional offices and product lines. We must ensure that after project planning, budgeting, and accounting are effectively managed, regional offices, product lines, and HQ departments can build on and support such work. This is why we need to develop a planning, budgeting, and accounting system at both field and back offices. *(Ren Zhengfei: Minutes of the Meeting on Developing a Planning, Budgeting, and Accounting System, EMT Meeting Minutes No. [2007] 024)*

Since our profits come from customers, our budgets should also come from customers. Only when we create an accurate budget for customer-facing sales teams can we break the budget into reliable, accurate annual budgets for product lines and regional offices. The rules for budgeting and accounting should be the same. When we use a certain rule for budgeting, we also need to use this same rule for accounting. This is how we achieve closed-loop budget management. *(Ren Zhengfei: Focusing on Strategy and Streamlining Management, Huawei Executive Office Speech No. [2012] 041)*

11.2.2 Proper Planning: Integrated Operating Plans Are the Foundation of Effective Management

Success is the result of proper planning. We need to break plans down to those who implement them and ensure they understand their tasks. Only when information is passed down accurately can we ensure effective execution at all levels. Managers must make their goals, intentions, methods, standards, and measures understood by their subordinates. Managers should be held accountable if their subordinates don't understand. *(Ren Zhengfei: Seizing Historic Opportunities and Welcoming Huge Development in 1998, 1997)*

The forecasts made by our planning system are not curves. Data cannot be fully relied upon to make completely accurate forecasts. During execution, we can adopt a breakdown method to get a complete and rational plan. However, forecasts and high-level management of plans rely on intuition. This intuition often doesn't come from economic performance or market orders, but from other things. Sometimes, for example, it is based on an understanding of politics. Reliable contract forecasts must be based on estimations, tracking, and analysis. Our employees must become more sensitive to the factors involved. *(Ren Zhengfei: Strengthening Management of Revenue to Drive Productivity and Revenue Increase, 1998)*

How can we achieve fine-grained management? The key is to have a reasonable plan and avoid being blind. Proper planning can significantly reduce freight costs and travel expenses for engineers. Success is the result of proper planning. Those who make plans must understand our business. Regional offices need to establish a planning, budgeting, and accounting department, which must be headed by someone who knows our business. Planning is critical because it is the basis for budgeting. Plans and budgets can then be corrected and measured through accounting. Why can't we keep freight costs under control? If we have a good plan and raise the proportion of our ocean shipping, our freight costs will go down. *(Ren Zhengfei: Speech at the Report by the BT Account Department and the UK Representative Office, Huawei Executive Office Speech No. [2007] 015)*

The key to reducing backlogs at customs and warehouses lies in developing accurate and objective plans. Regional offices and representative offices must step up efforts to build their planning system. Regional presidents and representative office general managers should be the primary owners for planning. *(Source: Guidelines for Delivery, Working Capital Management, and Team Building, EMT Meeting Minutes No. [2008] 013)*

When we establish over 20 planning units, what will be the role of level-1 planning committees in the company? They will be responsible for macro-level control, becoming involved in forecasting and planning and guiding future development and basic capability improvement. Our HR policies must be adjusted to support planning. The planning department is more than a financial department. A plan is like a lighthouse, the bow of a ship, and the radar that guides the entire company forward. Our appraisal and reward mechanisms are implemented to help the company forge ahead. The planning department needs to talk with the HR department to figure out how our HR policies should be developed to help us implement plans. We must change our mindset and understand that the planning department represents the entire company, not just the financial department. *(Ren Zhengfei: Speech at the 2008 Mid-year Report by Regions to the EMT, EMT Meeting Minutes No. [2008] 028)*

When making plans, each business unit should use scientific tools that have restrictive functions and reflect the company's management philosophy. This way, they can create plans that are rational, objective, and fact-based. These restrictive tools include positive cash flow, growth in profits, and an increase in per-capita efficiency. *(Source: Minutes of the Report on Developing Plans and Budgets for 2009, EMT Meeting Minutes No. [2008] 036)*

The purpose of our transformation in warehouse management is to integrate all warehouse management processes. Simplifying our supply model requires that our site plans are developed correctly on their first try. In the future, our supply centers will go digital and we will gradually reduce the number and scale of supply centers. If we can't make accurate plans for shipping equipment to sites, how can we develop an accurate plan for shipping equipment to warehouses in representative offices? The number of base stations is small in small countries, so we should think harder about how to develop the right models that can ensure our data accuracy. *(Ren Zhengfei: Speech at the Report on the Integrated Management Transformation in Small Countries, Huawei Executive Office Speech No. [2014] 062)*

11.2.3 Making Business Forecasts More Reliable

Business plans are the most important thing we look at when creating annual budgets. We must reasonably allocate resources through annual forecasting and promptly adjust resource allocation based on business forecasts. This is the primary cycle of operations management. To manage expenses effectively, we must begin with closed-loop budget management. We must first check whether the expenses are within the scope of the approved budget and then check whether the expense baselines are reasonable or not. If expenses exceed the budget, there are two scenarios: If the business plan has changed, new opportunities have emerged, or there are unexpected risks, you can apply for a new budget. On the other hand, if there are no changes to the business plan, the expenses that exceed the budget will be covered by the administrative team (AT). *(Meng Wanzhou: Aligning Financial Settlements with Value Creation and Aligning Cross Charging for Incentive Purposes with Value Distribution, Huawei Executive Office Speech No. [2012] 040)*

Over the next five years, we aim to achieve 3.0 points in information management maturity. This is an important part of data governance. It means we need to ensure that all of our business data comes from a single source and is therefore traceable and that our business forecasts are reliable. *(Source: Minutes of the Report on Data Work, EMT Meeting Minutes No. [2014] 024)*

We will identify and manage business risks through rolling forecasts and business reviews, and then flexibly adjust resource allocation. The head of each responsibility center is the owner for making forecasts. *(Source: 2015 Budget White Paper, Finance Committee Notice No. [2014] 014)*

The reliability of forecasts reflects the overall capabilities of managers at all levels. So long as there is no significant change to budget assumptions, any huge deviation of actual and forecasted numbers in the short term from the annual budgets tells us that managers are not good at forecasting. For departments where forecasts deviate greatly from their annual budgets, the revenue and profits beyond their budgeted numbers should be included in the departments' contributions. However, during performance appraisals, the managers' ability to prepare budgets and make forecasts should be considered. *(Source: Minutes of the Meeting on the 2016 Q1 Performance Review, Finance Committee Meeting Minutes No. [2016] 019)*

11.2.4 Continuously Optimizing Expense Baselines, Reducing Operating Costs, and Improving Management to Increase Efficiency

Cost management: Focusing on cost structures to control costs in the end-to-end process

In the coming three to five years, our most important task will be to improve our management and increase our efficiency. Right now, our per-capita efficiency is only one-sixth of IBM's. Can we increase it to one-third or even half of IBM's within three to five years? If so, we will be realizing an enormous amount of potential and improve our core competencies. We must improve our management and increase efficiency. This is the only way to sustain and grow the company's business. *(Ren Zhengfei: Staying Prepared Against Adversities in Times of Peace and Working with Stamina and Diligence—Speech at the Work Meeting of the Technical Support Department, 1999)*

We cannot control management costs in just a few domains. Cost controls need to be pursued in the end-to-end process. We should focus on cost structures and analyze the costs of big domains and large departments. Don't focus on the costs of small projects. If we keep a tight grip on their costs, bottlenecks will be created. If we use our current review method, no small projects will pass review because none of them are profitable. Opportunities, market size, and market share are all financial data. The cost management department should not aim to control and cut down on costs, but to provide guidance. This department should let go costs that should not be controlled and provide guidance on how to control costs that should be controlled. The cost management department must not just do paperwork. It must identify the actual issues. Cost control is necessary, but it must not affect our strategy. *(Ren Zhengfei: Minutes of a Work Report on Annual Taxes and Budgets, 2001)*

Cost controls are mainly about providing guidance for cost management in business departments based on the company's overall goals. This work should be about providing concepts, awareness, and methods to business departments, which will make adjustments and figure things out by themselves while keeping in mind the company's overall goals and interests. *(Ren Zhengfei: Minutes of a Work Report on Annual Taxes and Budgets, 2001)*

We must study how feudal dynasties in China were overthrown. It often did not cost a new emperor much to overthrow the previous one because the children of the previous emperor often formed a huge parasitic class that dragged the empire down. The new emperor would, in turn, have dozens of children, each of whom would have their grand residence and needed to be supported by the dynasty. Dozens of generations later, this group of "parasites" would become too large for the country to bear. Following this cycle, eventually civilians overthrow the beleaguered dynasty. Each dynasty shared the fate of their predecessors. If Huawei follows this same path, it will not be long before it goes bankrupt. *(Ren Zhengfei: Guidelines for Human Resources Management Transformation, 2006)*

Separating functional department budgets from project budgets and keeping functional department expenses as low as possible

We need to separate functional department budgets from project budgets, and keep the expenses of functional departments as low as possible. The goal of functional department operations is to ensure that we promptly deliver high-quality products and services to customers at affordable prices. *(Ren Zhengfei: Integrating Project Estimation, Budgeting, Accounting, and Final Accounting to Support Project Operations—Speech at a Briefing on the IFS Project, Huawei Executive Office Speech No. [2010] 007)*

We will spend three to five years reducing our general and administrative (G&A) expense rate so that our sales, general, and administrative (SG&A) expense rate can match Ericsson's current status. How can our SG&A expense rate be reduced? We cannot simply go about it like wringing water from a towel. We need to build long-term mechanisms to continuously improve efficiency by optimizing our organizational structures and processes and automating our IT systems. *(Source: 2010 Key Work Requirements, EMT Resolution No. [2010] 007)*

Can we streamline our organization or not? The answer is yes. There is sure to be a lot of unnecessary work being done, such as asking and waiting for unneeded instructions before doing something, sending all sorts of emails, and holding unnecessary meetings. This is a great waste of time and energy and costs us a lot. We need to adopt a unified platform for our operations and let the department head take charge of everything. If things go wrong, the head will be held accountable afterwards. We will complete this task in three to five years and increase Huawei's overall efficiency by 20%. I think we have a good chance of achieving that. If we can do this, we will be able to increase our profit without the need to increase the price we charge our customers. We will not have to transfer our internal costs to customers by charging them higher prices. We should cut down on our internal costs based on market prices rather than set the prices for customers based on our internal costs. *(Ren Zhengfei: Speech and Comments at the Strategy Retreat on Competition and Cooperation, 2012)*

We must gradually shift from the existing process compliance system into a process ownership system. Warehouse management is a real mess under our existing process compliance system. Who is to blame? Why not distribute the scrapped engineering materials to you as your bonus? It is our unswerving principle to hold wrongdoers accountable, even for acts that were committed in the past. Those who falsify accounts or cause waste and loss will see the equivalent amount of money deducted from their bonuses. If the bonus for a given year is insufficient to cover the losses they cause, the money will be deducted from their bonuses for the next several years. If a representative office general manager who was involved in the misconduct has left their position, they will still be held accountable, and will be given a "negative bonus". This way, they will learn the lesson and improve. Only by doing this will we have a better future. *(Ren Zhengfei: Speech at a Meeting with Trainees at the First Training Session for the Project Management Resource Pool, Huawei Executive Office Speech No. [2014] 058)*

11.3 Implementing Flexible Budgeting to Adapt to Opportunities and Changes

11.3.1 *Reasonableness Analysis of Detailed Business Department Budgets and Strict Control of Functional Department Budget Caps*

We should approach budgeting for business departments that are responsible for expansion from the bottom up. Their budgets will be granted as long as they are reasonable. We also need to check whether their budgets are spent reasonably. People responsible for preparing budgets must become deeply involved in business departments so they can accurately check whether their detailed budgets are reasonable. If we simply increase the percentage of our R&D budget in total revenue without controlling or overseeing how the money is spent, the money may not be well spent. The budgeting department must check whether the detailed budgets for business departments are reasonable. The budget and headcount for functional departments must be controlled. We will squeeze the "excess water" out of the towel. General and administrative expenses must not increase at the same pace as our revenue. Functional departments must control their budgets from the top down. *(Ren Zhengfei: Speech at a Work Report on 1999 Budgets, 1999)*

There are two approaches to budgeting. For business departments that are responsible for expansion, including R&D, Sales, and Marketing, we need to analyze whether their detailed budgets are reasonable, rather than simply controlling their budget caps. Other departments are functional departments. Their expenses are fixed, and their total budgets are strictly controlled. Budgeting should vary by department. We should approach budgeting for business departments from the bottom up, and for functional departments from the top down. *(Ren Zhengfei: Speech at a Work Report on 1999 Budgets, 1999)*

We will grant resource budgets to field offices, and profit centers will cover those expenses and costs. HQ does not have any money; it only has a minimum budget to ensure its operations. HQ has to charge field offices for the services it provides. Our budget should be prepared from the bottom up. Who should call for support? Field operating teams, not managers in back offices. This support comes at a cost. Those who call for support should bear associated costs. *(Ren Zhengfei: Keeping Customer PO Information Transparent to Support Payment Collection, Revenue Recognition, and Project Budgeting and Accounting—Speech at a Work Report by the IFS Project Team on December 29, Huawei Executive Office Speech No. [2009] 002)*

There are bottlenecks at our company's HQ. We should reduce the authority of HQ and downsize the HQ platform. HQ must focus on providing services. They cannot have all the budgets and resources in their hands, and have all the say about where the budgets and resources go. This must change. We must build a budgeting and final accounting system based on profit centers. This year, you have decided that HQ expenses cannot increase. My requirement is that the total expenses at HQ decrease next year. If the expenses don't decrease, we will have to let some people go or cut salaries. We can also have all HQ staff take a one-month break to see whether our field teams can continue to get their job done. If the answer is yes, it means HQ is not that important, and should be downsized. *(Ren Zhengfei: Speech at the Self-reflection Session of the Executive Committee of the Board of Directors, 2012)*

We have to set compensation baselines for HQ and control costs at HQ. To make this happen, our HR department needs to develop the necessary policies. *(Ren Zhengfei: Speech at a Briefing on the Progress of the ISC+ and CIF Projects, Huawei Executive Office Speech No. [2017] 035)*

11.3.2 Preparing Flexible Budgets to Allow Field Teams to Obtain More Resources After Their Business Grows

All budgets must be flexible, including the company's total budget and every individual department's budget. We must gradually figure out the ratios between the total budget of the company and individual departments' budgets. *(Ren Zhengfei: Comments at the Meeting Regarding the Budgeting Work for 2004, 2004)*

We need to change from inflexible to flexible budgeting. When our business grows, the budget should increase accordingly. We also need to improve HQ's efficiency in providing services. They should complete all necessary approvals within a standard time frame to ensure that field teams can quickly obtain more resources they need after their business grows. *(Source: Minutes of the Meeting on Preparing for the Development of a Planning and Budgeting Audit Management Committee, EMT Meeting Minutes No. [2006] 021)*

What does it mean to delegate planning, budgeting, and accounting authority to regional offices? It means we will give you a plan and you must pool resources together according to that plan. Resource expenses should not exceed your budget. Accounting will be performed when the budget is used up. If sales volumes increase dramatically, your budget will soar as well. However, if you use up your budget, but your sales volume doesn't go up, that means you are incapable. If you don't spend any money, though, you will be unable to grow your market. How do we make informed decisions based on the specific circumstances around us? We need to have the right managers. They must be able to flexibly control actual business situations. If they lack flexibility when using the plan and budget, it will be impossible for them to be good managers. We will delegate planning, budgeting, and accounting authority to regional offices. It would be unscientific and unreasonable for us to apply the same standard allocation rate to all regional offices. The planning department should not only take care of planning, but also perform accounting to carry out closed-loop management. After accounting is done, we will explore different allocation rates for different products, countries, and regions. After that, our performance appraisal criteria will become clear. *(Ren Zhengfei:*

Speech at the 2008 Mid-year Report by Regions to the EMT, EMT Meeting Minutes No. [2008] 028)

We must gather experience in flexible budget management. For example, if your plan increases and profits grow, and you still have to get your headcount and compensation approved, how can the budget be flexible? If your business results improve, budgets will increase naturally, and you will be able to operate on your own. However, if your business results worsen, you need to cut your budget immediately. *(Ren Zhengfei: Speech at a Briefing of the Northern Latin America Region and Colombia Representative Office, Huawei Executive Office Speech No. [2014] 051)*

We must not do business around the world rigidly. Instead, we should adopt flexible strategies and tactics. Right now, we are not investing enough in many of the strategic opportunities we face, but are expending lots of energy on areas where we have no hope. This is wasting our strategic resources. *(Ren Zhengfei: Minutes of the Briefing on the Progress of Differentiated Appraisals for Regions, Huawei Executive Office Speech No. [2015] 050)*

We must continuously analyze the difficulties we face in all the countries where we operate, and find the right operating model for each country. Seeking to expand in all countries will cost a lot, and those costs will be passed on to other countries. This approach is too rigid. For regions where we have no room for further expansion, we must transfer our strategic forces away to strategic regions with more opportunities. When the environment improves and opportunities emerge, we can transfer our strategic forces back. In war-torn countries where conditions do not permit network construction, we can provide spare parts and services at higher prices so we can support our local employees. If our business shrinks in countries where we face extreme hardships, we need to strengthen our process-based management. This will make it possible to oversee business operations in these countries remotely. *(Ren Zhengfei: Minutes of the Briefing on the Progress of Differentiated Appraisals for Regions, Huawei Executive Office Speech No. [2015] 050)*

Our current flexible budgeting system does not effectively use the huge profits we earn. To effectively manage our profits, we must consider linking our SPs and BPs. We need to systematically and strategically plan long-term investment based on the company's financial forecasts for the next three to five years. In addition, we must develop a sound plan that guides on the pace and intensity of our investment based on annual business results. *(Source: Minutes of the Meeting on the 2016 H1 Performance Review, Finance Committee Meeting Minutes No. [2016] 032)*

11.3.3 Strictly Implementing a Process for Granting and Increasing Budgets

Huawei has always worked to lower operating costs and expenses. Through continuous improvements, we aim to increase efficiency, improve management, and boost profitability. Since the IT industry's last "hard winter", we have been very lax with our closed-loop budgeting and accounting management. Sometimes we don't even set a limit on expenses. Managers at all levels just want to hire more people. They are never worried about whether they have money or not. They never care about how much they have spent or assess the relationship between the money spent and the value and contribution it created. Operating costs and expenses are very flexible. While continuing to use a flexible bottom-up budgeting system, we also need to build a strict closed-loop budgeting and accounting management system to avoid manager-driven budget granting and management. *(Source: Resolution on Strengthening and Improving Administrative Expense Management, EMT Resolution No. [2008] 032)*

We are now doing a better job at managing expenses. However, we still need to reinforce our work in developing a long-term closed-loop budgeting and accounting management system. In particular, we must strictly implement a process for granting and increasing budgets. Our goal is to achieve flexible budgeting and flexible management and ensure that money is available only when a budget is in place. *(Source: Minutes of the Report on the 2009 H1 Performance Review, EMT Meeting Minutes No. [2009] 038)*

Every department has its responsibilities, and all work within the scope of their responsibilities must be supported by the department's budget. Departments cannot apply for an additional budget for work that falls within their normal scope of responsibilities. Department budgets must be managed in a closed loop. The annual budgets should be generated based on responsibilities, expense baselines, and management improvement requirements. Resources will be allocated based on budgets. If resources beyond the budget are needed, the department involved must specify what extra things they need to do and what value will be created. The extra budgets can be listed separately and the company will centrally generate and grant these budgets. These extra budgets will not be included in departmental budget baselines. *(Ren Zhengfei: Minutes of the Meeting on the Budgeting Work, Huawei Executive Office Speech No. [2014] 004)*

11.4 Accounting: An Important Indicator of Management Improvement

11.4.1 Overseeing the Exercise of the Delegated Authority Through Accounting to Ensure Field Teams Have Command Authority

At HQ, we should streamline our organization and keep our processes simple. We should reduce direct command and remote control from HQ, move command centers to field offices, and give field teams the authority to perform their own planning, budgeting, and accounting. This means we are delegating the management and sales decision-making authority to field offices. Field offices need to have more tactical mobility to flexibly deal with changes in actual situations. Back offices need to step up their efforts to provide services based on plans and budgets, and oversee the exercise of delegated authority through accounting. This can make sure field teams have the authority they need to get the job done and HQ doesn't need to worry about the authority being abused. *(Ren Zhengfei: Speech at the UK Representative Office, Huawei Executive Office Speech No. [2007] 027)*

The key to budgeting lies in closed-loop budget management through accounting. Whether departments have taken budgeting seriously and have prepared their budgets effectively is determined through the accounting and assessment of their actual business results. *(Ren Zhengfei: Minutes of the Meeting on the Budgeting Work, Huawei Executive Office Speech No. [2014] 004)*

Currently, the amount of resources a field team needs to win a project still needs to be approved by HQ. For example, when a field team asks for nine people, HQ may only send six people over, claiming six people are enough. However, with the six people, the field team might not be able to fully win the project. In the future, we should delegate authority to the field and provide whatever they request. After the battle is over, we can calculate the amount of resources used for the project. For example, we may find out that only three of the nine people sent over by HQ actually worked on the project, so we need to check with the field team where the other six people have been. We are still unable to implement such an authority delegation system because we have not yet achieved end-to-end project management. We will ultimately get there within the next five to ten years. *(Ren Zhengfei: Remarks to Candidates for Full-time Board*

Directors at the Board Director Enablement Workshop, Huawei Executive Office Speech No. [2014] 007)

11.4.2 Improving Management Through Scientific Accounting

The primary purpose of implementing independent accounting is to improve management through comprehensive accounting. Currently, accounting does not cover all aspects of our operations. Through comprehensive accounting, we aim to encourage departments to focus more on costs and numbers. *(Ren Zhengfei: Minutes of a Briefing on the Operating Mechanism of the Mechanical & Industrial Division, 1998)*

When we track IPD and ISC projects, accounting is of paramount importance. It is really not an easy task to do accounting throughout the IPD and ISC processes. The most important responsibility of Finance in IPD and ISC projects is to do a good job in accounting. If accounting is done properly, we will be able to accurately break down costs that can be used as the basis for project assessments. Currently, Finance should focus its attention on accounting to provide reliable data as an input for management. *(Ren Zhengfei: Speech at a Briefing on Four Unifications and 2000 Work Plan of Finance, 1999)*

HR and Finance must do a good job in project cost accounting related to personnel. I simply don't understand why we can't do accounting effectively. When you said the SAP system didn't allow us to do accounting, we switched to the Oracle system. But now we're still having trouble with accounting even two years after the switch. Management improvement at Huawei will be impossible if our personnel expenses are not charged directly to projects. We should strengthen the guiding role of planning, budgeting, and accounting in our business development. The accounting of personnel expenses doesn't have to be too accurate. Estimated numbers are also acceptable. *(Ren Zhengfei: Adapting the Manager Appraisal System to Challenges Facing the Transforming Industry, Huawei Executive Office Speech No. [2006] 036)*

Accounting is an important indicator of management improvement. It's impossible to know whether we are making progress if we don't do accounting. We need to first perform accounting by project, region, and product line. Thanks to our core value of inspiring dedication in our employees, we are very competitive now. This management philosophy works for Huawei. However, our current management efficiency is very low. *(Ren Zhengfei: Timely, Accurate, High Quality, and Low Cost Delivery*

Calls for Professional Process-compliant CFOs—Minutes of a Meeting with Trainees of the CFO Session of the Reserve Pool, Huawei Executive Office Speech No. [2009] 021)

We don't have to do extremely fine-grained accounting for everything. For example, whether accounting should be performed down to the last component depends on the applicable business scenario. For material purchases, it is of course necessary to account for costs down to the last component. But for engineering delivery and product sales, we only need to account for the revenue or cost at the site or device level. Considering the complexity of some forms of accounting, we are still not mature enough to achieve the granularity we should have, so I think properly investing more resources in this is the right thing to do. *(Ren Zhengfei: Minutes of the Meeting with Staff of the Romania Accounting SSC, Huawei Executive Office Speech No. [2011] 021)*

We must reinforce our management of customer- and supplier-facing roles and make related estimation, budgeting, accounting, and final accounting more effective. These are the sources of our profits. We need to follow our major processes to improve management and accounting of the resources called for by field offices, keep costs under control, and improve the quality of operations to ensure profitability. To manage expenses effectively, we should properly manage budgets and ensure that expenses are reasonable and compliant with applicable laws and regulations. We should focus more on the most important points when it comes to cross charging for incentive purposes. The primary purpose of financial management is to generate profits and eliminate corruption. *(Ren Zhengfei: Focusing on Strategy and Streamlining Management, Huawei Executive Office Speech No. [2012] 041)*

Open Access This chapter is licensed under the terms of the Creative Commons Attribution-NonCommercial-NoDerivatives 4.0 International License (http://creativecommons.org/licenses/by-nc-nd/4.0/), which permits any noncommercial use, sharing, distribution and reproduction in any medium or format, as long as you give appropriate credit to the original author(s) and the source, provide a link to the Creative Commons licence and indicate if you modified the licensed material. You do not have permission under this license to share adapted material derived from this chapter or parts of it.

The images or other third party material in this chapter are included in the chapter's Creative Commons licence, unless indicated otherwise in a credit line to the material. If material is not included in the chapter's Creative Commons licence and your intended use is not permitted by statutory regulation or exceeds the permitted use, you will need to obtain permission directly from the copyright holder.

CHAPTER 12

Service and Oversight Functions of Accounting

At Huawei, accounting is about keeping centralized records and is managed from the top down. Over the years, the company has kept accounting an independent function, hoping that it can serve as a "dam", overseeing business activities and applying checks and balances. Accounting does more than just provide services – it also takes on an oversight responsibility. Its oversight responsibility even outweighs its service function.

Accounting must ensure that data is accurate and reliable, with the motto of "answering only to the truth, not to customers, business personnel, or managers". Accounting is completely separate from business management organizations. The accuracy of financial data depends on standard processes and clean data at the source. Only by regulating business activities at the source can we improve the quality of financial data.

Financial oversight means firm commitments to process management. We must build oversight into every part of our processes. We must dare to expose problems and push for improvement. Oversight is not just the responsibility of Accounting. Every link in the process must play an oversight role. Managers of business departments are the primary owners for business authenticity and reasonableness. However, managers must not intervene in process operations. Instead, they can initiate or propose process improvements.

The company has made it clear that fund security is a clear requirement for the payment division. Sustained high work quality is the most important criterion for appraising the performance of payment personnel. The implementation of the daily reconciliation mechanism at three organizational levels ensures greater business authenticity and compliance.

Accounting personnel must get close to business, understand business, and oversee business, so that they can better serve and manage business. When serving business, accounting personnel must remember that business plays a leading role. However, this doesn't mean they have to be reactive in this process.

Institutional oversight and ethical constraints are complementary to each other. Accounting personnel must always observe professional ethics during their day-to-day work. Of course, professional ethics do not conflict with the company's oversight rules. Compliance with job-specific code of conduct is a prerequisite, and observation of professional ethics is the bottom line. No matter what, accounting personnel must not cross the bottom line during their routine work.

This chapter delves deep into key points of accounting management.

12.1 Keeping Accounting Independent from the Top Down and Letting It Serve as a "Dam"

12.1.1 Roles of Accounting: Service and Oversight, with the Latter Being More Important

For years, we have kept Accounting independent from the top down, hoping that it would serve as a dam, overseeing business activities and applying checks and balances. What does oversight mean? Let me give you an example. Accounting personnel should be fully aware of the delivery cost of a project. If there are abnormal fluctuations and discrepancies in the data provided by business personnel, accounting personnel should identify them and ask more questions or require business personnel to offer more supporting information. Accounting should make it clear to business departments that it does more than just provide services – it also takes on an oversight responsibility. Its oversight responsibility even outweighs its service function. Accounting's mode of vertical operations is like a sieve within Huawei's internal operating mechanism. This sieve lets compliant, well-grounded business activities pass through, but blocks those that are non-compliant and erroneous. Through approaches such as communication, asking for instructions, and reporting, Accounting helps us reduce errors. These errors are not incorrect financial data, but errors caused by improper business operations. *(Ren Zhengfei: Minutes of the Meeting with*

Staff of the Romania Accounting SSC, Huawei Executive Office Speech No. [2011] 021)

On multiple occasions, Mr. Ren has stressed that Accounting does more than just provide services; it also takes on an oversight responsibility. The revenue recognition issue of the China Region indicated that Accounting has failed to fulfill its oversight responsibility. To ensure accuracy of financial data, you not only need to do calculations, but also need to ensure that financial data truly reflects business on the ground. *(Meng Wanzhou: Minutes of a Meeting with Accounting Managers, 2011)*

Accounting must operate independently and ensure data is accurate and reliable. Even when business personnel tell you there is no need to check the data, saying that they have indeed spent 3000 US dollars. You must still check. Otherwise, how can you ensure that the data is accurate? If the upstream unit that provides financial data alleges water (meaning the financial data) is not polluted, will you agree to drink the water? What if the water has been contaminated? That's why we require our accounting personnel to remain independent when it comes to understanding data. If water in the upstream is not polluted, then why won't business personnel drink it? I've learned that today's financial data is much more accurate and up-to-date. This is based on your assumptions that business data is reliable and that the approvers are responsible. However, if business data is unreliable, your assumptions won't hold. So it's still possible that accurate financial data may not truly reflect business on the ground. *(Ren Zhengfei: Minutes of the Meeting with Staff of the Romania Accounting SSC, Huawei Executive Office Speech No. [2011] 021)*

Two things about oversight need to be distinguished. First, oversight-oriented subsidiary boards deal with the oversight of internal and external compliance and this is not procedure-based. We should also move our oversight function forward while delegating the business decision-making authority to the field. Second, we must never transfer our central authority over treasury, accounting, and auditing to lower levels. Of these three, treasury management authority is not about managing, blocking, and exerting pressure. Instead, it should be about providing fast and flexible services, so that representative offices can use funds flexibly. Accounting management authority is about keeping centralized records, with the motto of "answering only to the truth, not to customers, business personnel, or managers". Accounting is completely separate from business management organizations. Field operations services and shared services centers (SSCs) are divisions of these three types of authority, not centers of authority. Auditing is oversight after things have happened. *(Ren Zhengfei: Speech at a Briefing on Improvements and Future Planning for Carrier and Enterprise Regional Organization Transformation, Huawei Executive Office Speech No. [2017] 030)*

12.1.2 Oversight by Accounting: Comprehensive Oversight Throughout All Processes

If we want everyone to follow processes and systems in their work, we have to sell the idea and convince people. The SSCs should post the management issues they identify on *Xinsheng Community*[1] or publish them in *Improvement*.[2] It doesn't matter if their findings turn out to be right or wrong. If they're right, you'll need to resolve the issues; if they're wrong, the findings will serve as a warning. Without them, the company won't be able to make progress. You'd better send the cases you find to Huawei Executive Office, too. You don't have to dress them up, just explain them clearly. The Executive Office will forward and publish them to help our business managers understand the importance of data quality and process compliance. *(Ren Zhengfei: Speech at a Meeting with Staff in Mauritius, Huawei Executive Office Speech No. [2013] 016)*

The most important thing for Finance is to expose problems and to tell the truth. Where is there overstocking? Where are bad debts? Finance needs to expose problems with our internal operations through oversight reports. Managers will feel the pressure, and will improve their management and coordination to make internal operations more efficient. That is what Finance can do for them. Accounting must be bold enough to oversee; otherwise, it will not be the "dam" it is supposed to be. When you find issues with documents, you should ask business personnel to explain. If secret or sensitive information is involved, Accounting must check with the original approver's supervisor before performing accounting. Accounting cannot handle expenses without all necessary information. When providing accounting services, do not forget your oversight responsibility. *(Ren Zhengfei: Speech at a Meeting with Staff in Mauritius, Huawei Executive Office Speech No. [2013] 016)*

Financial oversight means firm commitments to process management. We must build oversight into every part of our processes. We must dare to

---

[1] *Xinsheng Community* is a company-wide open online forum at Huawei.
[2] *Improvement* is an internal publication at Huawei.

expose problems and push for improvement. *(Ren Zhengfei: Speech at a Meeting with Staff in Mauritius, Huawei Executive Office Speech No. [2013] 016)*

12.1.3 *"Accounting Plays an Oversight Role": Incorporating Service and Oversight into End-to-End Processes; Exercising Oversight While Providing Services*

By saying "accounting plays an oversight role", I mean we exercise oversight in the process of providing services according to laws and regulations. Laws and regulations are like a sieve. By having everything go through this sieve, we exercise oversight. Every effort we make must aim to help grow our business. When you have doubts, you need to ask for instructions, not just block it. Simply blocking others is not oversight. Service, service, service! We ensure smooth business operations through delivery of standardized services. Everything we do aims to serve business. That's what "business plays a leading role" means. *(Ren Zhengfei: Speech at a Briefing on Four Unifications and 2000 Work Plan of Finance, 1999)*

Oversight is not separate from financial activities. All financial personnel are also oversight personnel. Financial personnel manage business through payment, collection of payment, budgeting, and other activities. They are not performing business activities. In fact, they are overseeing the operations of business processes. Accounting's oversight of business processes is like a big sieve. This sieve lets compliant business activities pass through, but blocks those that are non-compliant. Accounting then will ask involved departments to assess these non-compliant business activities. After the assessment, clear rules will be set on how to standardize these activities so that they can pass through the sieve in the future. This way, the sieve will more rapidly allow more business activities through, and our standards for fast, accurate, and secure services will be more powerful. Most business activities will be compliant, only a small proportion of activities require further assessments. This is how you should oversee business operations through processes. *(Ren Zhengfei: Speech at a Briefing by the Finance Management Department on Manager Appointment, 2005)*

Accounting must establish a business credibility system. If a business department has a low credit rating, Accounting may spend more time checking every piece of its data and respond slowly to its requests. If a business department has a high credit rating, Accounting may respond quickly and check business data afterwards. This enables Accounting to ensure responsiveness and fulfill its oversight responsibility. Accounting is to business what a nose is to the sense of smell. Accounting personnel who are unfamiliar with business data is like having a stuffy nose that is unable to smell a rat. The Internal Audit Department is like a water inspection department, occasionally checking water quality. Therefore, Accounting must exercise its oversight responsibility. This is the only way for you to become more outstanding employees. *(Ren Zhengfei: Minutes of the Meeting with Staff of the Romania Accounting SSC, Huawei Executive Office Speech No. [2011] 021)*

What does oversight mean? Oversight plays a role in every node of a process: Regional presidents have the primary oversight responsibilities in their regions. Directors of account departments have the primary oversight responsibilities of their departments. Remember that oversight involves more than just Accounting. *(Ren Zhengfei: Minutes of the Meeting with Staff of the Romania Accounting SSC, Huawei Executive Office Speech No. [2011] 021)*

First, Accounting is Huawei's steward, so I don't think there's anything you should not have a hand in.

Second, business departments are accountable for risks and Finance must remind business departments of possible risks. When a business issue is identified, Finance should report it not only to the person responsible for the business, but also to other individuals related to the business. In this way, everyone, rather than business directors, has the authority and obligation to comment on the report.

Third, oversight naturally conflicts with efficiency. We could let things pass quickly and examine what happens afterwards. We could also exert controls before things happen and ask business departments to explain them clearly before they can be passed. The approach we choose depends on our own judgment and understanding of the risks we face.

Fourth, SSCs should prepare and post risk reports, which resemble a bulletin board and show what issues have been identified in business operations and how they have been resolved. Don't make these reports too lengthy. All you need to do is release several of these reports each week or month to reveal the risks, and the departments involved will take care of them, so that you are not hard pressed to coordinate on their handling. You should divide the reports into several parts: improvements made by business departments after the previous report was released; new issues, conclusions of communication, and improvement opportunities. These risk reports, together with the operation analysis reports, should be regularly incorporated into each business unit's business management mechanism.

Fifth, business organizations are responsible for making improvements, and SSCs also need to take partial responsibility. Business departments should prepare action plans for improvement and SSCs should check whether the expected results have been achieved. If not, SSCs should stop providing financial services to these departments. We advocate sticking to principles and maintaining our stance when providing financial services.

Sixth, it is better to report risks than to sweep them under the rug. Our intention is to uncover risks, not to accuse anyone. *(Ren Zhengfei: Minutes of the Meeting with Staff of the Romania Accounting SSC, Huawei Executive Office Speech No. [2011] 021)*

12.2 ACCOUNTING MUST GET DEEPLY INVOLVED IN BUSINESS OPERATIONS AND IMPLEMENT INTEGRATED FINANCIAL MANAGEMENT WHILE SERVING BUSINESS

12.2.1 Accounting Must Be Proactive While Serving Business

When important market opportunities emerge, Finance is one of the important teams to support our efforts to seize them. Finance can also participate in the decision-making process. You must extend your reach from the most basic level to every link of the company's processes. You must exert appropriate control. When your control is inappropriate, you can loosen the string a little bit and exert control in areas you find appropriate. This way, you will move in the direction of appropriate management. *(Ren Zhengfei: Speech at a Meeting with Financial Staff, 1997)*

When establishing financial rules, we need to be realistic. We must ensure that the procedure is impartial before we aim to produce impartial results. At the current stage, we must not pursue absolute accuracy and should be a little bit flexible and tolerant. *(Ren Zhengfei: Minutes of a Meeting on Audits of Write-off and Payment Collection Activities, 2004)*

Financial personnel must proactively serve business personnel. First of all, financial personnel must proactively guide and communicate with business personnel. Second, financial personnel must give more training to business personnel during the process of oversight. Third, financial personnel must not arbitrarily let violations slip through. *(Ren Zhengfei: Minutes of a Meeting on Financial Transformation Projects, 2004)*

1. When serving business, accounting personnel must remember that business plays a leading role. However, this doesn't mean they have to be reactive in this process. CFOs are the most important decision-makers of companies around the world. While serving business, Finance uses standards as a sieve to execute financial processes.
2. To better serve and manage business, financial personnel must first understand business. You need to establish and implement a closed-loop backtracking mechanism and a flexible management mechanism that cover planning, budgeting, and accounting. This is the best integrated financial management.
3. Financial personnel must fulfill their management responsibilities and shift their focus from accounting to real management. You must accurately calculate profits and losses, unearth what's really going on in business, and support business management. For example, you need to figure out the costs of labor outsourcing.
4. Business data and information must be made accessible to pertinent financial personnel, so that they can accurately calculate and better explain data about output (revenue and profit) and input (costs and expenses). This will enable financial personnel to better serve business improvement and decision making.
5. The priorities of financial personnel lie in guidance before, service during, and management after business activities. They must promote correct corporate values, ensure the smooth execution of major business processes, and encourage business to forge ahead.
6. Internal controls (including financial oversight) teams need to go out to the field and work closely with field teams to ensure efficient operations and appropriate oversight. Engineering inspection teams are currently tasked with combating widespread corruption. Internal controls teams need to work with engineering inspection teams to develop policies and methods that ensure scientific oversight. The purpose of oversight is to ensure smooth business operations. Oversight is the means to our end goal – business success.
7. Business departments are the primary owners for business authenticity and reasonableness. Finance must oversee business activities. Only when everyone plays their own part, can business run smoothly.
8. Financial personnel must spend their spare time on sites to gain engineering experience, get to know the basic parts of a site as well as procedures and issues about cost baselines, logistics, and engineering. They should be aiming to improve. You can go to sites near

our Bantian campus in Shenzhen to learn or engage in hands-on practice in Songshan Lake, Dongguan. *(Ren Zhengfei: Speech at a Meeting with Financial Managers, Improvement Issue No. 369, 2010)*

First, how do we define a "competent CFO"? A competent CFO has the ability to take over the job of the CEO whenever there is a need. That's what we expect of a competent CFO. CFO is what accounting personnel should aim to become. Accounting personnel who don't have adequate business knowledge are unlikely to become business savvy and are only likely to provide basic accounting services that lack flexibility, creativity, and principles, and can add no value to business. This is fine if you just want to be an accountant. But if you want to move up the ladder, you must learn the ropes of the business; otherwise, your career development will be limited. We have raised requirements for financial personnel. The bottom line is that they must be able to understand contracts. I've asked the Romania Representative Office to select several standard contracts to help financial personnel gain insight into different commercial terms, acceptance criteria, and product configurations. This time, I am introducing many colleagues from Sales and Services to you. I hope that you will get to know them, visit their sites, and lend them a hand on weekends. *(Ren Zhengfei: Minutes of the Meeting with Staff of the Romania Accounting SSC, Huawei Executive Office Speech No. [2011] 021)*

Accounting personnel must get close to business, understand business, and oversee business. That's when we can start discussing what your function as a dam really means. This dam not only needs to ensure that water moves in the right direction (correct attribution of revenue and accrual), but also needs to guarantee the cleanness of water at the source (reliable asset quality and accurate accounts payable and payments). *(Ren Zhengfei: Minutes of a Meeting with Accounting Staff, Group Finance CFO's Office Meeting Minutes No. [2015] 081)*

12.2.2 Accounting Must Get Close to Business and Establish a Multi-level Shared Service Model Based on Business Scenarios

In the past, financial departments served as "scorekeepers" when they performed basic functions like accounting, receipts and payments, and financing. They were handlers of data. However, today, our requirements for financial departments are to effectively execute key financial activities, actively collaborate with business departments to manage business performance and risks, provide fair and accurate financial information to help business departments continuously improve business performance, and balance the expansion of business with suitable controls. *(Meng Wanzhou: Finance – From a Scorekeeper to a Value Integrator, Improvement Issue No. 396, 2012)*

If we look back at the growth of financial departments, we will find that management transformation and process reengineering are important driving forces behind the growth. In 1998, KPMG helped us implement the "Four Unifications" project. This project ensured the unifications of financial processes, rules, codes, and oversight across the company, laying a solid foundation for our management transformation initiatives afterwards. In 2005, with guidance from IBM consultants, Accounting established six SSCs around the world. These centers not just improved operating efficiency and oversight quality, but also provided sound accounting support for the rapid development of our business outside China. In 2007, Huawei started to work with IBM on the IFS Program. Under this program, we rolled out the IDS1 on payment collection, revenue, and project budgeting and accounting among global offices, aligning finance with business from two perspectives – the sales contract and the procurement contract. In the meantime, we are steadily advancing IDS2 and IDS3. IDS2 aims to improve project operations management and IDS3 aims to streamline planning, budgeting, forecasting, and accounting to support business management of the responsibility centers at different levels. *(Meng Wanzhou: Finance – From a Scorekeeper to a Value Integrator, Improvement Issue No. 396, 2012)*

Accounting must get close to business and establish a multi-level shared service model based on business scenarios. When building financial departments, we must focus on what contributions they can make to the company rather than how much operating costs they can reduce.

1. During the process of building SSCs, there are many factors for consideration, including costs, religious beliefs, time differences, and talent acquisition. When Western firms establish an SSC, their major aim is to create economies of scale and save on costs. When we do this, we should also consider how to ensure our internal controls and preventative systems are effective, as these are also the responsibilities and contributions of SSCs to the company.
2. We need to establish multi-level shared accounting services centers that are tailored to our particular businesses. (1) Where comprehen-

sive processes have been defined and related data is relatively accurate, we can take steps to gain cost advantages. We can establish one or two global SSCs to centrally deliver accounting services and build up disaster recovery and backup capabilities pertinent to accounting services.(2) For businesses where processes and rules for business operations have not been standardized, we can establish small teams near business departments to provide accounting services. If you stay far away from business departments and know next to nothing about their businesses, how could you ensure your accounting is clear and data is accurate? (3) Built on our existing SSCs, we can also establish shared accounting services centers in regions, focusing on accounting solutions and compliance with local tax laws and regulations. These centers mainly aim to provide capability support.
3. Outstanding managers from these SSCs must actively get close to business and apply their knowledge. The biggest shortcoming of our outstanding young talent today is that they lack hands-on experience. If they work in a project to accumulate experience, they might get promoted. If they then participate in a larger project, they may get promoted again. Things never look tough until you do it. Genuine knowledge comes from practice. *(Ren Zhengfei: Speech at a Meeting with Staff in Mauritius, Huawei Executive Office Speech No. [2013] 016)*

12.3 Payment Management

12.3.1 Basing Performance Appraisals of Payment Personnel on the Quality of Their Work and Maintaining Appropriate Redundancy in the Headcount

1. We have made it clear that fund security is a clear requirement for the payment division. During the performance appraisal for payment personnel, we should focus on the responsibilities they assume and the results they deliver. Sustained high work quality is the most important criterion for appraising the performance of payment personnel.
2. The quality of our work must approach the highest level possible. Even if our quality of work is higher than financial institutions, we

should keep on improving. However, operating efficiency cannot be increased indefinitely and we should also avoid blind pursuit of improvement. Excessive pursuit of improvement might cause tension among our employees, which may result in mistakes. We should know where to draw the line for improvement. Proper resource allocation is a prerequisite for high work quality.
3. Currently, a payment employee needs to process 60,000 documents on average each year. This figure is 120,000 for a member of the treasury management team. We have roughly 250 working days each year. That means a payment employee processes 240 documents each day. Finance must adjust headcount for these two teams to be better aligned with our future oversight plan. That is to say, their workloads must be reduced to 70%–80% of the current level in the future.
4. Business is evolving and industry is changing. Payment personnel need to finish their day-to-day work and effectively plan how to keep abreast of advanced payment technologies, so that they can leverage technological advances to ensure work quality and boost operating efficiency.
5. The payment system needs to bring in conscientious, responsible, reliable, and meticulous employees from the GTS and supply department, and allow them to create value in new posts. *(Ren Zhengfei: Speech at a Meeting with Payment Staff, Huawei Executive Office Speech No. [2017] 042)*

12.3.2 Establishing a Mechanism to Ensure Daily Reconciliation at Three Organizational Levels

1. Daily reconciliation at the first level must be achieved during business operations. Financial departments must consider how to fulfill their oversight responsibilities while serving business. Business managers must be responsible for business authenticity and reasonableness. While serving business, CFOs at different levels must ensure that data generated from key business activities is accurate and reasonable. Financial teams of business units must work with their respective units to nail down the responsibility fulfillment plans for ensuring daily reconciliation at the first level and effectively implement the plans.

2. The responsibility for ensuring daily reconciliation at the second level lies in the Accounting Management Department. When performing accounting, this department must check whether all business documents are provided, whether they are fully in compliance with laws and regulations, and whether the company can start the payment procedure based on these documents. The department also needs to check whether all information about our accounts receivable is clearly documented, and then performs account reconciliation with customers.
3. The Treasury Management Department ensures daily reconciliation at the third level. This department needs to check all payment records of all our accounts to see whether they are consistent with accounting records. Any amounts paid must be reconciled the same date. Any errors made must be identified and corrected within one working day.
4. The consumer and enterprise businesses involve many scenarios and customers and highly-frequent payment and collection activities. Once an error is made during the payment or business process, it is difficult to recover losses. That's why we need to assign more people to these two businesses to ensure daily reconciliation.
5. The accounting team must build up its capabilities for identifying business risks that arise from massive amounts of data. It should also have the courage to alert business teams and regularly report to the company on these risks. If the work quality of a business department is low, we will give them time to improve, but we won't tolerate or tacitly approve the behavior.
6. The implementation of the daily reconciliation mechanism at three organizational levels ensures greater business authenticity and compliance. This demonstrates greater value of the financial departments, and is the greatest opportunity for you to develop. The three levels must build effective channels of communication, promptly notify business departments of issues, and push for the resolution of the issues.
7. We must orient ourselves towards responsibilities and quality, and give decent pay to employees working on daily reconciliation, if circumstances permit. *(Ren Zhengfei: Speech at a Meeting with Payment Staff, Huawei Executive Office Speech No. [2017] 042)*

12.3.3 Having a Correct Understanding of Error Rates

1. We must respect errors instead of fearing them. Zero errors are an ideal situation, so a certain proportion of errors is inevitable. Aiming to achieve zero error is not realistic. We must respect errors. When an error is detected, we must reflect on ourselves and try our best to improve and avoid the recurrence of this error. We must not fear, dodge, or cover up errors.
2. As long as payment errors can be corrected, they are not real errors and won't be included in employees' performance records. Only by doing so can we encourage employees to expose and report on errors. This will also help us leverage concerted efforts to correct errors and reduce losses, rather than covering up errors until losses are irretrievable.
3. How an error is made must be documented in the system. The purpose of doing so is not to penalize people, but to improve the process. Every error teaches us a precious lesson. We must draw a risk map that includes error types and causes. We will then drive improvement and strengthen enablement training to gradually put out fires on this risk map.
4. Employees with low work quality over an extended period must be transferred away from payment positions. However, we cannot attribute each error to a specific individual and punish them. This is the basic logic behind total management. If a single error occurs, we need to invest our efforts in making improvement and avoiding recurrence. If an employee makes errors frequently, we need to reassign them promptly. *(Ren Zhengfei: Speech at a Meeting with Payment Staff, Huawei Executive Office Speech No. [2017] 042)*

12.4 COMPLYING WITH ACCOUNTING ETHICS AND RULES

12.4.1 Being Bold and Able to Stick to Principles

Finance must improve its organizational capabilities and strike the right balance between the stringency of rules and flexibility. The standard for you to handle things should not be a thin line, but a belt of certain width. This belt tests how well our business managers and financial personnel handle things. It is understandable, given the costs, that a certain margin of error exists when you build the financial division. Approvers can be flexible when judging whether an issue is reasonable. However, financial personnel must not randomly perform accounting or make decisions all by themselves. Any flexibility or relaxation must be approved by a superior and must be recorded. Accounting personnel can be dogmatic or rigid, but cannot be flexible. You are more like a sieve and must strictly follow rules and business processes. You should not just let non-compliant activities slip through. However, you should be warm and amiable when engaging with people. We must stress rules and at the same time flexibility at the front end. However, the financial function at the back end must be rule-based and even dogmatic, allowing little flexibility. Managers at different levels must be aware of this, be decisive, and avoid becoming hands-off bosses. *(Ren Zhengfei: Building a Professional Financial Team That Has Solid Integrity, Dares to Shoulder Responsibilities, and Sticks to Principles, Huawei Executive Office Speech No. [2006] 038)*

Sticking to principles is the bottom line for all our financial personnel. Being adept at sticking to principles must be the direction in which we are moving. *(Ren Zhengfei: Minutes of a Meeting with Accounting Staff, Group Finance CFO's Office Meeting Minutes No. [2015] 081)*

SSCs deliver a wide array of routine accounting services in accordance with corporate rules and policies day after day. These rules and policies are applicable globally, so it is inevitable that some rules or specific requirements are not applicable to certain scenarios. When such issues arise, accounting personnel in the field must proactively provide feedback and help establish a transparent issue resolution mechanism. *(Ren Zhengfei: Minutes of a Meeting with Accounting Staff, Group Finance CFO's Office Meeting Minutes No. [2015] 081)*

Business organizations are responsible for making improvements, and SSCs also need to take partial responsibility. Business departments should prepare action plans for improvement and SSCs should check whether the expected results have been achieved. If not, SSCs should stop providing financial services to these departments. We advocate sticking to principles and maintaining our stance when providing financial services. *(Ren Zhengfei: Minutes of the Meeting with Staff of the Romania Accounting SSC, Huawei Executive Office Speech No. [2011] 021)*

Accounting should establish a correct view of service and stick to principles while providing services. Accounting personnel must proactively serve business departments and the company as a whole. For business departments, we stress high efficiency and premium quality. For business teams at different levels, we stress accuracy and reliability. In other words, Accounting must not give up on its oversight function just because it provides services. Accounting must stick to principles while offering standard services they promise and must ensure that services are delivered on time and with promised quality. Regarding one-off tailored services, you must not blindly roll them out without any careful analysis of the value they may bring and the resources they may require. The company has a clearly-defined process-based requirement review and management system. Why do we often choose a smaller path instead of the highway? We have recently reviewed the use of tailored reports and found that most of them have very low utilization rates. I don't know why we need to invest resources in them. Accounting must stick to principles and follow rules when responding to service requests. Otherwise, the massive amounts of requirements will cause you to drift off course. *(Meng Wanzhou: Minutes of a Meeting with Accounting Managers, 2011)*

You must apply *huidu* and become good at sticking to principles. We aim to leverage accounting to unearth loopholes in our management, seek inflection points for improvement, and make financial data more accurate and business requests more rational. Our aim is not to judge people. *(Meng Wanzhou: Minutes of a Meeting with Accounting Managers, 2011)*

12.4.2 Complementing Institutional Oversight with Ethical Constraints

Discipline must be made part of our CIAG efforts, with both an accountability system and an award system put in place to widen the income gap for different employees. We will begin to crack down harder on account falsification and business fraud, and impose stricter disciplinary action against violators. The falsified amounts must be repaid 120% higher. If everyone falsified data, achieving CIAG would be impossible. *(Ren Zhengfei: Speech at the Report on the Integrated Management Transformation in Small Countries, Huawei Executive Office Speech No. [2014] 062)*

Institutional oversight and ethical constraints are complementary to each other. Accounting personnel must always observe professional ethics during their day-to-day work. Of course, professional ethics do not conflict with the company's oversight rules. Compliance with job-specific code of conduct is a prerequisite, and observation of professional ethics is the bottom line. No matter what, accounting personnel must not cross the bottom line during their routine work. *(Ren Zhengfei: Implementing Oversight with Care, Huawei Executive Office Speech No. [2011] 013)*

We must calculate expenses after completing a project to check how much money was spent and how much money was provided – this is the essence of oversight. Personnel who engage in a project don't care who spent the money or how much money was spent; they really have no idea or inclination to care about this in the heat of the moment. However, if no breakthrough is made in the project even if 101,000 US dollars is spent and a project manager puts an end to the project because the Internal Audit might be on its way to investigating excessive expenses, it is a sheer dogmatist. When a small project succeeds by using 3,000,000 US dollars, far more than the usual 101,000 US dollars, Accounting needs to check whether the data is well-grounded and uncover possible risks. To do so, Accounting has to ask the business directors responsible whether that 3,000,000 US dollars was really spent and whether the spending was well-grounded. If so, we would think that things are reasonable and compliant with rules and regulations, so accounting personnel can go on to offset the costs. However, if only 500,000 US dollars was spent and the remaining 2,500,000 US dollars is still unaccounted for, accounting personnel must ask more questions and offset the costs only after data is clear – this is what we mean when we talk about oversight. *(Ren Zhengfei: Minutes of the Meeting with Staff of the Romania Accounting SSC, Huawei Executive Office Speech No. [2011] 021)*

Financial data that does not reflect the true state of business is inaccurate. Accurate data can only be extracted from business activities that have occurred. *(Ren Zhengfei: Minutes of the Meeting with Staff of the Romania Accounting SSC, Huawei Executive Office Speech No. [2011] 021)*

Open Access This chapter is licensed under the terms of the Creative Commons Attribution-NonCommercial-NoDerivatives 4.0 International License (http://creativecommons.org/licenses/by-nc-nd/4.0/), which permits any noncommercial use, sharing, distribution and reproduction in any medium or format, as long as you give appropriate credit to the original author(s) and the source, provide a link to the Creative Commons licence and indicate if you modified the licensed material. You do not have permission under this license to share adapted material derived from this chapter or parts of it.

The images or other third party material in this chapter are included in the chapter's Creative Commons licence, unless indicated otherwise in a credit line to the material. If material is not included in the chapter's Creative Commons licence and your intended use is not permitted by statutory regulation or exceeds the permitted use, you will need to obtain permission directly from the copyright holder.

CHAPTER 13

Treasury Management

Huawei has always been a private company. Growing from within is the core and major driving force behind its future development. The company adopts an asset-light business model, which means it builds wealth by fully extracting value from labor rather than by being asset-heavy. This underlying principle means that as Huawei grows rapidly, its capital needs are mainly satisfied from within, through effective management of its capital structure and indirect financing scale, as well as through increase in working capital efficiency. This business model has raised high requirements for treasury management. Treasury management though, is not the sole responsibility of the Treasury Management Department. Rather, it permeates the company's entire value creation process.

The 2008 financial crisis increased the financing and exchange loss risks each company faced. This pushed Huawei to continually improve its treasury management by emphasizing local financing, establishing diversified financing systems and cash settlement centers, enriching the financing structure, and dispersing financing risks.

To ensure fund security, Huawei establishes a unified treasury management system to centrally manage its funds, and implements daily reconciliation in accounting and treasury management departments. On top of fund security, Huawei embraces technological advances and uses IT systems and electronic means to continuously improve payment quality and efficiency.

The ability to deal with strict foreign exchange controls helps to guarantee the company's fund security. It is also a core competency that helps affected regions maintain their competitive advantages and robust business performance.

This chapter describes the treasury management system that Huawei uses to ensure corporate fund security.

13.1 Exploring a Capital Structure for the Company's Long-Term Development

13.1.1 Growing from Within Is the Core and Major Driving Force Behind Huawei's Future Development

Capital accumulation is a key management issue for all companies. Capital can come from two sources. One is to sell stock in the open capital market to raise money; the other is to accumulate capital on our own by expanding scale and increasing profits. The first way gets us money more easily, but it comes at a price, because investors may interfere with our system. Our system is based on labor, not on capital. We recognize high performers, and reward them with higher salaries, more shares, and other incentives. Therefore, when it comes to fund raising, we need to balance these two sources rather than prefer one over the other. *(Ren Zhengfei: Speech Regarding How Huawei Accumulates Capital, 1994)*

Our company will run out of cash if we don't open up our capital system. A cash-strapped company will lose its vitality and be unable to share its interests. If we open up our capital system, we can receive funds from external investors. Throughout this process, we must carefully balance the relationship between labor-based and capital-based value distributions, and deal with the conflict between the company's vitality and external investors' desire for higher returns. If we can't effectively manage this conflict, we will be unable to ensure fair value distribution, and the company will lose vitality and enter a vicious circle. *(Ren Zhengfei: Speech Regarding Corporate Organizational Goals and System Blueprints for the Future, 1994)*

We need to diversify our approaches towards financing and continue to maintain a reasonable level of debt to support our operations. We need to explore more capital sources, control capital cost, and speed up capital turnover. This will help cultivate financing partnerships that support the company's long-term development and ensure our strategic plans are implemented. *(Source: The Huawei Charter, 1998)*

We must have specific numbers in mind when designing all our supporting systems. For example, when our sales revenue reaches 10 billion US dollars in two or three years, what will our capital structure look like? How will it work as a supporting and assurance function? How much will we pay and how much will we collect? What will the overall situation look like? These are all questions we need to address. We should be able to map out these statistics on clear charts. We also need to have plans for our organizational structure and operations. *(Source: Minutes of the Report on Developing the Global Financial System, EMT Meeting Minutes No. [2005] 035)*

The company is in a favorable position regarding borrowings in 2009. It is key that we make sure our reports meet essential banking requirements. Moving forward, Finance still needs to explore ways to manage the debt ratio. *(Source: Minutes of the Report on a Few Key Financial Issues Facing the Company in the Next Two to Three Years, Finance Committee Meeting Minutes No. [2008] 004)*

The Corporate Capital Structure (CCS) is a key module of the IFS treasury project team. The company's business and financial risks are closely correlated with the recent financial situations at home and abroad. In response, we need to have long-term business and financial plans in place. The company's Finance Committee will fully support work related to the CCS. *(Source: Minutes of the Report on Industry Practices Regarding the Corporate Capital Structure, Finance Committee Meeting Minutes No. [2009] 001)*

We need to actively explore ways to make full use of existing mature properties and use fixed assets more efficiently. *(Source: 2010 Key Work Requirements, EMT Resolution No. [2010] 007)*

Growing from within is the core and major driving force behind Huawei's future development. *(Source: Resolution on Proposals for Capital Investment Policies and Decision-making Systems, Finance Committee Resolution No. [2011] 038)*

Is going public the only way for a company to grow? Can some companies accumulate capital slowly on their own? Such companies usually focus on management and operations rather than capital investment. There has been a lot of speculation about whether Huawei will go public. Let me clarify a little bit. Over the past 20-plus years, the Board of Directors has never seriously discussed company listing, because we don't think it's good for Huawei's development. I would like to share a few words Eric Xu told a senior executive of a carrier customer. I feel these words represent the will of the Board pretty well.

Eric said, "We will not go public, list through divestiture, or engage in the 'capital game' by means of M&A anytime within the next five to ten years. We will not invest in projects that external capital engages in. We take this stance to avoid being dragged down into the traps of the capital market. In the next five to ten years, we will be committed to management transformations to drive a shift in our operational model. Over time, we will move responsibility and authority forward to the field, with our centralized governance giving way to a system that allows those closest to customers to call for support. By doing so, our HQ will shift from a management and control role to a service and support role, and we will establish a company that has modern management approaches and meets modern requirements."

I totally agree with him. Rumors about Huawei's going public are simply groundless. *(Ren Zhengfei: Speech at a Meeting with the Representatives' Commission, Huawei Executive Office Speech No. [2013] 056)*

"Have we saved up sufficient energy over the past 20 years?" It's a good question. Like the strategic talent reserve we have built, a capital reserve is also necessary for the company. While increasing incentives, we also need to invest heavily in strategic areas. This creates a dilemma when we try to reserve capital. We need thick "clothing" to fend off the challenges of a stormy economic environment. That requires wisdom from our management and the combined effort of all our employees. *(Ren Zhengfei: Reply to Xinsheng Community Users' Comments on the Speech "Firm Belief and Strong Focus Lead to Greater Success", Huawei Executive Office Speech No. [2016] 006)*

13.1.2 Improving Working Capital Efficiency and Quality to Ensure the Continuity and Robustness of Operating Cash Flow

Payment Collection Problems can Lead a Company Into Peril
We must take cash flow very seriously, because it is a bottleneck that could choke the company. Over the next three to five years, there may be serious global crises. If we continue with our current approach, which lacks a proper level of granularity, where would we end up? The company will run out of cash and collapse. Cash flow is a tough nut to crack. To address the

issue, we must be determined and implement transformations. Starting from this year, interest losses caused by overdue receivables should be deducted from the bonuses of all involved employees, including sales, R&D, and global technical services (GTS) staff. Piecework staff and staff paid by the hour can be excluded from this. Payment collection will affect the company's survival over the next three to five years. This problem must be addressed. Front-end employees should assume responsibility. In fact, it is a responsibility that needs to be shared by all employees. *(Ren Zhengfei: Strengthening Payment Collection and Improving Cash Flow—Speech at the EMT ST Meeting on February 28, 2006, Huawei Executive Office Speech No. [2006] 007)*

Payment collection problems can lead a company into peril. It's not that we don't have money. We have plenty of money; the issue is that it hasn't yet been collected from our customers. Without cash inflows, the company will be in a very dangerous situation and we could possibly die. All regional offices must take cash flow very seriously. As long as there are goods sitting in our warehouses and as long as payments remain uncollected, we will always be at risk. We need to put in place an ownership system for payment collection and address the source of the problem. We need to establish a project ownership system which includes payment collection plans during project planning and bidding. We should end our practice of collecting payments on a contract basis; instead, we need a finer-grained approach. That means we need to collect payments by site, site group, or project progress. In this way, we are paid for what we deliver on time. All regional offices must take this issue very seriously. *(Ren Zhengfei: Speech at the 2008 Mid-year Report by Regions to the EMT, EMT Meeting Minutes No. [2008] 028)*

Apart from payment security, the most important for corporate fund security management is to ensure continuous cash flow. Both on-time payments and fast payment collection are important. Regional financial organizations need to establish baselines for collection cycles to push for customers to make payments promptly. *(Source: Minutes of the Report on Fund Security Monitoring of the Accounting Management Department, Finance Committee Meeting Minutes No. [2015] 045)*

Our meeting in Sanya has resulted in two core goals for our consumer business: increasing profitability and keeping inventory at a proper level. Today, these two goals still stand. Our consumer business must be profitable and profitability must be based on healthy cash flow. *(Ren Zhengfei: Speech at Consumer BG's Annual Meeting, Huawei Executive Office Speech No. [2017] 024)*

What does the future hold for us? We must have profitable growth and healthy cash flow in the future. We must aim to eliminate restlessness among our managers so that they can settle down and serve our customers earnestly. *(Ren Zhengfei: Speech at Huawei Market Conference 2017, Huawei Executive Office Speech No. [2017] 007)*

Working Capital Efficiency and Quality is an Important Source of Operating Cash Flow
Working capital efficiency should be managed by category: (1) Historical accounts—For projects that have already been delivered, we should manage their payment collection separately and collect payments as soon as possible. (2) Future accounts—When assessing the value of a project, we need to assess the project's profits and losses, cash flow, and working capital efficiency, and manage them against baselines. We will continue to improve end-to-end transaction quality and manage it as a top priority of the company. During project execution, we need to closely follow the project plan, stay on budget, and effectively manage project costs, profits, and cash flow to ensure delivery quality. *(Source: 2010 Key Work Requirements, EMT Resolution No. [2010] 007)*

It is customers that drive working capital efficiency to improve. The optimization of performance indicators such as Days Sales Outstanding (DSO) and Inventory Turnover (ITO) should be aligned with our customer strategy to continuously improve transaction quality. For example, in installed base markets where we aim to expand capacity, we should benchmark ourselves against industry leaders. For new networks or new carriers, however, we should ensure favorable contract terms during our initial bidding process to improve later-stage operating efficiency. *(Source: 2010 Key Work Requirements, EMT Resolution No. [2010] 007)*

We should improve the company's operating cash flow by improving contract quality and properly controlling inventory. All relevant departments must view this as a priority and contribute to these goals. We can benchmark ourselves against multinationals with medium- and high-level inventory management expertise to improve our inventory turnover, reduce our inventory losses, and set our standard inventory baselines. Inventories of each type in each region should be controlled to avoid tying up too much cash flow in inventory. Our standard inventory baselines should be detailed to regions, countries, and inventory types, with owners clearly defined. Inventory with low turnover should be effectively controlled. Departments who fail to meet these inventory baselines will have some of their bonuses deducted. *(Source: Minutes of the Report on the 2011 H1 Performance Review, EMT Meeting Minutes No. [2011] 011)*

Working capital efficiency and quality is an important source of operating cash flow and should be given due consideration in our future fund planning. We need to strengthen working capital management, ensure that cash tied up in working capital is kept at a reasonable level, and improve efficiency and quality to maintain sustainable and robust cash flow. *(Source: Minutes of the Meeting on 2011 Corporate Capital Structure Planning, Finance Committee Meeting Minutes No. [2011] 003)*

Balanced growth must be based on robust operations. There are only two metrics for appraising the performance of our consumer business. One is profitability, and the other is inventory. Inventory constitutes a risk, while profitability is our goal. If our shipments cannot meet customer needs, it's okay. If the customer says that they will pay extra, it's okay. But they need to sign a contract and pay. Then we can ship more products. This way, the inventory risk will be borne by the customer, not us. If they don't pay us when they place an order, please don't accept it no matter what they say. What if they ask for customized mobile phones and then later on decide they don't want them anymore? If inventory piles up, the company will go bankrupt. Didn't some mobile phone manufacturers in China collapse in this way? We can't make the same mistake. *(Ren Zhengfei: Comments to Staff of the Guangzhou Representative Office, Huawei Executive Office Speech No. [2013] 057)*

We need to manage asset liquidity effectively based on the distinct features of different business segments such as direct sales, channels, and devices. Set performance indicators against their respective benchmarked enterprises, including DSO, ITO, Days Payable Outstanding (DPO), asset turnover ratio, and operating cash flow (OCF). Net cash inflows and capital structures should be managed separately for network and consumer businesses. They should be continuously improved by benchmarking against leading enterprises in their respective industries. *(Source: Minutes of the Report on Corporate Funds and Financing Management, EMT Meeting Minutes No. [2015] 010)*

Liquidity ratios should be approached differently for different businesses. The liquidity ratios for the consumer business should be different from those for the network business. The two cannot be mixed up. A high liquidity ratio for one business does not mean that the ratio is also high for the other. We need to create ratio roadmaps for different businesses and benchmark against leading companies in respective domains. Ask yourself: Why is my turnover ratio low? What's the underlying problem? Can it be fixed? How? You must pay attention to these details. The point of setting a roadmap is to give yourself a goal. It doesn't matter if you can't immediately reach the goal. But you need a goal to motivate you to forge ahead and scale new heights. *(Ren Zhengfei: Speech at the EMT ST Meeting on August 28, 2015, Huawei Executive Office Speech No. [2015] 132)*

The only way to deal with crises is to speed up cash flow. Without an adequate level of cash, issuing bonds is no different from borrowing money and problems with the financial health of the company will persist. Therefore, making our cash flow faster is the key and improving our financial health is our only way out. The reason why the German economy hasn't been severely affected is that it has a healthy financial system. *(Ren Zhengfei: Speech at the EMT ST Meeting on August 28, 2015, Huawei Executive Office Speech No. [2015] 132)*

The company should set clear goals for asset turnover so it can gradually improve across the board. The growing importance of our consumer and enterprise businesses means that we must manage asset turnover of different business groups separately. The Treasury Management Department should analyze and measure the contributions of the Consumer BG and Enterprise BG respectively to our asset turnover ratio. *(Source: Minutes of the Report on 2015 and Mid- to Long-Term Corporate Capital Structure Planning, Finance Committee Meeting Minutes No. [2015] 015)*

We have some "customer warehouses" where customers stock goods. We must not allow this to happen if customers haven't bought the inventory. If this continues, the flow of our goods will suffer. We wouldn't be able to ship goods to regions that run out of stock. Though the warehouse may be built by our customer, it is essentially a Huawei warehouse. The customer only pays for warehouse management. We must come up with solutions to customer and subcontractor overstocking. We must control inventory risks, and properly manage the smartphone inventory. For example, we must ask our customers to pay for the goods they intend to stock to put some pressure on them. We can sort out arrangements like this with customers beforehand. If they stock goods in our warehouses, they must pay interest on those goods. If the inventory they stock with us is worth 100 million US dollars, they must pay higher interest rates because they are affecting our cash flow. *(Ren Zhengfei: Speech at the Report on Integrating the Process from Central Warehouses to Sites, Huawei Executive Office Speech No. [2015] 005)*

We should have a contingency plan in place to deal with financial crises that includes reducing long-term overdue inventory and accounts receivable (AR). Improving contract quality is the most important thing here. *(Ren Zhengfei: Be First to Know When Springtime Comes. Vow Not to Return Till We Reach Our Goals—Speech at an Oath-taking Rally for*

Reassigned Senior R&D Experts and Managers, Huawei Executive Office Speech No. [2016] 093)

13.2 Building a Global Treasury Management System to Better Manage Fund Risks

13.2.1 Scaling Up Financing, Enriching the Financing Structure, and Dispersing Financing Risks

To support the company's rapid growth, we must continue to push our financing to the next level. We need to build on our previous work and extensively diversify our financing channels, explore financing opportunities with banks overseas, and use multiple international channels and financial instruments to harness the power of international financial capital. *(Ren Zhengfei: Current Situation and Next Steps—Speech at the Review Meeting of the Marketing & Sales Department, 1995)*

We need to build on our last year's effort to diversify our financing channels and consolidate our work comprehensively. We need to work more closely with foreign banks on buyer's credit. This can help improve our market competitiveness and payment collection considerably, thus alleviating our financial burdens. In the meantime, we can use as many other financing channels as possible according to international practice to support the company's growth. *(Ren Zhengfei: Exerting Ourselves and Sharing Weal and Woe to Improve Management, 1997)*

Financing departments should keep the company's strategy in mind when approaching their work and use the input-output principle to build framework models and scale up financing. Don't be too obsessed with financing costs. The company has entered a stage of rapid growth. Our current priority is scaling up financing. In addition, we need to make full use of our internal resources and adopt a holistic approach towards financing. We need to improve our ability to make market forecasts and, if necessary, change the way we deal with funds in compliance with applicable laws and regulations. This will help lay a solid foundation for the company's rapid growth. *(Ren Zhengfei: Promoting Development Through Four Unifications—Minutes of the Meeting with Financial Managers, 1998)*

We need to establish global financing systems and diversify our financing channels. *(Source: Guidelines on Sales Priorities, EMT Meeting Minutes No. [2008] 014)*

We need to ensure that the company has sufficient financial support from multiple channels. Good partnerships with local financial institutions through our overseas subsidiaries will help us establish a balanced global treasury management system. *(Source: Several Requirements on Cooperation with Banks, Finance Committee Doc. No. [2012] 008)*

We need to work with valued banks in key countries more proactively. Our subsidiaries can take care of local financing. We need to establish multiple settlement centers to fully leverage the financial advantages of key countries. *(Source: Several Requirements on Cooperation with Banks, Finance Committee Doc. No. [2012] 008)*

We need to find more long-term financing channels in more regions and explore more financing products such as bond issuance. *(Source: Minutes of the Report on Corporate Funds and Financing Management, EMT Meeting Minutes No. [2015] 010)*

We need to actively cultivate stable financing channels overseas and maintain stable profit margins to support large-scale financing needs overseas and cope with future uncertainties. *(Source: Minutes of the Meeting on the Review of Corporate Capital Structure 813 Planning and Initial Budgeting of 2017 Debt Ratio and Cash Flow, Finance Committee Doc. No. [2016] 055)*

13.2.2 *Establishing Diversified Financing Systems and Cash Settlement Centers*

We need to spend more local currency to avoid accruing too much profit overseas. We need to streamline the payment channels of our overseas research centers. For example, expenses of our American, European, and Indian research centers can be paid in local currencies. Superfluous local currencies can also be used to build facilities such as office buildings, dormitories, training centers, canteens, and fitness facilities, especially in countries with high inflation rates. We need to comprehensively assess our global business presence. In addition to business needs and legal frameworks, we also need to figure out the direction of cash flow and profit distribution. *(Source: Guidelines on Improving Financing, EMT Resolution No. [2011] 015)*

We need to take diversified approaches to financing and settlement, and reduce foreign exchange losses by spending local currencies locally as much as possible. In Japan and Europe, a good proportion of local settlements are done in local currencies, which partially hedges our foreign exchange position. In these countries and regions, we don't need to convert local currencies into USD. In countries where local currencies have no way to be used, we will assume exchange risks. *(Ren Zhengfei: Speech at the EMT ST Meeting, March 30, 2012)*

We cannot change the fact that the external regulatory environment for finance is tightening. Therefore, we must pay special attention to settlement risks and revisit our strategy on cooperating with banks. Seek settlement in different currencies wherever possible. Establish regional settlement centers in places including Dubai, London, and Tokyo to secure more settlement channels and work with more local banks. *(Ren Zhengfei: Remarks During Visits to Countries Where Cash Is Trapped, Huawei Executive Office Speech No. [2015] 023)*

13.2.3 Guaranteeing Financing Capabilities with Stable Financial Policies

Over the past two decades, Huawei has invested more than 150 billion RMB in R&D. However, the R&D capabilities and intellectual property rights that have come out of this investment haven't been reflected in our company value. Thanks to our robust financial policies, we are not in too much debt. Our current indirect financing approach based on financial statements and financing capacity limits do not involve our actual asset status. *(Ren Zhengfei: Comments at a Meeting with Sales Financing Experts, Huawei Executive Office Speech No. [2012] 025)*

We don't have any issue with bond issuance; we just weren't ready to issue bonds before. Today our governance structure is maturing and our approach to corporate management is becoming clearer and more standardized every day. I think it's time to explore international financing channels and issue bonds. At present, I think it is feasible when we issue bonds to banks and other financial institutions. *(Ren Zhengfei: Comments at a Meeting with Sales Financing Experts, Huawei Executive Office Speech No. [2012] 025)*

13.3 CENTRALLY MANAGING FUNDS TO ENSURE FUND SECURITY

13.3.1 Centrally Managing Funds and Enhancing the Process Ownership System

All cash must "flow down the Yangtze River" and our accounts need to be consistent. We do not allow too many reservoirs because they would dilute the cash flowing down the river. If the funds going down the river are from banks, the cost of financing will increase. *(Ren Zhengfei: Minutes of the Report on the Work Approach of the Accounting Departments in China, 2001)*

Our treasury management is done at three levels: The Finance Committee designs and manages macro policies; the Sales Financing & Treasury Management Department takes care of financing and payment collection for sales projects as well as financing for production and supply; and the Accounting Department is responsible for execution but does not make decisions. We exercise oversight using checks and balances in this way. *(Ren Zhengfei: Financial Transformation Is About Huawei Rather Than Only the Finance System, Huawei Executive Office Speech No. [2007] 004)*

We need to gradually increase the company's capital reserve. In the future, BGs will operate independently, but treasury will still be managed centrally. *(Source: Minutes of the Meeting on 2011 Corporate Capital Structure Planning, Finance Committee Meeting Minutes No. [2011] 003)*

About 80% of financial decision-making authority will be delegated to BG and regional CFOs. Group Finance will retain the remaining 20% of financial decision-making authority, including the authority over issues related to treasury and budget management. *(Ren Zhengfei: Remarks at the Briefing on Finance Process Building, Huawei Executive Office Speech No. [2013] 091)*

Cash inflows and outflows are centrally managed by the Treasury Management Department. *(Source: Minutes of the Report on Corporate Funds and Financing Management, EMT Meeting Minutes No. [2015] 010)*

HQ centrally manages treasury, accounting, auditing, and internal controls. The authority to make business decisions will be delegated to operating teams as long as they keep their data transparent. *(Ren Zhengfei: Speech at a Meeting in Paraguay, Huawei Executive Office Speech No. [2017] 025)*

All departments, except some centrally managed functions of HQ, exist to serve business departments. This includes Finance, Supply Chain, and HR. These departments oversee how things work in business departments, but are not centers of authority. *(Ren Zhengfei: Speech at a Briefing on Improvements and Future Planning for Carrier and Enterprise Regional Organization Transformation, Huawei Executive Office Speech No. [2017] 030)*

The company centrally manages three lines of oversight: treasury, accounting, and auditing. These lines are built into and made transparent in all departments. *(Ren Zhengfei: Speech at the Meeting on Extension of the Company's Oversight and Management Control System, Huawei Executive Office Speech No. [2017] 041)*

We should shift our focus of treasury management from process compliance to efficient exercise of authority and enhance the process ownership system by overseeing how authority is exercised. *(Source: Minutes of the Report on Overseeing Exercise of Treasury Management Authority, Group Finance CFO Office Meeting Minutes No. [2017] 016)*

13.3.2 Standardizing Account Management and Establishing a Unified Treasury Management System

We need to clean up our bank accounts. Too many accounts require high oversight and management costs. We must also move away from small- and medium-sized banks that do not have clear intent for cooperating with us. We must strengthen fund security and reject corruption. *(Source: Minutes of Discussions on Treasury Management System Building, EMT Meeting Minutes No. [2007] 013)*

Over the next five years, the company needs to continuously focus on fund security. Fund security should start with daily reconciliation. We must resolutely conduct daily reconciliation. If it's difficult, bring in more people to get it done. We need to establish a unified treasury management system. *(Source: Minutes of the Report on Corporate Funds and Financing Management, EMT Meeting Minutes No. [2015] 010)*

The treasury management function has already been established in Finance. Daily reconciliation has two layers. The first layer is the Accounting Management Department. Accountants, rechecking accountants, and payment approvers work in sequence when handling daily reconciliation. The second layer is the Treasury Management Department, which reconciles our payment records with bank statements on a daily basis. In certain countries, reconciliation can be done on a weekly basis and settlement on a daily basis. *(Ren Zhengfei: Minutes of the Report on Treasury Management System Building, EMT Meeting Minutes No. [2015] 022)*

We must resolutely perform daily reconciliation and make sure we have enough people to ensure fund security. For e-commerce transactions, we need to carefully attend to our bank account balances during daily reconciliation to ensure fund security. *(Ren Zhengfei: Minutes of the Report on Treasury Management System Building, EMT Meeting Minutes No. [2015] 022)*

Financial personnel are not responsible for the reasonableness of business requests. They do not decide whether cannons should be fired. Finance only provides financial support as requested by business departments, keeps records, and prepares reports. *(Ren Zhengfei: Minutes of the Report on Treasury Management System Building, EMT Meeting Minutes No. [2015] 022)*

To enter into new businesses, we must have associated financial systems and rules in place, especially when it comes to e-commerce and peer-to-peer engagement. *(Ren Zhengfei: Minutes of the Report on Treasury Management System Building, EMT Meeting Minutes No. [2015] 022)*

Financially, we are a conservative company. Our top priority is to ensure financial security. After hearing the Financial Risk Control Center's (FRCC) report on risk control, I think that we were right to place our FRCC in London. Originally, we just thought that London, with its centuries of history as a financial hub, would be a better choice than China. In contrast, scientists must be bold in both thinking and action, and must have the courage to take risks. Their approach is completely different from our conservative financial approach. At 2012 Laboratories, Huawei accepts a failure rate of over 50%. In terms of fund security, we do not tolerate any errors. We must focus on developing, selecting, and attracting outstanding financial talent, allowing them to fully unleash their potential. *(Ren Zhengfei: Remarks at Meetings with the UK R&D Center, Beijing Research Center, and Financial Risk Control Center in London, Huawei Executive Office Speech No. [2015] 075)*

To ensure fund security over the next five years, we must first solve the problem with payment security. To do this, we have to firmly implement daily reconciliation. If a region can't manage to do this, we can send more senior managers and allocate more resources to help them. If our accounts are reconciled every day when we clock out, we will be confident in what we did that day. Do not leave a problem to the next day. Second, we need to build a unified treasury management system. Third, we are a company held by employees. If Huawei is in trouble one day, will our employees voluntarily support the company at their own expenses? If we can ensure this kind of support, how would Huawei collapse? *(Ren Zhengfei: Speech at the EMT ST Meeting on August 28, 2015, Huawei Executive Office Speech No. [2015] 132)*

On top of fund security, we need to embrace technological advances and use IT systems and electronic means to continuously improve payment quality and efficiency. When it comes to payment security, we must take all corporate functions into consideration. We need to establish a unified treasury management system to ensure fund security and reliability. *(Source: Minutes of the Report on Fund Security Monitoring of the*

Accounting Management Department, Finance Committee Meeting Minutes No. [2015] 045)

Fund security is a clear requirement for payment personnel. Their performance appraisals should be centered on the quality of this work. We should have more payment personnel than we need. *(Ren Zhengfei: Speech at a Meeting with Payment Staff, Huawei Executive Office Speech No. [2017] 042)*

Accounting and treasury departments should manage payment error rates in a scientific, reasonable, proactive, and positive way. Payment security relies on both system controls and our payment staff's meticulous work and dedication. *(Ren Zhengfei: Speech at a Meeting with Payment Staff, Huawei Executive Office Speech No. [2017] 042)*

13.3.3 The Ability to Deal with Strict Foreign Exchange Controls Helps to Guarantee the Company's Fund Security. It Is Also a Core Competency That Helps Affected Regions Maintain Their Competitive Advantages and Robust Business Performance

We can conduct more business in countries with strict foreign exchange controls if we can repatriate more money. We need to adopt a pragmatic approach in these countries. What are real customer needs? Those are the needs of customers that can pay. In these countries, payment collection is our biggest difficulty. If we can collect payments, we won't worry about sales; we may even raise prices. We must remember that our team that deals with strict foreign exchange controls is an important operating team. Regions must rethink this issue. In countries with strict foreign exchange controls, we must view people dealing with this issue as being part of important operating teams and invest in improving their capabilities. *(Ren Zhengfei: Minutes of the Work Report by the Algeria Representative Office, Huawei Executive Office Speech No. [2014] 070)*

In countries with strict foreign exchange controls, transferring money out of these countries is more important and difficult than sales. That's why people who deal with this issue are more important than sales personnel. Personnel dealing with foreign exchange controls in regional centers of expertise are business partners of business departments. Their performance appraisals should be mainly determined by how much cash they repatriate. They are also responsible for management and control of the entire business process. We also need to establish a "Contribute and Share" system, providing timely incentives to those who hit performance targets for dealing with strict foreign exchange controls. *(Source: Minutes of the Discussions on Mr. Ren's Remarks During Visits to Countries Where Cash Is Trapped, Finance Committee Meeting Minutes No. [2014] 045)*

The US remains a very powerful economy, and emerging markets continue to lack stability. Therefore, strict foreign exchange controls will remain a long-term issue. Huawei needs to quickly train and develop personnel who are capable of dealing with this issue. *(Ren Zhengfei: Remarks During Visits to Countries Where Cash Is Trapped, Huawei Executive Office Speech No. [2015] 023)*

The ability to deal with strict foreign exchange controls helps to guarantee the company's fund security. It is also a core competency that helps affected regions maintain their competitive advantages and robust business performance *(Ren Zhengfei: Remarks During Visits to Countries Where Cash Is Trapped, Huawei Executive Office Speech No. [2015] 023)*

Open Access This chapter is licensed under the terms of the Creative Commons Attribution-NonCommercial-NoDerivatives 4.0 International License (http://creativecommons.org/licenses/by-nc-nd/4.0/), which permits any noncommercial use, sharing, distribution and reproduction in any medium or format, as long as you give appropriate credit to the original author(s) and the source, provide a link to the Creative Commons licence and indicate if you modified the licensed material. You do not have permission under this license to share adapted material derived from this chapter or parts of it.

The images or other third party material in this chapter are included in the chapter's Creative Commons licence, unless indicated otherwise in a credit line to the material. If material is not included in the chapter's Creative Commons licence and your intended use is not permitted by statutory regulation or exceeds the permitted use, you will need to obtain permission directly from the copyright holder.

CHAPTER 14

Tax Management

Paying taxes is a company's social responsibility. Huawei believes that the biggest contribution a company can make to society is to serve customers earnestly, do its work the best it can to survive, and pay its fair share of taxes.

Paying taxes is also a basic tax management requirement. Tax management must ensure taxes are reasonable, risks are well managed, and operations are secure.

Huawei prioritizes tax security for the company as a whole over that for regional and country offices and/or subsidiaries. Their tax planning must not undermine the overall tax security for the company. Huawei strives to avoid implicit tax costs when pursuing explicit tax benefits, and long-term tax burdens when pursuing short-term tax benefits. Improper tax planning is strictly prohibited at Huawei.

The company effectively performs intercompany transactions in compliance with external laws and regulations as well as industry practices. Transfer pricing (TP) positions are defined based on the functions performed, risks assumed, and assets invested by the involved parties during value creation. Intercompany transaction risks can spread easily, which requires the company to pay special attention to intercompany transaction quality.

Relationships with tax authorities are not the same as relationships with customers. Through close connections with tax authorities, the company takes more initiative to work out tax solutions. Managing tax authority relationships is not the same as managing people. It is in fact building up our expertise to manage things.

The company aims to build an effective tax risk management mechanism. By identifying, assessing, addressing, and closing risks, the company manages tax risk exposures on an ongoing basis.

This chapter dives deep into the policies and principles that Huawei follows in tax management.

14.1 Paying Taxes Is a Corporate Social Responsibility

14.1.1 A Company's Biggest Contribution to Society Is to Pay Taxes and Do Its Work the Best It Can

As long as we comply with national laws, maintain a healthy, dynamic, and well-coordinated internal management system, serve our customers earnestly, do our work as best as we can to survive, and pay our fair share of taxes, then we are making the biggest contribution to society. *(Ren Zhengfei: Notification on the Status of Human Resources Management Transformation, Huawei Executive Office Speech No. [2007] 037)*

Paying taxes is a company's social responsibility. *(Source: Minutes of the Report on the Company's Effective Tax Rate, Group Finance CFO Office Meeting Minutes No. [2016] 024)*

We must pay taxes, maintain a good brand image and corporate reputation, and ensure secure global business operations. *(Source: Tax Management Policy, Group Finance Business Directive No. [2016] 027)*

Tax management must focus on three goals: to ensure taxes are reasonable, risks are well managed, and operations are secure. *(Ren Zhengfei: Minutes of the Report on the "Manage Tax" Process, "Manage Finance" GPO Meeting Minutes No. [2016] 002)*

14.1.2 Abiding by Applicable Tax Laws in All Business Activities

Paying taxes according to applicable laws

To ensure accounting and tax compliance, we must make an ongoing effort to improve our rules, processes, data, and IT systems, and establish a long-term local tax compliance mechanism at a legal entity level. Tax rules must be built into business and accounting processes. Tax data must be accurate, verifiable, and traceable. Tax filing data must be accurate and completely recorded. *(Source: Minutes of the Report on the Progress of the*

Accounting and Tax Compliance Project, Finance Staff Team Meeting Minutes No. [2014] 117)

We must pay taxes according to applicable laws. When it is unclear whether tax laws and rules apply to us, we must develop a tax compliance solution based on standard tax practices. *(Source: Tax Compliance Management Policy, Group Finance Business Directive No. [2016] 020)*

We must accurately interpret existing tax laws and practices, and develop clear, accurate tax instructions specific to our business scenarios. We also need to keep track of changes in tax laws and prepare contingency plans in advance. We must update tax guides, processes, and work instructions before new laws come into effect. *(Source: Tax Compliance Management Policy, Group Finance Business Directive No. [2016] 020)*

The Integrated Tax Compliance (ITC) project aims to ensure local tax compliance by subsidiaries. This will help us create a positive business environment and avoid the spread of risk from one country to another. We must ensure 100% legal compliance and fulfill all our social responsibilities. This is a minimum requirement for us. To fulfill our economic responsibilities, we should analyze possible risks and compliance costs based on ROI on a case-by-case basis. *(Source: Report on the Progress of the ITC Project in Germany and the Decision on Tax Risk Acceptance, Finance Committee Resolution, 2017)*

We must embed tax compliance requirements into our business activities, and ensure tax compliance through data sharing and process interactions. Tax filing data must be based on accounting and real business data to ensure the data source is reliable, traceable, verifiable, and can be easily evaluated. Documentation is key to tax compliance. All tax payment supporting documents must be effectively managed. *(Source: Tax Management Policy, Group Finance Business Directive No. [2016] 027)*

Performing tax planning based on Huawei's business plan and in compliance with global tax laws

Tax planning must be in compliance with applicable laws, including the tax laws and conventions in countries where the tax payer is located as well as international tax laws and conventions. *(Source: Tax Planning Management Policy, Group Finance Business Directive No. [2016] 021)*

In our tax planning, we prioritize tax security for the company as a whole over that of regional and country offices and subsidiaries. We must avoid implicit tax costs when pursuing explicit tax benefits, and must not ignore long-term tax burdens when pursuing short-term tax benefits. *(Source: Tax Planning Management Policy, Group Finance Business Directive No. [2016] 021)*

No improper tax planning

The Tax Management Department must perform tax planning in a way that ensures Huawei's operational security. Business arrangements must be real and reasonable. *(Source: Resolution on Global Profit and Tax Distribution, Finance Committee Resolution No. [2008] 012)*

Improper tax planning includes designing tax solutions that break tax laws and regulations, fabricating or concealing business information, distorting business activities, or misusing preferential tax policies for the purpose of reducing or avoiding tax obligations. Improper tax planning is strictly prohibited at Huawei. *(Source: Tax Planning Management Policy, Group Finance Business Directive No. [2016] 021)*

14.1.3 Performing Intercompany Transactions in a Standard and Effective Way Based on External Laws and Industry Practices

Intercompany transactions must meet the requirements of external laws, including applicable local tax laws and international laws, such as TP instructions and Base Erosion and Profit Shifting (BEPS) issued by the Organization for Economic Co-operation and Development and the United Nations. We must be familiar with the law enforcement practices of local tax authorities and business operations of the industry, and analyze future development trends so as to ensure our intercompany transactions are appropriate. *(Source: Intercompany Transaction Management Policy, Group Finance Business Directive No. [2016] 022)*

Intercompany transactions must be designed based on actual business activities. Intercompany transaction profits are determined based on the functions undertaken by subsidiaries and their roles in value creation. This pricing must follow the "arm's length principle". *(Source: Tax Management Policy, Group Finance Business Directive No. [2016] 027)*

Intercompany transactions must follow the "arm's length principle". In other words, these transactions must be priced in a way similar to the pricing for similar transactions performed by comparable and independent third parties. *(Source: Intercompany Transaction Management Policy, Group Finance Business Directive No. [2016] 022)*

Intercompany transactions must be designed based on actual business activities. TP positions must be defined based on the functions performed, risks assumed, and assets invested by the involved parties during value creation. *(Source: Intercompany Transaction Management Policy, Group Finance Business Directive No. [2016] 022)*

Intercompany transactions must be designed based on actual business activities. A clear, holistic transaction architecture must be established at the corporate level to flexibly and effectively address BEPS challenges. During intercompany transaction design, we shouldn't just aim to cut short-term costs; we must also ensure that transactions benefit Huawei in the long term and meet external compliance requirements. The design must be clear and simple. *(Source: Minutes of the Meeting on Intercompany Transaction Planning, Group Finance CFO Office Meeting Minutes No. [2015] 001)*

To cope with the impact the BEPS Action Plan may have on international tax laws and address the increasingly complex challenges that we face in our intercompany transaction management, the company has decided to comprehensively transform intercompany transactions, establish a clear intercompany transaction architecture, and clarify relevant rules. This will support business compliance and efficient operations. *(Source: Minutes of the Discussion on BEPS Interpretation and Intercompany Transactions, Finance Committee Meeting Minutes No. [2015] 031)*

After the intercompany transaction transformation project is deployed, both field office and the tax COE must respect the rules. *(Source: Minutes of the 2017 Work Report by the Tax Management Department, Finance Staff Team Meeting Minutes No. [2017] 020)*

14.1.4 Establishing a Long-Term Transformation and Operation Management Mechanism to Ensure Taxes Are Paid According to Law

The deployment of the ITC project has ensured tax compliance at the technical level. We must also ensure tax compliance at the operational level by focusing on the responsibilities that are assumed and results that are delivered during performance appraisals. *(Source: Minutes of the Report on the ITC Solution for Huawei COOP, Group Finance CFO Office Meeting Minutes No. [2015] 084)*

Tax compliance key control points (KCPs) are part of our key controls over financial reporting (KCFR) and will be continuously improved alongside internal controls over financial reporting (ICFR) after the ITC project passes its acceptance checks. *(Source: Resolution on the Report at the Concept Decision Checkpoint of the ITC Project, Finance Business Transformation & IT Management Team Resolution No. [2015] 024)*

The ITC project's key deliverables for the initial and final acceptance stages should be assessed using the 5-phase and 18-step methodology. We will use the final acceptance report as our operations quality management baseline after the project is completed. *(Source: Minutes of the Report on the Progress of the ITC Project, Group Finance CFO Office Meeting Minutes No. [2016] 042)*

After the ITC project passes its acceptance checks, the corresponding regional and country CFOs must gradually improve their operational quality. Those improvements need to be reflected in their ICFR results. *(Source: Minutes of the Report on the Acceptance of the ITC Project, Group Finance CFO Office Meeting Minutes No. [2015] 079)*

Whether or not we deploy ITC, tax compliance is the responsibility of our country managers. *(Source: Minutes of the Report on the Deployment Strategy of the ITC Project, Group Finance CFO Office Meeting Minutes No. [2015] 085)*

We need to identify positions that are responsible for tax compliance in key countries, and train and incentivize people in those roles to ensure that our local offices continue to benefit from the ITC project. *(Source: Resolution on the Report at the Plan Decision Checkpoint of the ITC Project, Finance Business Transformation & IT Management Team Resolution No. [2016] 001)*

We must take effective managerial steps to ensure that Huawei meets the requirements of the preferential tax policies. *(Source: Tax Management Policy, Group Finance Business Directive No. [2016] 027)*

14.1.5 Creating a Positive Business Environment to Support Huawei's Global Operations

Legal compliance is the most important basis on which we survive, provide services, and contribute worldwide. We must strictly abide by rules and laws, and use the certainty of legal compliance to tackle the uncertainty of international politics. We must strictly monitor internal and external compliance, and operate within the boundaries of our business. *(Ren Zhengfei: Dedicated to China's Century-old Dream of Revitalizing Science and Technology, Huawei Executive Office Speech No. [2016] 067)*

We must stay on top of changes in the financial laws of the countries where our subsidiaries are located and make appropriate risk assessments. *(Source: Work Priorities for Subsidiary CFOs from 2017 to 2019, Group Finance Notice No. [2016] 039)*

We need to proactively communicate with local tax authorities and other government departments, leveraging our expertise and professionalism to respond to their inquiries and audits. *(Source: Tax Management Policy, Group Finance Business Directive No. [2016] 027)*

Our relationships with tax authorities are not the same as our relationships with customers. Through close connections with tax authorities, we can take more initiative to work out tax solutions. Managing tax authority relationships is not the same as managing people. It is in fact building up our expertise to manage things. *(Source: Minutes of the Report on the Organizational Restructuring of the Tax Management Department, Finance Staff Team Meeting Minutes No. [2015] 071)*

The Tax Management Department must not only function as a tax COE – it should also manage tax compliance, establish an effective mechanism for assessing local tax compliance, and regularly assess tax compliance. *(Source: Assessment Results of Finance's 2015 Work Priorities, Finance Staff Team Meeting Minutes No. [2016] 026)*

The Tax Management Department has brought in many high-end experts and is building up its capacity, and moving in the right direction at a fast but steady pace. The department must continue to bring in professionals and build a positive work environment, enabling them to unleash their potential as soon as possible. The department must also retain sufficient Chinese employees in each of its domain-specific teams. *(Source: Minutes of the 2017 Work Report by the Tax Management Department, Finance Staff Team Meeting Minutes No. [2017] 020)*

14.2 Proactively, Effectively, and Appropriately Managing Tax Risks and Costs

14.2.1 Clarifying Goals and Responsibilities of Tax Risk Management

The goal of tax risk management is to reduce tax risk exposure through specialized and reasonable risk assessment, proactive, effective, and appropriate risk management, and ongoing improvements on the business side. *(Source: Tax Management Policy, Group Finance Business Directive No. [2016] 027)*

We must develop a responsibility matrix for tax risk management. With clearly defined job responsibilities and efficient collaboration, we can work to reduce tax risk exposure. To further reduce risk, we must drive ongoing improvements on the business side because it is the source of tax risks. *(Source: Tax Risk Management Policy, Group Finance Business Directive No. [2016] 009)*

When business needs and tax rules conflict, we must identify potential or possible risks and manage those risks until they are eliminated by following a standardized decision-making process. We must also take the initiative to regularly review tax risks so as to identify potential risks, make improvements, and eliminate risks. We must keep improving our tax compliance management with ICFR and process controls tools. *(Source: Tax Compliance Management Policy, Group Finance Business Directive No. [2016] 020)*

To effectively close tax audits, we need to establish a collaborative approach. We also need to drive improvements based on audit findings. *(Source: Tax Management Policy, Group Finance Business Directive No. [2016] 027)*

We must build an end-to-end tax audit management approach. Specifically, we need to analyze existing rules and create contingency plans before tax audits; fully leverage our expertise and documentation to defend ourselves during audits; and take corrective actions when audits end. *(Source: Minutes of the Report on the Approach to Tax Risk Management, Finance Staff Team Meeting Minutes No. [2016] 066)*

14.2.2 Effectively Developing Global Tax Plans and Keeping the Company's Taxes at a Reasonable Level

We must truly reflect our effective tax rate (ETR). *(Source: Resolution on the Company's Annual Effective Tax Rate, Finance Committee Resolution No. [2011] 044)*

Our goal in ETR management is to ensure the ETR is reasonable, stable, predictable, and manageable. *(Source: Minutes of the Report on the Company's Effective Tax Rate, Group Finance CFO Office Meeting Minutes No. [2016] 024)*

We must clearly define non-standard taxes and their scope, and remind all relevant business departments to effectively manage losses that result from such taxes. Non-standard taxes are extra tax costs incurred due to trade-offs, operational violations, poor management, failure to comply with tax laws and regulations, and failure to comply with tax policies and guidelines. *(Source: Regulations on Irregular Taxes, Group Finance Business Directive No. [2016] 008)*

Open Access This chapter is licensed under the terms of the Creative Commons Attribution-NonCommercial-NoDerivatives 4.0 International License (http://creativecommons.org/licenses/by-nc-nd/4.0/), which permits any noncommercial use, sharing, distribution and reproduction in any medium or format, as long as you give appropriate credit to the original author(s) and the source, provide a link to the Creative Commons licence and indicate if you modified the licensed material. You do not have permission under this license to share adapted material derived from this chapter or parts of it.

The images or other third party material in this chapter are included in the chapter's Creative Commons licence, unless indicated otherwise in a credit line to the material. If material is not included in the chapter's Creative Commons licence and your intended use is not permitted by statutory regulation or exceeds the permitted use, you will need to obtain permission directly from the copyright holder.

CHAPTER 15

Internal Controls and Internal Audit

Huawei is committed to its fight against embezzlement, waste, jobbery, and corruption amongst senior managers. It seeks to receive income from a single source.

Huawei delegates authority to field offices, enabling them to have more autonomy and operate more flexibly and efficiently. Authority delegated must be exercised with effective oversight, and the purpose of oversight is to delegate more authority. To Huawei, oversight is the best way to care for and protect its managers. The company values basic processes and systems, especially the internal control system. When building its internal control system, Huawei insists on "wearing American shoes" and starting from scratch, rather than patching up an existing system.

The company has established three lines of defense for internal controls. The first line of defense is to control risks in its business operations. This is the most important line of defense, with business managers and process owners serving as the primary owners for internal controls. The second line of defense refers to functional departments, which are accountable for internal controls and risk monitoring. These departments should streamline the management of major risks across processes and domains. The third line of defense is the Internal Audit Department, which establishes cold deterrence through independent assessments and after-fact investigations.

Process controls aim to plug the leaks in processes. ICFR ensures that data in financial reports is reliable, rule-based, and robust. All process activities that affect financial reports, including balance sheets, profit &

loss statements, and cash flow statements, fund and asset security, or ITC of Huawei or any of its subsidiaries, fall under ICFR. Financial report quality must meet stringent regulatory standards. To ensure the quality of its financial reports, Huawei must start by managing the quality of business data.

At Huawei, the Internal Audit Department plays an independent oversight role in anti-corruption, anti-fraud, and anti-waste activities. The primary goal of this is to establish cold deterrence. During internal audits, the company separates investigations and disciplinary actions. While investigations are rigorous, disciplinary decisions show leniency. The Internal Audit Department assumes people are innocent before proven guilty and maintain a sense of propriety in imposing disciplinary actions against mistakes made at work.

The Internal Audit Department focuses on individual issues and establishes deterrence by addressing these issues. Oversight is everywhere and focuses on business-specific issues, and partners with business departments to uncover, manage, and mitigate risks throughout the process. The Committee of Ethics and Compliance (CEC) focuses on company-wide issues and aims to create a favorable environment for ethical compliance.

This chapter outlines the big picture for Huawei's objectives, principles, ownership system, and policy boundaries related to internal controls and internal audit.

15.1 The Company's Oversight System: The Governance Structure and Three Lines of Defense

15.1.1 *The Oversight System: Governance Structure*

The Audit Committee is a specialist committee that operates under Huawei's Board of Directors. Within the scope of authority set forth by the Board of Directors, the Audit Committee oversees internal controls, covering the entire internal control system, internal and external audits, corporate processes, as well as the company's legal, regulatory, and *BCG* compliance. The Audit Committee is made up of members of the Supervisory Board, the Board of Directors, and relevant experts. Audit Committee membership must be approved by the Board of Directors. Internal audit organizations and our external auditor report to both the Audit Committee and the Board of Directors. *(Source: Audit Committee Charter (Provisional), Board of Directors Doc. No. [2012] 008)*

The Supervisory Board is Huawei's highest oversight body. On behalf of the company's shareholders, it exercises oversight authority over the company. It oversees members of the Board of Directors and other senior executives, and stands outside of the company's processes. Departments at different levels implement business rules; the Supervisory Board implements oversight rules. The oversight-oriented subsidiary boards of directors report to the Supervisory Board. *(Source: Minutes of the Dali Meeting on the Company's Future Governance Structure, BOD Executive Committee Meeting Minutes No. [2015] 015)*

In the future, the company's Supervisory Board should focus more on oversight of daily operations. Authority over human resources falls under the purview of the Board of Directors. The Supervisory Board can initiate and handle certain issues, but disciplinary actions against any personnel involved should be taken by the Board of Directors and the HRC. They will hand any personnel issues over to the HRC Disciplinary and Supervisory Sub-committee, which is the organization with personnel management authority. The Supervisory Board doesn't handle personnel issues directly. *(Ren Zhengfei: Speech at the First Meeting of the Fourth Supervisory Board, 2015)*

The company's senior management is ultimately accountable for internal controls of the entire company. They should set the tone for internal controls by emphasizing their importance and building and continuously improving the internal control environment across the company. *(Source: Internal Control System 3.0, Corp. Doc. No. [2012] 238)*

15.1.2 Internal Controls: Three Lines of Defense

As the company develops more rapidly, our management may not cover all aspects, and we will find increasing numbers of temporary loopholes. This is why we have established three lines of defense within our internal control system.

The first line of defense, which is the most important, controls risks during business operations. We should put over 90% of our effort into developing an effective first line of defense, which should be standardized but flexible. We need to flexibly respond to the service needs of different customers. The ultimate goal is to have business managers take responsibility for internal controls. For example, the manager of a certain business will also be responsible for the internal controls of that business. This approach should be extended all the way up to the top levels of the company. We must never waver in our determination to strengthen our first line of defense, and move towards the process ownership system one step at a time. This means we will gradually delegate authority to process owners. Country representatives will eventually become general managers who need to meet the basic requirements for overall business operations. The company's processes must be simple and effective. The majority of our oversight must be based on processes. Processes themselves are a line of defense, so if we develop our processes properly, we will already have a strong defense system. Streamlining processes is a goal we will pursue with resolve.

The second line of defense ensures consistent management of major risks across processes and domains. Functional departments for internal controls and risk monitoring must promote the application of methodologies. A large number of managers should be trained on internal controls before going to work in the field. The second line of defense must provide many methodologies and also add, rotate, and develop numerous managers for the first line of defense. We have to define what responsibilities process owners should have. The Semi-Annual Control Assessment (SACA) is an assessment of process owners, and we should help them launch some pilots, establish process control systems, define jobs and roles, and get the whole system working correctly. At the same time, we should plan and deploy a Golden Seeds program country by country to roll out iSales, streamline configuration, and manage delivery in the Enterprise Resource Planning (ERP) system. Once the program succeeds, the golden seeds can be divided into two teams, and transferred to other countries. If they succeed again, a new group of golden seeds will emerge. This acts like an upward spiral that constantly produces new golden seeds. A new cohort of these will be promoted into managers. If they all have successful track records, then why not let them take over representative offices? Why not let them take over HQ? They will be welcomed back to HQ in high spirits. Who says they can't be leaders in their twenties?

Our third line of defense assesses risks and internal controls independently through audits and investigations. The objective of the third line of defense is to establish cold deterrence. *(Ren Zhengfei: Speech at the Briefing on the Proposal for Optimizing the Three Lines of Defense for Corporate Internal Controls and Risk Management, Huawei Executive Office Speech No. [2014] 005)*

Our first line of defense should identify the vast majority of issues, but there may still be loopholes. This is where the third line comes in: It locates and closes loopholes to establish cold deterrence. We can also call in external organizations to review our processes. This third line will never vanish. Once the first line of defense is set up, the third line shouldn't have too much to do. However, this doesn't mean the first line should be careless and rely on Auditing to clean up issues for them. If a rotten apple gets no attention, it makes no sense. When we build processes and organizations, we should remove this apple. That is to say, once a problem is found, no matter how large or small, an audit must scour every speck of dirt, even removing ant eggs. That helps establish the cold deterrence needed to support the building of the first line of defense. *(Ren Zhengfei: Speech at the Briefing on the Proposal for Optimizing the Three Lines of Defense for Corporate Internal Controls and Risk Management, Huawei Executive Office Speech No. [2014] 005)*

We need to further define the responsibilities of owners for the three lines of defense.

The first line of defense is comprised of business managers and process owners, who are also the primary owners of internal controls. We must build internal controls, awareness, and capabilities amongst our employees, and ensure process compliance at checkpoints and during real practices. Process compliance ensures the quality of authority exercises. We need to implement a process ownership system that ensures process owners and business managers are truly accountable for internal controls and risk monitoring. This should eliminate 95% of risks during process-based operations. Business managers must be able to do two things: create value and effectively implement internal controls.

The second line of defense is comprised of functional departments that are responsible for internal controls and risk monitoring. These departments should streamline the management of major risks across processes and domains. They should also develop methodologies, promote their application, and ensure employees at all levels have the required capabilities. The inspection team should focus on real-time events and serve as a helping hand to business managers. The inspection team must not overstep its authority though, and should remember that business managers are the primary owners of management. The inspection team needs to help business managers manage their business in a mature manner, identify problems, make improvements, and effectively resolve problems. The inspection and internal controls teams are to exercise the authority of oversight while helping business departments work according to processes. One thing is clear: Neither the Inspection Department nor the Internal Controls Department is accountable for internal controls.

Our third line of defense is the Internal Audit Department. Like a government's legal branch, this department establishes cold deterrence through independent assessments and after-fact investigations. Once the audit team uncovers a small issue, it will dig deep into it, temporarily ignoring all other issues no matter how severe they are. The audit team will focus on that small issue, and thoroughly examine the risks it poses. There are two types of investigation: vertical and horizontal. There are no hard rules about this delineation and issues are not ranked based on severity. The audit team looks into any issues they discover to establish cold deterrence. This will discourage people from acting inappropriately. *(Ren Zhengfei: Internal and External Compliance to Generate More Revenue and Pave the Way for the Company's Future Success—Speech at a Meeting with the Oversight Team, Huawei Executive Office Speech No. [2017] 002)*

The three lines of defense for oversight need to operate smoothly under the management of the Supervisory Board and the Audit Committee. The key points to implement the process ownership system are that: (1) Process owners, managers, and key position holders fulfill their full responsibilities; and (2) Effective and closed-loop employee education, management, investigation, as well as disciplinary and legal actions address both the symptoms and the root cause. *(Source: Minutes of a Report on the Strategic Plan of the Internal Audit Department, EMT Meeting Minutes No. [2014] 025)*

The Internal Audit Department focuses on individual issues and establishes deterrence by addressing these issues. Oversight is everywhere and focuses on business-specific issues, and partners with business departments to uncover, manage, and mitigate risks throughout the process. The CEC focuses on company-wide issues and aims to create a favorable environment for ethical compliance. The CEC exercises oversight throughout the company. *(Ren Zhengfei: Minutes of the Meeting with Staff of the Romania Accounting SSC, Huawei Executive Office Speech No. [2011] 021)*

15.2 Process Controls

15.2.1 Oversight Aims to Prevent Corruption, Improve Operations, and Establish Deterrence

We must continue our fight against embezzlement, waste, jobbery, and corruption amongst senior managers. *(Ren Zhengfei: Working Effortlessly to Build Even Greater Prosperity—Speech at the Inauguration for Managers from Finance and Procurement, 1996)*

We don't perform oversight for the sake of oversight. Nor do we want everyone to be pure and innocent. Oversight acts as deterrence: It helps the company move forward in the right direction, following our pre-set policies and processes. It will keep the whole company from going down the drain because of the greed of some individuals. *(Ren Zhengfei: Implementing Oversight with Care, Huawei Executive Office Speech No. [2011] 013)*

We seek to receive income from a single source. Our EMT has made it clear that the income of our senior managers and key employees can only come from the salaries, incentives, bonuses, and other schemes offered by Huawei. Income from other sources is not allowed. We have established organizations and systems to prevent anyone at Huawei, from the most senior executives down to the execution level, from destroying our collective interest through conflict-of-interest transactions for personal gain. Over the past two decades, we have mainly received income from a single source, and through this have formed a team of 150,000 employees who are united and dedicated to the company's success. I am aware there are still many flaws in our management, but we are trying our utmost to improve. I believe our HR policies will become more scientific if we continue to receive income from a single source. Consequently, our employees will become more passionate about their work. Then, there will be nothing that we can't achieve. *(Ren Zhengfei: Working Together Towards the Same Goal, Receiving Income from a Single Source—2013 New Year Greeting, 2012)*

If we can work together towards the same goal and receive income from a single source, Huawei will not fail. If we abandon these principles, we will probably fail. *(Ren Zhengfei: Working Together Towards the Same Goal, Receiving Income from a Single Source—2013 New Year Greeting, 2012)*

I recommend that you all read up on the Enron scandal of 2001. This seemed like it was just a matter of some false accounting. However, this company, worth several hundred billion dollars, tampered with their books and, in the end, the CEO received a 150-year prison sentence and the company collapsed. The reason we have been determined and gone to great expenses to become fully compliant: When we dominate the global market, we must not have an Achilles heel for people to exploit and bring us down. *(Ren Zhengfei: Speech at the Mid-year Workshop on the Enablement of Subsidiary Board Directors, Huawei Executive Office Speech No. [2014] 074)*

Situations where our strategic competitor hooks or corrupts our employees to acquire information has now become more serious than we could have imagined. We must not treat this lightly and must have stricter controls over our core assets and the commercial and technical information in our contract bids. *(Ren Zhengfei: Speech at a Briefing on the Progress of Large-scale Elimination of Corruption, Huawei Executive Office Speech No. [2014] 010)*

If we don't improve our systems or strengthen employee education, corruption will fester and the company will be doomed. *(Ren Zhengfei: Speech at a Briefing on the Progress of Large-scale Elimination of Corruption, Huawei Executive Office Speech No. [2014] 010)*

After authority is delegated, we must strengthen oversight over its exercise and establish an accountability system. Approval is part of business processes and cannot replace oversight, as oversight is independent from business processes. *(Ren Zhengfei: Minutes of the Report on Contract Categorization Analysis and Recommendations, EMT Meeting Minutes No. [2014] 008)*

Over the last year or so, the "startup and innovation culture" has swept across China. Increasing numbers of employees are leaving Huawei to start their own businesses, but we must make sure that none of them are taking information assets from the company when they leave. They are not allowed to use the company's assets as the basis for starting their own businesses. We must deal swiftly and decisively with anyone who starts a business using Huawei's technical or commercial secrets. *(Source: Minutes of the Report on Current Problems and Challenges in Information Security, and Remedies, EMT Meeting Minutes No. [2015] 018)*

Our oversight system must be able to make good compromises and establish cold deterrence. The ultimate goal of compromising is to support business growth. *(Ren Zhengfei: Speech on the Audit Committee's 2014 Annual Work Report at the January Board of Directors Meeting, Huawei Executive Office Speech No. [2015] 017)*

Many people at Huawei still don't place much emphasis on internal controls. This might be caused by issues with our HR assessment system, which focuses heavily on how many contracts one wins. Most people don't do bad things, so they take it for granted that others don't, either. Why are we building an oversight elite team? We want business managers to receive training and practice so they come to understand what oversight is all about. We have to work hard and must not slack off. Our internal controls and oversight are not designed to slow things down, but to make our processes smoother and faster. As you know, high-speed trains run very fast, but imagine what it would be like if there were no internal controls!

High-speed railways have very good processes and internal controls. For example, the direct train from Beijing to Shenzhen does not stop anywhere in-between. Do you know how many checkpoints it passes in one night? Lots, but they don't slow it down. In addition, we will implement an approval system for large departments, and every department will have only one approval point with a specific time limit. After the deadline, things will be approved automatically. However, when problems arise, the approval point will be accountable. This will ensure that we operate as fast as high-speed trains. *(Ren Zhengfei: Internal and External Compliance to Generate More Revenue and Pave the Way for the Company's Future Success—Speech at a Meeting with the Oversight Team, Huawei Executive Office Speech No. [2017] 002)*

15.2.2 *"Wearing American Shoes" and Starting from Scratch to Build Huawei's Internal Control System*

The EMT sees great value in IBM's internal control system. To build Huawei's internal control system, we must "wear American shoes" and start from scratch, rather than patching up an existing system. If our organizational structure doesn't quite fit with processes, we should adapt our structure to processes. We can keep managers who understand this system, but those who don't, no matter how senior, will have to leave their positions. We need to assign some bright minds to learn from IBM and establish such a system in our company. *(Ren Zhengfei: Wearing American Shoes and Starting from Scratch to Build Huawei's Internal Control System—An Introduction to IBM's Internal Control Practices and EMT's Guidelines for Building Huawei's Internal Control System, Huawei Executive Office Speech No. [2007] 032)*

To ensure the transformation of our internal control management is implemented effectively, we must first build an environment that is conducive to internal controls. Our managers at different levels must set an example. Those who understand IBM's internal control management system will be appointed to managerial positions and managers who cannot understand this system will be reassigned. All managers must step up efforts to learn about IBM's internal control management processes, methods, and experience. They need to take exams, either online or during training sessions, to prove their mastery of essential knowledge about internal controls. Those who fail their exams will have their salaries frozen and will no longer have advancement opportunities. If they fail the exams a second time, or do not take the exams within a specified timeframe, they will be reassigned. *(Ren Zhengfei: Wearing American Shoes and Starting from Scratch to Build Huawei's Internal Control System—An Introduction to IBM's Internal Control Practices and EMT's Guidelines for Building Huawei's Internal Control System, Huawei Executive Office Speech No. [2007] 032)*

To continuously increase internal control awareness of business managers, we need to establish career development paths and mobility programs for managers, and assign managers with extensive experience in business operations to our audit and oversight teams. We also need to send internal control high-performers to serve as managers within business departments. *(Ren Zhengfei: Wearing American Shoes and Starting from Scratch to Build Huawei's Internal Control System—An Introduction to IBM's Internal Control Practices and EMT's Guidelines for Building Huawei's Internal Control System, Huawei Executive Office Speech No. [2007] 032)*

The company values basic processes and systems, especially the internal control system. We must also establish an accountability system, which needs to define what kinds of disciplinary actions will be taken for different violations. Disciplinary actions need to be taken against wrongdoers themselves and also their senior managers. *(Ren Zhengfei: Wearing American Shoes and Starting from Scratch to Build Huawei's Internal Control System—An Introduction to IBM's Internal Control Practices and EMT's Guidelines for Building Huawei's Internal Control System, Huawei Executive Office Speech No. [2007] 032)*

We will rework our *Internal Control System* document by strictly following IBM's internal control practices. This document will serve as our guidelines for improving our internal control system and does not need to be confined to the content in our approved documents. *(Source: Resolution on the Plan for Improving Huawei's Internal Controls, EMT Resolution No. [2007] 045)*

We need to study IBM's authority delegation rules, and its philosophy and methodology on how to apply checks and balances through oversight. We must not be too radical when delegating authority and must be careful when defining the scope of authority to be delegated and to whom it will be delegated. We will first delegate limited authority to domains where there is an urgent need for authority and management is relatively mature. In addition, we must build an oversight system to ensure checks and balances. The philosophy must be communicated across all levels and authority must be delegated step by step. After authority has been delegated and exercised, we can review and assess how things work. In mature domains, we can further delegate authority. By proceeding gradually, we can make the system run effectively within three years. *(Ren Zhengfei: Speech at the Report on IBM's Authorization Practices and Huawei's Direction for Improvement, EMT Meeting Minutes No. [2008] 004)*

Authority delegation must revolve around processes, as they determine the organizational structures. If a department's structure does not align with processes, then we will restructure the department to suit the processes. Departments involved in oversight and checks and balances must participate in the authority delegation project. *(Ren Zhengfei: Speech at the Report on IBM's Authorization Practices and Huawei's Direction for Improvement, EMT Meeting Minutes No. [2008] 004)*

15.2.3 Internal Control Management: Objectives and the Framework

Objectives of internal control management

Internal controls aim to improve our operating processes, procedures, and management, close the loopholes of processes, and summarize the lessons learned. Internal Controls must make friends with people, employees in particular. If there are any issues, Internal Controls must be able to provide methods for addressing these issues through discussion. Internal Controls functions like a business department. It looks at how we do business from a different angle in order to identify potential execution errors. Unless there is sufficient evidence to indicate individual wrongdoing, we should just focus on fixing what has gone wrong, not on assigning blame. If processes are well-defined, we won't face too many issues. Only when we have created a culture of teamwork, can we help the company develop on a large scale. *(Ren Zhengfei: Remarks at a Meeting with Procurement Managers, 2000)*

The purpose of internal controls is to ensure the company's funds and assets are secure, the company's financial reports are accurate, and the company is fully compliant with the law. Internal controls are meant to effectively control operational risks, improve operating efficiency and effectiveness, and help the company achieve its set goals. (*Source: Internal Control System 3.0, Corp. Doc. No. [2012] 238*)

During its meeting on April 29, 2015, the EMT defined Huawei's internal control targets over the next three years as follows:

1. By 2017, the company should achieve maturity in its internal controls, with a minimum internal control score of "Basically Satisfactory" (60%).
2. By H1 2015, the minimum internal control maturity score will be 30%. Any manager whose department's score is below 30%, and who is not making efforts to increase that score, will face impeachment.
3. Minimum internal control maturity scores for H2 2015, end of year 2016, and end of year 2017 are set at 40%, 50%, and 60%, respectively. The Worldwide Business Controls Department (WWBC) is authorized to adjust the scores of local offices. After approval by the Audit Committee, these scores will be published at the beginning of each year. *(Source: Resolution on Fulfilling the Internal Control Responsibilities of Managers and Process Owners, EMT Resolution No. [2015] 007)*

To achieve a "Basically Satisfactory" internal control maturity rating, a department must have:

1. Properly designed processes that are implemented accurately, resulting in no major risks and only suffering losses within normal bounds
2. Accurate financial reports, with no major discrepancies or post-reporting adjustments
3. No serious compliance violations during the reporting period, such as repeated violations. *(Source: Minutes of the Meeting on 2015 Internal Control Assessments and More Detailed Definition of the "Basically Satisfactory" Standard, Audit Committee Meeting Minutes No. [2015] 016)*

The internal control management framework

Layer 1: the Control Environment. This serves as the base of the internal control pyramid. The global end-to-end processes and ownership system act as the foundation for Huawei's internal control system and must be fully understood and implemented to ensure internal controls are successful. Global process owners have the primary responsibility for internal controls within their processes.

Layer 2: Control Tools and Indicators. This includes the compliance testing of KCPs, internal and external audit results, and other control tools and indicators that have been defined as essential inputs for the internal control assessment.

Layer 3: Assessments. Company management can view and use the assessment reports regularly. Through the use of the control tools at Layer 2 and associated reviews, the control indicators are converted into useful information with which Huawei's control posture can be assessed regularly.

Layer 4: Appraisal and Accountability. Guided by business controllers, business owners and managers complete performance appraisals and accountability assessments, applying the assessment results from Layer 3 and considering the process for fulfilling their oversight responsibilities. These responsibilities include reviews, discussions, business risk assessments, operations monitoring, communication, information sharing, and professional assessments. Internal audit personnel and business controls departments also combine these outputs with their own professional analysis. This allows them to produce reports on audit findings and the company's internal controls. These reports are delivered to the Audit Committee and the EMT who then implement appropriate rewards, or disciplinary or corrective actions.

Layer 5: Policies. Top management including the Board of Directors and the EMT is responsible for the effectiveness of internal controls and the company's control posture; and develops and reviews internal control policies. *(Source: Huawei Internal Control Framework V3.0, Corp. Policy No. [2014] 002)*

15.2.4 Implementing the Process Ownership System

Currently, authority is centrally controlled by management teams without constraints, especially in junior- and mid-level management teams far away from oversight of HQ. These teams can easily become independent "kingdoms". Process owners must therefore be given the corresponding authority to review salaries and bonuses and assess and promote managers. This ensures checks and balances. Level-1 departments at HQ are already set up by function, so next, we need to review and streamline level-2 and level-3 departments. We also need to restructure lower-level departments so there is a stronger focus on processes. This will prevent the formation of independent "kingdoms" in departments that are vertically managed instead of being managed under a matrix. We must delegate sufficient authority to process owners, avoid wasting resources, and tear down departmental silos. *(Ren Zhengfei: Minutes of the Report on Work Responsibilities of Business Controls and Internal Controls/Internal Audit and Their Relationships, EMT Meeting Minutes No. [2008] 034)*

We remain completely committed to a process-based management approach and to improving our process ownership system. We need to shift from process compliance to process ownership. Business managers and process owners need to be truly responsible for oversight. In the past, we focused on process compliance. This meant that you could do a good job just by following a process. Process ownership takes that idea one step further: Whoever signs off on the task is accountable for anything that goes wrong. We've made it clear that managers should have to sign off on things they are accountable for. Signing off means that you accept that accountability. *(Ren Zhengfei: Speech at a Briefing on the Progress of Large-scale Elimination of Corruption, Huawei Executive Office Speech No. [2014] 010)*

Normally, people think that the process ownership system will ensure that nothing ever goes wrong, and owners will be held accountable if something goes wrong, but they are not accountable for being slow. If this is what our process ownership system is all about, our company will slack off and even collapse. When I talk about a process ownership system, I mean timely and accurate services and greater success, not zero accidents. We want a system of fast trains, not a system that keeps trains in the station for the sake of avoiding accidents. If a person cannot achieve this, then they are not capable and we will replace them with someone who is capable. So, what do we do when accidents occur? We hold people accountable. Those who get trains running both fast and accurately should be promoted through fast tracks. *(Ren Zhengfei: Speech at the Oath-taking and Awards Ceremony of the Transformation Elite Team, Huawei Executive Office Speech No. [2015] 047)*

Processes will require multiple levels of responsibility, with each level being unique. A high-speed train that runs from Beijing to Guangzhou is an end-to-end service. But in Zhengzhou, train station personnel just have to make sure the train leaves their station on time. They do not have to worry about what happens all the way down to Guangzhou. *(Ren Zhengfei: Speech at the Oath-taking and Awards Ceremony of the Transformation Elite Team, Huawei Executive Office Speech No. [2015] 047)*

Processes are not perfect, so we need to move oversight downward. Increasing the number of checkpoints isn't the answer to everything. The same goes for the deployment of the process ownership system. We need to remove checkpoints that don't help us achieve strategic objectives. *(Source: Minutes of the Report on the Work Priority of the Company for Building an Oversight and Accountability System, EMT Meeting Minutes No. [2015] 013)*

15.2.5 Internal Control Ownership System

Managers at all levels serve as the primary owners for internal controls

Process owners are oversight owners and so must accept oversight responsibilities. The Oversight Management Department has to give process owners methodologies and templates to help them shoulder these responsibilities, and appraise their performance. This department should not perform the oversight responsibility that belongs to process owners. *(Ren Zhengfei: Speech at a Briefing on Regional Oversight, 2007)*

The EMT has decided that directors of business departments are responsible for oversight. First of all, it must be made clear that process owners shall take responsibility for three tasks: proactive reviews, internal control checks and assessments, and the development of an authority delegation system. *(Ren Zhengfei: Speech at a Briefing on Regional Oversight, 2007)*

In our company, management teams are the sole decision-makers. Process owners don't have a say in these decisions. Therefore, I want to suggest that, starting from today, management teams can only determine employees' salaries and personal grades, leaving bonus allocation in the hands of process owners. We need to assign both responsibility and authority to process departments. Process owners are primarily responsible for building processes, and cannot have much assistance from their own departments. They must therefore get this assistance from process building departments. *(Ren Zhengfei: Huawei's Internal Control Organizations Must First Implement a Transitional Plan to Avoid a Management Vacuum—Minutes of the Report by the IFS-Business Controls & Internal Audit Project Team to Mr. Ren and the EMT on the Organizational Restructuring Plan of Huawei's Business Controls Departments, EMT Meeting Minutes No. [2008] 017)*

Process owners shoulder major responsibility for internal controls. By appointing global process owners, business managers become responsible for process operations and must ensure the processes under their management are running in an efficient and controllable manner. Process controllers are process experts. They help process owners build processes and monitor routine process operations by setting KCPs, performing monthly compliance testing, and sending monthly testing and SACA results to Business Controls. *(Ren Zhengfei: Huawei's Internal Control Organizations Must First Implement a Transitional Plan to Avoid a Management Vacuum—Minutes of the Report by the IFS-Business Controls & Internal*

Audit Project Team to Mr. Ren and the EMT on the Organizational Restructuring Plan of Huawei's Business Controls Departments, EMT Meeting Minutes No. [2008] 017)

When we look at which managers to promote, particularly senior managers, we look closely at their conduct regarding key processes, and how they have tried to prevent corruption. Anyone who is not firm in preventing corruption will never be more than an ordinary manager. When we look for new senior managers, we need to emphasize this quality. Process owners and business managers in high risk areas who consistently fail to improve their internal controls will have to explain this to the Audit Committee. If a manager submits false reports about internal controls or does not take on their internal control responsibilities, they will be impeached immediately. *(Ren Zhengfei: Speech at a Briefing on the Progress of Large-scale Elimination of Corruption, Huawei Executive Office Speech No. [2014] 010)*

Business managers are responsible for inspections and internal controls. The purpose of creating new processes is to improve operations (performance and efficiency). *(Ren Zhengfei: Speech at a Meeting with the Managerial Control Elite Team, Huawei Executive Office Speech No. [2015] 060)*

Managers at all levels are responsible for internal controls. The Managerial Control Elite Team exists to empower managers through a combination of training and practice. With this help, managers should be able to better fulfill their oversight role during process execution. First, Huawei implements a process ownership system. Overseeing a specific business isn't the responsibility of the Internal Audit Department or the Supervisory Board. Instead, it is the responsibility of the manager of that business. Second, our management needs to be standardized and streamlined in order to increase efficiency. Process owners need to promptly and accurately provide services, and quickly check relevant issues based on simple and standard processes without exercising excessive oversight, letting them pass quickly like a high-speed train. Strategic business departments need to operate within a strong matrix management system. Matrix management means that they have separate business managers and process owners, with the latter assuming 95% of internal control responsibility. For departments outside the matrix system, process owners and business managers are the same people. *(Ren Zhengfei: Speech at a Meeting with the Managerial Control Elite Team, Huawei Executive Office Speech No. [2015] 060)*

The Business Controls Department is a key functional department for internal controls

The oversight department's work priorities are to oversee process execution and clarify the internal control responsibilities of major process owners in departments at all levels. They are doing something constructive and need to consider how to lay each brick and fill every gap between the bricks of the Great Wall. In the past, our Business Controls Department only oversaw financial processes, rather than addressing issues in company-wide, end-to-end processes. However, in the future, our quality and oversight management must extend to the end-to-end processes. *(Ren Zhengfei: Huawei's Internal Control Organizations Must First Implement a Transitional Plan to Avoid a Management Vacuum—Minutes of the Report by the IFS-Business Controls & Internal Audit Project Team to Mr. Ren and the EMT on the Organizational Restructuring Plan of Huawei's Business Controls Departments, EMT Meeting Minutes No. [2008] 017)*

The Business Controls Department is responsible for our internal control environment: As an oversight COE, this department provides process owners and controllers with control methodologies and tools, performs comprehensive oversight assessments and SACAs, and briefs the Audit Committee on the overall internal control postures of the company. The Business Controls Department reports to the corporate CFO, even though it oversees all businesses, not just financial matters. This department helps process owners create better process controls, and at the same time oversees process control status. It reflects how checks and balances are applied within the company. *(Ren Zhengfei: Huawei's Internal Control Organizations Must First Implement a Transitional Plan to Avoid a Management Vacuum—Minutes of the Report by the IFS-Business Controls & Internal Audit Project Team to Mr. Ren and the EMT on the Organizational Restructuring Plan of Huawei's Business Controls Departments, EMT Meeting Minutes No. [2008] 017)*

The Business Controls Department's mission, authority, and responsibilities are to:

- Provide advice and training on controls;
- Develop appropriate control tools;
- Offer guidance and training on controls for existing and new processes;
- Assess and support the improvement of process controls, including SACAs;

- Help business managers and process owners rank and prioritize control-related risks and defects;
- Help develop improvement plans;
- Monitor plan execution;
- Coordinate deployment of controls resources (i.e., business controls personnel);
- Optimize resource deployment. *(Source: Internal Control System 3.0, Corp. Doc. No. [2012] 238)*

Inspection personnel are there to support process owners and managers

Inspection personnel are there to support process owners and managers. These personnel check up on processes as they are taking place. Inspection teams should offer more training to process owners and managers. *(Source: Report and Discussions on Latest CEO Rotation, BOD Executive Committee Meeting Minutes No. [2015] 023)*

Inspections are in-process spot checks that ensure process compliance and eliminate fraud, thus establishing deterrence. A combination of training and practice can help business managers do the right things in the right way. *(Ren Zhengfei: Speech at a Meeting with the Managerial Control Elite Team, Huawei Executive Office Speech No. [2015] 060)*

Inspection personnel focus on events during processes. They offer important support for business managers to identify and solve problems. We are going to assign the responsibility of the Engineering Inspection Department for building a COE and the inspection function of the Internal Audit Department to the Transformation Project Management Office. This office will then be responsible for building up inspection capabilities across the company. Other functions of the Engineering Inspection Department will be transferred to the GTS, and an Engineering Inspection Department will be set up under the GTS to carry out inspections during engineering and service delivery. Hui Chun will become the Executive Steering Committee's executive deputy chair to support Guo Ping, chair of the committee. Hui Chun will take on responsibility for increasing inspection expertise throughout the company, improving inspection practices and ensuring that all related problems are properly followed up on. *(Source: Decision on Adjustments to the Reporting Structure of the Corporate Development, Engineering Inspection, and Regions Management Departments, BOD Executive Committee Resolution No. [2015] 012)*

Engineering inspection is the end-to-end inspection of any engineering delivery business. It is supposed to create corrective action plans for identified problems in collaboration with business departments. If any evidence of *BCG* violations is found during the inspection process, these violations are reported to the Investigation Department of the Internal Audit Department. The Internal Audit Department must focus on establishing deterrence, while the priority of engineering inspections is to promptly identify problems and push for improvements in different business departments. *(Source: Minutes of the Report on Organizational Building of the Engineering Inspection Department, EMT Meeting Minutes No. [2011] 010)*

15.3 Internal Controls Over Financial Reporting (ICFR)

15.3.1 *Building Sustainable and Profitable Growth with High-Quality Process Controls and ICFR*

ICFR is a system that was established to ensure that data in financial reports is reliable (accurate and fair), rule-based (internal and external rules), and robust (secure and healthy). All process activities that affect financial reports, including balance sheets, profit & loss statements, and cash flow statements, fund and asset security, or ITC of Huawei or any of its subsidiaries, fall under ICFR. *(Source: Minutes of the Report on Decisions Made Regarding Phase 2 of ICFR, Finance Staff Team Meeting Minutes No. [2015] 108)*

Financial reporting management aims to address all requirements of the Board of Directors, auditors, and government regulators. It primarily does this from three aspects, through company-level financial reports, subsidiary-level financial reports, and ITC. That means it needs to ensure that financial reports are accurate and fair, and that an ICFR mechanism is in place, so that satisfactory financial reports are consistently delivered. *(Source: Resolution on Objectives for Improving Quality of Financial Reports, Finance Committee Resolution No. [2016] 014)*

ICFR represents all of Finance's requirements for business. In other words, Finance has but one requirement for business – to manage ICFR based on the three types of financial reports.

1. ICFR is designed to continuously improve the quality of financial reports.
2. ICFR management requirements should include requirements on data quality, ITC, subsidiaries' compliance with local Generally Accepted Accounting Principles (GAAP), subsidiary financial reporting, and financial process control. A sustainable goal should be set to drive continuous improvement in all these areas.
3. Finance's requirements of business must focus on improving the quality of financial reports. ICFR should serve as a management platform that helps business and finance to continuously improve. *(Meng Wanzhou: ICFR—Shifting from Moving Targets to Fixed Targets, Improvement Issue No. 492, 2016)*

The key to ICFR and financial process controls lies in the establishment of long-term mechanisms. Only by doing so can we avoid starting all over again. *(Source: Minutes of a Work Report by the Brazil Representative Office on ICFR and Financial Process Controls, Finance Staff Team Meeting Minutes No. [2015] 105)*

ICFR can be neither a major campaign nor a sprint race. We shouldn't try to achieve our ICFR objectives so quickly that we neglect to build a long-term management mechanism. These efforts would make no sense. Achieving internal control targets must have the support of a set of effective management mechanisms. For example, many problems we see today seem like one-off issues and we assume they are caused by poor process execution. However, if we dig a little deeper, it becomes apparent that these problems are caused by missing processes, poorly adapted processes, or improperly integrated processes. Only through thorough analysis can we see the big picture and understand how to design our integrated solutions. This is how we should establish our long-term improvement mechanism. *(Meng Wanzhou: Ensuring the Consistency of Business and Accounts and the Accuracy of Financial Reports—On Signing the ICFR Commitment Letter, Improvement Issue No. 479, 2015)*

15.3.2 ICFR Is a Means, and Consistency of Business and Accounts Is an End

The company must first achieve consistency of business and accounts

Following the Enron scandal in 2002, the US Congress passed the *Sarbanes-Oxley Act*. The Act states that CEOs and CFOs of listed companies are responsible for making sure their company has an effective ICFR system that promptly and accurately discloses financial reports and information. The Act also made fraudulent disclosure and commitment subject to legal sanctions. Of the last 10 lawsuits that were filed in the US involving between US$2 billion and US$7 billion, seven involved false accounting or fraudulent disclosure. *(Meng Wanzhou: Ensuring the Consistency of Business and Accounts and the Accuracy of Financial Reports—On Signing the ICFR Commitment Letter, Improvement Issue No. 479, 2015)*

Consistency of business and accounts means all financial results must reflect the true state of our business operations. This is also a minimum requirement of law and accounting standards. Independent oversight and strict accountability systems help ensure the consistency of business and accounts. This approach is widely adopted across the industry. Consistency of business and accounts requires more than just consistency of inventory accounts and goods, but also requires reliability, accuracy, and timeliness in all financial reporting, including that of revenue, cost, expenses, payments, collections, and fixed assets. *(Source: Work Requirements for Fully Implementing the Consistency of Business and Accounts Targets (ICFR), Group Finance Notice No. [2015] 006)*

To achieve consistency of our business and accounts, business and financial personnel must work together to fight false accounting. Legal affairs personnel must also take due responsibility for handling this problem. Many international companies encounter nasty obstacles regarding this issue, garnering punishments that range from heavy fines to the imprisonment of their executives. We also have a major problem ensuring the consistency of our business and accounts. We must resolutely address this problem. In fact, the industry already has a mature management solution that solves this: the ICFR mechanism – applying process controls to ensure the consistency of business and accounts. *(Ren Zhengfei: Speech at a Meeting with Employees of the Legal Affairs Department, Secretariat Office of the Board of Directors, and Wireless Network Product Line, Huawei Executive Office Speech No. [2015] 015)*

Consistency of business and accounts is the foundation of financial report accuracy. This consistency has two primary requirements: appropriate accounting policies and methods based on complete business data, and business data that includes all business information that may affect the financial team's assessment (business information that truly reflects the nature of business). Only if these requirements are met, can we ensure the objectivity, reliability, and fairness of our financial reports.

(Meng Wanzhou: Ensuring the Consistency of Business and Accounts and the Accuracy of Financial Reports—On Signing the ICFR Commitment Letter, Improvement Issue No. 479, 2015)

We must seek to achieve consistency of business and accounts within five years, as we still aren't there yet. Because of this, on December 31 last year, we offered leniency to anyone who admitted creating false reports. We show leniency when wrongdoers admit their mistakes. In the end, 4000 to 5000 employees came forward to admit their mistakes. This shows we still have a lot of work to do concerning our internal governance. *(Ren Zhengfei: Speech at the World Economic Forum in Davos, 2015)*

ICFR assessment results as the acceptance criteria for consistency of business and accounts

ICFR is a means, and consistency of business and accounts is an end. ICFR assessment results will be used as the acceptance criteria for the consistency of business and accounts. The Accounting Management Department will be responsible for checking and accepting the improvements made to the consistency of business and accounts. *(Source: Work Requirements for Fully Implementing the Consistency of Business and Accounts Targets (ICFR), Group Finance Notice No. [2015] 006)*

Assessment methods should be reasonable, reliable, and feasible. They should not overemphasize precision. *(Meng Wanzhou: ICFR—Shifting from Moving Targets to Fixed Targets, Improvement Issue No. 492, 2016)*

ICFR assessment methods are based on common, company-wide practices at Huawei, and may not be appropriate for use in high-risk countries. Therefore, regional CFOs in high-risk countries must create their own ICFR assessment methods in accordance with general ICFR principles and methodologies. Local offices in high-risk countries can choose the same assessment methods or tailor their own methods. *(Meng Wanzhou: ICFR—Shifting from Moving Targets to Fixed Targets, Improvement Issue No. 492, 2016)*

Generally speaking, the assessment rating of internal control maturity should not be higher than that of ICFR. Exceptions can be justified with examples and facts. *(Source: Minutes of the Report on the 2016 H1 SACA, Finance Staff Team Meeting Minutes No. [2016] 113)*

Quality management of financial reports aims to ensure they meet stringent external regulatory standards

The objective of managing financial report quality is to achieve a "Very Satisfactory" rating (barring certain matters for which the company makes exceptions), according to stringent external regulatory standards, by

2020. *(Source: Resolution on Objectives for Improving Quality of Financial Reports, Finance Committee Resolution No. [2016] 014)*

Now that we have achieved the CIAG, the EMT has agreed to add one more corporate-level work priority – improving financial report quality to a "Very Satisfactory" rating. Efforts surrounding this goal will be made to drive representative office-oriented integration and achieve the Five Ones[1] and consistency of business and accounts. *(Source: Minutes of the Report on the Progress of Driving Representative Office-oriented Integration Forward and Achieving Five Ones and CIAG, EMT Meeting Minutes No. [2017] 003)*

15.3.3   ICFR: Starting by Managing the Quality of Business Data to Ensure the Quality of Financial Reports

Finance cannot create data out of thin air. Financial data is generated either from business data or business decisions. For this reason, the objectivity, completeness, and accuracy of business data directly determine the quality of financial reports. To ensure financial work quality, we must first manage the quality of business data. This is ICFR. *(Meng Wanzhou: ICFR Is a Means, and Consistency of Business and Accounts Is an End, Improvement Issue No. 460, 2014)*

The *ICFR Regulations* must clearly state the ICFR responsibilities of managers at all levels. The responsibilities of CEOs/CFOs and process owners for ensuring the data quality of their respective domains must be clearly defined. Also, in this document, the responsibilities related to managing different types of financial data must be clarified. The document must also contain information about a layered commitment mechanism for fulfilling ICFR responsibilities. Responsibility fulfillment needs the support of tools and methodologies. Key control over financial reporting (KCFR) is a key tool for supporting ICFR. What is KCFR? KCFR is a tool used to identify key control elements that impact financial report quality throughout processes. Internal control methods, such as compliance testing and SACA, are then used to regularly monitor KCFR compliance during day-to-day work. This way, we can determine whether key data and information from business domains are accurate and reliable. There is no

---

[1] "Five Ones": any PO from receiving to order generation in One day, any shipment preparation in One week, any product delivered at agreed location in One month, any software ready for download in One minute, and any site from delivery to customer acceptance in One month.

way to completely ensure that financial reports will always be of high quality, even if we clarify ICFR responsibilities, identify KCFR throughout processes, and regularly perform compliance testing and SACAs. This is because even if we keep each KCFR under control, there may be manual account adjustments to stock data and provisions for project losses. Manually adjusted financial data must also be managed. Data management coupled with KCFR assessments makes the ICFR mechanism complete. *(Meng Wanzhou: ICFR Is a Means, and Consistency of Business and Accounts Is an End, Improvement Issue No. 460, 2014)*

At the start of the ICFR project, we examined the issues that relate most to finance and business departments and have bigger impacts on the company's financial reports. This will allow us to help everyone understand what ICFR is and which business actions can affect the quality of financial reports. One such issue is related to revenue data accuracy. After identifying and analyzing all the elements that affect revenue recognition, from opportunity identification to contract closure, we identified problems and their root causes in business processes, and incorporated KCFR to quickly monitor revenue recognition quality. As our accounting for the last two years indicates, revenue data quality has improved significantly. *(Meng Wanzhou: ICFR—Shifting from Moving Targets to Fixed Targets, Improvement Issue No. 492, 2016)*

15.3.4 ICFR Management Should Shift Its Focus from Moving Targets to Fixed Targets

Let's compare our moving target-based management approach to seeing a medical specialist. When a certain part of our body hurts, we go to a specialist for specialized treatment. This type of management approach resolves existing problems, but cannot comprehensively assess our health. A fixed target-based management approach is more like getting a complete physical examination. Even if we don't have any specific health problems, we should still schedule regular checkups to identify potential risks as early as possible. To maintain sustainable, healthy development, Huawei must regularly undergo comprehensive checkups and take preventative or corrective actions as necessary. A fixed target-based management approach should be the ultimate goal of our ICFR. Regular and comprehensive assessments, analyses, and improvements will help ensure the fairness and reliability of our financial reports. The moving target-based approach to ICFR management is intended to help everyone learn the specifics of small sections of business and understand and embrace ICFR. The fixed target-based approach aims to manage all types of data that affects the quality of financial reports, thus ensuring their fairness, reliability, timeliness, and accuracy. Moving targets allow us to better understand business specifics, while fixed targets allow us to fulfill responsibilities from end to end. By shifting our focus from moving targets to fixed targets, we can actively fulfill our ICFR responsibilities, instead of merely embracing ICFR. *(Meng Wanzhou: ICFR—Shifting from Moving Targets to Fixed Targets, Improvement Issue No. 492, 2016)*

There are three major financial reports: profit & loss statements, balance sheets, and cash flow statements. These statements are complementary to one another and combine to reflect the entire company's financial health. Financial robustness is usually measured through financial performance and financial report fairness and reliability. The latter is guaranteed by effective ICFR. Therefore, all business and financial items that affect the three major financial reports must be managed as part of ICFR. The structure and internal control elements of financial reports are largely fixed, so items that affect financial reports must also be fixed – this is why we have adopted a fixed target-based approach to ICFR management. *(Meng Wanzhou: ICFR—Shifting from Moving Targets to Fixed Targets, Improvement Issue No. 492, 2016)*

We currently focus most heavily on the management of profit & loss statements. However, when standing in the shoes of the company to comprehensively assess financial results, we must pay attention to the health and fairness of our balance sheets and cash flow statements. While it is vital to manage business performance, asset safety and ITC are equally important. The company's financial reports reflect the company's overall strength, while subsidiary financial reports show our business performance in specific market segments. Financial reports are the results, and business and financial activities are processes. That's why all business and financial activities that affect financial reports must be managed under ICFR. *(Meng Wanzhou: ICFR—Shifting from Moving Targets to Fixed Targets, Improvement Issue No. 492, 2016)*

15.3.5 Finance: Building an Effective Internal Control System; Business Departments: Rigorously Fulfilling Their Internal Control Responsibilities

Huawei's CEO takes the most responsibility for the accuracy and reliability of the company's financial reports. The CFO also assists the CEO in building, implementing, and managing the ICFR system. *(Source: ICFR Regulations, Group Finance Business Directive No. [2014] 005)*

As the owner of financial reports and financial data, Finance is responsible for ICFR. This means it needs to establish an effective ICFR mechanism and roll it out in different departments. It would be impossible for Finance to be responsible for the quality of all business data. That's why an effective and complete internal control mechanism must be in place to encourage business managers and process owners to take responsibility for business data quality, accuracy, completeness, timeliness, and reliability in their domains. Finance is responsible for building an effective internal control system, while business departments are responsible for rigorously fulfilling its internal control responsibilities. *(Meng Wanzhou: ICFR Is a Means, and Consistency of Business and Accounts Is an End, Improvement Issue No. 460, 2014)*

Regarding ICFR, Finance must: establish an effective internal control system; regularly assess the effectiveness of internal controls; correctly understand business scenarios and process business data as per appropriate accounting policies; and create financial and internal control reports based on business departments' description of matters without defects or omissions. Regarding ICFR, business departments must provide accurate business data and key information, regularly and effectively carry out the internal control activities as required by the internal control system, and make commitments regarding internal controls. *(Meng Wanzhou: ICFR Is a Means, and Consistency of Business and Accounts Is an End, Improvement Issue No. 460, 2014)*

An ICFR accountability system is used to ensure the accuracy of financial reports. ICFR accountability systems are commonly used throughout the industry. IBM has an ICFR commitment mechanism that clearly states related responsibilities. Under this mechanism, all levels of IBM's management rigorously control all data and information that may affect their financial reports, fulfilling their obligations to manage ICFR. This system guarantees the reliability and fairness of the company's financial reports. *(Meng Wanzhou: Ensuring the Consistency of Business and Accounts and the Accuracy of Financial Reports—On Signing the ICFR Commitment Letter, Improvement Issue No. 479, 2015)*

Within our management teams, some people are still passing the buck. Ultimately, this is because our process ownership system is not yet fully in place. Process owners at different levels must proactively take on process building and internal control responsibilities for their respective domains. The Quality, Business Process, and IT Management Department will centrally manage business process architectures and process integration across domains. We can fundamentally ensure process compliance and data cleanness if we truly make the process ownership system part of our day-to-day work. *(Meng Wanzhou: Ensuring the Consistency of Business and Accounts and the Accuracy of Financial Reports—On Signing the ICFR Commitment Letter, Improvement Issue No. 479, 2015)*

It is key that business managers and process owners at all levels are held accountable for the consistency of business and accounts. They need to avoid recurring problems by developing and implementing processes. *(Ren Zhengfei: Speech at a Meeting with Employees of the Legal Affairs Department, Secretariat Office of the Board of Directors, and Wireless Network Product Line, Huawei Executive Office Speech No. [2015] 015)*

15.3.6 ICFR Is Designed to Continuously Improve the Quality of Financial Reports, Not Merely to Hold People Accountable

Huawei Audit Committee Doc No. [2013] 002 *Internal Control Impeachment System and Standards* states that process owners and business managers who commit fraud on ICFR or do not act upon known ICFR problems will be directly impeached. Those who fail to properly manage ICFR or cannot generate expected results, need to report directly to the company's CFO and Audit Committee. If the CFO and Audit Committee decide to reject two reports consecutively, the involved process owner or business manager will be impeached.

All employees must act with integrity, diligently fulfill their duties, and comply with all applicable laws and regulations, as well as Huawei's own *BCGs*. Huawei prohibits all business fraud, including but not limited to:

- Forging or altering seals or signatures, and signing false contracts or other false documents.
- Signing two different contracts at the Huawei side and the customer side for the same business transaction.
- Falsely recognizing sales revenue by falsifying delivery progress information or delivery documents, and hiding true business information.
- Forging or falsifying business documents and financial records, resulting in inaccurate financial statements.

Wrongdoers will be dismissed and will need to compensate Huawei for any losses in accordance with corporate regulations. Huawei will pursue legal action against any individuals who break the law. The immediate and higher-level managers of wrongdoers will be subject to joint liability. *(Source: Resolution on Disciplinary Rules for Business Fraud, EMT Resolution No. [2014] 030)*

ICFR is designed to continuously improve the quality of financial reports, not merely to hold people accountable. *(Meng Wanzhou: ICFR—Shifting from Moving Targets to Fixed Targets, Improvement Issue No. 492, 2016)*

15.4 Internal Audits and Investigations

15.4.1 Establishing Deterrence Through Internal Audits

Internal oversight is an indispensable part of the company's financial operations mechanism. The reason we have established an audit team is to build a reasonable and standardized business management system and build simple but reliable operating procedures. In the short term, the audit team needs to set rules and procedures, create a framework for managing and controlling funds and logistics across the company, and ensure rule-based operations one step each time. This team must also help to maintain a firm grasp on rule-based operations, control key procedures, and delegate authority level by level. We don't want a small audit team. Instead, we want automated reviews and sign-offs for each operating procedure. We must strictly control contract reviews to narrow and close gaps, and gradually create an effective oversight system. *(Ren Zhengfei: Speech at a Briefing on Four Unifications and 2000 Work Plan of Finance, 1999)*

Finance is rolling out its Four Unifications project. Audit also has a role to play in this project, which is to perform retroactive oversight functions. All processes must be audited in a reverse order to determine the root causes of any problems. The results of the Four Unifications project must also be audited. If a problem is caused by our financial system, Finance must be held accountable. However, if there are recurring problems, then Audit must also be held accountable. Audit personnel must fully engage in the Four Unifications project. When initiating an audit project, we need to invite a consulting firm to help us build an audit and internal control system. *(Ren Zhengfei: Speech at a Briefing on Four Unifications and 2000 Work Plan of Finance, 1999)*

The Audit Department must clearly understand its top work priorities. First, they need to make sure no serious issues occur. Second, they need to make sure the same issues do not keep reoccurring. Audit personnel must assess risks concerning process operations and controls. They must also exercise stringent oversight to ensure that the company is moving in the pre-set direction. The work of the Audit Department is part business and part accounting. Therefore, you must play your role in building both accounting systems and business processes. *(Source: Minutes of a Meeting Between the Finance Management Department and the Audit Department, 2002)*

The Audit Department is accountable for results and behaviors, but not processes. They must maintain a high level of independence. All functions related to behavior and results currently under the Oversight Department will be transferred to the Audit Department. The Audit Department needs to establish deterrence against violations. There may be 10,000 items that need to be investigated annually, but the Audit Department only investigates 100 a year. You have no way of knowing which items they will select for investigation. If they find your problems, they will investigate thoroughly. The Audit Department should not be creating policies and they are only responsible for results. They just need to determine who needs to be held accountable and hand them over to the Audit Committee. Despite this, the Audit Committee may pardon these wrongdoers. The final authority for determining guilt and punishment lies with the Audit Committee. The committee sets the policies; therefore, the Audit Department is there to create deterrence. *(Ren Zhengfei: Huawei's Internal Control Organizations Must First Implement a Transitional Plan to Avoid a Management Vacuum—Minutes of the Report by the IFS-Business Controls & Internal Audit Project Team to Mr. Ren and the EMT on the Organizational Restructuring Plan of Huawei's Business Controls Departments, EMT Meeting Minutes No. [2008] 017)*

The Audit Committee ensures the independence and deterrence of internal audits. Specifically, it reviews SACA and audit results, builds up an executive accountability system for internal controls, and provides guidance to internal audit personnel and process owners on strategies and directions for internal controls. *(Ren Zhengfei: Huawei's Internal Control Organizations Must First Implement a Transitional Plan to Avoid a Management Vacuum—Minutes of the Report by the IFS-Business Controls & Internal Audit Project Team to Mr. Ren and the EMT on the Organizational Restructuring Plan of Huawei's Business Controls Departments, EMT Meeting Minutes No. [2008] 017)*

During organizational restructuring, field managers may not strictly follow rules, regulations, or methodologies when exercising the authority delegated to them, so enhanced oversight is necessary. Finance and audit departments need to constantly perform spot checks at key checkpoints during the oversight process and establish deterrence to ensure the proper exercise of authority. *(Ren Zhengfei: Timely, Accurate, High Quality, and Low Cost Delivery Calls for Professional Process-compliant CFOs—Minutes of a Meeting with Trainees of the CFO Session of the Reserve Pool, Huawei Executive Office Speech No. [2009] 021)*

Audit must be lenient to those who admit their mistakes and be strict with those who don't. We can offer lighter penalties to those who admit their mistakes, to encourage others to do the same. Once a problem is found, Audit must keep chipping away at it until they uncover the truth. Do not try to get ideal results; instead, hold on to the truth using a targeted approach. Don't invest too much making everything 100% clear; instead, close a case when 20–30% of the evidence is sufficient to reach a conclusion. Even in such a case though, we reserve the right to continue investigations at a later date. This is an imperfect world, so it is impractical to seek perfection. *(Ren Zhengfei: Minutes of the Report on Work Responsibilities of Business Controls and Internal Controls/Internal Audit and Their Relationships, EMT Meeting Minutes No. [2008] 034)*

At Huawei, the Internal Audit Department plays an independent oversight role in anti-corruption, anti-fraud, and anti-waste activities. The primary goal of this is to establish cold deterrence. The Internal Audit Department must also help set rules, implement a process ownership system, and build a culture of integrity. *(Source: Minutes of a Report on the Strategic Plan of the Internal Audit Department, EMT Meeting Minutes No. [2014] 025)*

We currently have an inspection and audit system in place. The Inspection Department is responsible for spot-checks of onsite activities. They investigate thoroughly, identify loopholes, and create solutions. The Audit Department is responsible for looking deeper into issues once they have been identified. I once said that we must not investigate managers randomly, and that we must not use approaches such as eavesdropping or spying on the communications of others. We must use appropriate means to gather factual evidence, and the investigation approach needs to be voted on by the managers' upper-level organizations following the majority rule. We should put in place our inspection and audit system before issues arise. This is the right way to manage managers, show care to them, and protect them. *(Ren Zhengfei: Speech at the Mid-year Workshop on the*

Enablement of Subsidiary Board Directors, Huawei Executive Office Speech No. [2015] 082)
I have said that, "If an audit finds 30% of the problems, that's enough to draw a conclusion." When I said 30%, I meant that you have to get right to the bottom of a specific problem. Investigate thoroughly or not at all. If you get halfway through an investigation and then switch to a new problem, then the audit will be ineffective. When you are investigating one problem, if it leads to a broader set of problems and you lose your focus, then you're not achieving that 30% clarity. You're going the wrong way. What you have to do is find one thread and follow it right to its end. Be sure to understand every detail, and let the subject of the investigation see that you have both the capabilities and methods. Then when you turn to look at the next problem, they will know whether they ought to volunteer to tell you about other mistakes they have made. *(Ren Zhengfei: Speech at the Report on Optimizing the Delegation of Authority and Process for Internal Investigations, 2015)*

15.4.2 Strengthening Legal Deterrence and Tightening Accountability Criteria Every Year

We will strengthen legal deterrence, increase accountability criteria year by year, and align our internal regulations with the law within the next three years. We need to rely more on legal forces to ensure deterrence. As long as we find 30% of the evidence to prove that an employee has violated the law, we can turn them over to the relevant legal authorities. If the wrongdoer is willing to confess everything, we can reconsider their case, but if they don't, we will hand them over to the legal authorities. If law enforcement bodies get involved, it doesn't matter if the employee confesses or not. This is how we ensure deterrence. *(Ren Zhengfei: Speech at a Briefing on the Progress of Large-scale Elimination of Corruption, Huawei Executive Office Speech No. [2014] 010)*

The multiplier for repayments by wrongdoers to the company should be increased each year to raise the cost of wrongdoing. For example, this year it is 1, next year 1.1, and so on, increasing year by year. If someone confesses their wrongdoing, then their repayment amount can be reduced a little. In the future, we can consider making this multiplier public to establish deterrence, so that everyone knows the true cost of wrongdoing. *(Ren Zhengfei: Speech at the Report on Optimizing the Delegation of Authority and Process for Internal Investigations, 2015)*

We must not allow problems to continue unchecked. If a problem has become very serious, to the point where it could impact the company, then we must take action. If a case involves illegal activities, in principle we handle it as the law says. But we do not have to take things to extremes. Where we can, we will allow wrongdoers to turn over a new leaf. However, those who reject our generosity though are beyond our help. *(Ren Zhengfei: Speech at the Report on Optimizing the Delegation of Authority and Process for Internal Investigations, 2015)*

We need to improve our accountability system. During the transition, we established integrity accounts, which provided wrongdoers with an opportunity to correct their mistakes and gain a fresh start. We have now closed these accounts. You need to be stricter with yourselves. Closing the accounts doesn't mean we are relaxing efforts to fight corruption. Instead, we are further strengthening the constraints placed on our team. One approach we may also take is to turn cases over to the local legal authorities. By developing this accountability system, we hope that our employees will follow the right rules and work conscientiously. *(Ren Zhengfei: Internal and External Compliance to Generate More Revenue and Pave the Way for the Company's Future Success—Speech at a Meeting with the Oversight Team, Huawei Executive Office Speech No. [2017] 002)*

15.4.3 Separating Investigations from Disciplinary Actions

We should always keep a few key principles in mind. First, daily operations and human resources should be managed separately. The Supervisory Board and the Audit Committee have authority over daily operations. The HRC has authority over human resources. As for how the HRC delegates authority to lower levels, we can define another set of rules. The HRC needs to develop rules for managerial discipline. *(Ren Zhengfei: Speech on the Audit Committee's 2014 Annual Work Report at the January Board of Directors Meeting, Huawei Executive Office Speech No. [2015] 017)*

We must strictly follow the principle of separating investigations and disciplinary actions. Investigations must be rigorous, but we should remain lenient when taking disciplinary actions. We need to be both lenient and strict with our managers. Being strict means we are rigorous during the process of finding out facts. If there is something we ought to know about, then we need to find it out. But when it comes to taking disciplinary action, we will be as lenient as we can. This will ensure Audit uncovers and reports on the facts, including everything they think may be relevant, like the attitude of the subject of the investigation and whether they have made significant contributions to the case under investigation. Disciplinary actions will be taken by the HRC Disciplinary and Supervisory Sub-committee. This is the separation we want between investigations and disciplinary actions. *(Ren Zhengfei: Speech at the Report on Optimizing the Delegation of Authority and Process for Internal Investigations, 2015)*

When it comes to disciplinary actions, we must learn to put ourselves in the shoes of the wrongdoers, not just our own position. It is unjust to be overly heavy-handed with our discipline. You can talk as much as you want to the HRC Disciplinary and Supervisory Sub-committee, but our disciplinary actions must not be too rigid. We should allow a certain amount of flexibility, and we must listen to what the wrongdoer has to say. Even before we hand someone over to the legal authorities, we can still listen to what they have to say. Of course, if they are not willing to talk to us, then we will have to let the legal authorities talk to them. However, if a wrongdoer is willing to talk to us, we can be lenient with our discipline, within reason, even if they have committed a serious fault. Our primary purpose is to keep our organization clean and warn everyone against doing bad things. Our measurement of punishments is not designed to target particular individuals. *(Ren Zhengfei: Speech at the Report on Optimizing the Delegation of Authority and Process for Internal Investigations, 2015)*

We need to have strict principles and disciplinary procedures that specify which level of department can investigate which managers. Investigators can give their own opinions, but they do not have the authority to discipline those under investigation – this authority is held by the HRC Disciplinary and Supervisory Sub-Committee. *(Ren Zhengfei: Speech at a Meeting with the Managerial Control Elite Team, Huawei Executive Office Speech No. [2015] 060)*

When we investigate an incident, we can share all clarified results with management teams at all levels, but some say that sharing information leads to leaks. In that case though, if the leak makes the wrongdoer stop doing what they are doing wrong, then we will have achieved our objective. Catching someone doing something wrong is not our goal because our colleagues are not our enemies. We simply want to clarify the issue during the investigation and wipe the slate clean for those involved so they can start again and become heroes. *(Ren Zhengfei: Speech at a Meeting with the Managerial Control Elite Team, Huawei Executive Office Speech No. [2015] 060)*

In addition to one or two spot audits during a manager's tenure, we should also conduct an audit when they leave their position. Then, everyone will feel that audits are normal at Huawei. *(Ren Zhengfei: Speech at a Meeting with the Managerial Control Elite Team, Huawei Executive Office Speech No. [2015] 060)*

At every key decision point of an investigation, decisions must be made according to the majority rule.

First, you must stick to the principle of collective decision making through votes by majority rule at every stage of an investigation, from launching the investigation, communication, and approval, to deciding on legal involvement. Business decisions can be left in the hands of the manager, but investigations into people cannot be the responsibility of only one person. No individual has the authority to approve or reject investigations into people. We stick to the majority rule, but the department head can chair meetings. We must avoid anyone abusing their authority to form cliques. No single manager has the authority to directly order an investigation into someone. Investigations must not become a tool for making people with different ideas suffer; otherwise, we will start to get cliques within the company. On this issue, we'd better be a bit conservative. We are all in favor of proactive auditing, but there have to be checks on authority, and the majority rule creates checks and balances.

Second, once an investigation has been started, it must reach a conclusion, and must be strictly confidential while it is ongoing. Every investigation must produce a result. Preliminary inquiries are not investigations. In general we do not accept anonymous complaints, but if an anonymous tip seems to have some substance, you may make preliminary inquiries. This does not constitute an investigation. As with the legal authorities, once an investigation is formally launched, it cannot be abandoned. There must be a conclusion. During an investigation, we must ensure that there are no leaks, neither from the decision-makers, nor from the investigators themselves. If information is leaked before the facts of a matter have been gathered and a conclusion has been reached, then how are the subject of the investigation and their manager supposed to work? *(Ren Zhengfei: Speech at the Report on Optimizing the Delegation of Authority and Process for Internal Investigations, 2015)*

In the future, we must have boundaries for our oversight. Daily operations and human resources must be managed separately, and we must be careful when investigating people. We cannot arbitrarily oversee or snoop on our managers. Investigation into managers is a process of collecting facts and reasoning things out. The higher-level management team of the manager under investigation should make decisions by following the majority rule. If a consensus cannot be reached, the matter needs to be escalated to the management team at a higher level, which still needs to follow the majority rule. *(Ren Zhengfei: Speech at the Report on Optimizing the Delegation of Authority and Process for Internal Investigations, 2015)*

We know that some managers are not good enough. It is fine that you voice your opinions about them, but you must have evidence. You cannot randomly accuse someone of stealing your axe when it is missing. Investigations into managers must follow the proper approval procedures. Once the facts have been gathered, you can submit the case to the HRC Disciplinary and Supervisory Sub-Committee for disciplinary actions. *(Ren Zhengfei: Speech at a Meeting with the Managerial Control Elite Team, Huawei Executive Office Speech No. [2015] 060)*

Showcasing contributions and enumerating merits are not the responsibility of our audit personnel. These activities are the responsibility of the highest levels of management. Contributions and mistakes are two different things. Auditing should be based on facts and aim to bring clarity to a situation. The HRC Disciplinary and Supervisory Sub-committee is responsible for discipline. This separates investigation from discipline. We should also separate contributions from mistakes. If we tolerate the mistakes of those who have made contributions, we will not be able to establish iron discipline. Our audit personnel should be independent, stick to principles, and adopt appropriate approaches. I hope that our audit personnel will have both the courage and tact to fight against corruption. We need to develop a team that is courageous and able to stick to principles. This is very important to the company. *(Ren Zhengfei: Internal and External Compliance to Generate More Revenue and Pave the Way for the Company's Future Success—Speech at a Meeting with the Oversight Team, Huawei Executive Office Speech No. [2017] 002)*

15.4.4 Oversight Is the Best Way to Care for and Protect Our Managers

While making our anti-corruption policies stricter, we will continue the policy of allowing employees to declare their own wrongdoing. This is a principle of being both strict and lenient, aiming to cure the disease and save the patient. Don't suppose that we will not hold people accountable for past wrongdoings. Without accountability, we won't establish cold deterrence. We need to establish cold deterrence so that our employees will not violate the *BCG* rules in the first place. Therefore, if you have already done something wrong, please report this voluntarily as soon as you can. Get them off your chest. Senior managers should take the lead in doing this to set an example. We should publicize it so that people know, through the offices of ethics and compliance (OECs), to send the message of a harder crackdown on *BCG* violations across the company. Cases which have been passed on to the legal authorities can be published on the company's bulletin board as well. *(Ren Zhengfei: Speech at a Briefing on the Progress of Large-scale Elimination of Corruption, Huawei Executive Office Speech No. [2014] 010)*

When it comes to overseeing managers, we need to be both strict and lenient.

1. We don't exercise oversight for the sake of oversight, but to scale new heights for our business.
2. We need to develop documents that give specific details about the standards that we can use to discipline managers. We should let employees know what will happen to them after their wrongdoing is discovered. They should also be aware of how lenient we can be. Making our standards public is a kind of deterrence. We want employees to know that they must not cross the line, as that will ruin their career. However, they will be all right if they choose to step back. This is a good way to prevent wrongdoing among our employees in the first place.
3. When we deal with managers, it's not an "us or them" situation. We have to apply a certain amount of *huidu*. We have to give managers, or any employees, the chance to correct their mistakes and move on. We are becoming increasingly scientific in our management, which makes major problems less likely to occur. When we do have to slap their wrist, we can do it with a feather duster, not a baseball bat. Make no mistake though, there must be penalties. The CEC needs to rate the severity of integrity issues in its files; during disciplinary actions, we must also distinguish serious issues from minor ones. If someone manages to keep their nose clean for long enough, their record can be wiped clean. That way we are both strict and lenient. Everyone will correct their mistakes, and with the past behind them, they will be more determined to forge ahead. *(Source: Minutes of the Report on the Work Priority of the Company for Building an Oversight and Accountability System, EMT Meeting Minutes No. [2015] 013)*

An audit is like a medical intervention: The goal is to cure the disease and save the patient. The company and business departments can decide how to deploy wrongdoers according to the nature of their violations and their improvements. Even a wrongdoer should be given the chance to clearly explain themselves and correct their mistakes. Once a person has made things right, their past should be left behind. They should have a way to move forward and an opportunity to showcase their better side. *(Ren Zhengfei: Speech on the Audit Committee's 2014 Annual Work Report at the January Board of Directors Meeting, Huawei Executive Office Speech No. [2015] 017)*

The right way to go about this work is to be responsible for the people under investigation. You need to help them understand their mistakes and get issues off their chest. Second, you have to select the right investigators based on the seniority of the people involved and the severity of the incident. You need the right strategy for the investigation. To be explicit about it, when the subjects of your investigation are senior and older members of staff, you have to send experienced investigators, even including their department heads in your investigation team. Where an issue does not involve any illegal activity (for example, claiming private expenses from the company), you should apply *huidu*. Not everything has to be dealt in absolute black and white. You should let the person involved retain a bit of dignity, and believe that Huawei employees are prepared to correct their mistakes once they are aware of their wrongdoings. *(Ren Zhengfei: Speech on the Audit Committee's 2014 Annual Work Report at the January Board of Directors Meeting, Huawei Executive Office Speech No. [2015] 017)*

To err is human. When we find that a manager makes a small mistake, we can take appropriate disciplinary actions against them to remind them not to do so again. This way, the manager may grow into a great man in the future. This is how we care for our managers. However, if we do not let them know they've made a small mistake, this manager may make a bigger one later and ruin their future. This is not caring for our managers. *(Source: Oversight Is the Best Way to Care for Managers, EMT Resolution No. [2016] 007)*

Developing a manager is not easy. I feel it a great pain each time the Board of Directors Executive Committee reports the disciplining of a manager. In fact, managers benefit more from contributing to the company than from fraud or corruption. Total reward at Huawei is competitive, even more so for senior managers. It isn't worthwhile for them to engage in wrongdoings for small gains. The way we audit managers upon their departure and during their tenure is actually a kind of care for them. This helps them avoid doing irredeemable things. If they commit a crime, they might end up in prison, which is miserable. They will feel even worse after we change our approach and turn cases over to the local legal authorities. *(Ren Zhengfei: Internal and External Compliance to Generate More Revenue and Pave the Way for the Company's Future Success—Speech at a Meeting with the Oversight Team, Huawei Executive Office Speech No. [2017] 002)*

15.4.5 Audit: Assuming Innocence Until Proven Guilty and Taking Appropriate Disciplinary Actions Against Mistakes at Work

In our company, Audit must assume the subject of the investigation is innocent until proven guilty. You must be responsible for employees and managers. Whatever you do, don't turn it into a battle against the person under investigation. Policies and strategies are our lives. The audit results must help unite our employees. *(Source: Requirements of Audit Work, EMT Resolution No. [2010] 019)*

The requirements of the company regarding auditing and audit personnel are outlined as follows: Audit must implement organizational controls and create rules for their work. These rules should cover the selection of a subject, the content and scope of auditing, ways to obtain evidence, ways to assign someone to talk with the subject, the content and scope of communication, and so on. All these things must be approved by the organization. Approval levels will vary by grade, depending on the seniority of the subject and the content of the audit. An audit of the president of a level-1 department or a more senior position must be approved by the Huawei Executive Office. An audit of the director of a level-2 department or a more senior managerial position must be approved by the HRC. Audits of other employees must be approved by level-1 management teams. As for financial *BCG* violations, audit personnel cannot speak with the subject unless they have irrefutable evidence. Such communication must also stay within the scope of their authority. When you perform an audit, be careful not to go beyond the scope set forth by the organization. There must be an end to every audit; otherwise, employees would just live in fear. The subject of an audit is not our enemy. If new clues outside the approved work scope are found during the audit, you must ask an appropriate manager to decide whether to continue or adjust the audit. The audit scope must not be extended at will. Audit must operate within the scope of authority of the Internal Audit Department. Currently, Audit manages problems related to violations of the law, and company rules and regulations. Other issues are still in the hands of management teams at all levels. Audit must not go beyond the scope of their own authority. *(Source: Requirements of Audit Work, EMT Resolution No. [2010] 019)*

Audit personnel must build up their strength. You auditing people must learn how to treat others with respect. Get off your high horse. You must be committed to principles and follow them well. *(Source: Requirements of Audit Work, EMT Resolution No. [2010] 019)*

I think our audits should be based on the following four principles. First, our basic assumption should be that the vast majority of Huawei employees and the vast majority of our activities are good. Individual instances of rule breaking are not the result of ill motives; they are more often caused by ignorance or unawareness. The number of people who intentionally break the rules is very few. This means that we should exercise oversight out of care for employees. Second, we should value facts and evidence. We must stand in the shoes of the subject of the audit and avoid subjective judgment. Don't rush to a conclusion. We should make employees and managers feel relaxed, instead of terrified. Even if someone breaks rules, we need to give them the chance to fully explain themselves and correct their mistakes. Third, we should allow leniency when wrongdoers admit their mistakes. Once a person has corrected their mistakes, their past should be left behind. They should have an opportunity to showcase their better side. If we fail to do this, many people will be forced to take the road to ruin. Fourth, Audit must be a department that unites our employees together. *(Ren Zhengfei: Implementing Oversight with Care, Huawei Executive Office Speech No. [2011] 013)*

I believe that our company is increasingly open-minded. However, our oversight is becoming more stringent. We are opening up on the basis of this increasingly stringent oversight, rather than doing so randomly. *(Ren Zhengfei: Implementing Oversight with Care, Huawei Executive Office Speech No. [2011] 013)*

We must delegate appropriate authority to lower levels, align their authority with their responsibilities, and build an environment in which everyone is taking on greater responsibilities. Managers at all levels must fulfill their job responsibilities. On top of this, the company needs to delegate appropriate authority to them. When it comes to accountability, we must distinguish between *BCG* violations and mistakes at work. The company has a very clear accountability framework in place for *BCG* violations. If a mistake is made during work, we must analyze it in detail and take appropriate disciplinary actions. *(Ren Zhengfei: Unite as Many People as Possible—Speech at the Self-reflection Session of the Board of Directors Executive Committee, Huawei Executive Office Speech No. [2013] 143)*

The purpose of investigations is to save our managers. First of all, don't be too fast to divide the world into friends and enemies. There are a lot of gradations between those two extremes, and you don't have to scour this company for every last speck of dirt. Relax that hair trigger a little. You need a sense of moderation. Second, we should value the careers of our managers. Since the goal of an investigation is to save our people, we should begin to increase transparency in our work. The company is gradually becoming more disciplined, and what we need when resolving many problems is transparency, not covert investigations. Our goal is to save our managers, not to punish them. Don't tell me that we have to be covert to catch them in the act. Letting them know that the company sees what they are doing will stop their wrongdoing. That is one of our objectives. We have to value our managers. We have invested a lot of time and effort developing them, so now we have to remind them that they still have the chance to correct their mistakes: They can admit what they've done, return any corrupt earnings, and make good the company's losses. That at least will stop them from making any more mistakes. At the end of the day, our objective is to motivate everyone to fight hard, rather than turning Huawei into a kindergarten. Kindergartens are full of pure, innocent kids, but Huawei is not a kindergarten. Third, we must not snoop on our managers. We must treat people with respect, and respect their human rights. If you're watching over people left, right, and center, then no one will feel safe. And then how will the company function? If you have evidence, present it. *(Ren Zhengfei: Speech at the Report on Optimizing the Delegation of Authority and Process for Internal Investigations, 2015)*

The primary responsibility of the CEC is to discover good people. Don't twist it to help those who aren't keeping up. When it comes to manager oversight, our starting assumption must always be that they are all good people, so we help them to work better, and to steer clear of high-voltage lines. Another aspect is employee education (this includes identifying and promoting good people, guiding the majority through praise, encouraging self-education, and providing remedial training). The CEC will be responsible for this. *(Ren Zhengfei: Speech at the Meeting with the*

CEC on Improving the Use of Non-monetary Incentives, Huawei Executive Office Speech No. [2014] 085)
The ability to compromise is invaluable to the company, and the audit system must be able to compromise. It is this compromise that helps establish cold deterrence. Slap their wrists with a feather duster. Managers are wise people and will get the message. What exactly does this deterrence do for us? To answer this question, we can look at the company's return on investment and our financial report. Overall, we have a very fine team of managers in this company. There are problems, and we should deal with them, but we need to think about how to go about this. We need to be gentle. It is not easy to develop a manager, so unless there are ill motives, we should educate the wrongdoers for the majority of problems and let bygones be bygones. The HRC needs to develop rules for disciplining managers. *(Ren Zhengfei: Speech on the Audit Committee's 2014 Annual Work Report at the January Board of Directors Meeting, Huawei Executive Office Speech No. [2015] 017)*
In the reporting outline, there should be a section explaining things from the perspective of the person under audit. We must fully understand their circumstances and their responses. At the same time, we have to stick to the facts. Sticking to the facts may just be four words, but it is not an easy thing to do, not easy at all! Whatever you do, don't turn the process into a battle against the person under audit. We still need to motivate more people to fight on our side. It's easy to impose penalties; but it's hard to help a person with a checkered past get back onto their feet. Many heroes from our history books had huge flaws, and there is no such thing as a perfect person. The reason Wang Anshi[2] failed was that he insisted drawing a clear line between black and white. With our managers, we must assume they are innocent until proven guilty. China is a country that places great emphasis on the rule of law, and we have to respect human rights. It is better to leave some things unclear than to harm our own people. You must not walk into someone's home and start insulting them. Above all, don't let the children of the person under investigation know the investigation is going on. This can be emotionally damaging. *(Ren Zhengfei: Speech on the*

---

[2] Wang Anshi (December 8, 1021–May 21, 1086) was a Chinese economist, statesman, chancellor, and poet of the Song Dynasty who attempted major and controversial socioeconomic reforms known as the New Policies. His reform program was doomed to fail because too many interest groups resisted the reforms.

Audit Committee's 2014 Annual Work Report at the January Board of Directors Meeting, Huawei Executive Office Speech No. [2015] 017)
Audit personnel need to make friends with the subjects of investigations. Audit has to help the subjects find evidence to prove their innocence and clear them of any mistakes. You can't get to the bottom of things unless the subjects see you as a friend. You have to remember this truth: Audit personnel must not be afraid to be by-the-book in order to obtain the truth. *(Ren Zhengfei: Speech on the Audit Committee's 2014 Annual Work Report at the January Board of Directors Meeting, Huawei Executive Office Speech No. [2015] 017)*

The HRC Disciplinary and Supervisory Sub-committee should be lenient and rescue people by curing their diseases. But the ATs of business departments should make stricter suggestions. We can't expect leniency at every layer of management. There have to be limits to our leniency; otherwise, how would ATs manage other employees? *(Ren Zhengfei: Speech at the Report on Optimizing the Delegation of Authority and Process for Internal Investigations, 2015)*

First, our audit aims to conclude that someone is innocent. You must have evidence. Without evidence, you must not randomly discredit a manager. You also need to adopt a scientific approach, base your judgment on facts, and respect human rights. Managers should be strict with themselves and try not to make mistakes. When mistakes are made, sympathy won't help. If we showed sympathy to those who made mistakes, we would ultimately harm good people. Currently, over 90% of Huawei employees are good people, so we must not let a few bad apples ruin our company. Even if you have evidence, you should still be reasonable, forceful, and moderate. You should never consider your actions to be a merciless blow, as such an approach does not solve problems. *(Ren Zhengfei: Internal and External Compliance to Generate More Revenue and Pave the Way for the Company's Future Success—Speech at a Meeting with the Oversight Team, Huawei Executive Office Speech No. [2017] 002)*

Open Access This chapter is licensed under the terms of the Creative Commons Attribution-NonCommercial-NoDerivatives 4.0 International License (http://creativecommons.org/licenses/by-nc-nd/4.0/), which permits any noncommercial use, sharing, distribution and reproduction in any medium or format, as long as you give appropriate credit to the original author(s) and the source, provide a link to the Creative Commons licence and indicate if you modified the licensed material. You do not have permission under this license to share adapted material derived from this chapter or parts of it.

The images or other third party material in this chapter are included in the chapter's Creative Commons licence, unless indicated otherwise in a credit line to the material. If material is not included in the chapter's Creative Commons licence and your intended use is not permitted by statutory regulation or exceeds the permitted use, you will need to obtain permission directly from the copyright holder.

CHAPTER 16

Digital Financial Management

Data is the company's most important asset. We must manage data in the same way as we manage capital. Data is our strategic resource. As we comprehensively mine our data and use it more effectively, we are constantly uncovering and creating new opportunities and new value. High-quality data delivers multiple benefits: effective deployment of human resources, streamlined management, integrated business processes, higher operating efficiency, and more transparency in our business performance.

Data accuracy is the foundation for effective internal controls. To ensure the quality of our data, we need to ensure that all of our business data comes from a single source and is therefore traceable and that our business forecasts are reliable. Business process owners take full responsibility for the quality of the data generated from business transactions.

What should our financial management system look like in the era of big data? It should deliver data-driven business insights and ensure a balance between efficiency and control. The core goal of this system is to support sustainable and profitable growth. Finance needs to explore how to use data to provide business insights for all other departments across the company. Finance also needs to explore how to ensure effective control and risk management through optimized business models, resource allocation, and capital structure, as well as business and process transformations. The ultimate goal of Finance is to improve efficiency and drive sustainable and profitable growth of the company.

The motto of our IT department is "Building roads is the first step to wealth." A large company needs to rely on automation, IT, and digital technologies to ensure smooth operations. In the field of accounting, it should actively pilot automation and the use of AI, handing over the accounting for standard scenarios to machines.

This chapter briefly describes how Huawei's Finance is going digital with clean data in the era of big data.

16.1 Data Is a Strategic Resource

16.1.1 Managing Data in the Same Way as Managing Capital

Data is one of the most critical elements in building the company's processes and management system. Smooth data flow is key to integrating our processes and supporting efficient operations of our management system. Data is our strategic asset, and data accuracy is the foundation for effective internal controls. Effective data management helps ensure data consistency, integrity, and accuracy throughout a process. It can also help improve operating efficiency, make well-informed decisions, ensure ICFR, and achieve other management goals. *(Source: Resolution on Data Management, EMT Resolution No. [2016] 001)*

We must take a holistic view at advances in our overall management system. We should build a well-coordinated management system and integrate processes from end to end in order to avoid silos caused by isolated transformations. We must also respect facts and prevent lies to ensure the consistency of business and accounts. Whenever possible, we should try to skip steps in the handover of internal operations data, as long as the necessary separation of duties is observed. This can help increase operating efficiency. *(Ren Zhengfei: Applying the Spirit of the Tortoise to Catch up with the Dragon Spacecraft—Speech at Huawei Annual Management Conference 2013, Huawei Executive Office Speech No. [2013] 255)*

Data is the company's most important asset, and data accuracy is the foundation for effective internal controls. Effective management of data value and risks can help streamline internal management, integrate business processes, improve operating efficiency, and create a clearer picture of actual business performance. *(Source: Huawei Data Management Overview, Corp. Doc. No. [2014] 005)*

In the era of big data, data has become a new type of economic asset, like hard currency or gold. We must manage data in the same way as we manage capital. We should use data to support our management, decisions, and innovation, which will drive sustainable and profitable growth of the company. Data is the most dazzling gem in our company's commercial crown. *(Guo Ping: Financial Management in the Era of Big Data—Speech at the 2013 Annual Meeting of Finance, Improvement Issue No. 423, 2013)*

Why do we place so much emphasis on data? The reason is quite simple. In today's business world, companies are like large ships afloat on an ocean of data. Only those that are able to sail on the blue ocean by leveraging big data capabilities can get rich returns. *(Guo Ping: Financial Management in the Era of Big Data—Speech at the 2013 Annual Meeting of Finance, Improvement Issue No. 423, 2013)*

Here are our takeaways regarding the implementation of the IPD process. Streamlined information in business flows is the basis for defining a process and an IT application architecture. This information is also the foundation for developing IT systems. Integrating major processes is essentially about smooth data flows. Data management is at the very heart of process and IT management. That's why we should take data seriously. *(Xu Zhijun: Thoughts on the Relationships Between Business, Processes, IT, Quality, and Operations, Improvement Issue No. 421, 2013)*

William Edwards Deming, the father of modern quality management, said: "In God we trust, all others must bring data." Data is the lifeblood of a company, and is the very soul of Finance. It is the smallest and the most accurate building block for logic within a business. *(Guo Ping: Financial Management in the Era of Big Data—Speech at the 2013 Annual Meeting of Finance, Improvement Issue No. 423, 2013)*

16.1.2 Fully Leveraging Data Resources to Create New Competitive Advantages

Data is our unique resource. Our IT systems, processes, and organization may be copied or imitated by others. Our employees may find a new job in another company. Only data truly belongs to us. If we can fully leverage our data resources to create innovative products and provide differentiated services to our customers, we can build core competencies that set us apart from our competitors. *(Guo Ping: Financial Management in the Era of Big Data—Speech at the 2013 Annual Meeting of Finance, Improvement Issue No. 423, 2013)*

Data has become an increasingly valuable resource in the information society. As we comprehensively mine our data and use it more effectively, we are constantly uncovering and creating new opportunities and new value. During his two presidential campaigns, Barack Obama fully leveraged data analytics and data modeling. This enabled him to see the big picture and allocate resources to locations where he was most likely to win votes. *(Meng Wanzhou: Discovering the Beauty of Data, 2013)*

Finance must shift its focus from the past to the future. To make this shift, Finance must consider how to use data to better understand business trends and better support decision making. This will allow Finance to play a bigger role in driving the company's sustainable and profitable growth. *(Guo Ping: Financial Management in the Era of Big Data—Speech at the 2013 Annual Meeting of Finance, Improvement Issue No. 423, 2013)*

We can use data analytics to enhance our customer- and supplier-facing roles. This way, we can create new competitive advantages and improve our sources of profits. In particular, we can determine the most suitable contract terms and payment terms based on in-depth analyses of our customers and suppliers. We can also provide them with customized financial solutions through our analytics platform. We can collect and analyze post-sales data in real time, and provide inputs for post-sales services, product quality control, and product design. We can also improve our demand forecasts and supply plans to increase inventory turnover. *(Guo Ping: Financial Management in the Era of Big Data—Speech at the 2013 Annual Meeting of Finance, Improvement Issue No. 423, 2013)*

We can use big data analytics to fully mine and analyze massive amounts of data regarding what our customers need. This will help us better understand our customers and work with them to create value. We need to analyze the massive amounts of data about contracts, orders, projects, configurations, inventory, and logistics within our company. This is vital to support timely, accurate, high-quality, and low-cost delivery. By applying big data analytics to human resources, we can optimize our approach to staffing and ensure that high-quality resources are allocated to valued customers. *(Ren Zhengfei: Speech at the Awards Ceremony for Whiz Kids, Huawei Executive Office Speech No. [2014] 039)*

16.2 DATA CLEANING IS THE MOST EFFECTIVE APPROACH FOR INTERNAL CONTROLS

16.2.1 Ensuring Data Quality from the Source

We must take data quality seriously and manage it from the source. There is still a lot of room for improvement when it comes to financial data accuracy and reliability. Data is not created by Finance; instead, all financial data comes from business. This is why I emphasize that data accuracy must be managed at the source in our business. If those who create data provide distorted data, Finance will be unable to effectively support operations and manage risks. *(Meng Wanzhou: IFS: Working with Business Teams to Comprehensively Improve the Capabilities of Financial Staff, Improvement Issue No. 407, 2012)*

Our business and financial teams must assume joint responsibility for data accuracy. The business team must hand over complete, accurate, and clear data to the financial team, and the financial team must process this data following the established regulations, rules, and processes. Managers should not interfere with process operations. They can only propose or initiate process optimization. The authenticity and accuracy of financial data depends on standardized front-end processes and clean data. The accounting department should face difficulties head on, assigning their best employees to field offices and integrating accounting requirements into their operations. Accounting personnel should get involved in the business to implement accounting requirements. The quality of financial data will only improve when front-end operations are standardized. *(Ren Zhengfei: Speech at a Meeting with Staff in Mauritius, Huawei Executive Office Speech No. [2013] 016)*

Business management at Huawei is data-based. Inaccurate basic data will result in inaccurate reporting data for business management activities. Inaccurate data doesn't truly reflect the nature of our business, nor can it serve as an effective guide for business management. *(Xu Zhijun: Thoughts on the Relationships Between Business, Processes, IT, Quality, and Operations, Improvement Issue No. 421, 2013)*

Key data must come from a single source. Data must be entered at a single point and made available at multiple points. Data quality must be assured from its source. *(Source: Huawei Data Management Overview, Corp. Doc. No. [2014] 005)*

Ideally, every procedure will create unique value, deliver exactly what the downstream procedure needs, and meet the quality requirements during this procedure. *(Xu Zhijun: Thoughts on the Relationships Between Business, Processes, IT, Quality, and Operations, Improvement Issue No. 421, 2013)*

There are many factors that may affect the quality of data. Specifically, there are issues with data itself (like architecture, standards, integration, and IT compliance), business execution (unclear rules or improper execution), and BCG compliance (business fraud or provision of false information). *(Meng Wanzhou: Minutes of the Report on Data Work, 2015)*

To get the process flowing, we first need smooth data flows. Why is a river crystal clear? Because fresh water flows from the spring. Data must be transmitted accurately and efficiently if we want to make it visible and easy-to-use throughout the process. That is what will make our management transparent. Currently, our data is not accurate and sometimes flows even more slowly than physical goods. This is mainly because we have not paid enough attention to data recording. The responsibility for keeping data flowing is not clearly defined. To address these problems, we first need to make sure data is recorded and recorded accurately, and that records are kept by experienced employees. Academic credentials should not be overemphasized. Data also needs to flow fast. Let's learn from high-speed rail networks. They have an ownership system every step of the way, ensuring things run on schedule and by the book. *(Ren Zhengfei: Speech at the Oath-taking and Awards Ceremony of the Transformation Elite Team, Huawei Executive Office Speech No. [2015] 047)*

In 2017, we aim to reach the level of "Basically satisfactory" for our overall data quality. That means we need to ensure that all of our business data comes from a single source and is therefore traceable and that our business forecasts are reliable. *(Source: Resolution on Data Management, EMT Resolution No. [2016] 001)*

High-quality data is the prerequisite and foundation for the use of AI. When we finish each procedure in our work, our first job is to look at whether high-quality data has been delivered. AI relies on data collected by thousands of employees, and then analyzes that data to find underlying patterns. Therefore, it is critical that we obtain clean and accurate data in the field. *(Ren Zhengfei: Speech at the GTS Workshop on the Use of AI, Huawei Executive Office Speech No. [2017] 034)*

16.2.2 Whoever Creates Data Must Be Responsible for Data Quality

Business managers must be responsible for process compliance, ensure that business data is accurate, timely, and standardized, and prevent their departments from committing fraud. They also need to have basic financial management capabilities and should take responsibility for oversight.

Inaccurate and non-standardized business data will make it impossible to produce accurate financial reports. *(Ren Zhengfei: Building a Highly Competitive Team—Speech at the Q3 Regional Presidents' Meeting, Huawei Executive Office Speech No. [2013] 093)*

Whoever creates data must be responsible for the quality of the data. Data owners should develop data quality criteria that are in line with users' requirements and gain consent from any key departments that use the data. *(Source: Huawei Data Management Overview, Corp. Doc. No. [2014] 005)*

Data quality needs to be managed at two levels. The first level involves transformation teams and GPOs, who must manage data structures, standards, integration, and sources. The other level is the representative offices and SPDTs, who must be responsible for data quality at the source. GPOs must take overall responsibility for data quality, and establish and implement effective management mechanisms. The aim is to ensure all data items created within their domains are of high quality. Whoever generates or inputs data must be responsible for the quality of that data. Representative offices, SPDTs, and all their subordinate operating teams are the major sources of data, and therefore must be responsible for the quality of the data they generate. *(Source: Resolution on Data Management, EMT Resolution No. [2016] 001)*

Data is the company's most important asset, and data accuracy is the foundation for effective internal controls. Data owners need to manage data roadmaps, information architecture, data ownership systems, and data quality. They also need to release a termbase for data to unify all language related to data. All transformation projects must be managed in line with the data architecture. Data quality should be assessed by the departments that use the data. Those creating data should be held accountable for any data quality issues. We must clean our data sources and ensure that data is entered at a single point, and made available at multiple points. This can help ensure the quality of company data. *(Source: Minutes of a Report by the Data Work Group, EMT Meeting Minutes No. [2014] 024)*

Business process owners take full responsibility for the quality of business transaction data. They must ensure the accuracy, compliance, timeliness, integrity, and consistency of the raw data generated from business transactions. *(Source: Financial Data Quality Management Policy, Finance Staff Team Doc. No. [2013] 048/Business Process & IT Management Department Doc. No. [2013] 015)*

We must build a unified data foundation at the logic layer to provide accurate, reliable, and consistent data. By doing so, we can support Huawei's digital operations. We must also extensively mine data and extract its value in order to open up our data capabilities. We must manage data based on objects, and define the single source and owner for every piece of data. Data must be shared from the same source and provided as a service to ensure information consistency across platforms and systems. (*Xu Zhijun: Improving and Complying with Our Enterprise Architecture to Support Agile Operations and Deliver a ROADS Experience—Speech at Huawei Enterprise Architecture and Process Management Conference 2016, Improvement Issue No. 518, 2017*)

16.3 MAKING ROUTINE FINANCIAL MANAGEMENT AUTOMATED AND INTELLIGENT, AND LEVERAGING BIG DATA ANALYTICS TO IMPROVE FINANCIAL MANAGEMENT

16.3.1 *The Basis of Scientific Management: Rational Analyses Based on Data and Facts*

We must underline the value of financial data. Financial reports are a window into how business units are doing, and must mirror their business performance in the current period. In financial reports, we should analyze gaps and develop and implement action plans according to the annual budget and rolling forecasts. While referring to historical data and checking against cost baselines, expense baselines, and targets on sales gross margins, we also need to analyze the data trends from multiple perspectives. We need to verify whether the management measures that we have taken are effective. Therefore, data rules must be able to guide management improvements. In addition, the rules must be stable and able to support comparisons with historical data. (*Meng Wanzhou: Aligning Financial Settlements with Value Creation and Aligning Cross Charging for Incentive Purposes with Value Distribution, Huawei Executive Office Speech No. [2012] 040*)

Rational analyses and decision making based on facts and data is actually a process of critical thinking. Critical thinking encourages us to be objective, humble, and fair. Critical thinking is also where creative thinking starts. Complexities in our business management can't be tackled by simply having a willingness to improve or by increasing headcount. This is why we still need to learn from the Whiz Kids. We must leverage the data-

and fact-based scientific management approaches advocated by the Whiz Kids to analyze the root causes of problems and find methodical solutions. *(Ren Zhengfei: Speech at the Awards Ceremony for Whiz Kids, Huawei Executive Office Speech No. [2014] 039)*

Our delivery efficiency needs to be improved. You must begin to improve your own capabilities that are closely related to your work: correctly understanding customer needs; correctly drafting contracts; correctly entering contract information; correctly shipping items; correctly delivering items; and correctly providing services. Every step matters. In the first half of 2015, we had 6.4 million data entry errors. If your data was wrong during this period, then how could you possibly make a correct delivery? Do you have a crystal ball? Once our contract information is correct and the information is properly recorded, there is no excuse for shipment errors. Our stock managers must have enough experience. If they ship the wrong goods because they are unable to understand the orders, then that is enormously wasteful. Therefore, we must first of all correctly understand customer needs in order to get the contract right. But if we don't record the correct contract correctly, there is no way we can ship correctly. And if we don't ship correctly, it is impossible to make the correct delivery. *(Ren Zhengfei: Generals Are Born of Battle—Speech at the 2015 Project Management Summit, Huawei Executive Office Speech No. [2015] 118)*

Our Site Information Database should centrally manage information on sites and site operations (survey data, configuration, inventory, etc.). Data must be entered accurately to minimize the need to re-do any work. We need to achieve consistency of business and accounts. *(Ren Zhengfei: Speech at the GTS Report on the Development of the Site Information, Geographic Information, and Dynamic Network Operations Databases and the Integrated Delivery Platform, Huawei Executive Office Speech No. [2015] 124)*

We must have a standardized form, perhaps in an electronic format, for site information collection. Every person who visits a site should fill out this form, even if it's an emergency visit. It doesn't matter if it is filled out perfectly, and the next time someone goes to the same site, they can download the form filled out previously, and add any items they may have missed. In this way, the accuracy of data will improve. After repeating this process for three to five years, we will have a clear view of all our old accounts, and information regarding our new accounts will be fully available. *(Ren Zhengfei: Speech at the GTS Report on the Development of the Site*

Information, Geographic Information, and Dynamic Network Operations Databases and the Integrated Delivery Platform, Huawei Executive Office Speech No. [2015] 124)

After the IT system is established, we need to make sure that data is carefully recorded every step of the way by people in every position, as this is necessary to reduce waste. There are several reasons for incorrect deliveries. First, the contract may be inaccurate because customer needs are not clearly understood. Second, if the contract is correct, its terms may be incorrectly entered into the system. Third, if the contract terms are correctly entered, the ordered products may be manufactured incorrectly. Finally, if the products are manufactured correctly, they may be shipped to the wrong recipient. Why does this happen? Because the people who ship the items cannot understand the contract. All of these problems result in huge waste for the company. If we can prevent these problems, we can achieve consistency of business and accounts and increase profits. Therefore, we require information to be strictly and accurately recorded. *(Ren Zhengfei: Speech at the GTS Report on the Development of the Site Information, Geographic Information, and Dynamic Network Operations Databases and the Integrated Delivery Platform, Huawei Executive Office Speech No. [2015] 124)*

16.3.2 *Establishing a Future-Proof Data Governance System*

Data management involves three main elements: ICFR data quality, data management system building, and business operations data. Data should be managed in two stages. In the first stage, we should focus on managing ICFR data quality and building a data management system. In the second stage, we should focus on managing business operations data. When setting data quality targets, we should rely on what is being managed, as well as the specific stage of implementation. *(Meng Wanzhou: Minutes of the Report on Data Work, 2015)*

We must always ensure our accounts reflect the true picture. But in the era of big data, we need more than that. We must also provide the smallest and the most accurate set of data, especially baseline data. This is the basic requirement you must meet as a business partner. All financial personnel should let the data speak for itself. Finance should establish business rules, and fully consolidate and analyze data. By doing so, Finance can support business management and help create business models geared toward the future. The era of big data presents both new challenges and opportunities for Finance. This is the biggest opportunity for Finance to leverage data to support company management. *(Guo Ping: Financial Management in the Era of Big Data—Speech at the 2013 Annual Meeting of Finance, Improvement Issue No. 423, 2013)*

We must ensure data is at the very heart of finance. To achieve this, Finance must build a future-oriented data governance system, develop a team of analysts with analytics expertise, and launch a big data strategy that relies on the smallest data set. *(Guo Ping: Financial Management in the Era of Big Data—Speech at the 2013 Annual Meeting of Finance, Improvement Issue No. 423, 2013)*

Data governance should be part of the operations management of the iSee system. We should enhance data governance through the use of data. Without data, there will be no iSee system. *(Source: Resolution on the iSee System, Finance Staff Team Resolution No. [2013] 002)*

Raw data can be processed and converted into information or statements by following pre-set rules. The key is to generate easy-to-understand and valuable information. Information or data can be used, analyzed, and then converted into intelligence that can support business management activities, inform decision making, and reveal risks. The key is to ensure that this intelligence can be effectively leveraged to deliver value. *(Source: Resolution on the iSee System, Finance Staff Team Resolution No. [2013] 002)*

We need to collect, consolidate, and classify data following basic financial rules and the paths of data generation, to prepare basic financial information. Then by combining financial personnel's understanding of data logic and business, we will identify opportunities and set objectives for management improvement during the process of data consolidation, gaining insights, modeling, and data analytics. This is the beauty of financial data. *(Meng Wanzhou: Discovering the Beauty of Data, 2013)*

CFOs have three key roles. They participate in and support strategic decision making, appraise performance and assess value, and act as a chief communication and coordination officer. To effectively fulfill these three roles, CFOs need solid, accurate, and reliable financial data. Financial analysis personnel and CFOs should go beyond data accuracy and delve deeper into the logic of data generation. They need to see both the trees and the forest. *(Meng Wanzhou: Discovering the Beauty of Data, 2013)*

16.3.3 Leveraging Automation, AI, and Big Data Analytics to Reduce the Complexity and Uncertainty of Financial Management

In the era of big data, the core goal of our financial management system is to drive sustainable and profitable business growth

The core value of big data lies in its role in supporting forecasting. Forecasts help us understand business trends and track value transfer trends and their direction. This allows Finance to play a bigger role in future-oriented initiatives like driving sustainable and profitable growth, and optimizing resource allocation and the capital structure. *(Guo Ping: Financial Management in the Era of Big Data—Speech at the 2013 Annual Meeting of Finance, Improvement Issue No. 423, 2013)*

What should our financial management system look like in the era of big data? It should deliver data-driven business insights and ensure a balance between efficiency and control. The core goal of this system is to support sustainable and profitable growth. Finance needs to explore how to use data to provide business insights for all other departments across the company. Finance also needs to explore how to ensure effective control and risk management through optimized business models, resource allocation, and capital structure, as well as business and process transformations. The ultimate goal of Finance is to improve efficiency and drive sustainable and profitable growth of the company. *(Guo Ping: Financial Management in the Era of Big Data—Speech at the 2013 Annual Meeting of Finance, Improvement Issue No. 423, 2013)*

We need to use digital technologies to improve our internal operations and management, enable the fast flow of standard and digital information, and make the information flow transparent throughout the process. We should share information and enhance internal communication while fully mining and analyzing the massive amounts of company data. High-quality resources should be channeled to field offices, to support timely, accurate, high-quality, and low-cost delivery. We must create value together with our valued customers. *(Guo Ping: Transform Continuously and Improve Field Operating Capabilities to Ensure the Company's Sustainable and Profitable Growth—Speech at Huawei Annual Management Conference 2013, Huawei Executive Office Speech No. [2014] 020)*

In the past, one of the hardest jobs in the world was captaining a tanker. You had to know where the shoals lay, how ocean currents flowed, and the right moment to turn the rudder. There was danger everywhere.

The Straits of Malacca are only 24 meters deep, but a 300,000 ton oil tanker might require 24.5 meters of water to prevent it from being grounded, so it must wait for high tide to get through. When the captain steps on the gas pedal, it takes more than 20 minutes for the tanker to actually start accelerating. How does the captain manage the tanker during this 20-plus minutes? I was recently in the Caribbean aboard a 170,000-ton American vessel, and I never saw the helmsman pilot the vessel, even docking was automated. Effectively and safely helming a vessel weighing hundreds of thousands of tons demands digital systems and automation. In the same way, managing a large company requires automation, IT, and digital technologies. *(Ren Zhengfei: Speech at the GTS Report on the Development of the Site Information, Geographic Information, and Dynamic Network Operations Databases and the Integrated Delivery Platform, Huawei Executive Office Speech No. [2015] 124)*

I often say to our IT department that if you want to get rich, build roads first. Our top priority is to solve the issue of broadband support in field offices and build experience centers more quickly. We should not hesitate to invest resources to solve this issue. It would even be worthwhile to rent satellites at high prices. We said we need to show more concern to our employees in hardship countries and regions. The first thing we should do is arrange for high-speed office networks and increase their bandwidth. Without a network, employees there may find it harder to finish their work, making them less efficient and progress more slowly. Broadband is a type of basic infrastructure, so expenses for broadband deployment and continued maintenance need to be borne by the company. Aren't all our offices in smaller countries equipped with telepresence systems? We can use the Experience Cloud to connect all our offices, enabling us to make experience and expert resources remotely accessible, worldwide. *(Ren Zhengfei: Building Advanced Tools and Enhancing Core Competencies to Achieve Success at a Higher Level—Speech at a Carrier BG Briefing on the Service Experience and Phased Acceptance of the "Three Cloud" Platform, Huawei Executive Office Speech No. [2015] 099)*

We encourage experts at all levels to analyze data to uncover patterns in their work. We can improve our work by automating or digitizing some processes. We also encourage AI research experts to become enablers for optimizing work throughout the company. We understand and support our scientists' theoretical research, but we also encourage them to use existing mature methodologies to improve our work. They can use these methodologies to automate or digitize some of our work processes, and help build the company's competitiveness for the future. Working smarter is one of our main goals. *(Ren Zhengfei: Comments to "The Future of Artificial Intelligence Lies in Applications", Huawei Executive Office Speech No. [2017] 039)*

When it comes to investing in AI, our strategy should be small applications first, to meet the most urgent needs. We should focus on businesses of certainty and projects that require large amounts of labor. At the beginning, less is more. We first need to apply AI in one or two scenarios, check whether it is really benefiting us, and then apply the technology to other scenarios. In the initial stage, we should not expect to apply AI too broadly or to go intelligent across many domains. Casting our net too wide will dilute the effect and result in failure. *(Ren Zhengfei: Speech at the GTS Workshop on the Use of AI, Huawei Executive Office Speech No. [2017] 034)*

In the field of accounting, we are actively piloting automation and use of AI, handing over the accounting in standard scenarios to machines. Currently, we handle an annual average of approximately 1.2 million expense claims from employees. Employees handle expense claim processes themselves, and machines directly generate accounting vouchers based on pre-set rules. There are 746 accounts in 98 countries that are now interconnected, with payment orders able to be transmitted to any given bank around the world within 2 minutes. Our payment accuracy is more than 100 times higher than that of banks. In four business scenarios in the accounts payable (AP) field, we have launched automated processing. Pilots have run for half a year, and parallel validations are being done manually. The results have thus far demonstrated an accuracy rate of 100%. *(Meng Wanzhou: Looking Back on the Path from Whence We Come, We See Only the Verdant Green Shimmering in the Majestic Setting Sun, 2017 New Year Greeting, 2016)*

Our global program of radio frequency identification (RFID) asset management through the Internet of Things (IoT) is now implemented across 140,000 fixed assets at 2382 sites in 52 countries. RFID tags are attached to fixed assets that need to be managed. Every 5 minutes, the RFID tags automatically report a location signal, and once per day we update the usage load (or idle) data for the fixed assets. After deploying RFID, the time required to carry out fixed asset inventory work was reduced from a scale of months down to only a few minutes. For each year's asset inventory work and asset inspections, we saved upwards of 9000 person-days of workload. The timely update and sharing of asset location information and asset idle data really got us on track in our asset

management. *(Meng Wanzhou: Looking Back on the Path from Whence We Come, We See Only the Verdant Green Shimmering in the Majestic Setting Sun, 2017 New Year Greeting, 2016)*
Building an integrated financial architecture ready for the next five to ten years

1. We are dealing with numerous services, changing models, an increasingly uncertain macro environment, and multiple business models. Therefore, Finance should be flexible and responsive to a wide range of requests.
2. Finance needs to leverage new technologies and architecture to enhance its capabilities and work more efficiently.
3. Finance should scientifically manage risks to meet the requirements of operations and compliance.
4. Finance should provide better support to business development with its responsiveness, smart decision making capabilities, foresight, and deductions.
5. Finance should expertly design a blueprint to help the company reach its goal of US$200 billion in revenue, and design system integration based on that blueprint.
6. When designing an integrated financial architecture, Finance should give full consideration to the nature of our business, the logic of architecture, and the feasibility of technologies. We should use a distributed IT architecture to meet a range of needs; build 3 centers, 2 types of applications, and 2 platforms; and ensure our capabilities are real-time, automated, online (secure), agile, and able to achieve self-service and sharing. *(Men Wanzhou: Minutes of the Workshop on the Integrated Financial Architecture to Support Huawei in Becoming a 200-billion-dollar Company, 2016)*

Open Access This chapter is licensed under the terms of the Creative Commons Attribution-NonCommercial-NoDerivatives 4.0 International License (http://creativecommons.org/licenses/by-nc-nd/4.0/), which permits any noncommercial use, sharing, distribution and reproduction in any medium or format, as long as you give appropriate credit to the original author(s) and the source, provide a link to the Creative Commons licence and indicate if you modified the licensed material. You do not have permission under this license to share adapted material derived from this chapter or parts of it.

The images or other third party material in this chapter are included in the chapter's Creative Commons licence, unless indicated otherwise in a credit line to the material. If material is not included in the chapter's Creative Commons licence and your intended use is not permitted by statutory regulation or exceeds the permitted use, you will need to obtain permission directly from the copyright holder.

CHAPTER 17

Making Financial Management Process-Based and Professional

Finance must be process-based and professional; otherwise, it will incur high costs for the company. We need to standardize and streamline routine matters through processes and professional work. This will help reduce our management and operating costs.

At Huawei, Finance is positioned to be a global team that provides services, management, and oversight. To align with this positioning, Finance must develop as a professional global team that has solid integrity, dares to shoulder responsibilities, and sticks to principles. To better serve and manage business, financial managers must first understand business. We need to build a stronger PFC team. Project finance is the best place for financial personnel to hone their skills. Being involved in a small project from beginning to end can help financial personnel better understand finance and business, and get prepared for becoming CFOs.

Progress in finance is the basis for all management advances. Without robust financial management or reliable oversight, it will be impossible for a company to delegate authority to field offices; nor will field offices be able to call for support directly. In the end, the HQ will become increasingly bureaucratic and bloated. Such a company will not be able to survive and thrive over the long term. Huawei always remains customer-centric, focuses on value creation, continues to streamline management, and works hard to reduce period expenses.

This chapter discusses how Huawei builds a professional financial team.

17.1 Financial Personnel Should Understand Business and Business Personnel Should Understand Finance

17.1.1 *Financial Personnel Can Help Business Grow Only by Understanding Business*

After you have mastered many modern tools and gained a deeper understanding of the business and people you serve, you can help improve efficiency. In that case, there will be hope for the company. You need to better understand the business and people you serve, and also customer needs. If you really understand the needs of your front-end customers, you will get promoted. *(Ren Zhengfei: Speech at a Meeting with the IFS Project Team and Staff from Finance, Huawei Executive Office Speech No. [2009] 004)*

I think staff at shared services centers need to be familiar with the business they serve. Otherwise, these shared service centers will become bureaucratic. If our financial personnel know nothing about business, they will not be able to communicate with field employees. Our financial personnel must step up efforts to upskill themselves and understand business as quickly as possible. I encourage those working in the shared services centers to become familiar with business. Otherwise, how can you possibly improve yourselves and do well in finance? The shared services centers are doomed to fail if they are composed only of financial experts who know nothing about business. *(Ren Zhengfei: Speech at a Meeting with the IFS Project Team and Staff from Finance, Huawei Executive Office Speech No. [2009] 004)*

CFOs should know how to make presentations on data and how to tell the stories behind the data. They need to analyze data to identify the patterns in business operations, and to develop methods to optimize business operations. This is how they can truly become business partners and help business grow. *(Ren Zhengfei: Quickly Building Our CFO Team to Support IFS Deployment, Huawei Executive Office Speech No. [2009] 023)*

Our financial team must be closely integrated with our business team. Business personnel must master financial knowledge, and financial personnel must acquire business knowledge. Financial personnel must have a clear and comprehensive idea of both finance and business, as this is the only way for them to effectively support project financial management. *(Ren Zhengfei: Speech at a Work Report by the IFS-PTP Project Team, 2010)*

In recent years, we have constantly required our financial personnel to get closer to business and be deeply involved in projects. This is because we expect you to be more than bookkeepers. We hope you can truly understand the nature of our business and effectively support our business management. You may set on the right track only when you truly understand business. It is not an underestimation of your capabilities; rather it is our expectations of you. *(Ren Zhengfei: Speech at a Meeting with Financial Staff, Huawei Executive Office Speech No. [2011] 032)*

Huawei expects its CFOs to be result-oriented and work with business departments to sustainably produce maximum output with minimum input. *(Ren Zhengfei: Speech at a Meeting with Financial Managers, Huawei Executive Office Speech No. [2012] 029)*

Finance must deploy the right people to the right positions to ensure effective financial management and oversight. They should also ensure our talent and business structures are appropriate. *(Ren Zhengfei: Speech at the Work Report by Finance, Huawei Executive Office Speech No. [2013] 234)*

17.1.2 Managers Are Also About Managing Finance

In recent years, we have hired and transferred many business or financial personnel to managerial positions in Finance. If these people continue to know only about their own domain, either business or finance, they can no longer serve as managers. That's why this transformation project involves both our financial and business personnel. Financial personnel, either managers or employees, must understand accounting principles and know how to do specific financial work. These personnel also need to understand business. Otherwise, they are unable to better serve the company. We must realize that financial and business personnel must help and learn from each other. These two are not opposites, despite having some conflicting elements. Instead, they are an organic whole. *(Ren Zhengfei: Minutes of a Meeting on Financial Transformation Projects, 2004)*

M is for manager, and M is for money. If a manager doesn't understand how money flows in a business, then they can't possibly be an effective manager. *(Ren Zhengfei: Speech at the Annual Meeting of the Chinese Market Finance Department, Huawei Executive Office Speech No. [2006] 002)*

We will focus on profits during our performance appraisals. Representative office managers should understand management, finance, and operations. They should also continuously improve internal management and reduce operating costs. We aim to establish a management model under which business plays a leading role and finance plays an oversight role at account departments and representative offices. *(Ren Zhengfei: Speech at the Report by the BT Account Department and the UK Representative Office, Huawei Executive Office Speech No. [2007] 015)*

We live in an age of professional managers; the age of founders and heroes has passed. If we don't adapt to this trend, we will fall behind the times. During the transitional process, we need to work together closely as a team and cooperate with one another to achieve synergy. We must remember that nobody is good at everything. Those who never seek help are inefficient, and those who seek only individual success are destined to fail. *(Ren Zhengfei: Timely, Accurate, High Quality, and Low Cost Delivery Calls for Professional Process-compliant CFOs—Minutes of a Meeting with Trainees of the CFO Session of the Reserve Pool, Huawei Executive Office Speech No. [2009] 021)*

Business managers do not qualify as managers if they only have business knowledge. They also need to have the most basic financial knowledge. To have a future, we need a lot of enterprising successors. Where does our future lie? It lies with financial personnel who understand business and business personnel who understand planning, budgeting, and accounting. *(Ren Zhengfei: Minutes of the Meeting with Staff of the Romania Accounting SSC, Huawei Executive Office Speech No. [2011] 021)*

Managers should become familiar with each other's domains. Financial managers should understand business, and business managers should understand finance. We will have well-organized mobility for managers across these two domains to facilitate knowledge transfers. Field teams with mixed knowledge and experience are better positioned to seize opportunities more efficiently, quickly, and confidently, to balance project wins with robust operations, and to make full use of the LTC and IFS processes that have been deployed. The closed-loop management mechanism will be used to improve how managers are appraised and selected. *(Ren Zhengfei: Applying the Spirit of the Tortoise to Catch up with the Dragon Spacecraft—Speech at Huawei Annual Management Conference 2013, Huawei Executive Office Speech No. [2013] 255)*

Employees in all fields should rotate through R&D, Sales, Finance, GTS, and other functions. Financial personnel must understand business. It is not enough for them to just passively read code. They need to take the initiative. Otherwise, they won't be able to become senior executives. Senior executives should have financial knowledge. Which of our senior executives don't understand finance? Apart from some Fellows and technical experts, who should delve deeper into their specific domains, the majority of our employees should rotate to improve their integrated capabilities. Our company now enjoys good business performance, so we will allow the Strategic Reserve to consume some profits. This will lay a solid foundation for the company's sustainable development. *(Ren Zhengfei: There Will Not Always Be Flowers Along the Road Ahead—Speech at the H1 Huawei Market Conference, Huawei Executive Office Speech No. [2016] 079)*

17.1.3 Financial Personnel Can Become Well-Rounded Managers Only by Knowing How to Manage Projects

I think the most important task for financial personnel is to learn and gain experience in project financial management. Only those who know how to manage projects can become well-rounded managers. *(Ren Zhengfei: Minutes of the Meeting with Staff of the Romania Accounting SSC, Huawei Executive Office Speech No. [2011] 021)*

I think project finance needs to perform effective accounting and ensure that projects generate reasonable profits. Foxconn has standardized production processes, so their people do not need to have very sophisticated skillsets. However, our projects are very complicated, and we expect all of our employees to be deeply involved in project operations. You are more than just data collectors. You must be deeply involved in business. Only by doing this can you provide valuable suggestions. *(Ren Zhengfei: Minutes of the Meeting with Staff of the Romania Accounting SSC, Huawei Executive Office Speech No. [2011] 021)*

I don't think CFOs need the same level of accounting knowledge as accountants. If accountants knew as much about business as CFOs, they might also become CFOs. However, it is much more difficult for them to gain business knowledge, than it is for you to acquire accounting knowledge. So this year, I hope we can select 20 to 30 CFOs from employees at our regional offices and key account departments. I hope that our project teams can effectively manage planning, budgeting, and accounting. However, our financial personnel haven't developed the required capabilities yet. We can't even select CFOs in our regional offices. We hope you can take the initiative, make your voice heard, and help the company establish a financial management system. *(Ren Zhengfei: Remarks at a Meeting with Senior Managers at a Project Management Summit, Huawei Executive Office Speech No. [2009] 007)*

We need to develop a stronger PFC team. In the future, our project financial team should include members from both business and finance departments. In particular, we will select some employees who have more than three years of engineering and technical experience and are also familiar with business, as well as some employees from Finance who are very familiar with business. We will train them quickly and send them to the field to enhance the roles of PFCs and business finance controllers (BFCs) within account departments. Project CFOs should also be selected from the project financial team. In the future, CFOs of representative offices or regional offices who are not familiar with finance or business should make up for their lack of knowledge. If they fail to do so, they can no longer hold managerial positions. *(Ren Zhengfei: Integrating Project Estimation, Budgeting, Accounting, and Final Accounting to Support Project Operations—Speech at a Briefing on the IFS Project, Huawei Executive Office Speech No. [2010] 007)*

Project finance is the best place for financial personnel to hone their skills. Being involved in a small project from beginning to end can help financial personnel better understand finance and business, and get prepared for becoming CFOs. *(Ren Zhengfei: Speech at a Meeting with Financial Staff, Huawei Executive Office Speech No. [2011] 032)*

Scientific management requires the support of Finance. Budgeting and final accounting are still our weak links. We should prioritize the development and sufficient deployment of PFCs. We can consider rotations between financial managers and business managers, in order to develop a team of managers and experts with integrated management capabilities. *(Ren Zhengfei: Minutes of a Briefing on the Progress of the Project for Changing Function-centered Operations into Project-centered Operations, EMT Meeting Minutes No. [2014] 019)*

We should deploy PFCs to effectively manage project delivery and reap the benefits of business management. Our project management is not yet very effective. In our early years, we knew nothing about delivery. Later on, after we understood delivery, we began to deliver as much as we could, and didn't care whether we made money or not. Today, we should continue to learn about delivery and also pay attention to delivery results. This calls for more PFCs. *(Ren Zhengfei: Speech at a Meeting with Employees of the Central Asia & Caucasia Region, Huawei Executive Office Speech No. [2016] 063)*

PFCs must understand business to better manage projects. To become better PFCs in the future, new graduates should visit sites with engineers and see how equipment is installed. These graduates can use stopwatches to measure the time required and then calculate how much they earn each second. Then they can calculate how much we need to pay if an "express delivery man" does the same. This will show the benefits we can reap from business improvement. As our delivery becomes more standardized, we will become more open, and our software commissioning will become standardized. The first thing that a PFC needs to do is to go to the field and learn about business. This is the only way for us to achieve the three-procedure loop – application, review, and approval. Otherwise, PFCs will be like "air force pilots" flying high in the air. If we don't give them the support and "fuel" they need, then they will fall to the ground. *(Ren Zhengfei: Speech at a Meeting with Employees of the Central Asia & Caucasia Region, Huawei Executive Office Speech No. [2016] 063)*

17.1.4 Developing a Mixed Financial Team

Why do we transfer managers from business departments to Finance? The purpose is to help Finance get deeply involved in business, and change the way they think and work. Finance was widely known to be simple but stubborn. Managers had been working hard, but now they need to start working smarter. By adding some "sand", we aim to make you strong like concrete, rather than just replacing you with another manager. Those who want to transfer to Finance need to pass accounting exams. For middle managers, job rotations are conducive to their career development and comply with our zigzag development program. *(Ren Zhengfei: Speech at a Meeting with Financial Staff, Huawei Executive Office Speech No. [2011] 032)*

We need to build a diverse CFO resource pool that includes both financial and business personnel. We should not be too rigid or dogmatic when selecting CFOs. Rather, we should flexibly apply performance ratings, giving full consideration to the macro environment and the maturity of the markets in which CFOs are working. *(Ren Zhengfei: Speech at the Work Report on Criteria for CFOs and the Mechanism for Their Development, Huawei Executive Office Speech No. [2011] 038)*

We need to transfer some employees from other departments to Finance in order to build a stronger and more diverse financial team. This is like making concrete from pebbles, sand, and cement to make it more solid. We also need to recruit more talent from outside the company. However, Finance must not simply focus on vacancies; otherwise, those who are incompetent may never be removed from their positions. *(Ren Zhengfei: Speech at the EMT ST Meeting, 2011)*

Excellent financial managers can be transferred to business departments. This can provide them with more growth opportunities and drive integration between the financial and business teams. Excellent country CFOs can become general managers. Excellent project financial personnel can become project managers. This expansion of their career paths will exert a positive impact on business management. *(Ren Zhengfei: Speech at the Work Report by Finance, Huawei Executive Office Speech No. [2013] 234)*

We are rotating managers on a large scale through the JCR, placing managers in new positions, and adjusting our approaches and resources. We also aim to deploy our managers around the world. We believe that we will achieve these goals within the next three to five years. In the future, we will select some individuals from project finance and appoint them as project directors. Then, we will select some business personnel to do financial work for projects. Through such an exchange, we will be able to develop the managerial candidates that we want. If senior managers do not read or study corporate documents, they may be replaced by younger managers. *(Ren Zhengfei: Growing from a Soldier to a General Within Three Years, Huawei Executive Office Speech No. [2014] 031)*

17.2 Building a Process-Based, Professional Financial Management System

17.2.1 Reducing Costs Through Process-Based and Professional Financial Management

Our administrative management system used to be very disorganized. Although the impact of functional departments is weakening, it's still not practical to implement a process-based management system. Our upstream and downstream processes are not yet effectively integrated, and our process-based management system still needs to be optimized. In terms of organizational behavior, we have yet to achieve repeatable, predictable, and continuously reliable results in our operations. *(Ren Zhengfei: Digging In, Widening Out—Speech at the Commendation Meeting of the Operations and Delivery Division, Huawei Executive Office Speech No. [2009] 009)*

Finance must be process-based and professional; otherwise, it will incur high costs for the company. CFO is a universal term known internationally and we do not have a specific interpretation for this term. Our CFOs have the same job responsibilities as those defined in the industry. We need to standardize many aspects of our business through processes and professional work. This can reduce our management and operating costs. *(Ren Zhengfei: Timely, Accurate, High Quality, and Low Cost Delivery Calls for Professional Process-compliant CFOs—Minutes of a Meeting with Trainees of the CFO Session of the Reserve Pool, Huawei Executive Office Speech No. [2009] 021)*

In the industrial age, a military's effectiveness was measured by its ability to quickly assemble large forces and maintain maximum strength. In the twenty-first century, the US military became worried about difficulties such as increasing complexity and uncertainty, as well as demand to take quick action and win quickly. To address these challenges, the US military proposed the "forward presence" strategy, which is still in place today. With this strategy, US forces are deployed in hotspots to continuously gain onsite and real-time intelligence, and perform combat exercises with live ammunition. If an order is issued, the US forces can respond quickly to deal with enemy forces. The relevant reinforcements can then be sent by central command, which enables the military to quickly and decisively win the battle. We are attempting a similar strategy by gradually establishing CFO organizations for our industry-specific teams, regional offices, functional departments, account departments, projects, and customer groups. With these organizations in place, we aim to maximize the value of our financial personnel in our field business. Doing so will enable them to accurately identify and respond to changes, and become true, reliable business partners. *(Ren Zhengfei: Comments to Huawei Finance Doc. No. [2011] 018, Huawei Executive Office Speech No. [2011] 025)*

I think our major processes should be streamlined, allowing things to be completed quickly. When it comes to our strategy, our approach is to review our data pipes and remove any unnecessary parts to make the pipes transparent and ensure data flows through them quickly. We developed the pipe management system into a simple, clear, and transparent operating system. We then removed functionality from pipes and converted them into modules. This allows us to add them back to the pipes as needed. We should adopt the same approach with our major processes. I think our major processes are now burdened with heavy oversight tasks, leaving too many checkpoints throughout our major processes. This has made these processes very ineffective. In my opinion, these checkpoints should be set in our sub-processes, rather than major processes. *(Ren Zhengfei: Speech and Comments at the Strategy Retreat of the Business*

Process & IT Management Department, Huawei Executive Office Speech No. [2012] 026)
When our major processes are clean and transparent, we can streamline our major sub-processes. After all unnecessary functions are removed, our sub-processes will also become open and flexible. *(Ren Zhengfei: Speech and Comments at the Strategy Retreat of the Business Process & IT Management Department, Huawei Executive Office Speech No. [2012] 026)*
More flexibility should be allowed in our back-end processes. For example, if our command center is located in Shenzhen, and it gives an order requiring all employees to wear a T-shirt, our colleagues working in the Arctic would freeze to death. Why does this happen? Because we are being too rigid and dogmatic and not allowing flexibility in field offices. So we now emphasize that back-end processes should be more flexible. *(Ren Zhengfei: Speech and Comments at the Strategy Retreat of the Business Process & IT Management Department, Huawei Executive Office Speech No. [2012] 026)*

17.2.2 Building a Professional Financial Team That Has Solid Integrity, Dares to Shoulder Responsibilities, and Sticks to Principles

Our company will face great opportunities and challenges in the coming years. Finance must provide effective support. Finance needs to build a financial system more rapidly and improve its ability to provide services and make professional decisions. This is the only way for Finance to more effectively support the company's business development. Finance needs to position itself as a global team that provides services, management, and oversight. To align with this positioning, Finance must develop as a professional global team that has solid integrity, dares to shoulder responsibilities, and sticks to principles. *(Ren Zhengfei: Building a Professional Financial Team That Has Solid Integrity, Dares to Shoulder Responsibilities, and Sticks to Principles, Huawei Executive Office Speech No. [2006] 038)*

What is professionalism? It is doing the same thing under the same conditions, but at a lower cost. *(Ren Zhengfei: Digging In, Widening Out—Speech at the Commendation Meeting of the Operations and Delivery Division, Huawei Executive Office Speech No. [2009] 009)*

17.3 Progress in Finance Is the Basis for All Management Advances

17.3.1 Financial Transformation Is Not Limited to the Finance System, But a Company-Wide Effort

We need a global financial team that is well beyond our HQ and manages all finance-related matters around the world. We are going to establish the position of regional financial management director. They will not be accounting directors, commercial managers, tax managers, or market finance managers. Instead, they will be commissioners assigned by Finance, International Marketing, and the company to regions. They should have a clear idea of accounting, regulations, revenue, and tax systems. *(Ren Zhengfei: Speech at the Third Quarter Meeting Regarding Marketing in China, 2004)*

Progress in finance is the basis for all management advances. The good news is that Finance has no longer been a drag on our business in the past few years. Without robust financial management or reliable oversight, it would be impossible for us to delegate authority to field offices; nor could field offices call for support directly. The result could be that the HQ becomes bureaucratic and bloated. If that happens, how can we survive and thrive? We must unwaveringly support the IFS[1] transformation program. We need to build a stronger financial team. Our financial personnel need to upskill themselves and remain responsible, dedicated, integrated with business, and growth-oriented. They also need to better serve business, support business development, and manage planning, budgeting, and accounting from end to end. Only those who dare to make a difference can secure a place in the company. Departments can have growth opportunities only when they create value throughout the process. *(Ren Zhengfei: The Market Economy Is Best for Competition; Economic Globalization Is Inevitable—Speech at the Commendation Meeting of Finance, Huawei Executive Office Speech No. [2009] 005)*

We are now developing a process-based and professional management system. It is time for us to begin building a CFO management system. We expect that CFOs, once they come on board, will help cut down on

---

[1] IFS: Integrated Financial Services. This is Huawei's transformation program in the financial domain. It supports and oversees Huawei's end-to-end business processes from R&D to marketing & sales, supply chain, and delivery.

waste and costs while maintaining rapid business growth. They will also help avoid partial optimization that can cause damage to the overall situation. We should always keep the big picture in mind. *(Ren Zhengfei: Timely, Accurate, High Quality, and Low Cost Delivery Calls for Professional Process-compliant CFOs—Minutes of a Meeting with Trainees of the CFO Session of the Reserve Pool, Huawei Executive Office Speech No. [2009] 021)*

The top priority for CFOs is to establish and implement financial processes that effectively support the operations of business processes. Both CFOs and CEOs need to properly understand and master company operations rules, and work together to help the company succeed and achieve sustainable and profitable growth. CFOs and CEOs are in the same boat, with the same goals and the same overall direction. However, they assume different responsibilities. Without the support of CFOs, CEOs cannot move forward. CFOs are not supposed to oversee CEOs; CFOs are there to establish and implement financial processes in a process-compliant and professional manner. This is necessary to support the effective operations of business processes and achieve sustainable and profitable growth. That means positive profits, positive net cash flow, and efficiency improvement. *(Ren Zhengfei: Timely, Accurate, High Quality, and Low Cost Delivery Calls for Professional Process-compliant CFOs—Minutes of a Meeting with Trainees of the CFO Session of the Reserve Pool, Huawei Executive Office Speech No. [2009] 021)*

What is the key to integrating the LTC, PTP, and OTC processes? It's the involvement of financial personnel in business, who are supposed to act like the glue that binds all people together. In the end, all processes will be integrated. *(Ren Zhengfei: Speech at a Work Report by the IFS-PTP Project Team, 2010)*

Over the past two decades, Finance has focused on developing vertical functional modules. This has helped build the right systems and processes. However, it has failed to provide effective, integrated management and strong support. Therefore, we need to further clarify the responsibilities and improve the capabilities of CFOs at representative offices and on projects. The aim is to improve the integrated management capabilities of financial organizations. *(Ren Zhengfei: Speech at the Work Report on Criteria for CFOs and the Mechanism for Their Development, Huawei Executive Office Speech No. [2011] 038)*

Financial transformation is about Huawei as a whole, rather than just the financial system. All senior management teams at Huawei must get involved in financial transformation. If a business department thinks it can transform successfully without any support, I would assume that this department can make profits without any expense. I do not think the director of this business department will go far. Similarly, Finance must not stay behind closed doors and think it is unnecessary to get business departments involved, give presentations to them, or listen to their opinions. *(Ren Zhengfei: Financial Transformation Is About Huawei Rather Than Only the Finance System, Huawei Executive Office Speech No. [2007] 004)*

We have made a lot of progress in our management. It's hard to imagine that a Chinese company could achieve such large revenue without encountering many problems. Over the past 28 years, we have put in place almost all the necessary processes, with our IT systems improving and management being streamlined. *(Ren Zhengfei: There Will Not Always Be Flowers Along the Road Ahead—Speech at the H1 Huawei Market Conference, Huawei Executive Office Speech No. [2016] 079)*

17.3.2 There Will Not Always Be Flowers Along the Road Ahead

Our management must remain customer-centric and focus on value creation. We must gradually streamline our management and endeavor to reduce period expenses. If we make customers pay for product features they do not need, we will drive them away. Therefore, transformation must be measured by whether more crops can be harvested both in the short term and long term. *(Ren Zhengfei: Our Transformation Goals Are to Harvest More Crops and Increase Soil Fertility—Speech at the 2015 Huawei Market Conference, Huawei Executive Office Speech No. [2015] 016)*

Our financial management is already ahead of the pack within the industry. We are now able to check regional site inventories. The CIAG in central warehouses and sites has reached 99.89% and 98.17%, respectively. A number of top experts and managers with successful field experience are continuing to develop and grow, but we should not rest on our laurels. *(Ren Zhengfei: Be First to Know When Springtime Comes. Vow Not to Return Till We Reach Our Goals—Speech at an Oath-taking Rally for Reassigned Senior R&D Experts and Managers, Huawei Executive Office Speech No. [2016] 093)*

Black swan events are emerging in great numbers around the world. There may be unexpected ups and downs, and we have yet to ensure strict internal and external compliance. We still need to step up our efforts to ensure more effective operations and ensure our financial systems are robust. *(Ren Zhengfei: There Will Not Always Be Flowers Along the Road Ahead—Speech at the H1 Huawei Market Conference, Huawei Executive Office Speech No. [2016] 079)*

Open Access This chapter is licensed under the terms of the Creative Commons Attribution-NonCommercial-NoDerivatives 4.0 International License (http://creativecommons.org/licenses/by-nc-nd/4.0/), which permits any noncommercial use, sharing, distribution and reproduction in any medium or format, as long as you give appropriate credit to the original author(s) and the source, provide a link to the Creative Commons licence and indicate if you modified the licensed material. You do not have permission under this license to share adapted material derived from this chapter or parts of it.

The images or other third party material in this chapter are included in the chapter's Creative Commons licence, unless indicated otherwise in a credit line to the material. If material is not included in the chapter's Creative Commons licence and your intended use is not permitted by statutory regulation or exceeds the permitted use, you will need to obtain permission directly from the copyright holder.

Epilogue

This book is the third in a series about Huawei's management philosophy. It elaborates how the finance department serves and oversees the company's business expansion in the role of a value integrator. This book aims to unravel the concepts, policies, and rules that Huawei adopts in its value creation process. The three books are separate in their own right, and have their own structures and flows.

As with its two predecessors, *Dedication: The Huawei Philosophy of Human Resource Management*, and *Customer Centricity: The Huawei Philosophy of Business Management*, all the content in this book comes from speeches and articles by Huawei's founder and other executives, as well as documents issued by the company's Executive Management Team (EMT) and finance department. Sources are provided for each extract. In each chapter, the content is arranged chronologically, from the year the company was founded to June 2017. The purpose is to help readers understand how Huawei's finance management philosophy has evolved, and give insight into its inner consistency.

This book was compiled based on the first and second versions of *Pursuing Sustainable and Profitable Growth: Huawei's Finance Management Philosophy*, an internal managerial training reference prepared under the leadership of Huawei's Rotating CEO Guo Ping and

CFO Meng Wanzhou. The editorial board has revised the structure of the training reference by dividing it into two parts: "Part One: Expansion and Control" and "Part Two: Value Management". The editorial board also fine-tuned the titles of each section and updated the content.

Guo Ping served as the director of the editorial board for the first version of the training reference. Meng Wanzhou was the deputy director. Other members of the editorial board were Huang Weiwei, Yin Zhifeng, Ye Xiaowen, Shen Shengli, Tu Jun, and Zhang Kai.

For the second version of the training reference, Guo Ping continued to serve as the director of the editorial board and Meng Wanzhou the deputy director. Other members of the editorial board were Huang Weiwei, Yin Zhifeng, Cheng Weihua, Zhao Minglu, and Peng Jianling. Cai Liqun, Zhang Ying, and He Xinyuan contributed to the revisions in the second version.

Huang Weiwei served as the editor-in-chief of this book. Other members of the editorial board for this book were Yin Zhifeng, Cheng Weihua, Su Baohua, Zeng Jinliang, Ye Xiaowen, and Zhu Xiaoyan, with Huang Maochang, Tu Jun, Li Feng, and Shen Shengli serving as executive editors. In addition, Shi Yanli, Zhang Xiaoqing, Gao Aozhan, Zhang Yinchen, Du Jilin, Zhang Hongmei, Sun Jian, Li Haipeng, Zhang Guo, and Li Zhaofeng made significant contributions to the content of Chapters 4, 5, 9, 12, 13, 14, 15, and 16 respectively.

The training reference was approved in January 2013. Since then, it has been used as teaching material at the Huawei Senior Management Seminar held each year. Over 60 sessions have been held on the topic of finance management at the seminar and have been attended by more than 2000 middle and senior managers at Huawei. These managers have shared a wealth of hands-on experience, unique perspectives, and critical ideas that have been essential to improving the training reference, and also made important intellectual contributions to the compilation of this book. We would like to extend a special thanks to these managers.

Chinese Version Editorial Board
June 30, 2017

The English translation of this book was produced by a Huawei translation team led by Zhang Linyan. The team ensured the translated text is faithful to the original Chinese in both content and style – especially the speaking style of Huawei founder and CEO Mr. Ren Zhengfei. In addition to Zhang Linyan (Chapters 1, 6, and 7), the translation team also included He Yanghong (Chapters 2 and 11), Feng Wenchao (Chapters 3, 4, and 10), Du Xiaolian (Chapters 5 and 8), Chen Xiahuan (Chapters 12 and 15), Guo Yanjuan (Chapters 9, 16, and 17), Gong Jing (Chapters 13 and 14), and Chris Pereira and several other native editors (editing of the English translation). As the owner of this translation project, Ms. Zhang Linyan also reviewed the accuracy of each chapter and proofread the entire book. The English text was confirmed and finalized by Huang Weiwei.

Translation Team
December 15, 2018

ACRONYMS

PREFACE

AP	Accounts Payable
CIAG	Consistency of Inventory Accounts and Goods
IFS	Integrated Financial Services
INSS	National Social Security Institute
IoT	Internet of Things
ITO	Inventory Turnover
OTC	Opportunity to Cash
PO	Purchase Order
RFID	Radio Frequency Identification
SSC	Shared Services Center

CHAPTER 2

BG	Business Group
BOD	Board of Directors
CC3	Customer Centric 3 is a project-based cross-functional team, consisting of three roles: Account Responsible (AR), Solution Responsible (SR), and Fulfillment Responsible (FR).
CEO	Chief Executive Officer
CIO	Chief Information Officer
CMO	Chief Marketing Officer

COE	Center of Expertise
EMT	Executive Management Team
GTS	Global Technical Services
HR	Human Resources
ICT	Information and Communications Technology
IPD	Integrated Product Development
IPMT	Integrated Portfolio Management Team
ISC	Integrated Supply Chain
IT	Information Technology
KPI	Key Performance Indicator
LTC	Lead to Cash
PC	Personal Computer
PR	Public Relations
PSST	Products & Solutions Staff Team
R&D	Research and Development
SDC	Strategy & Development Committee
ST	Staff Team

Chapter 3

AI	Artificial Intelligence
BOD	Board of Directors
CDMA	Code Division Multiple Access
COE	Center of Expertise
EMBA	Executive Master of Business Administration
EMT	Executive Management Team
GTS	Global Technical Services
IT	Information Technology
LTC	Lead to Cash
LTE	Long-Term Evolution
PHS	Personal Handy-phone System
TD-SCDMA	Time Division-Synchronous Code Division Multiple Access

Chapter 4

CVC	Corporate Venture Capital
IVC	Independent Venture Capital
M&A	Merger and Acquisition

Chapter 5

CAPEX	Capital Expenditure
FC	Finance Committee
FRCC	Financial Risk Control Center
HRC	Human Resources Committee
OEC	Office of Ethics and Compliance
SDC	Strategy & Development Committee

Chapter 6

CRM	Customer Relationship Management
FC	Finance Committee
IFS	Integrated Financial Services
IPD	Integrated Product Development
ISC	Integrated Supply Chain
IT S&P	IT Strategy & Planning

Chapter 7

AR	Accounts Receivable
BCGs	Business Conduct Guidelines
CC3	Customer Centric 3 is a project-based cross-functional team, consisting of three roles: Account Responsible (AR), Solution Responsible (SR), and Fulfillment Responsible (FR).
CIAG	Consistency of Inventory Accounts and Goods
IDS	Integrated Deployment Solution
IFS	Integrated Financial Services
OTC	Opportunity to Cash
PTP	Procure-to-Pay

Chapter 8

AP	Accounts Payable
AR	Accounts Receivable
BBOM	Build Bill of Materials
BC&IA	Business Controls and Internal Audit
BMT	Business Management Team

BP	Business Plan
BPE	Business Process Executive
BU	Business Unit
CBOM	Customer Bill of Materials
CIAG	Consistency of Inventory Accounts and Goods
CMA	Capability Maturity Assessment
COA	Chart of Accounts
CRM	Customer Relationship Management
CSO	Contract Support Office
DCP	Decision CheckPoint
DSO	Days Sales Outstanding
DSTE	Develop Strategy to Execute
ERP	Enterprise Resource Planning
GTS	Global Technical Services
IFS	Integrated Financial Services
IOI	Invoice Only Invoice
IPD	Integrated Product Development
IPMT	Integrated Portfolio Management Team
ISC	Integrated Supply Chain
ITO	Inventory Turnover
ITR	Issue to Resolution
KCP	Key Control Point
KPI	Key Performance Indicator
LTC	Lead to Cash
OTC	Opportunity to Cash
PAC	Preliminary Acceptance Certificate
PDT	Product Development Team
PFC	Project Financial Controller
PO	Purchase Order
PTP	Procure-to-Pay
ROI	Return on Investment
SBOM	Sales Bill of Materials
SOD	Separation of Duties
SP	Strategic Plan
SPDT	Super Product Development Team
SSE	Self Service Expense

CHAPTER 9

BFC	Business Financial Controller
PD	Project Director
PM	Project Manager
SDT	Sales Decision-making Team

ACRONYMS 455

Chapter 10

BG	Business Group
CIAG	Consistency of Inventory Accounts and Goods
CIF	Cost, Insurance, and Freight
ISC	Integrated Supply Chain
JCR	Joint Committee of Regions
KPI	Key Performance Indicator
MET	Marketing Execution Team
PO	Purchase Order
R&D	Research and Development
RC	Responsibility Center

Chapter 11

AT	Administrative Team
BP	Business Plan
BU	Business Unit
FU	Functional Unit
IRB	Investment Review Board
MU	Marketing Unit
SBG	Service Business Group
SP	Strategic Plan

Chapter 12

SSC	Shared Services Center

Chapter 13

AR	Accounts Receivable
CCS	Corporate Capital Structure
DPO	Days Payable Outstanding
DSO	Days Sales Outstanding
FRCC	Financial Risk Control Center
GTS	Global Technical Services
ITO	Inventory Turnover
M&A	Merger and Acquisition
OCF	Operating Cash Flow

Chapter 14

BEPS	Base Erosion and Profit Shifting
COE	Center of Expertise
ETR	Effective Tax Rate
GPO	Global Process Owner
ICFR	Internal Controls over Financial Reporting
ITC	Integrated Tax Compliance
KCFR	Key Control over Financial Reporting
KCP	Key Control Point
ROI	Return on Investment
TP	Transfer Pricing

Chapter 15

CEC	Committee of Ethics and Compliance
ERP	Enterprise Resource Planning
GAAP	Generally Accepted Accounting Principles
ICFR	Internal Controls over Financial Reporting
KCFR	Key Control over Financial Reporting
OEC	Office of Ethics and Compliance
SACA	Semi-Annual Control Assessment
WWBC	Worldwide Business Controls Department

Chapter 16

IoT	Internet of Things
RFID	Radio Frequency Identification

Chapter 17

BFC	Business Financial Controller